An Introduction to GameGuru

An Introduction to GameGuru

By Michael Matthew Messina

CRC Press is an imprint of the
Taylor & Francis Group, an **informa** business

CRC Press
Taylor & Francis Group
6000 Broken Sound Parkway NW, Suite 300
Boca Raton, FL 33487-2742

Printed on acid-free paper

International Standard Book Number-13: 978-1-138-61263-1 (paperback/) 978-1-138-61268-6 (hardback)

Library of Congress Cataloging-in-Publication Data

Names: Messina, Michael Matthew, author.
Title: An introduction to GameGuru / Michael Matthew Messina.
Description: Boca Raton : Taylor & Francis, a CRC title, part of the Taylor & Francis imprint, a member of the Taylor & Francis Group, the academic division of T&F Informa, plc, 2019.
Identifiers: LCCN 2019012483 | ISBN 9781138612631 (paperback : alk. paper) | ISBN 9781138612686 (hardback : alk. paper)
Subjects: LCSH: Computer games—Programming—Computer programs. | GameGuru.
Classification: LCC QA76.76.C672 M47 2019 | DDC 794.8/1525—dc23
LC record available at https://lccn.loc.gov/2019012483

Visit the Taylor & Francis Web site at
http://www.taylorandfrancis.com

and the CRC Press Web site at
http://www.crcpress.com

Contents

Acknowledgments

Quis et Deus? Thank you Father, Son, and Holy Ghost—for the opportunities, blessings, experiences, and people in my life.

Foremost, I do everything in my life for my family and children, so this book is for them. Special thanks to my wife for dealing with my mania as I finished this book near the end.

Special thanks to my proofreaders and those who assisted with this book directly: Johann Ertl (aka ertlov) for his interview; Jeffrey Thompson for letting me pick his math-addled brain; Amenmoses for assistance with physics, particles, and proofing Lua; Kevan Hampson (GraphiX) for particles and explosions; MStockton for his art and texture assistance; PirateMyke for answering all the questions everyone else missed; Mio Sejic for his general donation of materials; and tdreisinger and Len The Man for their full or partial proofing assistance.

Thanks to Wolf, Duchenkuke, and Bugsy ... members who have been a fount of information and inspiration for many years. Thank you as well for your technical assistance throughout the project.

Thanks to James Ellison, Esq., for his assistance with respect to legal inquiries.

Also a big thanks to Lee Bamber, Rick Vanner, Deb, and the crew at TGC games for providing a medium that prompted me to write a book!

Everyone on discord and on the forums—my blog readers, thank you all!

About the Author

Michael Messina is a central Pennsylvania native and proud father of three. His experience spans twenty years of professional Information Systems work. He currently serves as the Chief Linux Administrator for Rite-Aid Corp. His longtime interest in game development has resulted in mods for games such as "Quake 1" and "Mechwarrior 4," notably the Siege and Teambot mods. He is the author of the Game-Guru Report (http://gamegurureport.blogspot.com/), a weekly update blog that covers all things GameGuru.

Introduction: About 3D Games

Video games have been around a long time now, but they have evolved from a human history of game making and challenging ourselves in a competitive way. They encourage human thinking and ingenuity and improve our reflexes, coordination, and information processing. Mazes and puzzles are both exceptionally common and effective ways to improve our brains, and clinical research has shown that the human mind benefits from mazes and puzzles while also helping old brains stay young.

One specific subset of gamer, the FPS (or first person shooter) enthusiast, is typically better at processing information as they tend to process inputs faster and more precisely than those who are not FPS gamers. I've included links to references on this in the hyperlink reference guide at the end of this book.

When I first started with video games on the Atari® 2600 in the early '80s, I was thrilled by the concept of seeing moving pictures I could control evolve into more and more complex concepts. As we progressed onward to NES and PC gaming in the late '80s and early '90s… the technology improved such that we could really see some impressive works. However, most of the techniques and methods of game design remained the same. The game engines themselves have changed. Back in the '90s, 2D Mario®-style side-scrollers were all the rage on home gaming platforms. After Doom®, a whole market segment emerged of first person shooters and exhibited extreme dominance.

As the years have gone by, technology has grown exponentially. What were merely aspirations and dreams in the early '90s are now commonplace. Games commonly have physically based rendering, volumetric cloud systems, physics engines integrated into game engines, and cinema quality video. In return, the game industry has grown and grown, with publishers and studios resembling movie studios. We often refer to these studios and publishers as "AAA" or triple-A studios. They represent the highest level of capability a producer or studio can manage. While these can seem cripplingly difficult to compete against as an independent (or indie) developer, it's important to bear in mind that they have their own hurdles to overcome.

Unfortunately, they suffer the same issues that most modern movie studios have—that being a lack of creative gameplay or original plots in their stories. They consistently churn out lowest common denominator products that sell big numbers but frequently fail to provide a rewarding experience. These days we are seeing a constant trend toward less fun, more grind-oriented gameplay that is often little more than a thinly veiled cash grab. A corporation often casts a keen gaze toward focus groups, market demographic research, and consumer purchasing trends over things like good gameplay, control, and engaging stories.

This is where you come in.

Many independent game developers have a bold vision based on their own experiences with gaming. They know what they like and have a passion for making their dreams come to life. After all, who knows what gamers desire better than an actual gamer? The major hurdle, of course, is that most gamers lack the technical expertise to make their visions take shape. It's exceptionally difficult, if you have no experience in three-dimensional modeling, game design mechanics, game theory, or programming, to put together a game from scratch.

Being an independent (indie) game maker is a consuming experience, something that can be both overwhelming and exhilarating. There's a huge number of skillsets required. In no way can you be an expert in all of them, though it won't hurt to try your best. A partial list of the things you'll need to be is: an architect, a programmer, a graphic artist, a story writer, a sound engineer, a composer, a director, a marketer, a technical support representative, a quality assurance tester, a CEO, a 3D modeler, a texture artist, and much, much more. The more you can do, the better the product will be.

As such, a number of game "engines" have popped up on the market. Most of these engines are marketed toward people who have a wide range of experience ranging from beginner to expert. Generally speaking, the more advanced engines are functionally easier to use by experts. Some make very simplistic engines that have no real power and make huge promises. It can be difficult to know where, as an amateur, you slot in. This is where GameGuru shines; it's touted for its ease of use and ability to rapidly build levels by a member of any skill bracket.

Make no mistake, though, even with an "easy game maker" such as GameGuru, there will be a significant investment in time, energy, blood, sweat, tears, and possibly even money. Game making is not for the faint of heart and, while it's a fun hobby, if you want to turn it into any kind of profession, you will need to prepare yourself for the difficult days and nights that you might encounter as your development cycle reaches its crescendo.

GameGuru for Game Development

GameGuru is a game engine oriented toward newer developers and has a very simple interface, making it ideal for people just getting into game development. It fits neatly between the niches of hobbyists and professionals alike by providing a gentle learning curve while still offering some fairly advanced features. With a fairly robust Lua® interface, it provides scripting power for those who are looking to do more than simple object placement.

My personal background was with the Acknex™ A5-6 engines. I still hold a special place in my heart for it, due to its phenomenally powerful "Lite-C" scripting language. However, building a game in it required a significant investment of time and resources as you had to structure literally everything from scratch. This included physics models, first person shooter (FPS) controls, and even rudimentary things like making functional doors or enemies. EVERYTHING had to be scripted from the ground up by you. While that did allow a significant degree of control, it also virtually guaranteed that anyone who had a shortage of time would never make anything of real value.

GameGuru (originally called FPS Creator: Reloaded or FPSC: R) offers a tantalizing alternative to that if you are in the market to make a 3D game. Since you have a prebuilt framework with GameGuru, it is a very attractive offer for someone who doesn't want to invest months or years building just the basic tools before getting started. This is especially true of the developer who doesn't want to waste years of their life just building the toolkit before they can actually begin building levels. With GameGuru, you can literally install it and immediately begin snapping together a first person shooter game in minutes.

What is GameGuru?

GameGuru is the evolution of a series of First Person Shooter engines developed by "The Game Creators," a UK based company. This evolution has taken a long time to get to where it is and has grown from a rather simplistic configuration to something far more powerful and possibly more sinister, depending on who you ask. The older versions of the "First Person Shooter Creator" or FPSC, were extremely simple to use and allowed hundreds of users to make games in a situation when they would not normally be able to. This engine is built to expand and improve on that capability and functionality to provide accessibility for a whole new generation of users.

It is a very simplified 3D game development tool that will allow you to rapidly build detailed and interesting 3D levels and that maintains a particular focus on FPS games, though it can be used in other genres in a limited context. Third-person capabilities, while restrictive, do exist. A significant amount of higher-end features have been implemented in a limited context as well—such as SSAO (screen space ambient occlusion) and PBR (physically based rendering). These powerful post-processing and rendering features allow the game engine to produce striking visuals when time is taken to make best use of them.

Features:

- An extremely low price point for entry into 3D game development.
- Terrain generation both random and flat; terrain modification tools that are easy to use.
- Sixteen individual or blended tiles of terrain.
- Tons of material assets, literally tons. More than you will know what to do with. Most of these are available for free or via expansion packs at a very low price point. Alternately there's also the GameGuru marketplace, which has tens of thousands of well-priced assets that are a fraction of the cost of its contemporaries.
- Lua scripting, which is fairly well fleshed out and allows a significant degree of control over your games. The Lua engine is fast, lightweight, and efficient while using a C-style syntax that is both common and easy to learn.
- A shader enabled 3D engine.
- A reasonably competent static lighting system, which helps supplement the increasingly capable dynamic lighting system.

- Simple, though functional AI.
- PBR/DX11 implementation was most recently added as of the time of this writing, and while we haven't explored their full potential, it does bring this engine within striking range of more powerful editors like Unity or Unreal.
- An easy building editor, which is literally exactly as it says it is. You can design and build buildings with extreme ease. There are some caveats to this as we will discuss later.
- Steam® integration ensures smooth operation with the world's largest digital software distribution platform.
- A massive, well-priced store of assets, objects, and scripts. This really can't be understated, it allows you to get started and do some fairly impressive things rather rapidly.
- A tight-knit, friendly, and knowledgeable community with a long history.
- Source code available on GitHub®, with public community-driven development.

What is the History of GameGuru?

The history of GameGuru is actually fairly long and complex. It's most recently been called GameGuru since February of 2015. Prior to this, it was known as FPS Creator: Reloaded, as I previously mentioned. This change marked several differences in development direction and influence as well. During its life as GameGuru, we have had several major reworks in the product that have eaten considerable time and man hours in terms of development. Most notably there was a conversion of the code to C++ for performance reasons and a conversion from DX9 to DX11, which, while still relatively fresh, was a huge leap for the engine and should really open the floodgates for significantly more advanced features.

FPS Creator, aka FPS Creator Classic, aka FPSC

FPS Creator is grandfather of the GameGuru engine. It is now available open-source via GitHub but in many ways set the standard for what was eventually to be GameGuru. It had rapid prototyping, snap-together levels (Albeit at a 90-degree angle). Levels were constructed using *SEGMENTS*, an innovative yet limited method of level design. They allowed rapid construction of interior shapes and designs. That said, it was a limited game engine in a number of respects, and while it had a lot of functionality, it also had a lot of limitations. It still maintains a very active community and remains a respectable game engine, especially considering it's basically completely free at this point.

FPSC X10

X10 was an ambitious project that was developed as a successor to FPSC but fell short in many respects. Eventually it was abandoned in favor of FPSC: Reloaded.

FPSC X10 specifically was released in 2007, with early hints of its arrival showing in technical demos and tidbits on the The Game Creators' official newsletter prior to that. It made bold promises of a massive technical rework to DirectX® 10, which would significantly increase the function of the extremely limited DirectX 9 version of FPS Creator. There were a lot of (at the time) groundbreaking features such as reflective water, bloom, window refraction, better AI, and more shaders. Unfortunately, performance suffered with respect to these additional capabilities, and the system was never quite up to spec as a result. It also took on more of a closed source aspect that in some ways alienated FPSC Classic users. At this point in time, it was in some ways more advanced than GameGuru is today, but it needs to be considered that it remains a failed product despite the technological superiority of some aspects of it (such as volumetric soft particles) and due to its failure as a commercial offering.

This system, I believe, represents the final position of where I'd personally expect GameGuru's development to go now that DirectX11 is implemented. We can likely expect in the future many technological goodies such as volumetric particles, advanced shader support, and advanced anti-aliasing systems to come in future patches. It's mostly opinion but given the historicity of Lee Bamber's desire to add new and powerful features, we generally should expect more of that. Never forget that it's a boring job coding the same engine for 15 or more years. We're all human and, given he's not a robot, we can reasonably expect he will pursue things that interest him to keep his morale and motivation alive.

FPSC: Reloaded/FPSC: R

FPSC: Reloaded is the father of GameGuru in virtually every sense. Many of the older features from the original FPS Creator never made it into the newer development, which became highly structured around a functional terrain generation system. So while the original FPSC did a great job for what tools it had for indoor scenes, it failed miserably on outdoor scenes, whereas the contrary was true of FPSC: R. FPSC: R had a wonderful ability to build outdoor scenes but had virtually no provisions for building an indoor scene. You could do it, but there were numerous issues with the methods that had to be employed along with a number of promised features that unfortunately got scrapped because they couldn't be delivered within the budget and time frame allotted.

To explain, back in around 2012, The Game Creators, LTD (aka The Game Creators), decided they were going to revamp their very aged and tenured FPS Creator engine. This revamp was originally going to be funded via the Kickstarter®, but the Kickstarter failed.

At the time of the Kickstarter (https://www.kickstarter.com/projects/TheGameCreators/fps-creator-reloaded), the project seemed to be effectively a revamp of the failed FPSC X10 experiment. It was going to have a broad range of features, which were not clearly defined but seemed promising. Things ranging from improved AI to a terrain system, functional occlusion, and other things of that nature. It mostly looked to free the existing system from its constraints. I'm fairly certain, given the videos I've seen and demonstrations used that some of the early features of GameGuru were developed in this time period.

On a Purely Speculative Note

Please note it was a very short time frame, but one of the most noteworthy creations is that of a terrain system. Now this terrain system appears to have been developed outside of the original FPSC system, which used walls, floors, and ceilings segments that snapped together to create levels quickly and cleanly. This terrain system formed the core of what we know of today as GameGuru. It's also a big part of the reason why the system has so much ease at building outdoor scenes but so much difficulty at building indoor scenes. The two systems of development were never truly reconciled.

After the Kickstarter failed, they then decided to do a direct fundraising effort by preselling copies and accesses. I actually purchased it on a gold level of this pledger, and this provided enough funding to get the original copy off the ground. The stated mission at that time was:

> Our mission is to develop an open world game creator that is easy to use and produces very high quality results in all areas; such as superior art & animation, smooth gameplay and top class audio.

I'd say that after nearly four years of development, this has actually been a reasonably achieved success as far as goalposts go. A lot of features listed in the Kickstarter were met. Even simple things like ambient occlusion, occluding objects for performance, better AI (it's not much better but is still better), multiple weapon usage, and other functions were all achieved over time. However, at the time of FPSC Reloaded, there were a lot of "potential" add-ons that fell by the wayside. Things like an explosion system still remains elusive to this day. Of course, the legacy of these issues leaves a bitter taste in the mouth for some, but no engine is without its quirks. In development, it also dropped the legacy FPI code, which was a custom scripting language developed for the FPS Creator engine(s) but instead started using the more common, faster, and more powerful Lua language.

Lee Bamber, Creator and Founder of GameGuru and The Game Creators

By now you've read me mention the name "Lee Bamber." Lee is the chief programmer for The Game Creators and its driving force. He has to wear a lot of hats on any given day and as such it really can be an exhausting job. He's an Intel Black Belt, which means he's been selected as a distinguished member of the programming community by Intel.

Figure 1.1

"Relics of Deldroneye," Lee Bamber's Commodore Game.

The biggest issues, as always, are time and motivation. When you are motivated, you never have enough time. When you burn the candle from both ends to make the most of your time, you burn out on motivation. It's a difficult and tricky situation for any person, and Lee's been doing it for well over a decade.

He got his start with a Vic-20 before moving on to Amiga games and is known as the creator of the game "Relics of Deldroneye" (see Figure 1.1).

He gives a pretty good and detailed interview about his Amiga days over at Amigapd, an Amiga platform gaming website… You can find that link in the hyperlink reference guide.

In the '90s, he had a few titles, and he is credited with several games before he made some more serious stuff—an early game creation engine called "The Games Factory™." It's widely known as the successor to the much better known "Klik n' Play" engine.

I contacted Lee with some questions, and I was happy to get a very broad series of responses that he's allowed me to share with you.

MM: Why did you get into games; where was your first experience that you can recall?

LEE: My first experience with games was with an ancient console-like device I called the "intertelly," which had four games, which I played constantly. My first exposure to real computer games was visiting my uncle, who had a state-of-the-art computer called the VIC-20. It was not long before my nagging got me the most expensive Christmas present I ever had, my very own VIC-20. I was ten at the time. By the end of the day, I had created my first computer program. Back then, games and programming went hand in hand.

MM: When did you decide to go from playing games to making them?

LEE: Thanks to a steady stream of games from the aforementioned uncle, and pocket money, I was able to play most of the games on the VIC-20, and later on the C64. Back then, my uncle was already coding, and during my teen years we would talk programming a lot, and it was not long before BASIC and Assembly were second languages to me. By the time I left school for college, I had already made a lot of "mostly bad" games and had several small publishing successes in magazines and the shareware scene. As I got older, I found myself coding more and playing games less. It was actually more fun to make them!

MM: When did you go from making games to deciding to help others create games?

LEE: *Back in the day, most game developers had to create their own tools before the game could be finished. Level editors, asset creation, debugging tools, and usually built right into the games. One of the last games I wrote for the Amiga was "Relics of Deldroneye" which needed a full "graphic adventure editor" creating before I could create the scenes and logic for the game (think Monkey Island in Space). By the end of the game development, I considered releasing the game editor as a tool in its own right. Of course, this was around the same time I had to leave college and get a real job, so I put down the Amiga, picked up the PC and started writing games again for what was then called Klik & Create (now called Fusion). During my time at this publisher, I started creating a BASIC programming language in my spare time that would make 3D game making easier for PC users, it was called Dark BASIC. This was in 1999, and I've been making game makers ever since.*

MM: What sort of challenges do you have with respect to communities and expectations?

LEE: *A community will generally reflect the product, and expectations can vary wildly. A community based around a pure programming language is already tech-savvy and has the ability to make quick conclusions on the suitability of one tool over another and accept or reject the product on those terms. A community based on a product that claims to make game creation super easy needs careful management of expectations, and even then, such a broad product claim will surely disappoint a proportion of users come what may. We cannot control how users may react to the product, but we can respond quickly and clearly to any questions put to us, and make sure the information on our Steam page, website, and other channels reflects the current and true state of the software. Beyond that, it's a little futile trying to change such forces of nature, and the best you can do is understand the critique when it is offered and do something to address it with the resources available.*

MM: What are some of your favorite games made by users?

LEE: *There have been a lot of games over the years that I would hold above anything I have created myself, but I tend to like games that go that extra mile to impress. Even though I've provided hundreds of gigabytes of free game-making assets over the last 17 years, games that use custom media are the ones that really stand out and show that the game developer is serious about their craft. Games that took the basic foundations of the underlying game making technology, and then built on them to such a degree that it leaves me wondering how on earth it was done. Games that really understand how to set a scene, tell a story, and create an emotional connection with the player, or simply employ addictive and lasting game play so you keep coming back. These are the qualities that make me smile when I see them coming from one of my game makers, and if the game developer also gets to sell their creation and make a living at it, then that makes me smile even more.*

MM: What does the future hold for GameGuru? What is your vision for its projected course?

LEE: It is clear that three years was not long enough for a very small team to deliver on the expectations created when GameGuru was launched, not least because of the relentless march of games technology means that visuals that were acceptable yesterday are out of date tomorrow. As chart topping games get even better, the expectation that anyone can create games of that scale and quality is also prevalent, making the crash landing much harder on users who hope to create the next GTA™ or Uncharted™ in a few weeks. In the short-term, GameGuru needs to begin educating new users about the realities of game making and what is reasonable to expect when embarking on a game creation project. It also needs to up its own game in terms of the features it offers and attempt to resemble the visual and performance quality of games of not more than a few years old. I still believe there is a place for GameGuru in what has become a pretty crowded market of game-making solutions. Not many products attempt to make 3D game creation easy, favoring instead to hand the responsibility of coding the actual game to the end user. GameGuru has the potential to remove this barrier to entry, but until it can produce results with the quality of contemporary games, it will forever be regarded as a three-legged horse in a race that is only getting faster each lap. On a positive note, it is a unique product with a lot of potential, comes with a fantastic community, and has the benefit of a team that has been making game creation easier for almost two decades, so let's stay calm and make games!

I want to thank Lee for taking the time to answer my questions in detail. He's got a difficult enough job as it stands so it's always good when he can block time away to be able to really plot out his history for us. To me, it's crucial to understand where a chief developer comes from to know how you got to where you are. It also helps you determine where you'll be going.

Note from the Author: At the time of this interview, it was clear Lee was being somewhat cagey though I couldn't tell specifically on what. I prodded him a bit more and never got anywhere. In the time of this writing, however, he made the source code publically accessible so it was clear he was trying to keep his cards close to his vest. Ironically, as we approached publication of this book, it became clear he had a lot of news he was hanging onto, notably the move to GitHub and all of the resultant tectonic shifts that came with it. This last year (since the interview, which was done a scant two months before the move to GitHub) has brought more change to GameGuru's base code than the last four years preceding it.

So from my standpoint, I have to say the future is looking a fair amount brighter than it had been previously. Gains are rapidly being made toward a much greater sense of legitimacy by mainstream game studios, which is an impressive feat for such a short period of time. Since this update, we've had actual water code added, in-game control of water, better AI, better lighting, PBR materials, and a host of other features. Things are coming along at a record pace, so much so that by the time this book is printed, there will likely be a vast amount more!

As I neared the end of this book, I returned back to ask Lee some further questions to help clarify his earlier answers from nearly a year prior.

MM: Do you have any changes in how you feel the direction of GameGuru will be going forward?

LEE: No change in direction; I think we have a pretty good system set up now for the community to actively contribute to the project both in terms of code and art, and it will be exciting to see what we add in 2019.

MM: How are you feeling about the increased community involvement so far?

LEE: It has been fantastic, we are seeing features and improvements that simply would not have been done had it not been for the repository contributions.

MM: What's one thing you'd like to see from the community in the future?

LEE: More freelancers taking on some of the tasks so we can spend more of the donation pots that have been building up. I think the community wants to see the donations spent and new features and fixes appearing.

MM: Any additional thoughts on GameGuru in general?

LEE: I still think it's a pretty unique product that allows someone with no interest in coding or art creation to have a 3D game up and running very quickly, giving them a great start into the games industry. It will never replace the professional tools, and maintaining such a product is a daunting task, but we have a strong community and a growing product, and the future looks good.

2

A Brief History of FPS Games

What is a "FPS?"

FPS is an acronym for "first person shooter" as well as "frames per second," so context is fairly important here. The FPS (first person shooter) genre of games is a common genre that has evolved as a subset of 3D gaming. It typically is a three-dimensional representation of a one-versus-many conflict involving mazes and simple puzzles such as "find the key" or "get the information." It's a shooter in that it often involves gunplay, and the guns actually serve as a form of "problem-solving implement." Your obstacle can be anything from zombies, to evil Nazis, or even mere barrels that explode when you shoot them.

They range from reactive fast-paced shooters to slower-paced survival-style games and cover a massive range of environments, scenes, and genres. This broad nature allows them to function fairly well as a story-telling implement though, admittedly, they do that almost secondarily; FPSs almost always are a "Gamer's Game." They tend to revolve around a loose story but feature solid and fun gameplay, along with interesting and innovative game mechanics.

While they often can feature grotesque depictions of hyper-violence such as in the "brutal doom" add-on, they are often fairly tame to maximize market appeal. The use of firearms as a problem solver is not without its controversy but overall has become more acceptable to the mainstream world. Granted, your problems to be solved are usually "bad guys," zombies, space monsters, or the like. The firearms, however, solve the difficulty, often at cost in the form of noise attracting more attention or increased enemy aggression. Frequently, games will reward more cunning behavior such as sneaking by opponents or using your intellect to lure them into a minefield.

The Godfathers of 3D Gaming: Romero and Carmack

A company called "id Software®" (yes, it's deliberately lowercase: like the Freudian "id") had developed 3D engines for several games before Doom®. Each game's engine had progressively more advanced 3D technology. This company is well known for the "two Johns": John Romero and John Carmack. They were typically regarded as "the rock star developer" (Romero) and "genius 3D coder" (Carmack). It's relevant to understand though that Romero was originally a coder as well, so this helped cement their partnership early on and contributed to their early success. Entire books and articles have been written on these two alone. I own one, in fact: the venerable "Masters of Doom™" (David Kushner, Random House, 2004) in hardcover. It's pretty much a must-read if you're into the history of two of the most famous independent game-makers of all time.

Vast tomes have been allocated to covering the work id contributed to the broader 3D FPS movement, but I do feel it's important to at least have a rudimentary understanding of how we got to here so you know what is out there. Their early works started with ray casting engines and went in a very linear progression, at least for a while.

Carmack really broke the mold in a lot of ways. He created or popularized several crucially important methods of game development ranging from "adaptive tile refresh" ("Commander Keen®"; 1990), "ray casting" ("Hovertank 3D™"; 1991/"Wolfenstein 3D®"; 1992), "binary space partitioning" ("Doom"; 1993), "surface caching" ("Quake®"; 1996), "Carmack's reverse (shadow algorithm)" ("Doom 3®"; 2004), to "MegaTexturing" ("Enemy Territory: Quake Wars®"; 2011).

Romero, while being a programmer, designed some of the most memorable levels for some of the most memorable games in early FPS history. So while Carmack created some absolutely fantastic algorithms, it's important to note that Romero brought them to life. In GameGuru, you will effectively be playing the role of Romero as you are not coding the engine itself (most likely, though, given that the code is on GitHub® these days, anything is possible).

Eras of FPS Games

As you can tell, I'm a fan of history. I feel that if you know where something came from, you can better understand how to work with it. I've been a huge fan of id software's work since I was an awkward teen. They invented the FPS genre as we know it, so it's worth understanding what drove them and how they in turn drove us.

Early Games: Battlezone™

It's widely agreed upon that the first real "FPS" for home gaming came in the form of a game called Battlezone. Battlezone was a 3D tank simulator that was surprisingly advanced for its time. However, due to its perspective of simply having a gun, it often looks very much like a very primitive FPS. There were, however, many other examples of maze-based first-person games in the early '80s and '90s, such as maze wars, Faceball, midi-maze, and a few others.

Really though, it all started with Maze in 1973. A group of computer geeks at NASA's Ames Research Center made a maze-based two-player game. It continued development over time and became a spectator viewable shooting game placed in a maze. This, in fact, was functionally almost identical to what id's "Wolfenstein" presented visually, though it didn't have a fraction of the graphics. Maze represented the purest idea using the most limited hardware available. At the time, it was groundbreaking, but given the lack of home computers would never achieve any notoriety beyond the occasional mention in a book such as this one.

Titles like "Midi-maze™" and "Faceball®" had much better graphical functionality but typically lacked any real story or gameplay beyond "shoot the giant face." On top of that, the earlier titles such as midi-maze lacked the distribution, advanced features, and ambition that really made id Software's offering as noteworthy as it was. As a result, the FPS genre stagnated for many years before finding its legs in the early '90s.

The Ray Caster Era (1991–December 1993)

A ray casting engine is the most simplistic form of making a raster in a 3D space. What? Huh? Raster?

Ok, let's start at the beginning.

A raster is a very simplistic image structure, specifically a rectangular grid of pixels that contains image data, as shown in Figure 2.1.

That is literally it. Just a grid with information about what color goes in what square. A ray caster literally throws simulated lines of light out from a central point (the camera) and computes how far away an intersection is with a wall. Then it reads the raster image data and draws them at a scale proportionate with their distance from the camera. I go into this in significantly more detail in Chapter 9.

id's first go at 3D technology was a game called "Hovertank 3D" (1991). It used a rather simplistic system of solid-color drawn walls and scalable sprites. This, at the time, was approximately on par with other competitors such as "midi-maze" or "Faceball" and as such provided little in terms of ground-breaking capabilities. This did, however, provide a crucial backbone for later works.

"Catacomb 3D™" (1991) added texture mapping to the walls and as such represented a tremendous step forward technologically, despite its crude 16-color palette. The ability to take a picture and put it on the formerly solid colored walls was a natural progression but presented a real step forward for the genre. Unfortunately, the dated colors and graphics meant the audience still remained limited.

Figure 2.1

A close up of pixels in an image.

"Wolfenstein 3D" (1992) increased the color palette from 16-color Enhanced Graphics Adapter (EGA) to 256-color Video Graphics Adapter (VGA). The game engine was also licensed out to other companies, which further fueled the early '90s 3D gaming craze. This game and engine was fast, efficient, and beautiful compared to previous 3D game iterations.

Just prior to Doom's full-blown release, a company called "Raven Software™" got cozy with id and licensed their upgraded Wolfenstein engine. They created a game called "ShadowCaster™" (1993), which featured diminished lighting, texture mapped floors and ceilings, walls with variable heights, and sloped floors. It was, in a sense, "Wolfenstein 2.0," and while it is a lesser known title remains a fantastic game in its own right. It also, much like "Catacomb" and "Hovertank," represented an important stepping-stone.

"Wolfenstein" and "Catacomb" used this simplistic method of scanning a two-dimensional grid map to draw three-dimensional representations of their environment. Prior to this point, most of the 3D gaming graphics were done via very primitive polygons, which were computationally expensive and in general resulted in poor fidelity as well as poor performance. The ray casting systems used by "Wolfenstein 3D" and "Catacomb" were able to produce a 3D representation of a 2D map with stunning speed and impressive graphics for their time. This was a big reason why "Wolfenstein" was able to propel id Software to its place as a leader in the market.

The fact it ran on everything more powerful than a toaster didn't hurt either; the game literally had 286s running it, which, considering the game involved, is an impressive achievement. That level of capability meant it was highly portable and ended up on a number of systems including the Apple IIGS, a non-Intel platform. "Wolfenstein" sold a total of 200,000 copies by 1993 on a six-month development cycle and a $25,000 dollar investment in rent and salaries. It generated a massive income for the fledgling company and allowed them to really push forward with some generational leaps. At one point, it was literally making $200,000/month and a profit of nearly $45 per copy (due to the shareware method being used to market it). This was not only groundbreaking for a 3D game but for independent game developers in general. In a sense, it set the bar for others in the market to aim for.

"Wolfenstein" had broken the mold, and others were eager to follow it. Clones came out as fast as you could think, and the market was flooded with duplicates and lookalikes that wanted to get their fingers on some of the money flowing toward id. Games like "Blake Stone: Aliens of Gold®" used the Wolfenstein engine on license which meant more money flowing toward id.

Doom Era (December 1993–1996)

As has been said before, it will be said again: if "Wolfenstein 3D" broke the mold: Doom evaporated it. No one, not a single person, was prepared for what Doom brought to the table. People simply weren't accustomed to the types of massive leaps forward that a game like that embodied. Doom housed a generational increase in engine flexibility with a total engine type change. Gone were the clunky raycasters of "Catacombs" and "Wolfenstein." In was the new "2.5D" engine with odd wall angles, and unique variably sized wall heights, floors, ceilings, an advanced lighting system, and many other improvements meant this game completely obliterated its predecessor.

The z-axis, while not completely represented, gave us the equivalent of a 2.5-D engine. This level of flexibility cannot be understated, however, as it literally resulted in a generation-defining difference from the mere 2-D side scrolling games from a scant few years before.

Doom's source code was released to the public on December 23, 1997, under a license allowing noncommercial use; in 1999, it was rereleased under the GNU General Public License. This led to the development of numerous source ports adding new features to the engine. It continues to see community-led development in the form of new ports, mods, and maps. Even John Romero came back to it recently many years later and released several new maps on Twitter for his most die-hard fans to try out (like me). It's amazing that a game that captivated so many still holds the attention of us almost 25 years later.

Some Quick Facts

It was the first 3D game engine that allowed variable heights for floors and ceilings. However, it only allowed one floor or ceiling per area, making multistoried levels impossible. It also was id's first game to include a multiplayer component called "death match" that made the game wildly popular. My first experience with the game, for instance, was playing at a local college, where several Comp-Sci college kids had setup a local area network (LAN) and were playing four-man death match. At the time, this was absolutely mind-blowing to me and was something I had to have.

John Carmack experimented with 16-bit textures but found the overhead unacceptable for the game. This meant some downsizing but gave Doom a very unique look and feel, which I believe carries itself very well to this day thanks to some very intelligent palette color choices by their lead artist (Adrian Carmack: no relation to John!).

Doom's inherent success really set the tone for shareware developers everywhere. Its model was exceptionally successful and, as a result, people everywhere couldn't wait to imitate it. Clones appeared everywhere, virtually overnight, with most of them being on par with being something along the lines of "Wolfenstein's" level of technical capability.

Around this time, one of the first clones decided to break the mold and offer its development tools for purchase. This system was called the Pie 3D GCS™. It was spawned from a game called "Terminal Terror™" and was available in PC gaming magazines for an exceptionally low price.

While there were other game-creation systems, at the time, this game really presented one of the first viable methods of game development for the casual gamer. It was a true forerunner to the GameGuru engine and bore a lot of similarities to Doom. Though at the time, technologically speaking, it was only about as advanced as the Rise of the Triad engine, which itself was an improvement on "Wolfenstein 3D."

I myself remember fondly spending my hard-earned money on a copy of the Pie 3D GCS and making my own very amateurish games. It was a thrilling feeling and provided a lot of interesting days learning new languages like Forth, which was used for the AI system, and FORTRAN, which was used by the actual game engine itself.

Doom's success was highly dependent on the shareware model but sold so many copies it generated millions versus the hundreds of thousands that "Wolfenstein" had earned. It was literally everywhere. Pop culture had been taken over, and the FPS genre was here to stay.

Quake Era (1996–1998)

While all the Doom (and even "Wolfenstein") clones were making their run, John Carmack and John Romero were pushing ahead with a new project called Quake. This "id tech® 2" engine would shatter traditional game-development conception by providing a fully realized 3D game engine including actual Y-axis traversal and rapid engine capabilities with BSP (binary space partition) tree capabilities expanded tremendously from the Doom era. Binary space partitioning is a form of rapid data traversal that allowed Doom and Quake to create incredibly fast 3D environments.

Moreover, I still remember the first technical demo for it and waiting with baited breath. This was an exciting time where graphic horsepower was still limited, so coding geniuses like Carmack really created this whole new realm of possibility. In a few scant years, we'd gone from side scrollers to fully realized 3D gaming. Moreover, it was fast. It ran well and looked good. It covered the spread in every respect. For its time, it literally was so far ahead of the curve, it actually drove a lot of the push toward hardware acceleration for 3D graphics. At the time, no one could imagine a fully 3D game as possible for many years, but id had done it. "Quake 2®" followed much the same track "Doom 2" did; it offered mild technological improvements and mostly the same gameplay. There's no doubt Quake 2 was a vastly prettier game than "Quake 1," with a far more cohesive plot… but, generationally speaking, it was hard to put into words the shock factor that came from playing "Quake 1" after years of playing "Doom 1 or 2."

Goldeneye Sub-Era

It's rare that any game made a sufficient enough stamp on the FPS crowd to be noticed with id effectively owning the market upside down and sideways. There were a few exceptions, and one worth noting is the very impressive game for the Nintendo 64® console called "Goldeneye 007™." I still remember going over to my friend's house and playing it for hours. While it wasn't groundbreaking in terms of graphics or level design, what was impressive were the hugely variable game modes, weapons, player characters, and nuances available. Weapons ranged from fully automatic weaponry that decimated enemies to proximity based grenades. There was even a mode for "slappers only" where you literally ran around slapping your competition to death. It was an unbelievably comprehensive system that opened the doors to a significant amount of gameplay options.

At the time, it also had some impressive technical achievements such as location-based shooting and an awards system. With respect to location-based shooting, it recognized things such as head or leg shots, which had additional modifiers for them. Leg shots would actually cause an enemy to hop around. There was also mission-based gameplay, which was a bit of a first, allowing you to have specific mission objectives to accomplish and stretched the gamut from straight up "shoot 'em all and let God sort 'em out" to "blow up X object, sneak past object Y, get through the guards without raising alarms" and other more modern concepts. Bear in mind, this was all delivered on the extremely limited RAM of a Nintendo 64 cartridge containing 96MB of data. This type of technical achievement would be hard to pull off today, let alone in 1997!

On top of that, it offered a two to four person split screen game mode in which many a young teen spent hours huddled around a mid-sized or tiny television trying to kill his friends. It made for a fun afternoon and allowed several people to play without the hassle of PC-style communications (which were not nearly as refined as they are today).

This brief window in time is important because clones stopped being as similar as id's software. Games with real potential had stepped up to the plate with their own take on what FPS should be and had carved out chunks of their own market segments.

"Quake III®" Rules the Roost

"Quake III" was another bombshell game, which came out shortly after Goldeneye but ramped up rapidly as a fast, competitive game that evolved as a whole subset of e-sport. While the character models weren't particularly impressive, some of the innovations Carmack had wrought in the engine itself allowed some impressive graphical adjustments. It's hard to think of an engine that pushed the envelope as much as this one did at its time. It didn't include any software rendering and required a hardware GPU to function. It was groundbreaking in a lot of ways, from its use of shaders (a sort of scripting that modifies graphics in-game), in-model representation, and its "fast inverse square root function," which presented a fairly novel way of dealing with complex math for the engine allowing it to process difficult operations very quickly. As mentioned, it also helped evolve e-sports as a by-product of its game design. It's hard to understand how Carmack could take his own knowledge and build on it in such a way, but it paved the road for many great things to come.

The Post-Quake Era

From a technical standpoint, improvements in the "post-Quake era" haven't been as groundbreaking. The immersion of the games has gone up due to an increase in graphics quality and fidelity, and there are better physics and much more interesting lighting systems. But overall, the games offer little in terms of actual game design or functions that go beyond the hash of games that came out using the Quake engine tech. Games like "Duke Nukem® 3D," "Unreal®," "Unreal Tournament®," and "Goldeneye" had broken the mold that id had ironically created (after breaking the mold themselves many years before). From this point, we saw many different innovations in story and gameplay design. The quake engine was licensed out to many companies, including Valve®, the creators of the preeminent "Half-Life®" series, and it formed the basis for dozens of games and even technologies going forward; but in a sense, Carmack's ability to innovate so far ahead of the curve took a while for anyone else to really begin to catch up.

During these years, we saw many games move forward with interesting concepts such as the "Call of Duty®" and "Medal of Honor®" franchises, as well as the various iterations of Unreal and Half-Life.

As a result, engine design was relatively stale with no particularly mind-blowing technological increases for several years after this point until id dropped another lasting bombshell: Doom 3.

Doom 3 and the Era of Graphical Innovation

In 2004, Doom 3 arrived. It once again provided the sort of shattering change in graphic fidelity that was hard to fathom at first. In fact, it was so advanced it helped obsolete the DirectX® 7 standard along with a whole generation of graphics cards! For many years, running this game on Ultra was a luxury of the rich as it required more computing power than most people had available. While gameplay was nothing particularly amazing, its use of Bezier curved surfaces, subdivided textures, dynamic per pixel lighting, shadow volumes, skeletal animation, and MegaTexturing was groundbreaking: the gauntlet had been cast down. Though neither Carmack nor Romero survived the transition that id Software endured, their legacy would live on.

A New Generation is Born (Crytek®, "Unreal 4®") 2007

Carmack and Romero's achievements in programming, level, and game design should not be understated. They're covered here out of a deep admiration by one of their biggest fans (myself, obviously). However, all things must come to an end. Romero and Tom Hall had left id Software in 1996, taking some of the most innovative level and game design away from the company. Highly talented artist Adrian Carmack left in 2005. John Carmack left after 22 years with the company in 2013. In that time, numerous difficulties erupted, which are better left for another day.

In this period, other names came into prominence as well. The world is not without its geniuses, after all. Major advances were made in other engines, notably the CryEngine® and Unreal engines, spearheaded by their own groups of highly intelligent people. Of note are Tiago Sousa and Tim Sweeny, as well as countless subordinates and secondary developers. An interesting side note here is that Tiago Sousa eventually ended up at id Software to fill the shoes of John Carmack after he left!

FPS Gamedev and the Common Man

As game developers plodded unflinchingly forward with their ever-increasingly potent game engines, some realized that there was a unique opportunity that had never been adequately exploited. In other cases, there were game engines that simply couldn't compete against the top tier engines like Unreal or CryEngine; but they could be marketable as readily accessible game development engines.

These engines have come and gone; some remain. During this period of growth, though, there was a profound explosion of indie gamedev engines. Some of these are more noticeable, including the Unreal engine itself, which is a powerful tool—if a little unwieldly for the average user.

Unity came about, with its broad base of support and fairly well-thought-out graphical user interface (GUI). Other lesser-known engines such as Acknex (A6, A7, and A8), Leadwerks, CopperCube, S2Engine, and others all found their way into the market. It was during the initial period of this that FPSC came about as a truly down-to-earth way for absolute beginners to get into game making. Its subsequent evolutions like FPSC: Reloaded and GameGuru continue this tradition. It's an exciting time where anyone can work with any number of engines, trying what works and discarding what doesn't.

3

A Design Flow Document or Technical Design Document

GameGuru is a "WYSIWYG" engine. That stands for "what you see is what you get." It's very straightforward and allows very rapid prototyping of levels and even whole games with a minimum of fuss. Models are plentiful and cheap, common code components are included with it, and level design is very intuitive. So why then am I about to talk about making a technical design document (or TDD)? What's the point of using a "WYSIWYG" engine if you have to do planning? The answer is that more complex engines require more complex planning and with an engine as easy to use as GameGuru, such documentation could be seen as counterproductive, right?

I'll admit, I'm a little more structured than most. Indeed, I spoke to some of the more prominent mapmakers in the GameGuru world and discovered that a great many do build their maps on the by and whole intuitively. But with further digging, I quickly discovered that all of them would often write down even simple notes about levels, plans, and draw simple maps. Sometimes these would even be on the back of a napkin. It doesn't have to be much. Just something to orient your thoughts.

Imagine it as a journey on a ship. You are Magellan, sailing toward an uncertain future. You have a basic idea of what you need and how you want to get there.

You need to gather supplies, get a map, navigational aids (this book, for example), some competent crew, and most importantly, have a vision of what you seek to achieve.

So although game design seems like something you can walk into and be done with by simply slapping together a few models and assets, this is not the case, and a lack of planning will result in a product that often lacks polish at best or looks like poorly laid out slop at worst. Some game makers "create games organically." This, to me, is translated as "planning is boring, I just want to make stuff." That said, I agree, planning IS boring because I do just want to make stuff. But wisdom has taught me that I just so happen to make better stuff when I plan things. Your miles will inevitably vary.

Now when you're making your TDD, even the simplest TDD will do. It's often the difference between simply putting down something on a napkin and putting it into a Word document. It doesn't need to be much—even a list of enemies, level structure, pickups, and some basic information. Invest in some manila folders and some graph paper too if you want to do even more "pre-development" work.

So What Goes into a Design Document?

The first component you're going to work up is your general premise and a quick outline of the story. Start with a simple description of the situation, the main character, setting, and antagonists. Enclosed is a copy of the demo game's TDD, broken apart piece by piece.

Summary

> My game is going to be a sci-fi mystery game where you uncover the reason for your ex-wife's murder. It will take place in the future both on several planets and a space station. You will fight a combination of evil gang members, killer androids, and hostile alien creatures.

Now you want to establish the scene itself, in greater detail. I often do this by asking myself questions such as: What time does it take place in? Where are you? Why are you in that location? What special environmental components are there? Is this a low gravity space station? Are you in a primitive jungle with dinosaurs?

I like to break these out level by level. So, in our example, we have:

Level 1: Ex-Wife's home planet. Brown and green foliage, gray streets. Not particularly advanced, seems more run down and backwater than you'd expect from the future. You start at a hangar and advance through several areas, such as speaking with the corrupt local police, and then arriving at the ex-wife's residence to find the clues. Once you find enough clues, you can then move on to finding her killers. This level will have minimal combat.

Level 2: Off-planet hub satellite station. Rusty, dark, damp. Something has happened here, many dead piled up in the corridors. I want this to seem like a really dark place that people only go to because they have to. Grungy textures are a must. This is a combat-oriented level. A few scientist-types and others.

Architecture should be confusing and disorienting....

Level 3: Criminal's planet. This is a more upscale planet with mega-skyscrapers, possibly a dome-type sky, lots of neon, and criminals everywhere. Lots of alleys, cutaways, storefronts, and other areas that give it a cyberpunk feel.

Level 4: Alien planet where the secret aliens who were manipulating everything are from. Pretty crazy combat-oriented level.

Story

The next key element to address is the story itself. You should, as a game maker, expect to revisit this area often; it can and will be subject to change. One of the greatest examples of this was in the making of the original Doom game; there was a massive tome dedicated to an expansive plot called "The Tei Tenga Incident." This was eventually completely thrown out in favor of a fast-paced action shooter with minimal plot. It coincidentally became a worldwide sensation. Don't be afraid to modify or adjust your goals; you can't be expected to get it perfect the first time.

So some of the questions you want to be asking yourself are: Why are you doing what you're doing? What's the overarching flow of the story? Is this story too big or too small? Is there a clear ending? Does my character evolve? Is my character better at the end for having made the journey?

It can be as simple or as complex as you desire. Anything from "save the princess from the evil green reptile king" to a four-thousand-word essay with a complete story breakdown or more. It really all depends on how much you plan to implement in the game from your story and how much you need to plan before doing.

Monsters

Monsters are as much a part of the environment as the environment itself. Often you have to think of each area as its own sort of biome (e.g., a large area where animals and plants live). This organic location perhaps is a mechanical world and thus has robot enemies. Perhaps it's the previously mentioned jungle and is full of vicious old-world man-eating plants. Maybe it's in an unspecified area of the Middle East and you're fighting terrorists. It's good to map out your monsters at least a little to flesh out what types of challenges your protagonist (the player) will overcome.

Most FPS games thrive off enemies as an obstacle to overcome. While a significant amount of FPS games have followed the traditions of the puzzle game Myst from the '90s, a great many more love to add monsters or villains to contend with.

Example:

- **Pistol guy:** a basic, low hit point (HP) enemy
- **Shotgun guy:** a stronger, mid HP enemy
- **Uzi guy:** A machine gun-style enemy with low HP but high damage

- **Rocket launcher guy:** a rare, but tough, opponent with high HP and big damage
- **Giant scorpions:** An environmental mini-boss that can poison the player
- **Giant rats:** A mid-level environmental enemy that can swarm the player
- **The evil scientist genius:** hides behind machines and other enemies, final boss.

Weapons, Collectibles, and Other Objects

I like to break my collectibles into several components, first we have the weapons. Are there melee weapons? Historical weapons like bows and arrows? Machine guns? What types? Will you be using assets built in, custom made, or from the store?

In our demo game, we will have:

- A custom melee weapon.
- A modified or custom revolver.
- A custom machine gun.
- A very powerful shotgun.
- A projectile-based weapon.

Other collectibles will include health kits: some people use food, others use medical kits. Sometimes they even just use a giant plus sign. They also include things like ammunition for your weapons, keys for doors, custom objects like puzzle pieces, and other associated usable minutiae.

Other objects would be items that you pick up or interact with. Some games have readable notes, others have story objects. These should all be outlined and detailed so you can keep your thoughts in order.

Our game will need:

- Health kits that are collectible.
- Adrenaline kits that will act as a power amplifier.
- Keys and switches.
- Notes that can be read and collected.
- Puzzle pieces that allow areas to progress (multicomponent keys) and "clues," which are objects that once collected help complete a quest, thus allowing the game to continue forward.

Mapping Your Levels

From this point, I like to draw a preliminary draft of each level. As with all things in the game's TDD, this stands as an overview or a general point I want to aim for. Let's start with some basic questions, once again:

Are they indoor? Outdoor? What types of design features do they have?

I like to use graph paper when available for drawing out quick-and-dirty ideas of what my maps will look like. This helps me structure them when I actually go

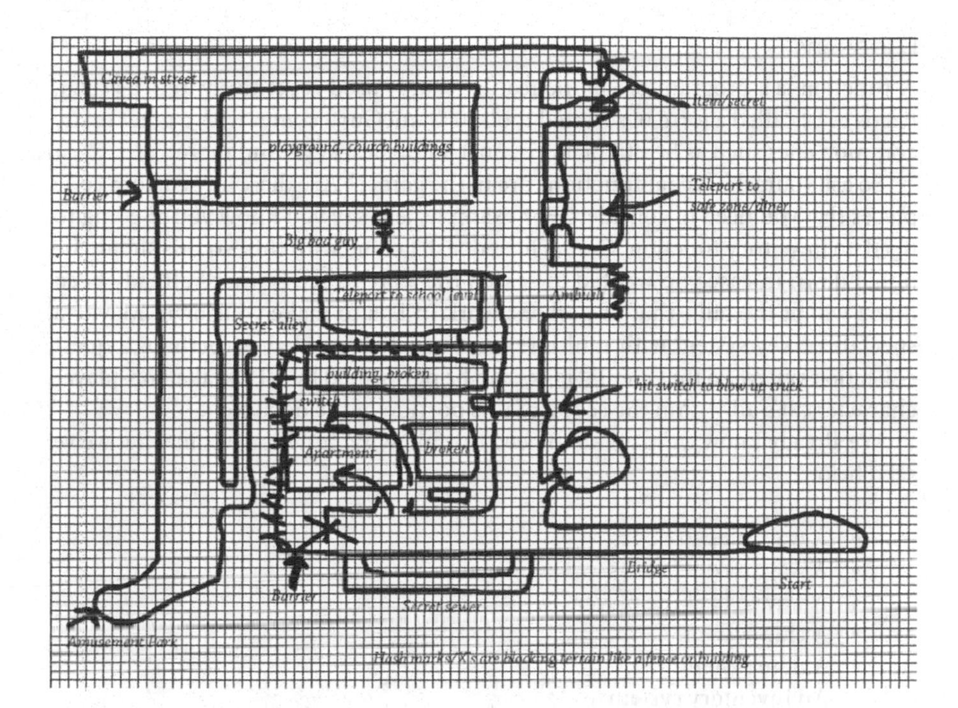

Figure 3.1

A hand-drawn map.

to make them later. It also gives me time to "develop" when I'm not actually at a computer (which happens more often than I'd like due to my other job of being an active father of two).

As you can see in Figure 3.1, there's not a lot of detail in this example. I'm simply illustrating that this particular method helps me shape my design later on. You may find it's better for you to just start sticking pieces together to get a sense of what you want to accomplish. Still, I recommend writing at least a bare concept on paper, even if it's just simple lines illustrating a path.

Individual Level Details

Maps are good, but often it's useful to put separate information about the level's specifics into a document for the level. It will include things like environmental effects (i.e., is it foggy, sunny, cold, wet, etc.). It will have a couple words about the level itself and what your intent is. A good example would be like this:

> Level 03: The underground ruins. This dark area will be wet, with many different types of fungi. Some will be illuminated but most won't. I would like some to be edible for the survival portion of the game. Inside the ruins will be numerous dangerous enemies and the walls should be wet and slick as if they are covered in slime.

Functions

A function is a program or engine feature that is used repetitively and, as such, needs to be called a form of scripted toolkit. GameGuru comes with a great many common ones such as health pickups, hurt/hit zones, keys, and more.

So ask yourself, "What functions are in the game?" Are there any custom code pieces that you need to consider? For example, let's say you know you're going to need an inventory function. GameGuru doesn't come with this, so this should be noted down in case you wanted to search the store to see if what's already been made will fit the bill—that or perhaps work in Lua to make your own. Maybe a specialized key system with multiple components is needed, or perhaps a quest collection system so that menial tasks can be performed by NPCs, aka non-player characters. It's all within the scope of this portion of the document.

We already know we're going to need the following functions from what we've seen before:

- A way to open doors.
- A way to collect keys.
- A way to heal the player.
- A clue system.
- A note system.
- An inventory system.

That means we'll be leveraging both built-in and custom Lua code to help create our final product.

These documents, which some might see as tedious, also give you a clear sense of not only what you need to achieve but also what you've already achieved by acting as a sort of checklist. It gives a clear sense of accomplishment, which can be very useful as your project continues to eat more and more of your free time. Sometimes just seeing a list and saying "I'm halfway there!" is a good incentive to keep working.

4

Using GameGuru

So now we have some idea of the product we're using, the history, the type of game we'll be making, and even a preliminary idea of what the game we are making will look like!

It's time to start using the tool.

When you first open GameGuru, you will see the screen shown in Figure 4.1.

This loading screen will open up the various component entities that comprise GameGuru. Each of the list files it is building is basically a subfolder inside of GameGuru that it has to check for changes and updates so that it knows what weapons are available and what skies, terrains, and so on can be integrated. This also means that if you make significant changes, you need to restart the editor entirely from time to time.

Figure 4.2 is a "welcome screen" on which you can tick off the little box at the bottom to disable it showing again. This welcome screen is comprised of three separate choices. First is learn, which brings you to the user manual you can find in the included documentation. It's a fairly straightforward manual that covers many of the things in this chapter such as how to make a simple level and place objects.

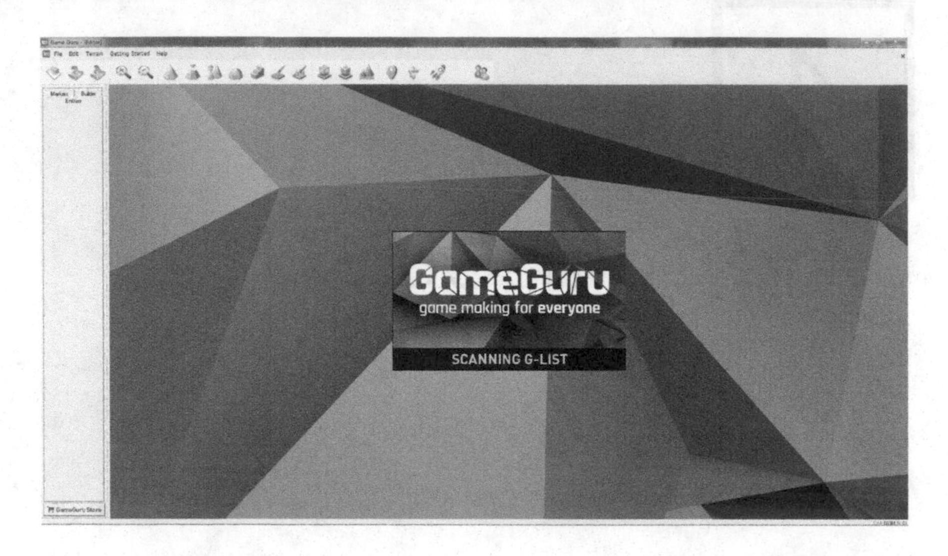

Figure 4.1

The initialization screen of GameGuru.

Play will bring you to a demo game that has a pretty thorough build to it using all stock assets. This game will allow you to see what you can do with GameGuru if you take the time to truly learn it, even when you are using the bare minimum of assets available.

Figure 4.2

The welcome screen of GameGuru.

Last is create, which simply drops you off in the editor so you can begin making your game. If you tick the box to not show the startup window, this is what it will default to.

Cheat Sheet

Undocumented

Numlock disables some key binds. If you suddenly find yourself unable to use certain functions, then hit numlock and see if they start working again!

Control-z initiates an undo on the last thing done.

Documented

F1: Key list.

1–6: Various rotations on 45-degree angles (x, x-, y, y-, z, z-).

Shift-1, 2, 3, 4, 5, 6: Fine rotation on 1-degree increments.

R: Rotate Y + 45 degrees. Same as 3.

T: Enter terrain editing mode.

LMB: Raise/lower terrain or paint.

LMB-shift: Lower terrain or remove paint.

E: Entity editing mode.

B: Grid mode cycle (snap, grid, and none).

LMB: Mouse select and paint entity.

Click and Drag LMB: Select group.

Delete: Delete if extracted or highlighted.

Y: Entity to dynamic or static (red/green)—locked?

Return/Enter: Put entity on top of other objects (cycles the mode).

PGUP: Move entity up.

PGDOWN: Move entity down.

U: Toggle auto flatten when placing entities, which creates a flat spot around the object so it isn't resting cockeyed on the terrain.

I: Spray entity mode, a spray-paint mode that allows you to randomly spray entities in varying quantities and positions.

Tab: Clip all entities; basically cuts everything in half so you can easily see insides of rooms, allowing you to do interiors with ease. You can adjust clipping height with "CTRL+Mousewheel."

L-Drag: Link entity. Hold down the L key, left-click, and drag while holding the L key. Everything that you select will be connected for the duration of that level being loaded in GameGuru as a "linked entity." This makes moving buildings with many pieces inside easier as they become one solid object from the editor's standpoint. You can still modify individual pieces, of course.

P: Waypoint path editing.

+: Increase size of circle.

–: Decrease size of circle.

<: Zoom in or cull draw distance.

>: Zoom out, extend draw distance.
Mouse wheel: Zoom in/out.
Hold shift: Increase speed of zoom.
RMB + move mouse: Free flight view.
RMB + WASD: Free flight move.
G: Top down view, very useful for streets, mazes, and waypoint editing.
F: Free flight view.

Test Game Mode

WASD: Move keys.
Mouse look: Allows you to look with your mouse.
LMB: Shoot weapon.
RMB: Zoom in weapon.
Space: Jump.
C: Crouch (hold).
Shift: Run (hold).
Tab: Framerate performance meter.
Tab again: Full settings of level (see Section"Tab settings" in this chapter).

SHIFT+F1: Simple lightmap. A quick lightmap using only real-time shadows. Use this for checking rough placement of objects.

SHIFT+F2: Advanced lightmap. This will bake the textures onto the meshes and gets the basic sun color for the scene mapped.

SHIFT+F3: Full lightmap. A lightmap for full lighting. This bakes the lights into the terrain and objects along with all previous lightmap functions. This is the preferred option.

SHIFT+F4: Full lightmapping and occlusion. This takes the longest amount of time to render but combines the other three lightmapping modes. The occlusion portion was removed, however, so this really is an unnecessary choice until any future integrations or until the keys are remapped or removed.

F9: Edit mode (in game paint, object movement, etc.).
F11: Hardware information and debug disables.
F12: Screenshot (stored in documents/GameGuru files).

A Blow-By-Blow Walk-Through of Every Button

Starting with the GUI

F1: A go-to button for your own cheat sheet list. This option presents everything you need in one neat, easy-to-digest format.

1-6: A simple and easy way to rotate an object. Select it and press the corresponding button to rotate the object in 45-degree increments along its X/Y/Z axis (corresponding to the button you push). If you hold shift while pressing 1–6, incrementation will occur by the degree allowing a finer degree of control.

R: A carbon copy of 3. Control-R does the same thing as Shift-3.

E: Entity Editing Mode (EEM). This mode allows for the selection of entities and the modification of their properties such as scale, rotation, or movement. This mode is functionally different from terrain mode, so while in this mode, you cannot modify the height, shape, or color of terrain.

B: Cycles Grid Mode type. This allows for the placing of enemies within the constraints of a grid system. Hitting B again activates snap-mode, which causes the entities to snap to each other. It is not perfect but for the most part is useful for getting repetitive entities to connect to each other. It will NOT snap two different entities to each other, only entities that are identical.

Hitting B once more will activate grid mode. This allows for the placement of objects in game measurement terms of "100 units" and ensures that they will be precisely the same distance no matter what. There are a significant number of vendors on the store, particularly ones who have been working with "FPS Creator Classic," who are intimately familiar with this system and build their construction kits around the use of 100-unit measurements.

Hitting B one more time returns you to non-grid mode (or default).

LMB in EEM will allow you to both place entities and select existing entities. Once selected, a context-driven menu will pop up. This menu will have a range of options depending on the entity being selected such as move, scale, rotate, properties, extract, and lock.

Move allows you to physically drag the object along the x-y-z axis if you use the endpoints on the arrow icons. If you click and drag on the boxes you can use a combination of axes such as X/Y or Z/Y.

Scale will stretch an entity or shrink it. Occasionally, this command will cause massive shrinkage or completely disproportionate growth. This is caused by being on the "wrong side" of the indicator. Simply change your viewpoint to be viewing the opposite side of the object and it will function normally.

Rotate is the most simplistic function; click and drag one of the rings corresponding to an X/Y/Z axis and it will rotate the object. This allows a much finer degree of rotational control than using the 1–6 or Shift 1–6 keys.

Click and Drag LMB will select everything within its selection box. This feature can be tricky to use so I typically go into top-down view mode first to ensure I'm getting a proper grab.

Delete: Deletes an object. This works if it's either selected or is currently being extracted.

Y: Entity to dynamic or static (red/green); you must extract the entity before this will work.

Return is a very useful key; it will cycle "on top mode" for an object. What this does is an in-game calculation and if the object is underneath a table, that object will be auto-placed on top of the table. This makes putting together interior scenes a lot easier. Hitting return or enter again will set it back to default mode, which simply places the object wherever you set it. If you are working in a building and all of your objects are not showing when you place them, try disabling this mode to get them to show up again.

Page up and Page down: Move a selected object up or down.

U: Toggles on/off the auto flatten feature. What this does is certain objects may place a big flat area of terrain around them. One scenario would be building a house on a hill but wanting part of it obscured by the hill. When placed, however, the terrain is raised, flattened, and the object placed. This can be avoided by hitting U and then placing the object.

I: Entity Airbrush. This is another supremely useful tool. Use plus or minus to adjust the size of the circle for spraying. For more densely packed objects, use a small circle, and for loosely packed objects, use a big circle; then just click and drag to "spray" an object on the terrain. What's awesome about this is it allows you to place a lot of repetitive objects quickly. It also rotates them randomly so they are not identically positioned.

Tab: Clip all entities; cuts everything in half so you can easily see inside of rooms. This cuts any entity over 50 units in height off of the view so that the insides can be seen. Hitting tab again toggles this mode off. CTRL+Mousewheel will control the clipping height.

L key-Drag: Links one entity to another. Inside of the editor if you hold the L key and drag, you will link entities to each other so they retain positional information relative to the other object. This allows you to place things such as windowsills, doorframes, etc. on buildings and keep them as one solid object for placement.

Inside of the editor there are several nondescript buttons that will stand out below your very common Windows command menu. The command menu is the text menu that comprises a series of pull-down menus that can be used to perform various tasks. Inside of GameGuru at the top, you will see a very simple command menu.

There are, as you can see in Figure 4.3, several pulldown options: File, Edit, Terrain, Getting Started, and Help.

The vast bulk of your work will not be done via this menu. There are, however, several very important functions you should be aware of here. Foremost is the File menu, which contains the following options:

> New Random Level, New Flat Level, Open, Save, Save As, Save Standalone, Download Store Items, Character Creator, Import Model, and up to four "recently opened" items.

New Random Level generates randomized terrain (see Chapter 5 on "Building your first game" for more information about terrains), whereas New Flat Level starts with a completely flat plane to work with. The default is New Flat Level. Open opens existing levels. A standard practice of successful

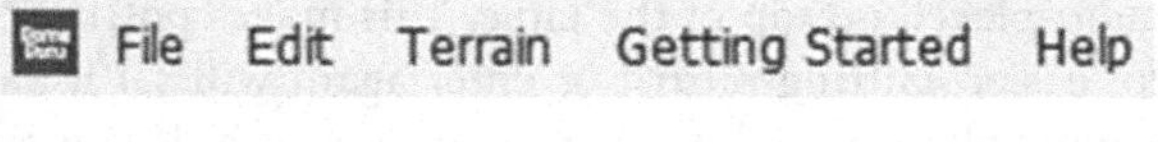

File Edit Terrain Getting Started Help

Figure 4.3

The GameGuru command menu.

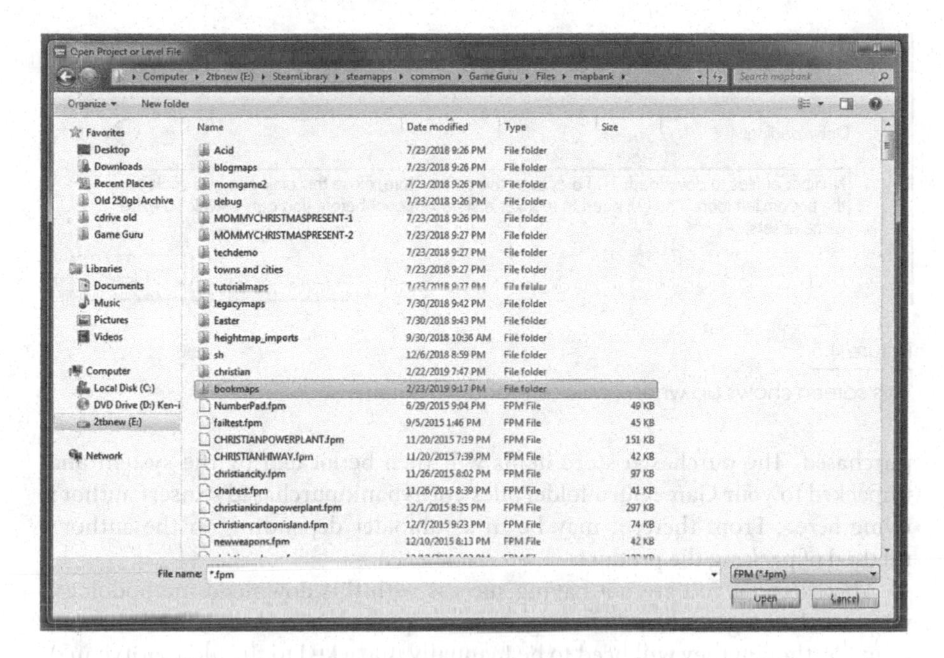

Figure 4.4

The open menu's browse screen.

developers is to separate work into subfolders in the accompanying "browse" screen (Figure 4.4).

The save menu item will save your game to the currently stored .FPM filename. If there isn't one, it prompts for the filename and location. The default location for all map files is in the GameGuru folder, under files, and then mapbank. This can be reached by hitting Alt-F and then S.

The save as menu offers the same functionality as save, although it will always prompt for a filename. This is useful if you are making multiple copies or instances of a level, such as if you want to test lighting without impacting your main copy. This can be reached by hitting Alt-F and then A.

Of particular note is the "Save Standalone" function. This allows for the creation of a GameGuru independent function that produces a working save that people can play without having to have GameGuru. This special export of your game will have a bare-bones menu and launcher as well. (See Chapter 18 on "Building a standalone" for more detailed information about this.)

Download store items will grab purchased items from the store (Figure 4.5). This does, however, require you to be logged into Steam. If you do not have Steam open, you will get an error message that says "you must be logged into the store."

The download process starts by counting your current inventory list TWO times. Once this is done, you have to hit download store items AGAIN. This will begin the process of downloading the actual new items from the store that you've

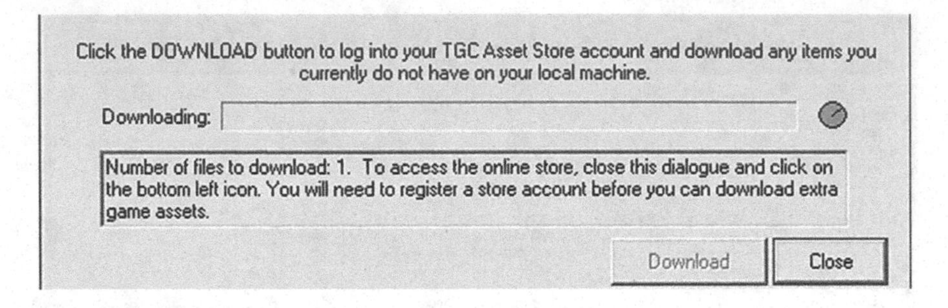

Figure 4.5

This screen shows up when you download store items.

purchased. The purchased store items will then be located by the system and unpacked to your GameGuru folder\files\entitybank\purchased\<insert author's name here>. From there, it may be in a subfolder depending on the author's method of packing the product.

Alternately, if you are not having success with this download methodology, you can always go to http://www.tgcstore.net/purchases and download them as a zip file, though they will need to be manually unpacked to the files\entitybank\purchased\<insert author's name here> folder.

Further menu items in the file menu are the Character Creator, which allows you to generate your own custom characters for games, and the import model function. Import model will bring you to the model importer, which has a unique interface and GUI. We will go over that item separately later, as well as the Character Creator, in greater depth.

The last few items are the various "recent" items and the Exit function, which operates the same as hitting X in the upper right corner of the window.

Edit Menu

The edit menu is the most simplistic of all the menus, boiling down to a scant two options: undo and redo. These two options are fairly common across most platforms and perform the same function you'd expect.

Terrain Menu

The terrain menu acts as a secondary way to access the same buttons seen across the top toolbar. While it doesn't get to all of them, it does allow for access to the typical terrain-based functions. The top item, shape, is a standard "terrain drawing" tool that allows for the raising and lowering of circles of terrain. Level mode is the flattener tool, arguably one of the most useful of the bunch. Stored level allows for terrain to be brought up to the height of your last shape-tool height.

Next is the blend tool, which allows for the equalization of terrain in a way that acts similarly to melting it down. This allows you to easily round sharp edges and blend terrain shapes seamlessly. Ramp requires clicking and dragging from one location to another and creates a ramp the width of the terrain circle from the start point to the end point based on the height between them. Paint texture allows for the painting of textures chosen from a palette on the bottom right.

This terrain palette consists of 16 different textures which will layer on top of each other starting with the one in the upper left and ending with the one in the bottom right (Figure 4.6). Simply click the one you want and then paint it onto the terrain to your discretion.

Paint grass is a vegetation spray tool that, unfortunately, is very limited in capabilities though still a wonderful tool. It allows for a single type of vegetation to be sprayed, which is dictated by the tab-tab settings. This spray allows for the painting of grasses, bushes, dead weeds, and much more directly onto the terrain.

Getting Started Menu

This menu is fairly simple, with two options like the previous edit menu. On this one, you can either revisit the welcome screen or access "Development Broadcasts."

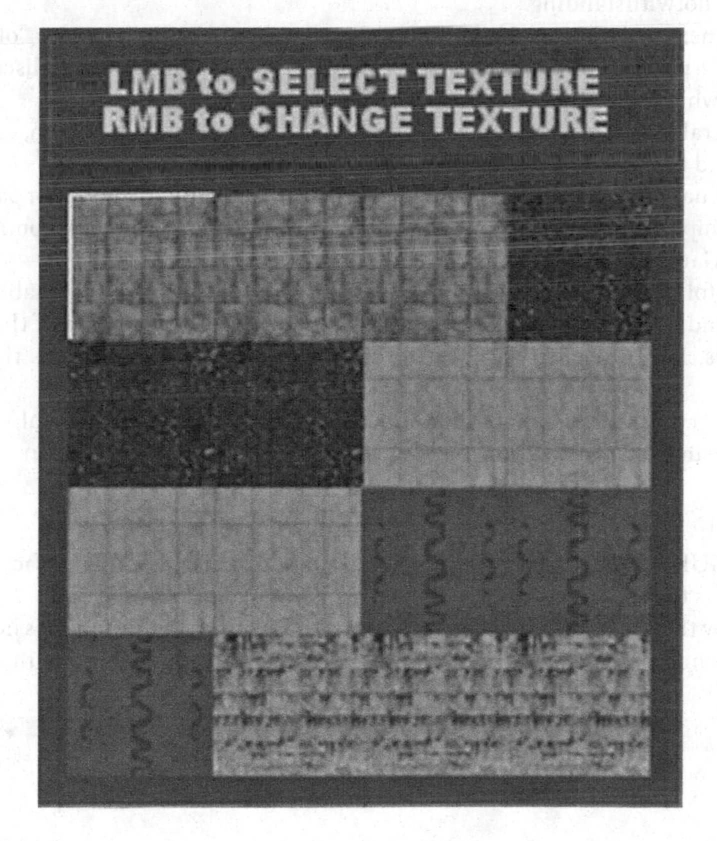

Figure 4.6

This is the terrain palette.

The development broadcasts menu item brings you to the video tutorials page on https://www.game-guru.com, which has a huge repository of video-based information on topics covering the full spectrum of GameGuru usage. Most of these consist of hour or so long "podcasts" with Lee Bamber, the lead developer of GameGuru, and they are very informative.

Help Menu

The help menu is a fairly heavily laden menu that carries a significant amount of relevant information.

The first item is "Editor Keyboard Shortcuts," which presents the same screen as the F1 key and gives a fairly comprehensive list of in-editor keys that can be used to access functionality and shortcuts.

The "About" menu gives detailed information about GameGuru, including the version (handy when multiple versions are installed).

Credits displays a full list of people involved with GameGuru's development, GitHub notwithstanding.

The next two items are for the two primary user forums, the "official" GameGuru forums located at forums.GameGuru.com and the steam discussion forum, which is linked to the game on Steam.

Generally, newer users can be found on the steam discussion forum, and the more "old hat" users hang out on the official forums.

The Lua scripting guide menu item links to an older guide that is not particularly complete but is still fairly useful for learning some basic Lua commands within GameGuru.

The following option "Toggle Restricted Content" allows the enabling of blood and gore effects, which admittedly are fairly tame and "out of the box" anyways. If you decide you want to disable them altogether, this is the way to do it.

The very last menu item of the pulldown menu is "Read User Manual," which has the same effect as clicking the "learn" button on the welcome screen.

Graphic User Interface (GUI) Details

In the GUI, under the status bar, is a fairly simplistic display and interface.

Across the top we have our menu bar, as discussed previously.

Below that is a toolbar of buttons (Figure 4.7) that, when the mouse is hovered over them, provides additional details on what they do. The first three are

Figure 4.7

The GUI's top menu bar.

"new level, open level, and save level." Then there's zoom in and zoom out. After that, we have our terrain buttons that are in the same order as they are in the Terrain menu at the top.

The next one is "Entity mode." Use this if you need to manipulate entities instead of terrain, such as bringing up their properties. It also provides access to the "I" key for spraying entities.

After that is a similar-looking item titled "marker mode." This one is of particular use if you are modifying a trigger, sound, music, or any other kind of zone. The five little points that are clicked and dragged for control can be exceptionally hard to click, if there are other entities nearby, without this handy little menu item.

The button with the two little hills shown here is actually a "terrain editing mode" button, which will allow for selection of either entity or marker mode while putting you back into directly editing the terrain. Please note: This same effect can be achieved by clicking ANY of the terrain tool buttons.

The next two buttons specifically pertain to the waypoint editor. The former allows for the positioning of a single waypoint and links them by shift clicking to create a path for the AI to follow. The other allows you to edit a waypoint or to modify existing waypoint paths.

Next up is the all-important "test game" button. This button will be used probably more than any other in this menu as it loads a test instance of the game that can be entered from the development editor. Inside of that, editor settings can be changed along with environmentals and skyboxes, and to edit the game directly if necessary.

The last button is a multiplayer launch button if you intend on playing your game multiplayer with others.

At the bottom of the screen is a very thin status bar with a wealth of information (see Figure 4.8).

On the left, it shows what "Mode" you are in. This will either say "Terrain Painting Mode" or "Entity Mode." To the right of that, details are provided on what the mode's specific information is, such as if you are using the Terrain Shape tool. If Entity mode is engaged, it shows the entity name and number as well as whether it's in static or dynamic mode. If you are in entity mode with nothing selected, "none selected" will be displayed. Waypoint editing shows further information, notably LMB="Drag Point," SHIFT-LMB="Clone Point," and SHIFT-RMB="Remove Point."

After that, we have the clipping information (leftmost on the right side), which indicates whether clipping is on or off. Next is cursor X and Y position, which is helpful for figuring out absolute position on the map for object placement.

Figure 4.8

This is the bottom status bar.

"Snap type" shows if you are in "Normal mode" (aka no snapping) or alternately will show "Snap," which means it's snapping to entities, or the "Grid," which is the 100-unit grid inside of the editor.

On the far bottom right are some indicators for if you have your NUM, CAPS, or Scroll Lock keys set. If it's in dark black, it's enabled, and if it's in gray, it's not enabled.

On the left side of the screen is a thin panel with three tabs on it. They are "entity, builder, and markers." These all have very specific functions that are isolated from each other.

On the entity tab, you can add new entities by clicking the "add new entity" item (Figure 4.9).

Once added, the entity can be found in a table that can be vertically scrolled. This can be difficult to navigate if you have a significant number of objects, so be prepared to have the Windows Explorer window open to assist with finding entities. The list is ordered chronologically in the order objects were added, meaning all the newest objects are at the bottom. Objects that are already on the list will not be added as separate entities, which means often it's faster to get new entities that are already on the list by clicking "add new entity" as this will take you immediately to the bottom of the list, allowing for easier and more efficient navigation.

The Markers tab gives access to special Lua-code-enabled zones such as trigger or win zones. It also gives access to lights.

The Builder tab is specifically oriented toward the "EBE" or easy building editor. This is a fast way to add custom 3D buildings. This will be covered in greater detail later on in this chapter.

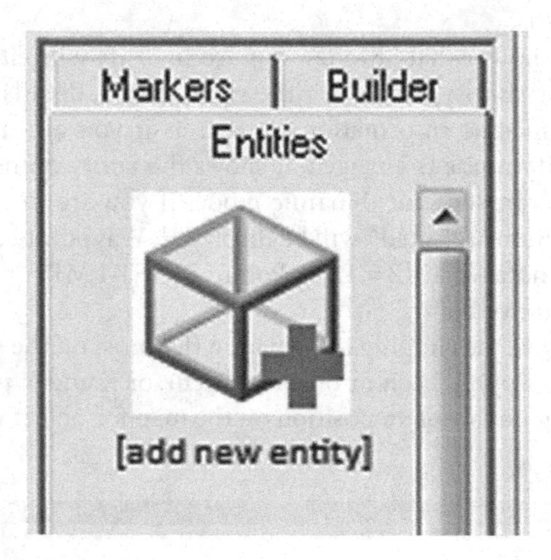

Figure 4.9

The sidebar's add new entity option.

Using the Character Creator

The character creator is a relatively new portion of GameGuru with great promise and potential. It essentially allows the layperson to put together characters rapidly and with great ease. This includes some very basic functionality to get you started, though more advanced users will likely move to more functionally complete third-party programs.

It has the following functions, as shown in Figure 4.10:

Slider1: Character view angle
Slider2: Character view height

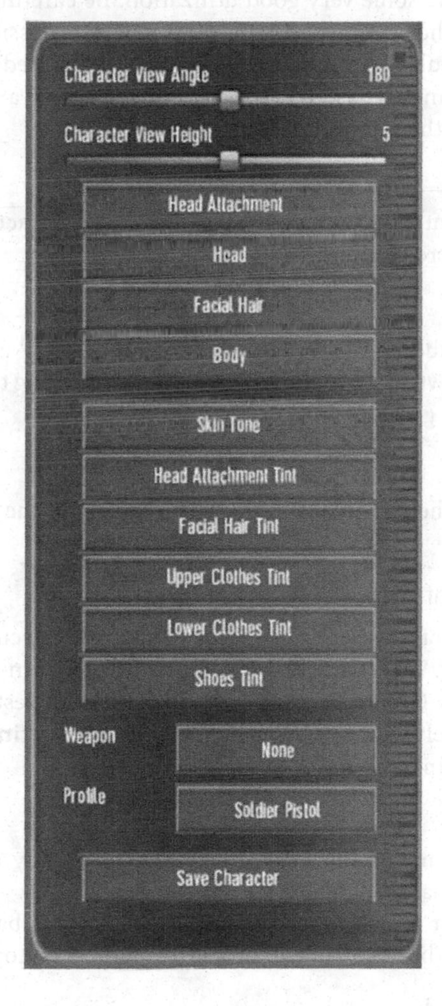

Figure 4.10

The Character Creator's selection menu.

Head Attachment

This defines what type of hair, hat, or helmet the character will use.

Head

Prebuilt into male and female types, these heads are preconstructed and included with the game engine. Certain downloadable content or DLCs allow for access to new heads such as the "Fantasy pack" or "Sci-Fi pack." There is also a "facial mapper"; click on the head item, then select the "off-sized" head. Choose the smaller female or the larger male one. Then choose a good graphic and line it up with the marks for eyes, nose, and mouth to "map" a face onto a head. It's an interesting concept that can have some very good utilization. Be careful not to infringe on other people's work, however, when using faces here. It is possible to achieve some fairly interesting results here if using screenshots of painted faces for instance. The system will automatically detect the color on the border and replicate that for the rest of the head (the side and back).

Facial Hair

This feature is currently useful if you are using a male character to provide some level of physical differentiation.

Body

Selects body type. Adding the fantasy and sci-fi DLCs will add a few bodies to this. Mostly boils down to male and female bodies of varying types. Most of these body types are fairly generic.

Skin Tone

Adjusts skin tone, where specified in the texture map, for the various body components and face.

Head Attachment Tint

This option allows you to select a tint layer to apply to the current base color of the head attachment. This frequently washes out the resulting color, so take care in your color choices. Grayscale selections will often work best due to it functioning more appropriately as a tint. When you choose a color tint, it will attempt to merge that colored tint over the existing color.

Facial Hair Tint

This operates the same as the head attachment tint, only applying the same change to the facial hair.

Typically, the hair is easier to adjust as it usually has a base color of gray or white, which allows the color tints to properly manifest on top of them.

Upper Clothes Tint

This adjusts the upper body's tinting.

Lower Clothes Tint

This adjusts the lower body's tinting.

Shoes Tint

This adjusts the tinting of the shoes.

Weapon

Selects a weapon type for the character. It unfortunately will only select from the ones that come with GameGuru and will not allow any selection beyond that. As a basic selection, the safest option is the Colt 1911. Later on you can edit the .fpe (also called the FPE) file, which contains the details on the custom entity that is created, and it can be edited manually to use custom third-party weapons. If parental controls are enabled, this removes weapon choice from the interface.

Profile

Profile allows a user to select the animation profile to use with respect to the character type. As such it is important to match it with the type of weapon and movement you anticipate the character to use.

Save Character

This will create a character in the entitybank/user/customcontent folder. This can then be used in any project. Be aware that character creator models sometimes don't export properly to standalone. Check Chapter 15 for specifics on how to check for standalone compiler errors.

Using the Model Importer

The model importer is a simple way to bring in .x models from a program such as blender and to automatically generate an FPE file for them so they can be used with GameGuru.

The model import tool is a massively powerful tool that allows importation of various types of model files into GameGuru. There are several stages to this process. First, select the File menu and choose "import model" to be presented with a rather common explorer window that allows the choice of a model file to import. It accepts three different formats:

.x files: These are DirectX models that are easily read by the engine. For many years, they were the sole model type that was acceptable by the importer and as such they have the most compatibility of any model type. They can be exported from programs such blender.

.3ds files: 3DS files are a common format created by "Autodesk®"; they are frequently found on third-party resource sites such as "Sketchfab®," "Clara®," and others. This is considered by many the "de facto" 3D format from an industry standpoint. 3DS files are comprised entirely of triangles, however, so some modelers don't like to use this format.

.fbx files: FBX files are a format that's risen to prominence recently thanks to a reasonably clean SDK (software development kit), which allows it be read across a number of platforms with a reasonably high degree of symmetry. It also allows animations to be packaged with the models, which provides some very tangible benefits for the model developer.

There's also one other type of format that can be read, which is the proprietary FPE file format. This format is the format used by the actual GameGuru engine when loading models into the engine. This allows loading from premade files for complex tasks. Some examples can be found in the entitybank\user folder, such as the fuse examples subfolder. This can greatly streamline complex tasks.

When using a 3D model format, the importer will then attempt to read the model and determine its core components. If there is a series of textures that are stored as references in the model file, it will then attempt to reference them and automatically load them into the importer. If it cannot, it will load a default texture that resembles a red-and-white checkerboard. Click on the corresponding square on the left and another explorer window will pop up and allow selection of a texture for that specific UV map. For multitexture objects, each corresponding gray box will be a different texture for the system.

As mentioned previously, the importer is actually an enormously powerful tool. It's capable of reading out all the various secondary textures after a diffuse is selected. This means it will load the corresponding detail, normal, specular, and illumination (DNIS) texture map into the engine as well. Illumination maps will not show in the importer.

PBR texture importing works much the same way. Select your model and the corresponding _color map for a diffuse texture. It will then begin reading the other files for your PBR mapping. They will show up with corresponding gray boxes in the following order from top to bottom and left to right (Figure 4.11).

Top left: _color
2nd: _normal
3rd: _metalness
4th: _gloss
5th: _ao
6th: _height (top right)

These should all automatically import based on the filename of the original. If the rest are in the same folder and follow the filename guidelines, they will automatically attach to the model.

Illumination maps and cube maps are not shown but are functional in the engine. Test them directly to figure out how they look with the model.

Afterward, import the model and textures to now have the opportunity to configure the relevant settings for the model. Notice that there is a red human model overlay where the model is. This is simply there for perspective and scale so users know exactly how big the model will look in game.

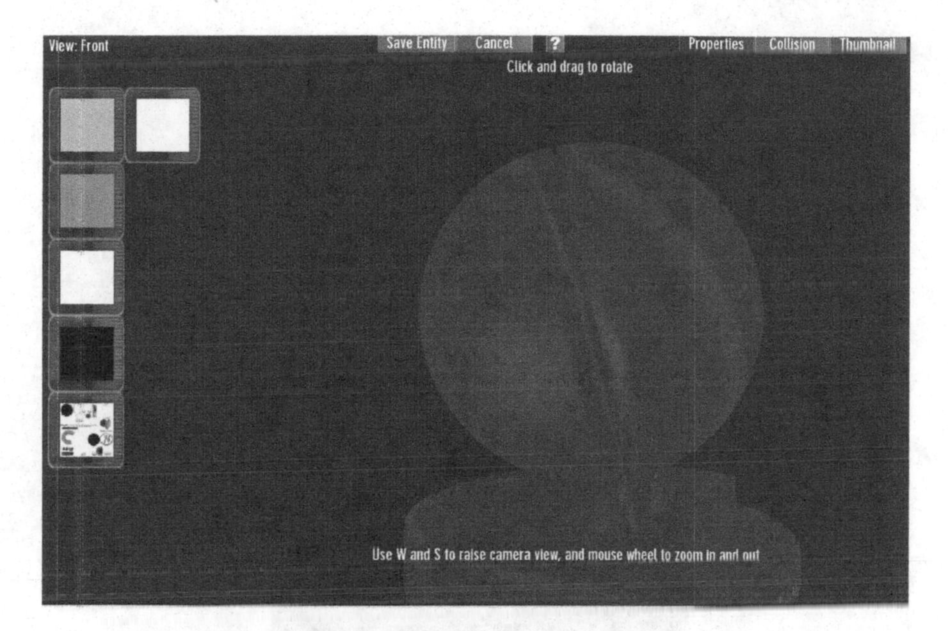

Figure 4.11

An example of the model importer with PBR textures.

Correspondingly, there's a scale option at the top right that can be used to increase or decrease the size of the model. This bar can be clicked or dragged to increase the scale percent, which can run from several hundred to several thousand percent, to accurately obtain the size desired.

Below that is a shader selection screen (Figure 4.12) with quite a few potential options.

There is a significant amount of them, though in general, when the model is imported, it will detect the necessary shader and select it. In most cases, it will be either a basic PBR shader or one that supports bones for movement if bones are detected. There are also some secondary ones such as illumination shaders that are holdovers from previous iterations of the PBR shader's development.

Below that there's a Y rotation bar, which allows rotation of the model for viewing so it can be seen as preferred. Click and drag in the main window to rotate the model. Vertical traversal along the Y axis is done by using W and D.

Underneath that slide bar is a "Collision Mode" box that allows the choice of the type of collision box this particular entity will have while interacting with the game. Bear in mind there are only three types of physics boxes that are tied to this setting. When choosing the sphere, it will be a spherical collision box. When choosing the cylinder, it will be a cylindrical physics box. Everything else, despite the listed type, will have a box-type physics box. This, however, does not

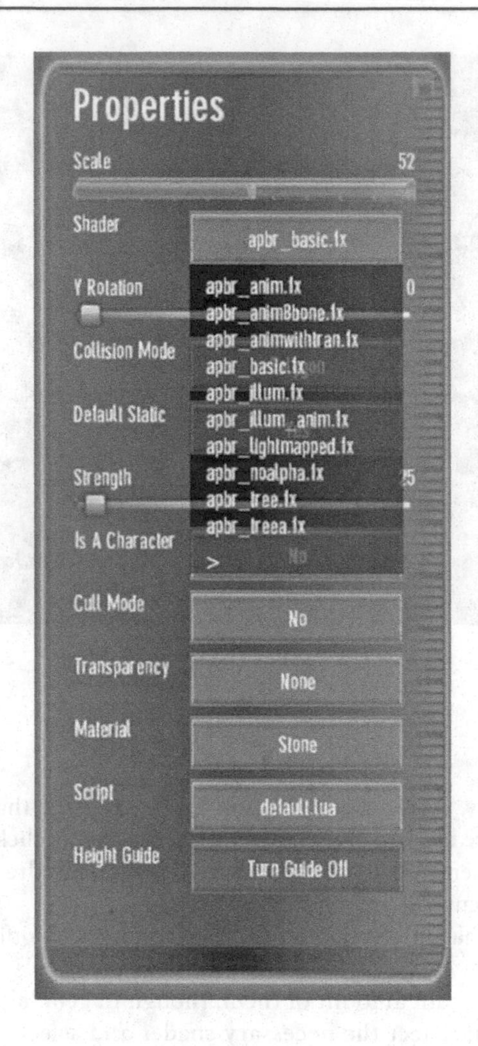

Figure 4.12

This screen shows the shader pulldown's options.

mean collision detection isn't as stated, merely that the physics interaction will be a box. It means that this is a dual purpose selection, so choose wisely.

Default static is a simple yes or no setting that allows the choice of whether this is a static or dynamic entity.

Strength is a slide bar that directly configures how many hit points this entity will have.

Another option is "is a character," which configures whether this will be an AI entity.

Cull mode exists for if the model has inverted culling. If it does, set this to yes. If it doesn't, leave it on no. As a default, no is the best choice.

Transparency is for if there are any transparent elements to the model. Leaving this on "no" will save CPU cycles, whereas turning it to yes will enable the transparency effect for alpha masks but can cause CPU drain, so it's best to only use this when necessary.

The material index has four options—generic, metal, stone, and wood. These are used with respect to sound and being shot—when shot, it will do an impact effect based on what you choose. The FPE file offers greater flexibility. (See the Appendix for details on alternate material types.)

Script allows configuration of a default Lua script for the entity. You will be prompted to select one with an explorer-style screen like when you selected the textures.

The last option is the height guide; this is a simple on/off toggle that shows the little man that is used as a height reference.

At the top, there are several tabs as well—there are the properties tab, the collisions tab, and the thumbnail tab. Properties is the default tab with all of the previously mentioned options. Collisions allows direct control of the size and shape of the collision box as it is managed by the engine. This is excellent for controlling the finer points of a box surrounding your entity. The thumbnail tab is the most simplistic, allowing control of the automatically generated thumbnail picture for your entity.

After hitting the save entity button at the top, a prompt for a name will appear. The engine will then begin to generate all of the necessary files for the entity to work within GameGuru. This means the FPE file and dark basic object (DBO) file that are used by the engine will be generated from the ground up. From there, the next step is to go and attempt to load it by adding it in the engine. Upon loading it, it's best to verify the import was successful in several stages. First, open it and look at it in the editor. If it does not show, look for a small white circle—this means that the model file was unable to open. In newer versions, it may not show at all (Figure 4.13).

If it doesn't show the white circle, click and drag to select and delete it. From there, check the FPE file directly to see if perhaps one of the file locations failed or reimport it again.

Assuming it did import and it shows, verify that the texture looks ok in the editor. Bear in mind that not every effect is fully enabled in the editor, so you will need to load the test game to completely validate it. This will give you a complete idea of whether the illumination maps, cube maps, normal maps, and other associated textures truly loaded properly.

If the model pops in and out, go back into the editor and modify the occluder and occludee settings to no, then try changing them one at a time to see which one is causing the issue.

All in all, this process is usually pretty painless. The FPE file gets generated, and just like that it is a functional entity. From there, there's simply the fine-tuning process of the entity properties or the FPE file itself, which acts as a "default setting" for the entity.

There are of course secondary ways to import files, and many users swear by them. One such method is the "FBX2GG" program. Another is a FPE file

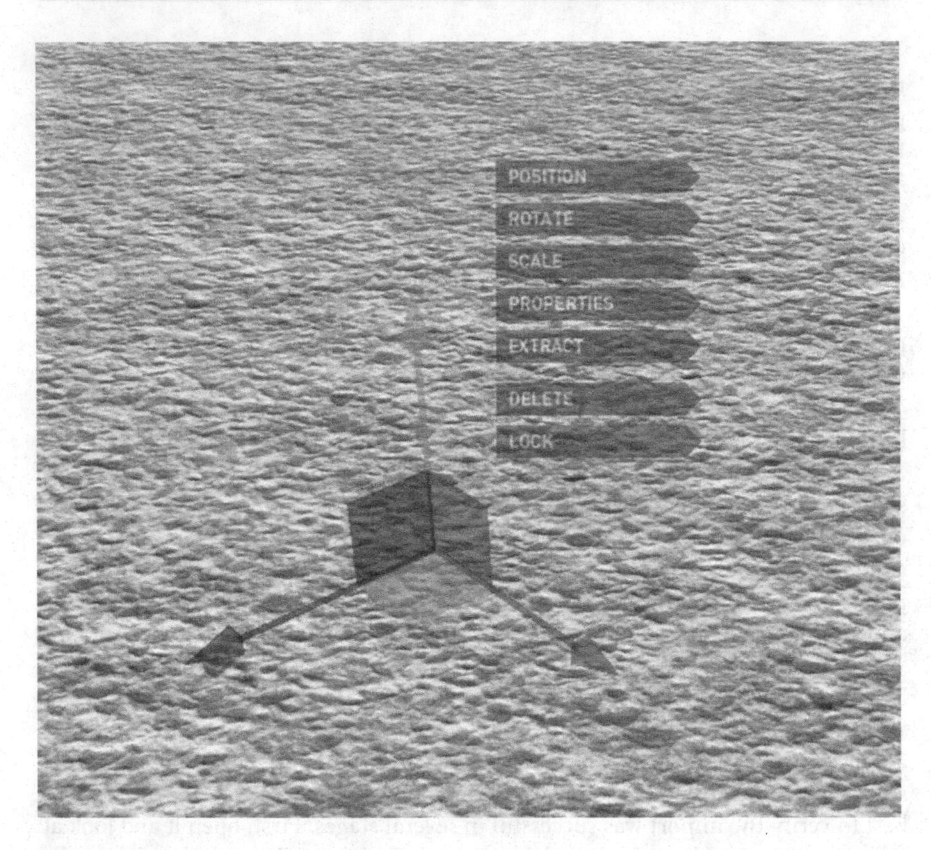

Figure 4.13

The object is missing but the widget still shows.

generator that is unsupported as well but can generate FPEs from .X files. Both of these have links included in the hyperlink reference list.

Reading Log Files

From time to time, an error in GameGuru can only be resolved by checking the log files. Perhaps you've added a new object that is breaking everything or a script that is failing. Maybe there's a graphical bug in a new model. It's difficult to tell from the error system inside of GameGuru itself. Instead, sometimes the best answer is to use the logging system.

The GameGuru log files are actually fairly substantial and noteworthy. They include two separate files:

- The actual game engine's log file.
- The level's log file.

These are especially useful if the GameGuru instance crashes. (We'll get into this in much greater detail in Chapter 20 on testing and troubleshooting, and Chapter 21 on optimization.)

Using the Easy Building Editor or the EBE

The EBE is the "Easy Building Editor," a simple, integrated way of building structures and static objects. It's fast, easy (as the name implies), and fairly thorough. A user can rapidly assemble anything from a skyscraper to a labyrinthine maze.

The method to access the EBE is on the left-hand-side toolbar; you have to find the "Builder Tab." When clicked on, it will display an "Add New Site" option, which when clicked will allow the user to place the southeast corner of the builder grid that will be worked on (Figure 4.14).

Bear that in mind when placing the grid. Make sure that it's going to have enough room to position so it's not got the east or north part overlapping other objects if you can.

The EBE, once placed, will drop a simple 2D grid. You will also get an invisible series of grids vertically aligned above this grid. They can be accessed by using page up or page down to go up and down through the grids. In the builder tab, there are a number of shapes that can be used to quickly lay down objects in a series along the grid by left clicking. If you notice, in the bottom right, there are a number of panels down in the corner and bottom edge that

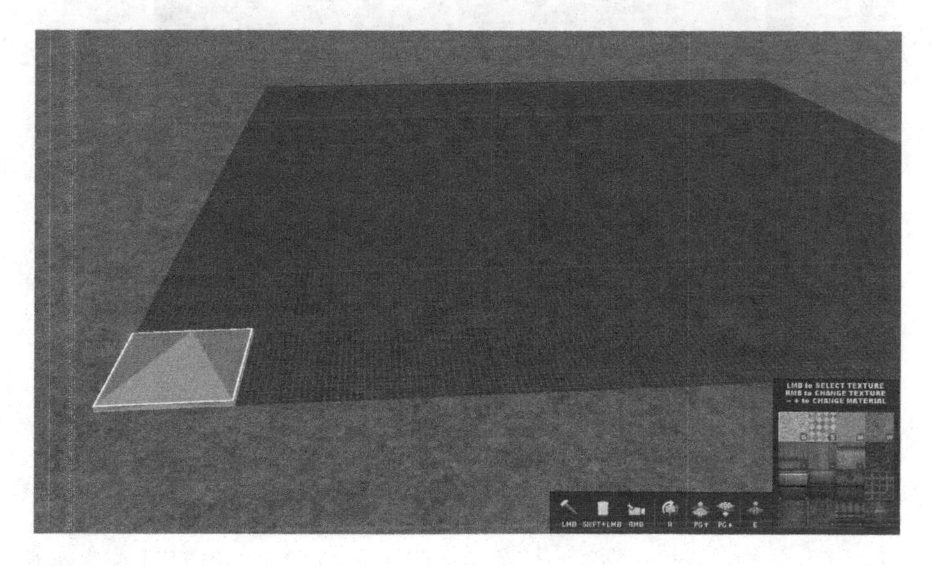

Figure 4.14

The EBE's initial starting screen.

provide additional controls. Please note in the bottom left corner of the grid is a small widget for manipulating the position and additional controls we will reevaluate later.

In the far bottom right (Figure 4.15), is a four-by-four tile set that can be used and applied to any of the shapes chosen. These tiles can also be modified with custom tilesets if you so desire by right clicking on a texture. Left clicking will select the texture for use. Note the M, W, S lettering. This lettering determines how the game engine will interpret this particular material. These signify (M)etal, (S)tone, or (W)ood. This selection determines the sound it makes for footfalls, the type of decal it creates when shot/hit, and other internal game functions. To modify a texture's material type, use the + and: keys, respectively.

So for now, we're going to pick the "WALL" shape and the green wall in the first column of the tileset, third down. Move your mouse over to the grid and click. A wall appears. Simple, right? Well, it gets easier. You can also click and

Figure 4.15

The EBE's tileset selection menu.

drag to draw lines of shapes. You can also "delete" shapes by using shift-left click. Using the R key will rotate the shape along the x/y axis.

For now, we're going to build a simple rectangular room. So let's lay down a four-by-two series of walls outlining a room. Now let's go on the left and select the "floor" shape. We're now going to "paint" a floor down by clicking and dragging to fill the rectangular room we made with a floor. Same thing with a ceiling, so let's click the ceiling shape and paint a ceiling on.

Congratulations! You made your first box. It's not quite a room though as it needs a door. This is where the ingenuity of the EBE really shines. What we're going to do is take the column tool and move it where we want our door to be. Now just SHIFT-CLICK and drag to create the door you want.

One useful tip is to undo and redo work when painting; if it's one continuous click, it will undo the entire action. This is useful if you're in a hurry and make a mistake.

Hit E to come out of the EBE and go out to your entity tab. Then go to add a new entity and find the EBE specific entities that come with GameGuru. Notably, there are windows, doors, and rooftops. These are all custom designed to work with the EBE and are typically found under the fixtures section.

Select an appropriate doorframe and place it on the building. If you hold the L key while you do this, it will LINK the frame to the actual EBE structure so that they form one cohesive entity for later use.

After you've placed the doorframe, go back in by clicking on the EBE widget and add or remove rows or columns using the CLICK or SHIFT-CLICK methods. By now, you've undoubtedly noticed some of the other tools in the Builder tab, specifically the stairs. Yes, you can build multilevel structures with ease in the EBE.

The answer here is to place a set of stairs, delete the ceiling (select the ceiling and SHIFT-CLICK to remove), and voila, you have a floor for a second level of your building. Now select the wall tool again and hit the PGUP key on your keyboard. The reason we have to hit the wall key is because the PGUP and PGDOWN will literally create a grid the size of the object you are using. So if it's only one unit high (such as your ceilings or floors are), it will only go up that exact distance. Since we want to create walls of the proper height, it's important to use the wall tool to select the height we'll be PGUPing to. An alternate way of doing this same process of raising or lowering the build floor is to simply use your mouse wheel. Personally I prefer the precision of the PGUP/PGDOWN keys, but this method may not be preferable. Give it a try and see which one you prefer!

This system can easily be expanded out to multilevel floors and heights, with interior walls, doors, and exterior windows. It's all rather simple but follows the same flow as previously noted. Click your tool, set your height with PGUP/PGDOWN (or mouse wheel UP/DOWN), and then CLICK to place or SHIFT-CLICK to remove. R will rotate your walls and that's really the whole shooting match.

Beyond that we have several extra tools to discuss with the EBE. One of which is that you can save these as actual models! This means once you design a building/object with the EBE, you can hit E to leave the editor, click on the widget, and choose SAVE. This will allow you to actually save the model as its own entity for reuse without having to remake it from scratch again! This ultrasimplistic tool suddenly becomes a very functional model creator and editor.

You can even use it to create voxel (voxels are three-dimensional pixels like in Minecraft®) objects with the "cube" item. The limit is your imagination, literally!

This is a really useful feature for new users who want to make their own objects, albeit in a rather limited fashion. There are a few negatives about it, which we'll discuss later, but for the moment dig in and see what you can create!

Tab Settings

In test game mode, there's a wealth of information that is not available anywhere else. You can't even see it in the editor itself! These settings are referred to as both the Tab settings and the "Tab-Tab" settings.

Tab settings are among the most important and probably least understood features of GameGuru. These settings allow a massive amount of control of content and quality. They impact the way a level looks, acts, and perform.

It's important to cover some of the more important ones, with the more specific ones (notably dealing with lighting) coming later in greater depth, notably in the Optimization chapter (Chapter 21).

TAB 1 Time

Brings up the performance panel on the left edge of the screen. This is shown in Figure 4.16.

Each of these bars will move and modify based on what's going on in your game. The first 11 bars are going to indicate roughly how much time is being used for each process. This can be useful in pinpointing a specific performance drain in late-stage game development but for the most part is generally nonhelpful. The most valuable from the standpoint of performance are Polygons and Draw Calls, both of which are specifically going to indicate how many ACTUAL resources are being used. Polygons are individual polygons being rendered by the game engine. The vast majority of the time this enormous number will be based on how large your in-game terrain is. The Draw Calls component represents the amount of times the CPU tells the GPU to draw a certain set of vertices or triangles with a shader. There's a delicate balance here, but typically, too few will result in your CPU being overburdened.

Too many draw calls results in your GPU being overburdened. If you are getting too many draw calls, often it comes down to something being incorrectly occluded. This will come to bear later, so just try to bookmark that in your mind for when we talk in depth about occlusion and optimization. Draw calls in general, though, are expensive, so it's better to go under than it is to go over. It's also hardware dependent as different hardware can handle different quantities of draw calls.

At this point, you are probably wondering about the utility of this screen. After all, didn't I promise you'd be able to do a significant amount of work here?

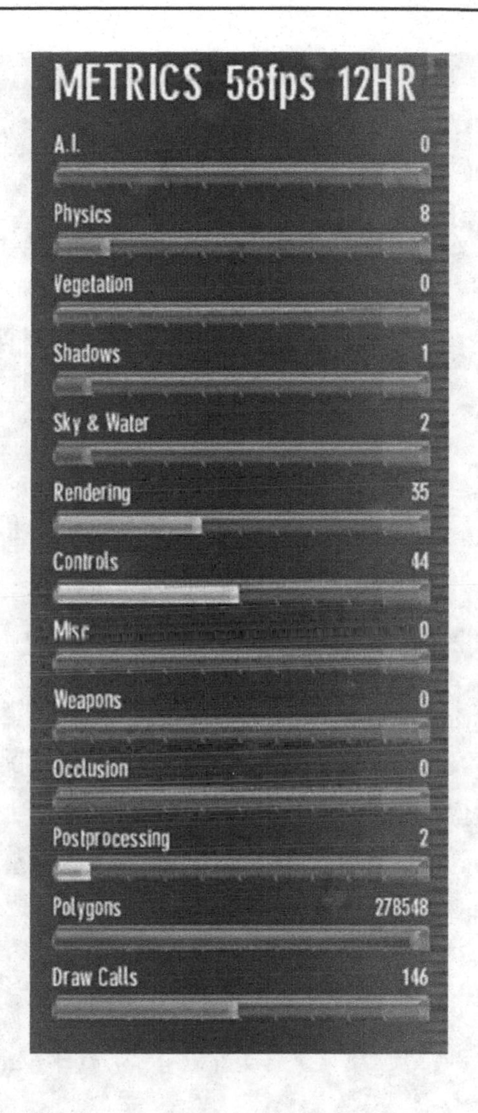

Figure 4.16

The tab menu's performance statistics.

Well, it turns out the Tab settings has another level of settings. Hit Tab again for an options menu.

TAB 2 Times Brings Up

Now there is a screen full of levers and sliders (Figure 4.17) that you can use to adjust your game. Each of these sliders or pulldowns can have a profound impact on your game's performance and visual quality. These are saved on a per-map basis. These settings are typically referred to as the "tab-tab" settings.

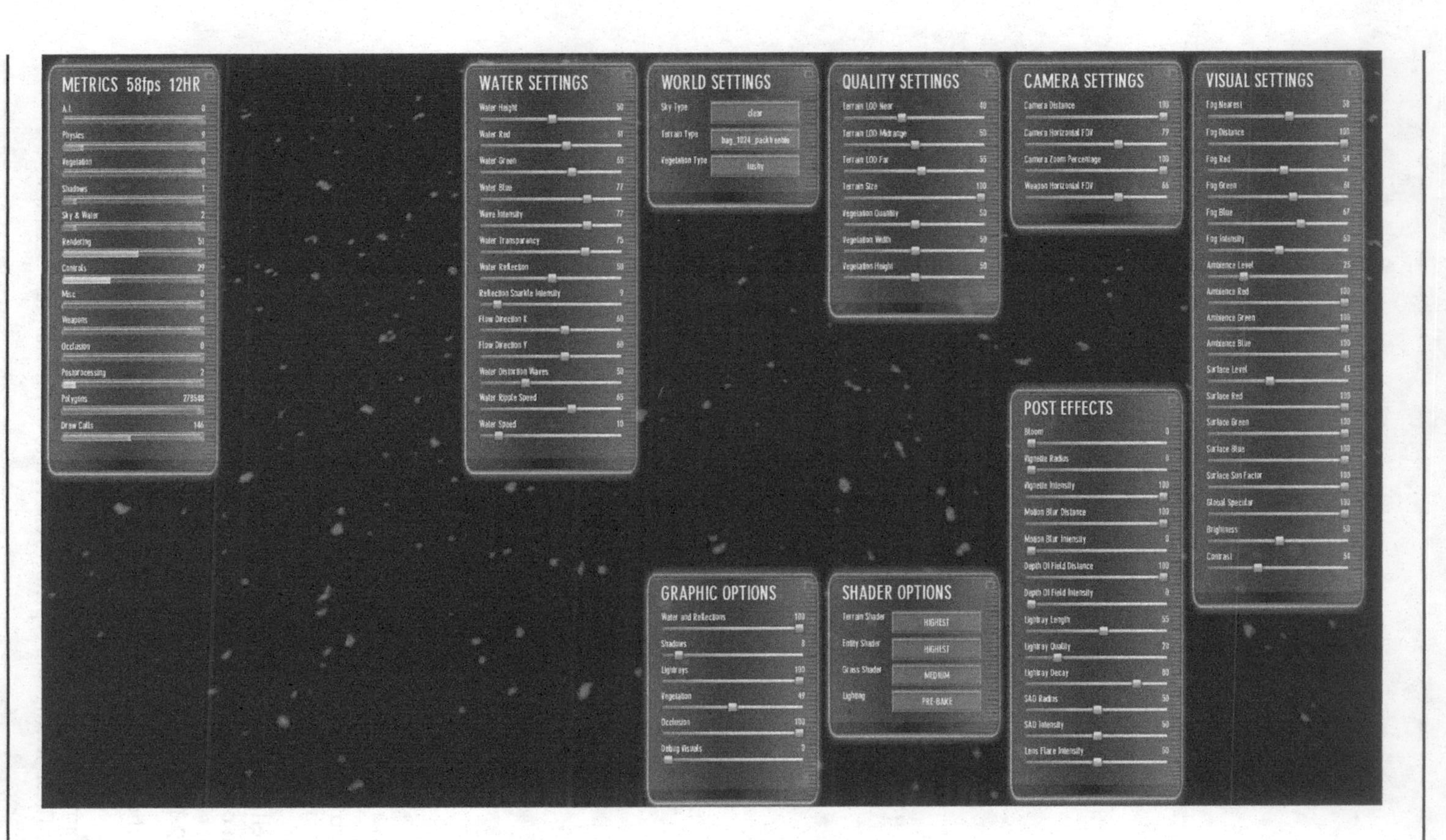

Figure 4.17
The tab-tab menu's full options.

Starting from the top left, there is metrics, which we've already discussed, and water settings which we will cover separately later.

World Settings

Sky type: This simple pulldown will parse the <GameGuru folder>\files\skybank folder to dynamically generate a list of skies for use. Please note, this list is generated only on the initialization portion of GameGuru, so if adding new skies, then GameGuru will need restarted.

Terrain type: This pulldown will parse the <GameGuru folder>\files\terrainbank folder to dynamically generate a list of terrain for use. Again, this is only initialized as a list on GameGuru's startup process. Adding or downloading new terrain will require a restart of GameGuru.

Vegetation Type: This pulldown selects a pattern of vegetation available parsed from <GameGuru folder>\files\vegbank and will only refresh upon a restart of GameGuru.

Graphic Options

This subheading has a host of very relevant options that will directly impact the game's performance and look. These settings are all pretty heavy-handed, so be aware they will very easily show the difference when selected.

Water and Reflections: This slider controls the water's visibility from a level of not visible at all to highly visible and highly reflective.

Shadows: This slider controls the alpha value of the shadows, thus controlling how "dense" they are. It runs from the low end of no shadows at all (useful for indoor scenes with pre-baked shadows or for a low performance setting) to a very dark black shadow.

Lightrays: This slider directly controls the quantity and density of so-called light rays, aka God Rays. These beautiful flows of light are best used in outdoor scenes, though beware, as they do carry a performance hit for the quality of them.

Vegetation: This slider controls the overall level of vegetation in the game as the amount of vegetation rendered via the grass drawing tool. This ranges from none (lowest) to maximum (highest). The difference is clearly visible if there is drawn grass. Changing this slider will impact the performance window's Polygons value.

Occlusion: This slider controls the level of occlusion in the game. It ranges from no occlusion (lowest) to maximum. It is generally recommended to keep this at the maximum value to ensure maximum performance. This particular type of occlusion is called SSAO (or screen space ambient occlusion). This shader ensures that objects that aren't visible (i.e., that are behind other objects) are not rendered, thus saving precious draw calls. These settings are governed by the "occluder and occludee" settings inside of the FPE files for entities.

Figure 4.18

Enabling "debug visuals" provides a wealth of details.

Debug Visuals: This slider is another binary slider with a low of 0 and a max of 1. It really is either on or off. When it is turned on, the screen will look like the image in Figure 4.18.

This screen illustrates several important components useful for troubleshooting. First of all, notice that it has a colored circle around the AI, shows bounding boxes, the current line the AI is taking, and also a node it's navigating to! This type of information is vital when troubleshooting issues with the level's design and AI's interaction with it. We'll be circling back to this piece later when we get into debugging our game.

Quality Settings

The quality settings are several quality settings, honestly. They control terrain and vegetation quality settings, and as such, can have a noticeable impact on the game's performance.

Terrain LOD Near: Level of detail (LOD) controls the quality of a texture's resolution as the renderer displays it. Reducing texture depth and quality at a distance can save some memory and draw calls by cutting what's actually being output. Distant things are less clear; thus they do not need to have high quality. So in this case, this controls the "near" value, which sets when the LOD system kicks in for the terrain system. Note, this doesn't impact anything but terrain.

Terrain LOD Midrange: This determines the mid-point value for LOD. LOD typically comes in three flavors—high quality, medium, and low. This would be where terrain transitions to a "medium" LOD. From here to the "far" value, in particular.

Terrain LOD Far: The last LOD slider is the "far" value, which sets at what point the lowest quality terrain LOD will be displayed. Default values should be sufficient for most users.

Terrain Size: Terrain size is literally the total terrain amount being rendered at any given time. It is the square of terrain rendered around the player. The default value is all of the terrain at all times. If you want to cut this down to reduce draw calls and poly count, which can be useful if there are a lot of blind corners, then it is advisable to play with this value for some extra performance.

Vegetation Quantity: Vegetation quantity sets the density of the vegetation system as rendered. So while the "vegetation slider" controls total amount rendered and the respective quality, this will cause areas to look sparse or thickly populated. I recommend abusing the slider as much as possible for lush forests or barren deserts.

Vegetation Width: This controls the width of vegetation as a starting point. Now, in GameGuru, vegetation is randomized significantly, with widths being along a slight range to help provide visual differentiation. This slider controls what the median value is.

Vegetation Height: Likewise, this controls the median height as height is also randomized, with some outlier plants that are significantly tall or short. This slider provides a large amount of differentiation.

Water Configuration Settings

Water, for many years, was a long-standing issue in GameGuru. Function was minimal, consisting of a singular water plane that was spread uniformly across the entire map. Indeed, when GameGuru was first introduced as FPS Creator Reloaded, it actually had zero controls at all and existed at all times even if you weren't using it. To access the water level, a user would need to dig down into the terrain and then spread it out using the terrain tools.

This caused excessive framerate loss in a lot of cases as it was still functioning even when water had no viable use, such as being indoors. Along came GameGuru, however, and eventually some rudimentary controls in the form of Lua commands were added that allowed us to "go indoors" or "go outside." This was accomplished by choosing to enable or disable the terrain and water planes.

More recently, water control was expanded when several forum members figured out some of the settings that could be used to configure the effects shader for the water directly by modifying the file itself. This allowed us SOME level of control over the water plane, but still, it was limited to configurations outside of the game engine itself. This meant no on-the-fly adjustment of water, yet. No simple fixes would resolve this lack of function.

Then, of course, came the great awakening that came with the release of the engine to GitHub earlier this year.

During this period, a significant amount of function was added, even during the writing of this tome, specifically addressing the exceptionally weak (at the time) water system.

Now we have the image shown in Figure 4.19 on the tab-tab screen.

As you see, there are several powerful controls for water, allowing significant variability where once there was none. There's also a "swimming" system added, whereas in previous iterations of GameGuru, players simply died when they went into the water. The swimming system is a big improvement and allows for even more gameplay types, should you be so inclined.

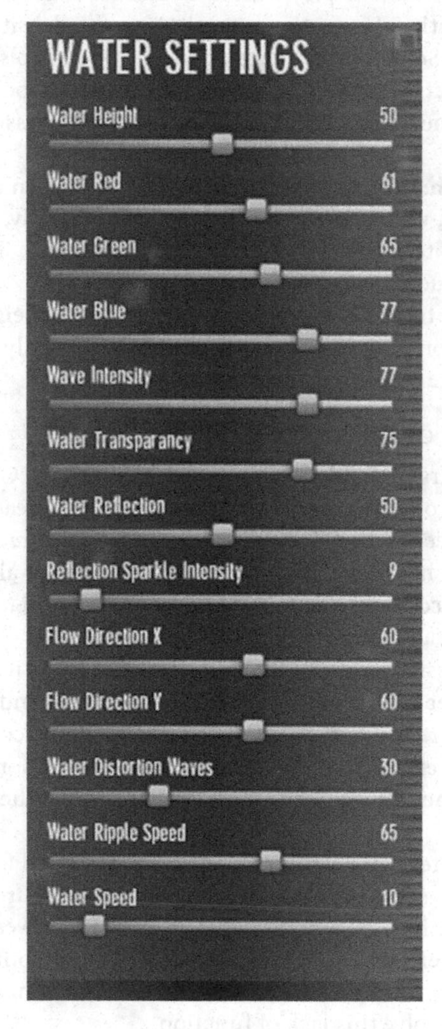

Figure 4.19

Water settings allows great variability in your water plane.

These settings, starting from top to bottom are:

Water Height, Water Red, Water Green, Water Blue, Wave Intensity, Water Transparency, Water Reflection, Reflection Sparkle Intensity, Flow Direction X, Flow Direction Y, Water Distortion Waves, Water Ripple Speed, and Water Speed.

First and foremost is the Water Height. This setting is of vital utility, allowing players to move the actual physical height of the water plane (it still does exist as a level-wide plane, unfortunately). This height adjustment allows users to easily create oceans, islands, or even city streets with just a tiny bit of water on top of them. It's a massively powerful setting that has very clear and direct effects.

Water Red, Green, and Blue are all simple color controls that allow adjustment of the intermingling of color shades that the water applies, allowing simple lakes, toxic chemical dumps, or even vivid red lava! Now adjust the sliders to where the color value will match for the particular level. Unfortunately it is a zone-wide shader change, so bear in mind that ALL of the water in the level will take on the appearance selected here. This applies to every change in the slider bar.

Water Intensity is the thickness of the wave quantity or how tranquil the water is essentially on its surface. Think of the surface of the water as a combination of textures, surfaces, and noise, this is the noise component on a large scale. The intensity will control the size of the noise on the water (which gives it the appearance of, say, a whitewater rapid).

Water Transparency is exactly as it sounds—how transparent the water is. It controls how see-through the water is when staring down at it. When looking at water, there's a lot more going on than most people realize. There's the water itself, sure, but there's also the surface boundary layer, which is a border between air and the volume of water.

Try to visualize it like the image shown in Figure 4.20.

Game developers attempt to mimic this methodology through various tricks so the natural environment is properly duplicated or at least that it's reasonably

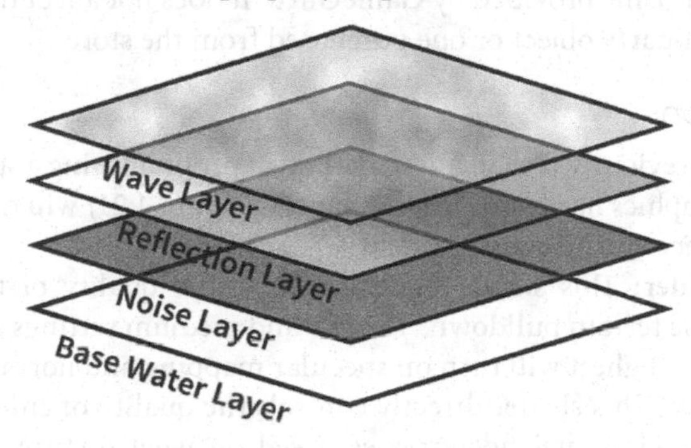

Figure 4.20

A simple example of the layers used in the water system.

close. In this respect, remember that the water has several components to it and, in the case of water transparency, it's the density of the color that the game applies to the water. Imagine it sort of like a fog. A good value for most standard applications is 20 or 30 percent on the slider.

Water Reflection is a blending level among a reflection of the sky, environment, and a layered water texture.

This gives a nice mirror effect or a duller look for when a hazier feel is desired. With clear skies, use a high value for the water reflection setting. There's also the issue of performance, which—when testing—may show a performance hit from the reflection on the test computer(s). Careful configuration of this will yield excellent results.

Reflection Sparkle Intensity is the specularity map control for the water; this links with water reflection to make the actual specular changes. Think back on the discussions about textures and specularity from before. This slider is how "shiny" the reflection is at its peaks. It is most noticeable when the water reflection value is set to a high level already.

Flow Direction X/Y determines the "flow" of the water, with respect to movement. This doesn't impact the player at all but creates the illusion of flow on the surface of the water.

Water Distortion Waves make the "noise" of the surface of the water finer at a higher level; it is a second control for intensity. This secondary control gives detail to the initial noise provided by the intensity slider.

Water Ripple Speed controls the speed of the "noise" on the surface of the water, thus controlling the "speed" of the synthetic rippling waves.

Water Speed controls the texture layer's movement on the water, giving it a sense of current in combination with the flow settings. Again, bear in mind all of these controls impact ALL water throughout a level. If there are multiple water sources, then it will show all of them moving at the same velocity. This can be problematic if the player is supposedly going from looking at a tranquil lake to looking at a fast-moving river. It can be one but not both. Please note this only affects the water plane provided by GameGuru. It does not affect the water plane added as a third-party object or one purchased from the store.

Shader Options

As mentioned previously, a shader is a method of programming a specific rendering effect on graphics hardware. These shaders (Figure 4.21) will directly impact your performance and also visual fidelity.

Terrain Shader: This shader controls the visual quality of the terrain as selected from the terrain pulldown. The low and medium settings are minimally different, but the highest will turn on specular mapping and normals.

Entity Shader: This shader directly controls the quality of entities in a game and how high their visual fidelity goes based on what texture mapping they have. High is reserved for specularity and PBR, medium, and low have those two graphics options disabled.

Figure 4.21

The shader options submenu of the tab-tab screen.

Grass Shader: This shader has a slight impact on grass. Here again though, every bit of performance matters, and users may find that the engine functions best with a low setting with only minimal loss in fidelity.

Lighting: The lighting pulldown has two settings: pre-bake and real-time. It's typically in real-time unless compiling a static light map. Users can disable this static light map by setting it to real-time if encountering an issue.

Camera Settings

The settings shown in Figure 4.22 directly impact how the camera views and displays things on the monitor. It can have performance and gameplay ramifications.

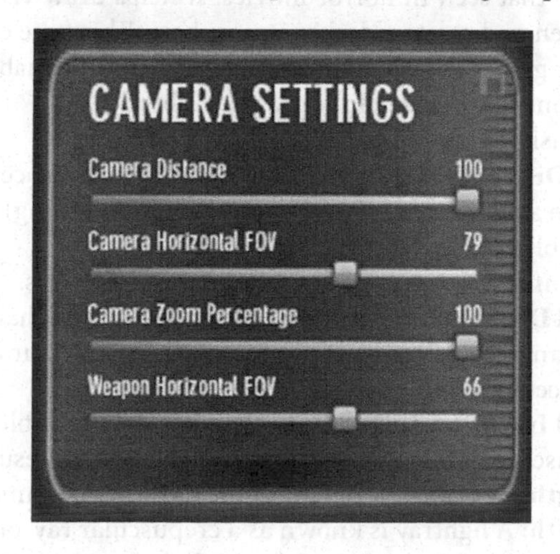

Figure 4.22

The camera settings submenu of the tab-tab screen.

Camera Distance: This slider controls how far the engine displays as a screen percentage. This is especially useful for performance and runs from 1–100%.

Camera Horizontal FOV: This controls the in-game FOV (field of view). This setting can give anything from a narrow field of view to a wide one akin to a fish-eye effect.

Camera Zoom Percentage: This controls how much the initial view is zoomed in. The basic setting is a good default, but in some instances, users might find it works better zoomed in/out (such as when making a third-person-view game).

Weapon Horizontal FOV: This controls the FOV when wielding a weapon on its default view level. This works similar to Camera Horizontal FOV but only functions when a weapon is selected.

Post Effects

Post effects (Figure 4.23) are industry terms that define graphical effects run AFTER the initial rendering is done, mostly to help beautify a game. Post effects are always CPU and GPU consumers of the highest order and as such should only be used with caution due to their performance considerations.

Bloom: Bloom is an important feature that will provide a level of visual light-blending in the game that, if carefully controlled, can create beautiful effects and help contribute toward making the game look absolutely stellar. The Bloom slider controls a number of secondary functions as well, such as the lens flare effect. If you find that you need to eliminate these effects, then you can disable Bloom to remove all of them at once. Bloom's overall function is to blend brightly lit colors together. It has a huge impact on FPS in GameGuru. See Chapter 21 on optimization if you are having difficulty with performance after enabling this.

Vignette Radius: This is a graphic effect that causes a dark ring around the screen to emulate that seen in horror movies. It helps draw visual focus to the center of the screen and create a darker atmosphere. This type of visual effect is popular in horror games as well and is available for you to enable or disable via this slider. This controls the size of the graduated border.

Vignette Intensity: This controls how dense the border is.

Motion Blur Distance: Motion blur is a popular post-processing effect that blurs objects when a player is in motion (typically when turning) to help approximate the real-life blur of movement.

Motion Blur Intensity: Controls how severe the blurring is.

Depth of Field Distance: Depth of field simulates the way that distance causes blurring for human vision. This creates an ever-increasing blur effect beginning at the distance specified by this slider.

Depth of Field Intensity: This controls the intensity of the blur. This is a powerful feature, so use small increments to achieve the desired result.

Lightray Length: Controls the length of the lightrays in-game.

Lightray Length: A lightray is known as a crepuscular ray, or God ray, which is an atmospheric phenomenon caused by sunlight being blocked by an object such as a cloud. This results in a line of light pointing back to the light source.

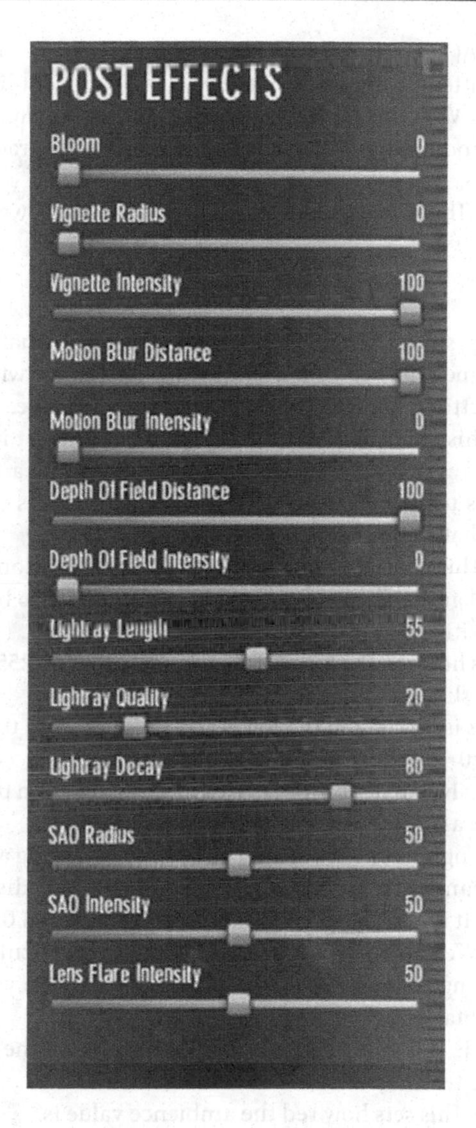

Figure 4.23

The post effects submenu of the tab-tab screen.

The emulation of this effect in GameGuru is controlled in part by this setting which configures how long the lines for the lightrays are.

Lightray Quality: This controls the overall graphical quality of the lightray itself.

Lightray Decay: This controls how strongly the lightray's visual effect continues on towards its maximum length. Setting a high decay value means it rapidly fades, gaining a higher alpha transparency value as it approaches its endpoint.

SAO Radius: SAO stands for Scalable Ambient Obstruction, a form of post processing which attempts to simulate the effects of ambient lighting on objects by approximation. What this means to you is that it will create small shadows on the texturing to produce realistic shadows on objects. The radius controls how large these will be.

SAO Intensity: This controls how darkly the SAO shadows will show on the model.

Visual Settings

The Visual Settings sliders (Figure 4.24) control most of what you see environmentally in the game. They control a significant portion of what is displayed to the player. These settings are fine-tunable and even scriptable.

Fog Nearest: This controls when the fog first starts to set in in the distance. It ranges from 1 to 255, yet in the editor only displays as a 0-100 percentage. So while it appears to only be a simple 0-100 value, there is significantly more nuance to it than that when accessing it via Lua.

Fog Distance: This controls when the fog ends its transition. If you set it over a long range, it will gradually go over that range. When set to be close to nearest, it will rapidly transition to the densest fog.

Fog Red: This is how red the fog is. This ranges from 0 to 255 in Lua, but again displays as a 0-100 slider on this screen.

Fog Green: This is how green the fog is. This ranges from 0 to 255 in Lua, but again displays as a 0-100 slider on this screen.

Fog Blue: This is how blue the fog is. This also ranges from 0 to 255 in Lua, yet again displaying as a 0-100 percent slider.

Fog Intensity: Fog intensity controls the opacity of the fog at the height of the transition. This means it starts opaque and maximizes at fog distance to whatever this value is set to. It is another percentage-based slider from 0 to 100.

A note on fog: We will be revisiting these sliders in particular as they have an extremely broad range of applications. For now, familiarize yourself with them through experimentation!

Ambience Level: This controls the overall saturation of the ambient intensity levels across all the textures.

Ambience Red: This sets how red the ambience value is.

Ambience Green: This sets how green the ambience value is.

Ambience Blue: This sets how blue the ambience value is.

Surface Level: Surface level controls how bright the lights show on a texture surface and controls how much static lighting shows on a surface.

Surface Red: This affects red surface value. A safe setting for most applications is 100.

Surface Green: This affects green surface value. A safe setting for most applications is 100.

Surface Blue: This affects blue surface value. A safe setting for most applications is 100.

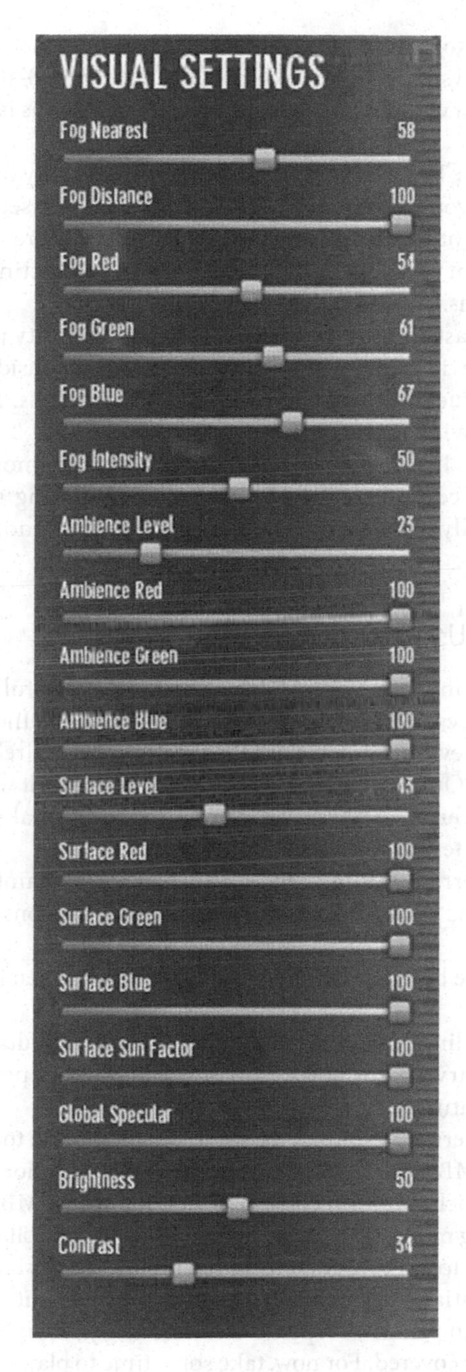

Figure 4.24

The visual settings submenu of the tab-tab screen.

Surface Sun Factor: This value controls how much impact the shader applies the static sunlight system to your textures. It ranges from 0-100 percent. At the lowest value, the sun will not impact your textures at all. This is useful for indoor scenes.

Global Specular: This controls how "shiny" a specularity map is. It will have no visual impact if your terrain/entity/grass shaders are not set to high, however.

Brightness: Brightness brightens a game by adding more white values to it. Unfortunately, it can easily wash out a picture. The best settings are under 50% for most applications.

Contrast: Contrast controls how strong the color intensity is. A high contrast will result in very vivid colors that have very little variance aside from their peak brightness. Low values will make a game virtually colorless. Most applications will benefit from having this at 50%.

Just on an aside, it's worth noting that a significant amount of these controls can be adjusted and modified via the Lua scripting system. This can allow for some really impressive effects in-game that cannot be achieved any other way.

In-GUI: How to Use the Terrain System

The terrain system in GameGuru is one of its most powerful features. Making advanced terrain does take time and effort, as well as some understanding about the system itself. Previous versions of FPS Creator were entirely focused around indoor feature sets. Outdoor terrain was a hack at best, and it was reflected in the level design. GameGuru has always been oriented toward making really effective levels with outdoor terrain.

T enables the Terrain Editing Mode. This will allow "painting" terrain onto the terrain field. This allows users to raise hills, carve canyons, or drill out holes for lakes and rivers.

LMB: Left mouse button will allow raising elevation when in Terrain Editing Mode (TEM).

LMB-shift: Holding shift and pressing the left mouse button will lower terrain. This allows carving out holes, canyons, and making pockmarks or other common terrain features.

With respect to terrain painting, the same system is used; to paint grass or terrain colors, hold LMB. Users can remove grass or terrain colors (it will configure it to the default, which is terrain color 1) by holding shift-LMB.

In terrain editing mode, there is an adjustable circle controlled by using the –/+ keys. This is critical to making good terrain with fine details and for large mountains. When you initially are making terrain, it will come out looking very much like a mashed potato pile. In Chapter 6 on "Building your first game," advanced methods for use are covered. For now, take some time to play with it and get a feel for how the various elements of the Terrain Editing Mode work.

New Flat Level Versus Random

The GameGuru editor has several modes of level creation. The first is the "new flat level," which is a full-size flat level a few units above the waterline.

The random level feature will generate procedurally a terrain. This terrain will ripple and wave and can save you a lot of time when looking to get a pre-made terrain done quickly. The default setting will create a fairly good amount of large mountains and flat spots. Use the flat spots as a guideline for creating water features to obtain a more natural feel. These long flat areas are perfect for lowering down and using the terrain flattener tool to make massive lakes or rivers.

There is a second, undocumented random terrain feature. In the early days, the terrain generation system for random was as previously mentioned. This is going back to the time of FPS Creator: Reloaded. During that time, the terrain generator was pretty well liked. However, at some point, Lee Bamber decided to modify the algorithm for it and created a new random terrain. This change was roundly disliked. It had no low flat spots, the terrain was bumpy but on a fairly regular basis. This gave terrains a sense of sameness despite the randomization. This mode was sidelined in favor of the original mode.

The other method can still be accessed if users go to FILE/New Random Level again. This will cause the GameGuru editor to make a new map that is the older type of random terrain. It does however have plenty of use. It's just a matter of preference. So give it a try! If users continue to go back to FILE/New Random Level, it will alternate the type of map between the preferred and non-preferred types of random terrain (see Figure 4.25).

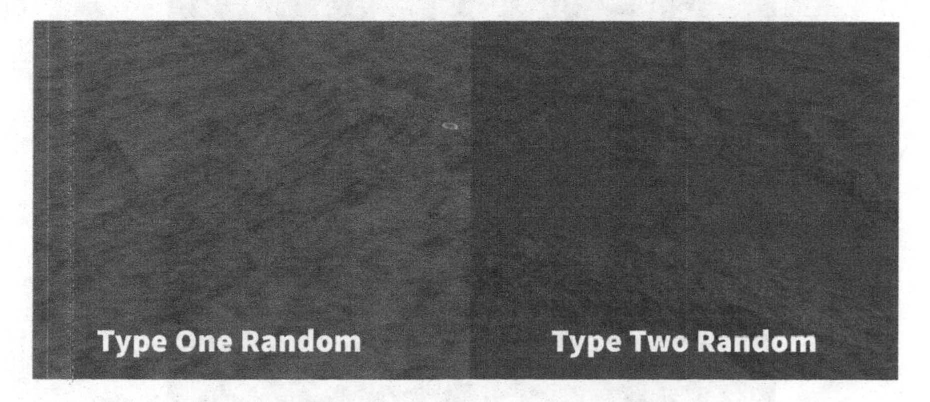

Figure 4.25

The two different types of random level terrain generated.

Importing a Heightmap

Another method of creating a terrain is actually with a third-party tool called the Heightmap Importer. A heightmap is a relatively modern way of creating detailed terrain using a tool specifically designed for it. Most of the hyper-realistic terrain seen in modern games is created using tools like this. Some of the more advanced game engines have heightmap importers built into them.

Please be aware that a heightmap is most generally suited toward long sloping areas. Sharp surfaces and angles (such as really rocky mountains) don't typically generate correctly when read from a file. As always, building it by hand will often produce the best results. That said, this is a very fast way to generate realistic terrain.

While this may yet be a feature for GameGuru to incorporate, currently it relies on an external tool to produce this functionality. A heightmap file is a simple color or grayscale image of 1024 × 1024 pixels. Colors will be converted to grayscale, and it will then be converted to terrain data and saved as a map file in the GameGuru\files\mapbank folder. As of this writing, it will be the _GGRANDOM.fpm file.

The logic behind a heightmap is simple. It is a graphical file that uses colors to translate to a number. Using black and white colors means that a black color is a low spot (numerically 0) and a white color is a high spot (255), as shown in Figure 4.26. Gray colors in between create your gradual slopes and the like.

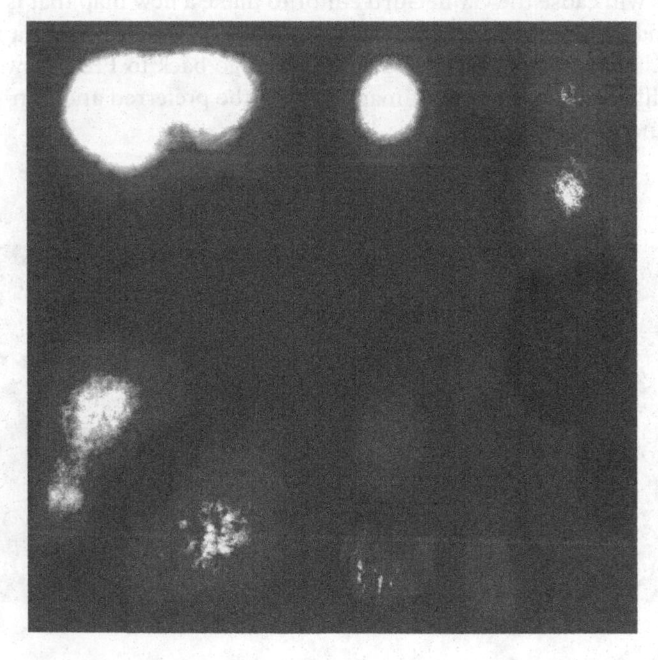

Figure 4.26

A heightmap for importation into GameGuru.

Upon opening it, the terrain frequently will have significantly jagged edges. This will require hand-fixing in the editor, mostly with the blend tool, to help clean up the terrain. Regardless, it can allow users to do some very interesting things, especially if you are using third-party terrain-generation tools. Some of these tools can run into the hundreds of dollars but will create impressive and realistic terrain.

For more details, please check the GameGuru forums and find BOTR's third-party application heightmap importer. A link to it can be found in the hyperlink reference guide portion of the Appendix.

This particular application is fairly simple in function. First unzip the file to a folder on your desktop. Open the folder, and run the application. It will ask for an input image. Make sure there is a heightmap ready to go. Using a program like TerreSculptor® or importing one from http://terrain.party can provide very high-quality results with minimum effort.

Several example files are included with this book for use. Each one will demonstrate a variety of suitable terrains that demonstrate principles from words on a background to real-world locations.

In the future, possibly by the time this book is printed, GameGuru may see an actual in-engine heightmap importer. With the code being available freely to modify on GitHub, this gives significant power to community-driven efforts.

Placing Your Entities

After making mountains, setting up flat areas for buildings, and generally having terrain completed, it's time to start placing some entities! If terrain is the body of the game, then entities are the game's lifeblood! They help bring every scene to life.

Time to start with some very basic entities.

Every GameGuru installation comes with a default set of entities. These entities are useful for prototyping a level but tend to be extremely limited when actually designing something that will stand the test of time. This is not to say they cannot be used; however, the optimal use for them is to prototype a level before replacing them with higher quality assets.

Included with this book is a large collection of assets. These assets have a wide variety of styles and shapes that you can use for any of your future projects, free of charge.

Basic Positioning

Placing entities in GameGuru is exceptionally simple. Start by adding the asset on the bar on the left. Then place it in the live view on the right by left-clicking it. Of course, there's more to it than that, but the overall flow is almost always the same.

Or is it?

There is a lot of nuance with using a product like this.

Let's start with the actual entity itself.

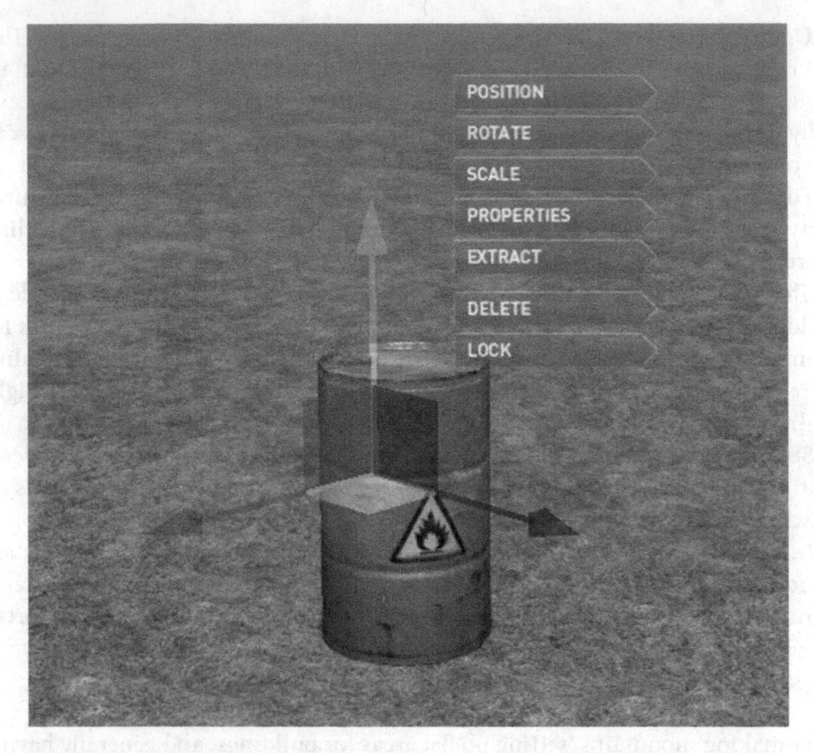

Figure 4.27

The movement widget in GameGuru.

Once you place it, you'll get the image shown in Figure 4.27.

This is called a widget. It's a term for the tool that allows manipulation of the entity. Note there are two separate portions. The first is the actual widget itself; the other is a context menu. This menu will change based on the type of object that is being manipulated. Each object has a separate, though mostly similar, menu.

Pay attention to the top three items: Position, Rotate, and Scale.

Each one of these has a separate visual widget for manipulating the object (Figure 4.28).

Notice there are three colors given. This is a fairly standard industry format. Green is Y, red is X, and blue is Z. This applies to all three modes of widget: position, rotate, and scale.

For now, focus on the move tool. When initially taking an object and placing it, the default configuration will be set to this method for the widget. On the widget, pay attention to both arrows pointing along the various Cartesian axes and that there are also several squares. These both operate in a different fashion. The arrows will slide the object along the axis that you select, thus making positioning very precise! It can never accidentally move off this invisible railway line that it will be attached to, so long as the mouse button is held down while moving it.

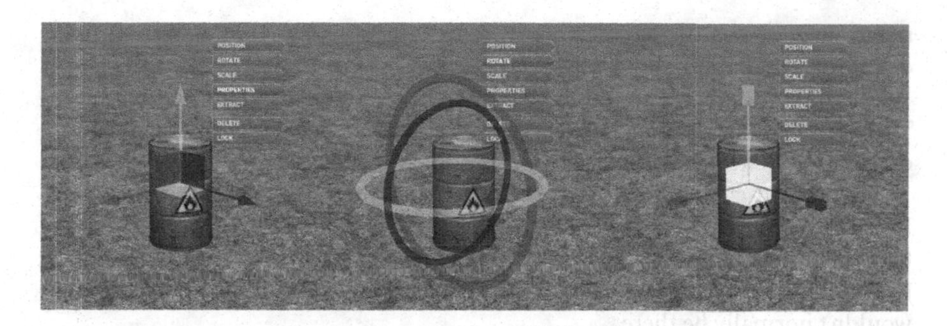

Figure 4.28

The three different widgets in GameGuru.

An alternate method is a less precise way where the user clicks and drag the square to position the object. This method tends to favor the plane for the square grabbed but will allow dragging it almost anywhere on any axis. This is great for quick positioning but typically will need some finer tuning.

A fast way to set an object placed at floor height is to hit the ENTER key. The exception to this that the ENTER key will also place the object on top of things already on the floor. So if it's an empty floor, it will go to floor height, but if for example, it's under a table, it will instead go on TOP of the table.

TIP: The ENTER key sets objects to either floor height or to the top of an object already resting on the floor such as a tabletop or roof.

The next widget is the scale tool. This tool looks similar to the movement tool, but the ends of the lines have several rectangles instead of arrows. This tool will allow some very interesting stretching or compression of a model. By stretching models one can get significantly more life out of them by reusing them for multiple tasks. Unfortunately, there are side effects to this, notably the quality of the object will typically deteriorate as you stretch it.

With this tool, users can stretch along the specific axis that is selected, such as the green Y axis slider. This will cause the object to increase in height but not in width or depth. The other sliders work similarly. One function easily overlooked is when clicking in the middle on the white square in between the various lines on the widget, it begins what's called a "global scale." This global scale will cause a uniform growth of the object in all three Cartesian directions. So in a sense, it will make the object look like a larger or smaller version of itself without causing it to flatten out, like using the actual sliders would.

All of that aside, there's a lot of utility in the slider. Users can turn unassuming boxes into flat walls, cola cans into billboards, or create the appearance of depth by resizing objects to look further away than they are. The sky is really the limit here, literally!

The last widget tool to evaluate is the rotation tool. Now at this point, the tool will look drastically different. Recall that the keyboard can be used to rotate some objects along 45-degree increments. Also, it can be used with the shift-keys to move along in one-degree increments. This tool, however, allows an even finer degree of control than those methods.

The three rings correspond to the different axes that are used by the object. This rotation will allow operation at very fine increments of movement on a level of precision unavailable to any other method.

The human eye will often see perfectly symmetrical shapes as "unnatural." In fact, think about the world at large: every single building, tree, park bench … they are slightly asymmetrical in position. By using the rotation tool and adding just the tiniest shred of rotation, it provides a sense of reality to the scene that wouldn't normally be there.

This doesn't just apply to rotation either. Slightly modifying repetitive objects via scaling or moving them around so they're not perfectly lined up can really help give a better sense of realism. One method for example is to lower sidewalks and curbs so they don't line up perfectly. It changes very little in terms of the game itself but really helps give cities a sense of depth and character.

It is important to remember the "little details" to help produce the highest quality levels.

Properties Panels

The properties window will show when clicking on "properties" on the context menu. This will then produce a white frame on the left of the screen filled with information unique to this particular object (Figure 4.29).

The properties pane is a completely dynamic menu generated off of the type of entity being used. Virtually every single component in GameGuru will have a separate and different properties menu. This includes but isn't limited to: static entities, AI entities, lights, physics-enabled objects, start markers, trigger zones, win zones, sound zones, and much more. For now, focus on a standard entity pane and the menu that goes with it.

Inside of this pane look for several bold headings with several subheadings that have editable fields. Each bold heading can be collapsed by clicking the [-] sign next to it.

Beginning in the "General" category are the "Name" and "Static Mode" fields. Name is an alphanumeric name that is applied to this specific object. Please note that name is not a unique field so it's possible to have SEVERAL entities with the same name. Alternately, it might have several identical entities with differing names.

Next is "Static Mode," which is a simple binary toggle of "yes" or "no." Static mode is an important configuration property. It controls whether the object will be able to be interacted with (when set to no), if it can receive baked on shadows (when set to yes), and can also impact the processing of your game by dedicating it to static = yes. A general rule is "if it's moving, choose no, and if it is staying in one place, choose yes."

TIP: If it's moving, choose no, and if it is staying in one place, choose yes.

Figure 4.29

The properties panel for a normal entity.

Next is the category "AI System." This has only one item underneath it for a standard entity: "Main." Main controls what Lua script is assigned to this entity. The default Lua script (unless specified in FPE files) is going to usually be "default.lua," shockingly enough. This file is an empty file that specifies that there is no code functioning on this object. For now, just make a note of it and move on.

Under this is another heading of "AI Automated." This section applies to the Lua code above it. The "Use Key" field specifically applies to door and key Lua files. It is the name of an entity with the "key.lua" script attached to it. Any other time it is blank.

The If Used field controls what happens in the code if the object is "used." It will point at another object via name, similar to how the Use Key field works. Here again, by default, it will be empty.

Respawn/Spawn At Start controls whether this entity comes into the game spawned in or is only summoned by Lua code.

Statistics is another heading with several subheadings of Strength, Speed, Anim Speed, IsImmobile, and LOD Modifier. Strength is a simple raw hit point value. Speed is how fast the AI entity will move. Anim Speed is how fast the animations cycle. IsImmobile allows configuration of whether this entity has functional ragdoll on death or not. LOD Modifier is for entities that have "level of detail" or LOD enabled and, in most cases, will not be useful.

Under the Physics heading are several subheadings of Physics On, Always Active, Physics Weight, Physics Friction, Explodable, and Explode Damage.

Physics On enables physics with a binary yes or no option. Always Active configures whether the entity disables after 3000 units of distance or not. This is useful for performance considerations. Physics Weight and Friction will be covered in Chapter 15 on physics. Explodable configures whether the entity will explode, removing its body, upon death. Explode Damage merely configures how much damage the explosion will do upon its subsequent demise.

Last is the Media heading with several subheadings of Sound0, 1, etc. We will cover this in Chapter 7 on sounds and music.

When to Use High-Quality Entities

Many users love the extremely reasonable price of the asset libraries available in the GameGuru store. This can grow into a rather unwieldy collection. Unfortunately, the assets are not always of the same quality either. There are significant amounts of objects that are good, but just not good enough to be placed right under the user's nose for close inspection.

I recommend following a few simple rules for determining an asset's quality.

The first is to know whether the assets are LOD enabled. This makes the job simple as LOD means "level of detail." This means that it will automatically control the number of polygons based on how far or near it is to the player. This little factoid will often show on the asset's page on the store. If it has LOD, then place the object at any range and it will automatically regulate the quality level of the model.

Most objects, especially older ones, do not have LOD, however. This leaves us in a dilemma. What happens when you have out-of-date objects that you paid good money for but couldn't rightfully use as a primary object? The answer boils down to placement. If you place the object in the background, the lack of detail will actually enhance the scene as typically things further away from the viewer are less detailed and more smudged. This lack of detail works to the developer's advantage while at the same time preserving a valuable polygon count to reduce performance impact for the player. This will be covered in more detail on that particular gem later in the optimization chapter (Chapter 21). For now, just try to get into the habit of putting the "uglier" models further away from the player's main viewing area. There are, of course, a few exceptions to this, such as objects reused over and over will often benefit from having a lower quality to them as otherwise they will consume unnecessary resources. With a 32-bit engine like GameGuru, it's critically important not to overload with too much detail on objects that simply might not need it. Sure, it's nice to have that 20,000 poly model with 4k texture depth in the game, but how often is the player really going to stand around and admire the world's prettiest garbage bin?

So the truth is it's often a balancing act. In general, you are safe with moderate-quality textures everywhere, low-quality textures far away, and high-quality textures up close. The high-quality (HQ) textures will often be less used unless it's an area being showcased as well. Dark areas, for instance, will not need many high-quality textures.

The player's opening area, however, would do well to get the HQ treatment as it will often impact the player's initial impression of your game and tilt their opinion toward a positive view. We will go over this in significantly more detail in later chapters on adding ambience and optimization.

Where to Find Additional Documentation

Obviously, this book counts as unofficial documentation. However, with respect to actual documentation for GameGuru. it's generally all over the place. There are old forum posts, hour-long streams by Lee, blog posts, and anything in between.

The starting place is actually within a GameGuru installation itself under the "Docs" subfolder (Figure 4.30). This subfolder has a fairly enormous amount of literature in it, allowing information of various elements such as material index values or scripting with Lua. All of these have a significant amount of utility, but it can be time consuming to go through each one, so use it as a reference when all other sources are exhausted.

There's also about ten or so demo games you can examine, some of which have an absolute wealth of information, like Morning mountain stroll.

As you may have noticed, when you first opened GameGuru, it gave you a tutorial screen with a great many options for video tutorials and demo games.

Name	Date modified	Type	Size
DarkAI Documentation	7/23/2018 8:56 PM	File folder	
Weapon Hand Files	7/30/2018 9:42 PM	File folder	
Building Editor Guide	7/30/2018 9:30 PM	Office Open XML ...	24,886 KB
Building Editor Guide	7/30/2018 9:30 PM	Adobe Acrobat D...	2,504 KB
CharacterKitSampleParts	7/30/2018 9:30 PM	Compressed (zipp...	8,666 KB
CollisionModeValues	7/30/2018 9:31 PM	Text Document	2 KB
EBE Material Types	7/30/2018 9:31 PM	Text Document	1 KB
ForceObstaclesValues	7/30/2018 9:31 PM	Text Document	1 KB
GameGuru Weapon MAX Files	7/30/2018 9:30 PM	Compressed (zipp...	23,153 KB
Importing models into GameGuru	7/30/2018 9:31 PM	Office Open XML ...	41 KB
Importing models into GameGuru	7/30/2018 9:30 PM	Adobe Acrobat D...	507 KB
Projectile Types	7/30/2018 9:31 PM	Text Document	1 KB
Scripting With LUA	7/30/2018 9:31 PM	Microsoft Word 9...	95 KB
Scripting With LUA	7/30/2018 9:31 PM	Adobe Acrobat D...	227 KB
Terrain Palette	7/30/2018 9:30 PM	Adobe Acrobat D...	754 KB
The Music System	7/30/2018 9:31 PM	Microsoft Word 9...	53 KB
The Music System	7/30/2018 9:31 PM	Adobe Acrobat D...	45 KB
Water Lua Command List	7/30/2018 9:30 PM	Adobe Acrobat D...	525 KB

Figure 4.30

The docs folder has a great deal of additional info.

These are all very useful examples of what can be done in a very short period of time by virtually anyone. The tutorials in particular are a godsend for first-time use and cover a lot of the introductory material provided in this book.

There's also the "GameGuru" channel on YouTube, which has literally hundreds of demo videos illustrating many topics. Some of them are rather lengthy, but they often contain information not found elsewhere. There's a significant amount of very useful information available in those channels.

Other fantastic reference locations are the GameGuru forums. Now this can be divided into two primary areas. The first is the actual forum site on http://forum.game-guru.com and the other is the steam discussion forum available on the steam page for GameGuru. While the former is definitely the better source of information and free stuff in particular, there's occasionally a good piece of information available on the steam discussion forums as well.

GitHub is a long-standing website where coders can get together to collaborate on projects. GameGuru's code is constantly being refined there as of this writing by both TheGameCreators crew and willing members of the community. There's a lot of high-end talent that uses GameGuru, and it's starting to show as the access has opened significantly for us. Prior to this, coding was limited to Lua scripting, and the actual engine itself was a closed box. Since being opened up on GitHub, things have really started flying along. Even to the point where sections of this book had to be rewritten because new things came online as it was written! GitHub has an issues section to track trending problems and bugs. You can also submit found bugs or issues. Not to mention there's a significant body of documentation there as well.

Then, of course, there is my own blog (which features regular updates about all things GameGuru) and lastly the discord channel. Discord® is a communications program that's extremely platform agnostic and allows a massive range of free methods to connect. It can be obtained on phones, on a pc, in a browser, in a program, etc. Once inside, there are channels of discussion, chats, direct messages, voice chats, etc. It's really quite impressive how much comes from there. Often things show there that can't be seen anywhere else, such as new works in progress or technical answers to difficult questions (such as how to use PBR assets).

Part of using a game engine is using the available assets to their fullest, to ensure that you are able to maximize your knowledge on the particular elements being put together. It's not uncommon for indie gamedevs to have stacks of manuals and reference materials on their desks as they work. No matter how powerful the game engine is, what's more important is how knowledgeable, capable, and imaginative the actual creator is.

Take for instance, Five Nights at Freddy's®. This series was created with an incredibly simplistic game engine, something that would have honestly been at home in the late '90s. The success is directly attributable to the creator's finesse with the engine, marketing, story, and game development capabilities. With all that said, take a look at the resources provided and check the reference section in the back of this book for a list of important hyperlinks.

5

Building Your First Game

Priorities for GameGuru Games

Foremost: This is an outdoor game engine. Like it or not, if you are going to make a primarily indoor game, you will be fighting an uphill battle. This will go MUCH easier for you if you try to "go with the flow" of the engine and build it around its strengths instead of its weaknesses.

This is not to say you cannot add indoor areas or even make indoor maps. It is simply to say you must expect it's going to go much, MUCH easier to build the game around outdoor areas.

That aside, the demo materials will illustrate both methods of building a level and what's involved with the process.

So first, we've got to start by defining an area we will be working in. When I begin, I typically use the terrain paint tool to "mark" areas such as borders, buildings, or landmarks (Figure 5.1). This way I can know exactly where I want to place things later without having to spend extra cycles trying to be creative on the fly.

However, the first place I always begin is where the level will be "contained" in. Typically, you don't want to use the ENTIRE map in GameGuru, merely a

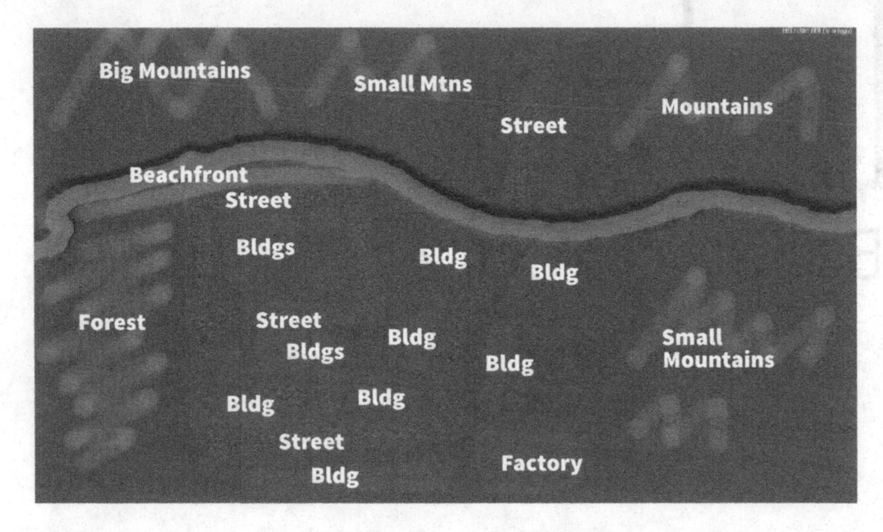

Figure 5.1

Rapidly defining a level for even quicker prototyping.

fraction of it. This allows you to ensure there's terrain past the viewing area for the player but also limits the amount of resources you're going to spend on terrain, which can easily eat up available memory or processing power.

So determine the box you have for your "working area," then decide if you will need visible background elements such as buildings, mountains, or other objects that will be parallaxed for the player (Figure 5.2).

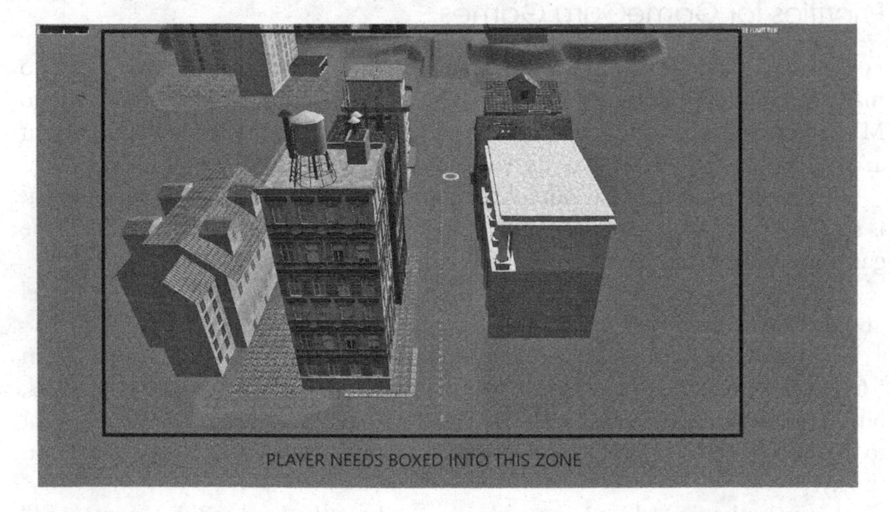

Figure 5.2

Demonstration of playable area and need for barriers.

Very early games had difficulty rendering outdoor scenes because they're incredibly resource intensive. There is no exception here; you have to take care to use the most of your resources. While you can build indoor scenes with GameGuru, in particular some pretty phenomenal ones with static lighting, they generally tend to be resource intensive and slow. This is because the occluder (which shelters objects from loading that are not in view) is generally not that great. It does work, mind you, but typically tends to function secondarily to good level design. Good level design effectively ensures that your level never has too many objects in view, which will prevent them from overloading the system.

Building Something Memorable

There are a few key facets to making a game that you want to try to keep in mind. While you'll have specific environments that you may aim to create in, there are certain elements that will remain central to your game.

First of all: Make it memorable! You don't want your game to be relegated to obscurity because it was too generic and too boring. Try to put something in that will build a sense of awe in a player because those are the things they remember. Of course, this can work in a negative fashion as well if you build a terrible map. This sense of awe should be worked into your environments as something sincerely impressive or even just massive. Sometimes having an enormous monument somewhere central is sufficient, other times it's a sense of scale brought on as you gaze out into a town that stretches miles. The key element here is to try to remember that as you work forward.

Second, and perhaps just as importantly, you want your levels to be fun and interesting! While this feeds into the first point, not everything has to be memorable. The rest of the time though, we want our levels to have a good feel to them that makes players have a good time. Keep the scenery and interactions interesting to keep the player engaged with your story.

Third, you want to "show, not tell." This is an old creative writing "rule" that also applies very well to game design. As a thought exercise, imagine opening up a fairly bland "store" with a big sign that says store above it. Then a narrator comes on and tells you that this was a family run store where obviously a murder has occurred.

Kind of boring, right?

Instead, what you want to do is show the story to the player by building all of the elements that detail that particular story inside of the scene. This means you'll need a body, of course, with blood, maybe some knocked-over furniture to show a struggle, and perhaps some notes that indicate this is who owned this store. Sometimes this can be done by having "family pictures" in the shot or other personal effects for the now deceased NPC. This type of storytelling can be difficult if you let it but really take the time to try to make each area shine for maximum player experience.

The fourth thing you want to keep in mind is that your expectations may not always match your implementation. This can be difficult to deal with as often our mind's eye sees it very differently than how our ability to create brings it to life. Obviously, we want to try to match our mind's eye as often as possible but, due to limitations in our assets, the engine, or even our own proficiency, it may not be possible. Do the best you can within your limitations!

The last stage of any level's design is optimization and polish. These two stages will take nearly as long as the actual design of the level in many cases but are well worth it to provide an optimal player experience. So for that reason, don't worry too obsessively about the details while you are making the level. Many AAA developers design their levels with "placeholder" objects that they then later go back and put in with greater levels of detail. In fact, throughout this book you'll get a very clear idea of how I build my levels, which typically starts at a large "abstract" level that is then carefully and meticulously added to in layers of detail.

Having a Plan

As mentioned previously, it's important to have at least a basic plan of what you intend to do with your game. A written account of your intended design will get you closer to your objective. The more you flesh out, the easier it is know what to do!

Part of this book is a walk-through of a whole game build, from start to finish. I've included a simple TDD to help speed things along. If you open the Chapter 5 folder, you can see the TDD enclosed on the media. For the purposes of our development in this game, I will walk you through relevant components of each level in our demo game, as well as the subcomponents of it such as menu design, custom assets like sounds, and AAA quality lighting techniques on each level and map. Full copies of each finished level will be included as well, for your direct examination. Please see the licensing documentation for rules and legal information about the copying and use of these items.

TDD Start

Our project is going to be a science fiction game set on a faraway planet. Our protagonist will be Drake Ironglass. He's a hard-boiled cyber-detective looking for clues on his ex-wife's murder—with some revenge thrown in, of course. She'd gotten herself into trouble with her new boyfriend and sent Drake an inexplicable message asking for you to visit before her death.

Spoiler alert: Her boyfriend was a smuggler for a local gang that got involved in helping an outside group prepare an uprising by smuggling thousands of illegal arms onto the planet.

The setting of a faraway planet will have a few caveats. We'll have a few different planets and a space station-based level (with no terrain on that one).

Our enemies will consist of both environmental enemies (fire, poison gas, wild animals) and actual aggressive enemies, such as gangsters and robots. There will be optional enemies as well, such as scientists who don't like you interrupting their work and peacekeeping robots that may not like your activities.

We'll add more to the documentation as we go.

Level 1: Home planet, spaceport to constabulary to your ex-wife's home, back to spaceport.

Level 2: Space station Quebec-X-ray-Foxtrot (QXF).

Level 3: Gangster's planet.

Level 4: Your home planet, in ruins (revolution, fires, etc.).

Level 5: Last level, enemy planet.

TDD End

Our first level will be the site of your ex-wife's murder. It's a small, agrarian planet close to some major trade routes. We'll have some farms, some hills, and mostly gentle terrain. There's a small town, a spaceport, and of course, your home.

It's going to consist of a relatively simple terrain with some navigable terrain features. First, we need to create a center point—something people can fixate on to help them navigate. In this case, it will be a large mountain with a facility on top of it.

This mountain will dominate the area around it, giving a sense of scale and shape to the area. A landmark like that is hard to miss and gives people a sense of awe.

We're off to a good start, I think. Next, let's create a flat area for our little town and spaceport. This will give us a good area to start with. We're going to line it with some buildings and miscellany.

When building our city, we want to design some streets first and use them as a guideline for the path the player will take. Our first objective will be to see the city constabulary. They will have some information on Drake's ex-wife and her death. We'll have some NPCs there who will tell the player their hands are tied, but we'll get into that later. For now, we're just planning the actual design and build of the city itself. We're going to use the terrain tool and our custom terrain to "draw" some roads. This will give us the latitude of some very natural-feeling roads that are worn as they won't be perfectly flat and instead can have bumps, potholes, etc. Even speed bumps are viable.

We're going to use this system to build some simple roads, along with some side roads. Then we'll fill the dead areas with some buildings that will add flavor and "life" to the area.

(NOTE: Later, we will add an objective about getting your equipment from customs, which will keep us from having a weapon on this first map.)

Let's work on the spaceport next. We'll need a landing pad, a terminal, a warehouse, and a hangar.

Again, we need a large flat pad to start with. This time we're going to use the metallic texture in the texture tool to draw on a realistic looking area for the spaceport to operate on.

Now we're going to place several buildings and the landing pad.

We'll start by placing the large objects first. These large objects are sort of the low-hanging fruit of the level. They're easy to place and take up a substantial portion of the real estate.

As we add these objects, try to leave room for other, smaller objects to get put in. The smaller objects are referred to as "clutter objects" and help give each scene a distinct feel and flavor.

On Clutter Objects

Clutter objects are a critical component of making a level feel less amateurish and making it look and feel more professional. These objects are often "filler" on a screen. They don't actually provide any measurable value beyond tying the piece in aesthetically. That said, though, when you see a game that doesn't have proper use of clutter objects, it will seem very unprofessional. Imagine walking through a forest with a hundred trees... but no rocks, animals, or plants. It seems unnatural and weird. We as humans are programmed to look for these types of oddities as a sort of survival mechanism.

One of the little tricks that AAA game companies use is they will design each area as its own scene. They don't have to be significant scenes, just a minor backstory to each room. Is this the "dirty bathroom that has seen one too many airport travelers" room? Perhaps the back alley will have mats and empty bottles to make it look like it's the haunt for a particular group of homeless people. Rooms should all have their own personality; it helps give each area a sense of being alive and really lends to the feel of it being a complete game. This goes back to the idea of "showing, not telling."

As with all things, though, a little restraint is in order. It might be fun to go through and decorate every single thing from wall to ceiling, but the reality is we're working with a strict memory limit for a 32-bit game engine. There are limits to what we can do and achieve, so we want, as often as possible, to reuse clutter objects. For instance, what's the point of having 18 different trash bins or skips? We can easily have one or two models for that and reuse those with some slight variation to make them feel differentiated.

Take the trash bins shown in Figure 5.3, for instance. This particular image shows how one model can be used three different ways to provide a completely different experience for the player. We have your basic trash bin on the left—very plain Jane, but a common sight through most towns and cities. In our second picture, we have the same skip, adjusted slightly by rotating it about 5 degrees on its X-axis. I've added some trash bags and broken boxes make it look full. You get the sense it's nearly garbage day since trash has literally begun piling up outside the dumpster. The last picture shows a dumpster thrown on its side, trash spilling out into the street. Perhaps this is a postapocalyptic setting. Remember, it's all

Figure 5.3

Creative re-use of assets is critical for resource management.

about context clues. If we were to put a car crash adjacent to it, then people would assume the dumpster had been knocked loose by the wreck.

So for now, we're going to add some larger "set pieces" to our world. These bigger clutter objects are things that are more recognizable than individual things such as bricks, empty cans, etc. We want to work downward from largest to smallest when doing clutter. The method is as follows:

Build a large-scale landmark for navigation and to help stage the scene.

Place the most important locations first.

Draw roads between the important locations, using these to create your initial "maze" design.

Place large secondary objects next. These are your primary "blockers," which will prevent players from being able to move forward through an area. It's important to not only make them seem natural to terrain but also to use them as landmarks as well. Obviously, if you just use consistently repetitive terrain, it becomes boring and disorienting as well. If you position the large objects in a meaningful way, it will give the player a more navigable experience while at the same time funneling them where you want them to go.

Smaller secondary buildings are placed after this. During this phase, we will typically begin to "wall in the player" so that they only can go where we want them to. This is done by creating walls with buildings that are impassible, fences, and other roadblocks. Some games take this literally by destroying roads and creating falls that will force the player to commit suicide if they attempt to keep walking. Waterways with the terrain engine are another important piece of this and can be used to restrict the player's movement considerably. For now, in these initial phases of development, we want to really make the player sort of stuck in a box. We don't want to worry about inhibiting movement in individual areas. We want to only prevent them from leaving our "game play area" box.

Now we move on to clutter. Arrange the scene with large "set piece" buildings first (the type with no way into them that are there for show). Then move on to smaller buildings.

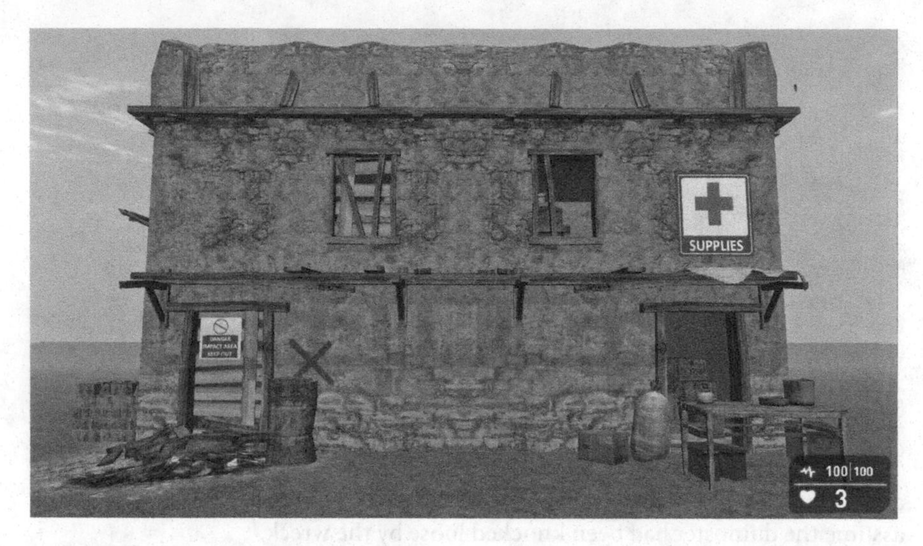

Figure 5.4

On the left an abandoned building, on the right a medical hut.

Large clutter pieces like vehicles, trash skips, benches, and trees should go in next. It's important to reuse these but not to overuse them to the point where the level becomes repetitive and bland. As these are large, they are the most easily noticed components for repetition.

Medium set pieces such as posters and signage, chairs, boxes, and trash bags should go in next. These help really differentiate areas into distinct scenes. By adding posters or signs, such as in Figure 5.4, we can set up the area to look like it "belongs" to an owner. Perhaps it's a pet store or a generic midnight market. Often, adding a sign is enough to help create this level of distinction. Adding other moderate pieces that contribute to that will guide the player further in their belief of the scene.

Small set pieces (detail pieces) go in last and typically consist of tiny objects that are spread around to really break up the differences between your areas (Figure 5.5). These help contribute to the overall mood of a particular location and, if necessary, can really provide a massive distinction (provided you use enough of them) for a particular area. The downside is the overall cost of having many different models so this is where you will typically run into memory issues if you get too out of control here.

We're not going to get too heavily invested in this portion for this segment of this book as we have a lot more to cover before we circle back to it.

This basic process, working from most important and largest to least important and smallest, ensures that our level will have a clean flow. This flow guides us through game design as much as it guides the player through the game itself. For now, don't worry about functional things. We're solely looking at designing the scene itself, creating the environment in which the player will operate.

Figure 5.5

On the left light clutter and on the right is heavy clutter.

In our example, I've included the demo level for this map in the corresponding chapter's folder on the enclosed media. In the chapters folder, we have our mapbank, and inside of that are the various iterations of the map itself as I laid down the pieces section by section so you can get some sense of how it's arranged and in what order.

Making Mazes and Puzzles

Most levels follow simple design features. They want you to follow a simple path, overcome some obstacles, and then proceed to the objective or finale for the map.

When you are designing your level, understand that no one likes a map that is a simple linear romp. Players like to explore, be rewarded for their exploration, and figure out the puzzle you lay out before them. It gives them a sense of accomplishment.

Mazes are one of the oldest paradigms in gaming and they remain, to this day, a fixture. Think back on classics like "Pac-Man®" or "Donkey Kong®." While the former had a very obvious maze, even "Donkey Kong" offered you a sort of maze by giving you many paths with varying rewards, despite a relatively linear design. This type of risk-and-reward system is its own type of maze, causing players to have to rapidly evaluate the choice of taking the minefield versus taking the scenic route.

For now, we're going to focus on building a simple maze, something that can be relatively easily navigated but can be added to later (as we will be coming back to it).

There are several types of simple mazes that we face in everyday life. There are mazes of boxes and mazes caused by confusing or repetitive terrain such as the mosaic city mentioned previously. Getting lost in a forest is equally confusing if you aren't used to taking a bearing or getting some orientation based off local landmarks. Similarly, repetitive terrain can be absolutely murderous on a person's ability to make decisions for navigation. As developers, we have to try to not only provide a challenging maze but also provide a few clues to help them along. Give the player a sense of achievement for completing your puzzle. Granted, some will look up a guide or know intuitively how to navigate the maze, but the fact remains that there's always a certain joy in being able to exercise your mental capabilities in a challenging way. There are, of course, limits to this. Mazes can rapidly become infuriating or tedious if overly complex.

Making Realistic Mountains

The terrain system in GameGuru is one of the best features about it. You can make fairly complex terrain features with some time and effort, as well as some understanding about the system you're using. In prior iterations of FPS Creator, they were entirely focused around indoor feature sets. Outdoor terrain was a hack at best, and it was reflected in the level design. GameGuru has always been oriented toward making really effective levels with outdoor terrain, so it's important to keep that in mind when designing your levels. Otherwise, you will be fighting the tide and that can really wear you out rather fast. Moreover, it seems rather foolish to disregard one of the strongest features of a game engine!

Given that GameGuru is a game engine oriented toward outdoor locales, it makes sense to familiarize yourself with how to use the built-in terrain editor. On the face of it, it is extremely simplistic (which of course is part of the appeal). The controls are simple enough, just select your tool (Figure 5.6) and start clicking.

Holding in the mouse button continues an action, so if you are raising elevation, then holding it down will continue to raise it. Holding shift usually causes something to do the opposite of what it normally does. For example, holding shift while using the elevation tool causes it to reduce elevation. This way you can carve valleys and rivers into the landscape. Holding control while clicking will often result in something happening faster when working with the terrain system.

T puts you into the Terrain Editing Mode. This will allow you to "paint" terrain onto the terrain field. You will be able to raise hills, carve canyons, or drill out holes for lakes and rivers.

LMB: "Left Mouse Button" will allow you to raise elevation when in Terrain Editing Mode (TEM).

LMB-shift: Now if you hold shift and hit the LMB, you will lower terrain. This allows you to carve out holes, canyons, make pockmarks, or what have you.

Figure 5.6

The terrain submenu of the GUI top menu.

With respect to terrain painting, the same system is used; you can paint grass or terrain colors with LMB. You can remove grass or terrain colors (it will configure it to the default, which is terrain color 1) by holding shift-LMB.

You will also notice in terrain editing mode that you will have a circle that you can adjust in size using –/+. This is critical to making good terrain as you will need to be able to both put fine details and create large mountains. When you initially make your terrain, it will come out looking very much like a mashed potato pile.

This is most likely not your desired outcome. However, achieving good results with GameGuru takes time and patience. It also takes a solid toolkit, which I have graciously assembled for you.

The first method I like to use is a big, then little, method. I use large circles to build the basic shape. This is where most people generally stop; they will create a fairly basic series of hills. These, however, have a very unnatural appearance and shape, which makes them stand out in people's mind as being "bad." What we want to do is create a realistic level of detail, so we first need a basis of comparison. Go do a search for "types of mountains" now in your favorite engine so you can have a good spread to look at.

Note also that these mountains aren't solitary. They are generally surrounded by other mountains. Moreover, those mountains aren't all in one neat, flat, little line. They are smattered all in a general area, which adds a sense of depth to the terrain feature.

There's a technical term called "parallaxing" that refers to the simulation of distance by moving objects that are further away at a slower rate than objects that are closer. This was typically more relevant in 2D gaming where it was important to create a sense of depth from a flat world. However, with 3D gaming, the parallax effect is mostly automatic as the renderer is developing a 3D picture for us every time it draws the screen. However, it's important to make the most of this by placing larger objects in the distance, which can be used as a reference for both orientation and also to provide a sense of depth.

When I say for orientation, I'm talking about providing a reference point for people to get a sense of direction. It's a fairly important navigational method for people. They often call it navigation by landmark. The reality is, though, as a human you are attuned to use your sense of depth perception and large landmarks as navigational aids. This is why it's crucial for us to start with big objects before we begin placing details. We want to provide solid sets of landmarks for our players.

So let's get back to our methods of making mountains and then we'll circle back to our method of map building. In this example, what we're going to do is choose a type of mountain and proceed to make it. We want to create it in a fashion that gives it a sense of depth, so we'll be giving a few separate peaks to it. This way we can be sure it appeals to our viewer's sense of parallax and creates a living breathing environment (also called a biome), which the player will be immersed in.

While GameGuru is a simplistic engine, this is arguably one if it's best features. Lee Bamber put a LOT of time into making sure the terrain system was capable. With a little work, you can really produce some stunning landscapes.

So let's begin.

I always start with a search of images of the type of terrain I want, in order to gain inspiration. So pick your favorite poison here and go to a popular (or unpopular, if you must) search engine's images section. We'll be searching for "sci-fi mountains."

You'll notice there are some truly impressive specimens here. The mountains are large and looming with jagged spires and massive spurs in their features. They are imposing natural castles. Pay attention to how many of them are important focal points. We're creating a sense of awe here, which is important in gaming for creating memorable scenes.

TIP: Always strive to create a sense of awe for your players.

We'll be making a mountainous terrain with dense forests. This is going to be an agrarian, backwater planet. It will have a few major features, notably:

The spaceport on top of a small mountain or hill, which will have a minor amount of interactivity.

The town with its police station, which will act as a backdrop and generally be noninteractive.

Finally, the outskirts of town, small farms, and the like. This is where our final destination for the first level will be. We will focus our efforts on interactivity here.

What we're going to need are some mountains and flat areas, maybe a river or two. These will provide us our setting. First, we'll work on the backdrop, so let's start by making a new flat level (file: new flat level).

From here, the first thing we want to do is head to the upper left corner of the map using the arrow keys. Now use the plus sign on your keyboard to expand the size of the circle to the largest. We're going to make a great big mountain here.

Hold your left mouse button to raise the elevation to a suitable height. In our example, it will be fairly large (Figure 5.7).

Congratulations! You have your first mountain… sort of.

This is… not quite what you were looking for, right? However, this is what most first-timers typically create, and it does serve as a suitable starting block. Try to be like the sculptor "freeing" the mountain from the pile of rock. To do that, we will need a mountain range. So let's add a few nearby lumps that we will then connect piece by piece.

This basic range will form the primary "monument" for our level, something players will see in the distance and use to understand their position and distance. It will act as a permanent landmark. Let's add a few more major circles nearby it, which will extend the mountain's range. Try to vary their height or location. Remember that nature is asymmetrical.

Let's start adding some slopes to it, by dragging slowly down the hill with the raise tool. Before we do, let's make the circle about half of the size it was

Figure 5.7

A simple lump, the base of our mountain.

before (Figure 5.8). These slopes are there to illustrate how the mountain "rose up" from the ground. It gives it a much more natural feel.

TIP: You can also use the ramp tool for this section if you want a more jagged appearance! Now click on some flat terrain and drag to high terrain to create a ramp of the precise length you need.

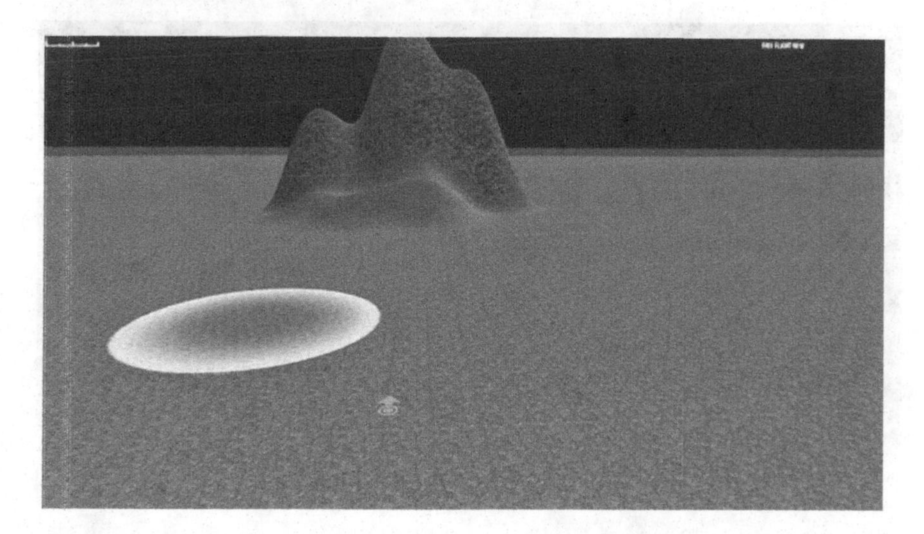

Figure 5.8

A few undefined lumps to help shape the core of our mountain.

We're going to be adding detail as we build, from the large to the small. This method will ensure that we get a very realistic feel as we add layer upon layer to our work. This is similar to how master painters in the Renaissance would slowly add layer after layer to their own canvases to create the great works we know and love today. Obviously, there's a learning curve involved but don't shoot yourself down—remember that detail added upon detail will reap the rewards. The tricky bit is to not get so mired down in said details that you forego the rest of the bigger picture. You need to be able to move on at some point to the next element and continue adding detail to those other components. An exception to this is items that are far away from the player do not require that level of detail; in fact, it's actually a negative, if you are drawing very distant mountains, to use too much detail.

The reason for this is because it will actually cause a performance hit for something the player literally cannot even see. So as a rule of thumb, try to add the most detail up close and the least detail far away.

Remember we're making slopes here that drag from the ground up to the peak. Just use your imagination! Try to picture a real mountain in your mind's eye and make it a reality (Figure 5.9).

Great! Now, in order to really cement the "feel" of a real mountain, we are going to add some hills in front of the primary mountain. This will give it a sense of depth, as mentioned previously. These hills don't require nearly as much work. Just make a few quarter- or third-height mountains at slightly varying distances in front of the primary mountain range.

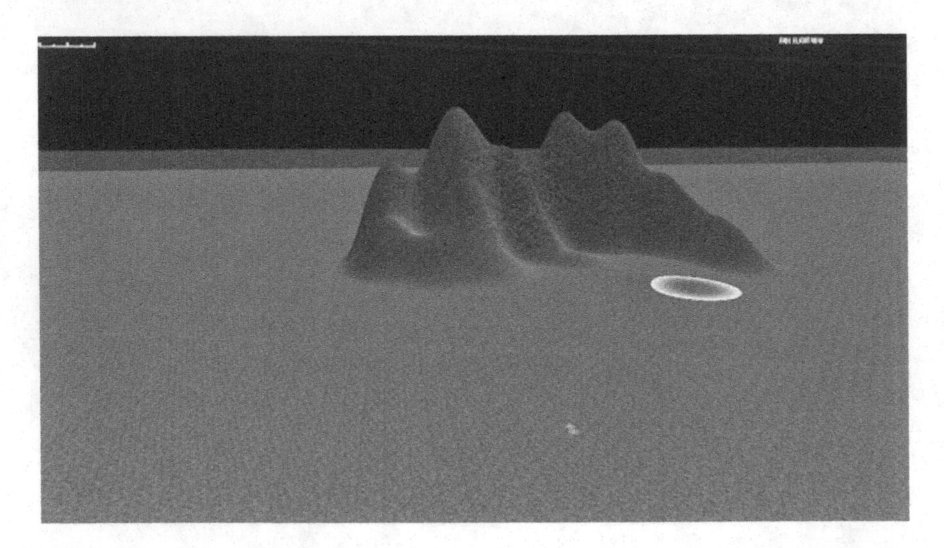

Figure 5.9

Adding depth by parallaxing a ridge behind it.

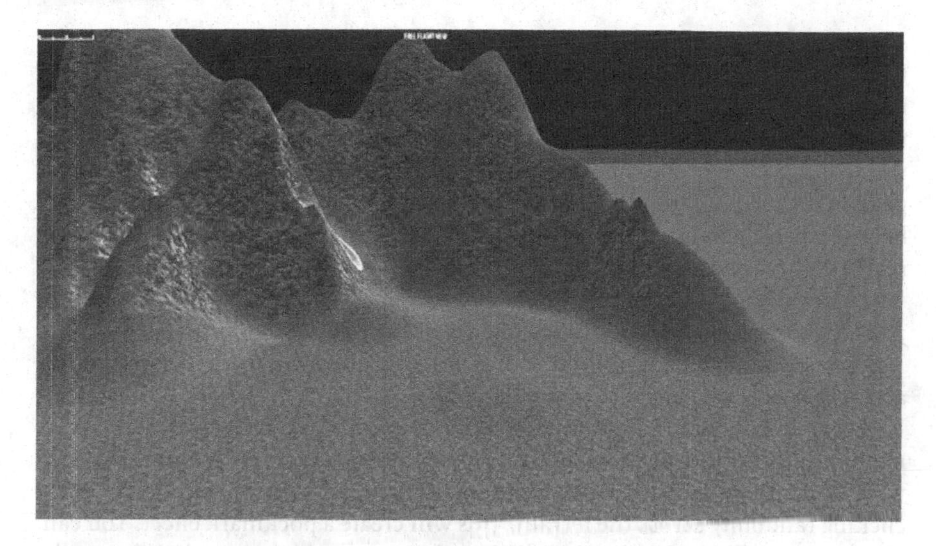

Figure 5.10

Adding definition by using a small terrain circle.

With these hills, we're not going to put as much time into them. This is primarily because we don't want the user to focus on them. Typically, humans have a specific focal range, so if they are looking at the mountains, the hills should appear blurry. This means we will be investing less time and energy into these secondary hills. They are literally only there to provide a necessary sense of depth.

For this exact same reason we'll be adding some half-height mountain ranges slightly behind and slightly in front of our primary mountain (Figure 5.10). These will be larger than the hills and have a bit more depth to them but should be looked at as part of the final mountain as it's very rare that a single monolithic mountain rises up out of flat terrain. Mountains come in groups and so we want to reflect that.

It's really coming along now, isn't it? You can almost see it looking like a real mountain range though it still has miles and miles of work to go. Let's taper the edges of these mountain ranges to help provide a realistic sense that they've come up as a sort of earthly fold to a peak. We don't just want to rely on the circle tool for this; we need to again create slopes with it by either using the ramp tool or slope tool.

Now if you've used the ramp tool to create your slopes, it's important to use the blend tool later to help blend those edges; otherwise, it's going to look really clunky.

The good news is this can wait for a bit while we work on providing more depth to our mountain. We'll be adding lots of slopes and detail. When you're done with your slopes, you should see a very jagged mountain range instead of a gently sloped one.

At this point, you've really not gotten much detail. It looks … ok, but definitively unfinished or amateurish. The way we're going to really differentiate our terrain is to now go back to the elevation tool and hold the minus key (–) until the circle is as small as it can get. At this point now, what we're going to do is use this to just click here and there along the slopes and ridges. This will cause a slight peak in the terrain. Run this tool at a brisk pace down the edge of your ridges to help sharpen them up. Click intermittently on flat surfaces to give them a more realistically varied appearance.

TIP: Don't hold down the elevation tool as a small circle in one spot too long or you'll get a very ugly spike … unless you want that.

Don't be afraid to play around with this at this point; try to allow some happy accidents (some call this serendipity) to occur.

At this point, your mountains should look significantly more refined. We're not done just yet though. Now it's time for us to simulate some erosion. The way we're going to do that is by using the small circle again and instead just shift-clicking randomly across the terrain. This will create a pockmark effect. You can also create small rivulets by shift-click and dragging down in a slightly erratic fashion to create what looks like places where water has run off.

After we're done making our pockmarks, we are going to now set our circle size to about half by hitting the plus (+) key. At this point, I want you to choose the blend tool and click-hold down the mouse button while dragging the circle across your mountain range. The longer you hold it, the more it will equalize the terrain—so try not to stay in one place too long. The exception to this is if you used the ramp tool to rapidly generate your slopes, this will likely require more time with the blend tool to help create a more realistic appearance.

At this point, the base terrain is basically done. We need to finish it, however, otherwise it will look much akin to an unpainted car. It needs finishing and fine tuning before it's ready to run. So we're going to begin by selecting a good terrain for this. I've included the one we're going to use which is a high quality texture of my own creation. This texture will have the appearance of the world we're building but will also provide a realistic height to the mountains (Figure 5.11). Thankfully, GameGuru will automatically detect the height of the slope and adjust the texture accordingly using a process called "tri-planar texturing." This allows very high mountains to look as if they have a more realistic texture.

In that respect, it's important to have a high-quality terrain map if you're using outdoor terrain (Figure 5.12). Once you've selected the terrain for this map, we'll continue by adding other fineries to the level.

By now you should have invested a scant 30 minutes or so of time into this. This type of build happens very rapidly and comes together well. It's a primary strength of GameGuru versus other engines. I've built similar terrains in Unity, which has significantly more terrain tools to work with, though it's hard to compare with the ease and simplicity that GameGuru allows you to put this all together.

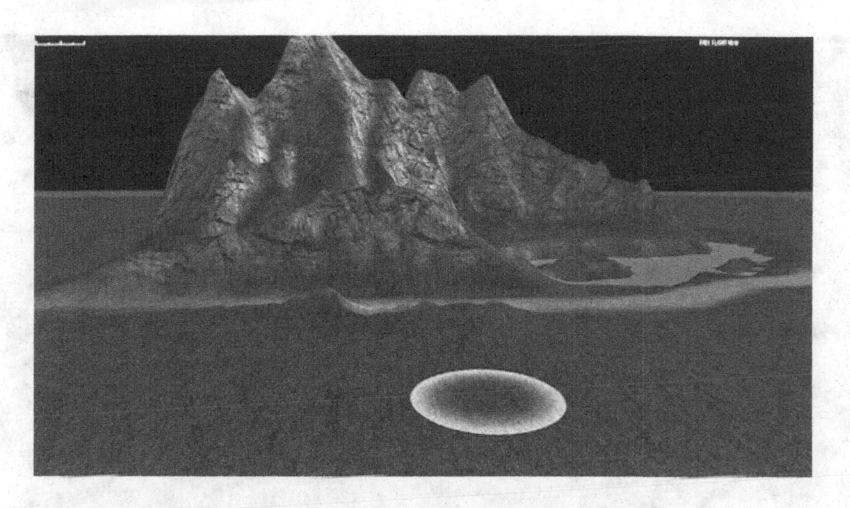

Figure 5.11

The nearly completed mountain, painted and detailed.

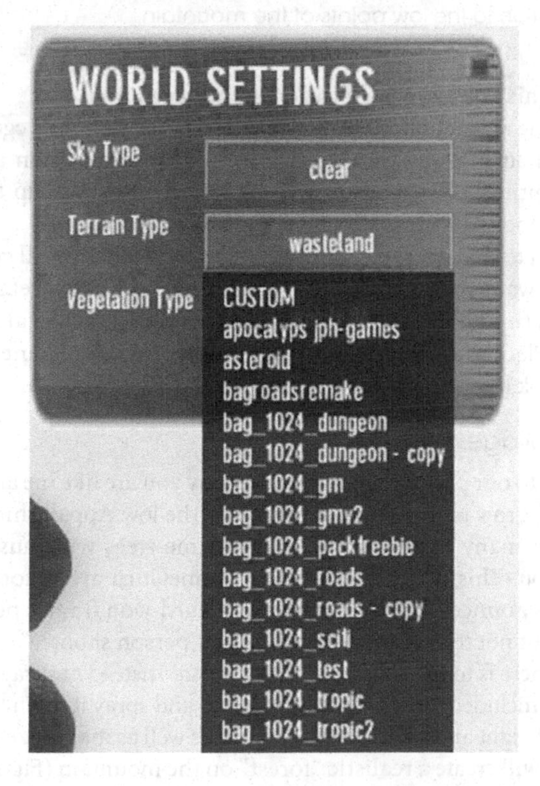

Figure 5.12

Choosing a custom terrain from the tab-tab menu.

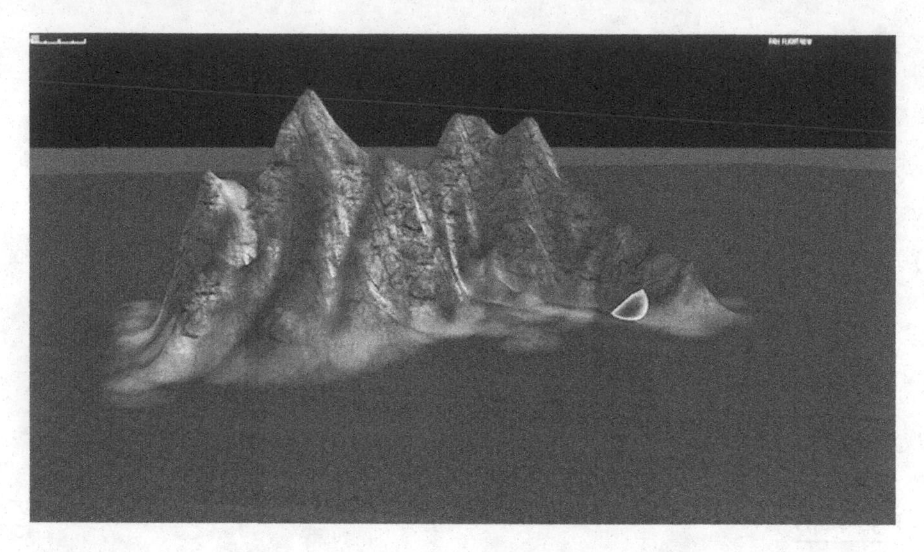

Figure 5.13

Spraying vegetation to the low points of the mountain.

However, at this point, we need to add some vegetation.

If you examine any actual mountains, you will see that the vegetation almost always grows in such a way that there is significant vegetation at the bottom. Decreasing quantities of vegetation will be found as you go up the mountain, typically in the nooks and crannies where water concentrates.

The exception to this is a mountain on a forested planet. We'll get to that later. For now, what I want you to do is choose a realistic type of vegetation (I've provided a few with this book) and use the vegetation spray tool all along the base of the mountain. Place grass anywhere you reasonably can imagine water collecting. It should look like the image in Figure 5.13.

Secondary Foliage and Rocks

Now going back to our previous example, let's say you are like me and live in a forested area. Trees grow in massive quantities on the low Appalachian Mountains, and placing that many entities as actual in-game trees will cause nothing but heartache for you. This is because trees in GameGuru are notorious FPS hogs that will eat every ounce of your precious and hard-won frames per second (also known as FPS but not to be confused with "first person shooter").

The solution here is to use the vegetation system! Instead of spraying vegetation, select one of my included "tree" vegetation types and spray it on the mountain. Set your vegetation height and width to maximum as well as maximize the quantity of vegetation. This will create a realistic "forest" on the mountain (Figure 5.14). Please note, however, that you will want to only use this technique for background mountains as the moment a player goes to navigate the terrain the ruse will be up!

Figure 5.14
Spraying trees as vegetation. (Courtesy of Duchenkuke.)

As you can see, the difference between making a mountain and a forested mountain is essentially the difference of filling in the entire mountain versus strategically placing where water would accumulate. By using this method, we can use the reasonably fast vegetation renderer to take the place of our highly intensive tree entities. This way we can speed up the process while still giving really good results.

The downside, of course, is that if you use this method, you won't be able to spray vegetation anywhere else. However, if you are clever, you'll find a way around it. I personally use vegetation objects and then use the entity spray tool (i) to spray them down as a separate set of foliage. This way I can ensure I get a wide variety of foliage.

As you are likely by now aware, GameGuru only supports one type of vegetation with its vegetation system. There are some inventive ways around this, but the simplest is to use the spray tool (i) to spray an object of grass or plant material around. This will provide a similar effect to the vegetation spray tool. It will not, however, have the heavy CPU cost associated with physics capable objects like trees. One of my preferred methods is to use the spray tool and make it a small circle using the minus key (–). This ensures that the density of the foliage will be quite thick. I then spray several clumps of it where I want, typically around the edges of objects (as that is where it frequently grows in reality). Perhaps I spray down a field of it somewhere to give the appearance of a field of wildflowers.

Afterward, what I do is go back with different foliage using the spray tool (i) again, only this time I increase the size significantly using plus (+). Then I just tap the button once over an area where I've sprayed foliage. This provides a nice interspersed foliage effect while at the same time providing variety. This same method can be used on the previously mentioned mountain.

Try to use rotation and randomness to your advantage. Remember that the human brain is superb at picking up patterns, especially visual ones. You want to avoid symmetry for natural shapes as often as possible.

TIP: Natural shapes are most often asymmetric and random; human built structures often are symmetrical.

If you must use tree entities, make sure you disable their physics settings in the .FPE file and ensure they are properly configured for occlusion. (For more details, see Chapter 21 on optimization.)

At this point, we've got a fairly reasonable mountain setup that will at least provide a convincing bit of terrain for your users to look at. Moreover, it's also large enough that it will act as a very capable landmark for the purposes of outdoor navigation. It's important you use other noticeable landmarks as well. I recommend terrain features such as rivers, lakes, pits, and hills. I also recommend combining them with specifically noticeable buildings as landmarks such as large towers, buildings with enormous signs, and areas that are specifically lit up. I'll reiterate this point more as we build our first level together.

The Flattener Method

Another method for building mountains is to use something I call the flattener method. This is because we'll be using the flattener tool rather extensively.

One popular method for putting together believable mountains is to do it in a random fashion. The trick is to make one large mountain, much as our previous example had. Then you take the flattening tool and stamp randomly all over the place. This causes a lot of elevation changes that are both abrupt and pointed. These pointy little peaks are then blended using the other tools to create something exceptionally realistic.

One method I use extensively is to use the ramp tool to make cliff sides and rock walls. While the tool itself is generally fairly inefficient, you can use this to your advantage by making very short ranged ramps that overlap each other, thus creating a very realistic texture.

Lastly, I recommend using the blend tool, which actually is more of a normalization tool. It helps add a level of erosion to surfaces that are otherwise too jagged, thus allowing the creation of more realistic terrain.

The Large to Small Method

This method is fairly simple but results in some excellent looking "peaky" mountains. If you are looking for looming, jagged piles of rock, this is probably the best choice for you.

The first step is to create the largest possible terrain circle. After you've expanded it to the maximum using +, start holding down the button to raise up the pile. Instead of going with it, though, we're also going to simultaneously begin holding or tapping the : key throughout the raising of the mountain. This will create a smoother, pointed tip. After you have this base shape, then use the typical method of dotting the mountain with further smaller peaks and channels as we did in the previous example.

Finishing Up

No matter how you chose to make your mountain—be it via my method, using the ramp tool, using the flattener, or with the "large to small" method—you will still want to touch up your mountain. The final touches here are to add a few rocks and other objects to provide a higher level of detail for your users. We also want to take the terrain paint tool and work on adding more of the "mountain" terrain (which is typically the last slot in the terrain palette) painted on the sides. This allows it to look far more like a mountain and far less like a mound of dirt (which is what the default settings will almost always end up as).

When placing your rocks, use shift-3 to rotate them incrementally until you find a suitable angle. Then place them at locations to help accentuate the naturally jagged appearance of the mountain. Try to imagine what your mountain's special story is. Maybe it had a rockslide with a pile of rubble. Perhaps a war broke out and over the past 20 years it's been growing vegetation that was lost, meaning it's still rather sparse. It doesn't have to be much. Just a little something to add character to it goes a long way.

Rocks and vegetation should generally be more frequent at the bottom and less frequent as you go up due to the natural mechanics of rocks rolling down hill and vegetation having an easier time at lower elevations.

Making a Realistic Forest

Despite the fact that GameGuru is, as I've said several times already, an outdoor engine, it has significant shortcomings at the time of this writing with respect to building a forest. These primarily center on performance issues. They can be remedied with proper design and configuration. That said, there are a number of complexities with building a convincing outdoor environment. These are in no particular order: the terrain, foliage's asymmetrical nature, coloring, and inert elements such as rocks.

During the process of writing this tome, I participated in a contest predicated on building a forest. It was among a few of us who are sort of regulars in the community, and some really fantastic stuff came from this contest.

I realized that I didn't have time to do a proper forest, so I wasn't going to be able to put forward what I'd consider my full effort on it. So instead, I took my regular method, as you will learn later in this chapter, and opted to go

Figure 5.15

A fungal forest I made for a competition.

with an unusual theme. The theme was an alien mushroom forest, as shown in Figure 5.15, instead of a traditional forest.

There you can see, not too bad. That said, it's important to remember that this is a screenshot. Anyone can stage a screenshot. A screenshot, after all, doesn't need to run a smooth 28 FPS. A screenshot could, for example, run like an absolute pig and still look great. As this one did.

Still, despite the performance limitations, it's important to know how to set up a realistic looking forest. It all starts with the terrain. Let me explain this in the form of an anecdote for you; I live in Pennsylvania. In the United States, this is known as "Penn's Woods." It's incredibly overgrown, even in the urban areas with vegetation.

There is an area I visited as a young man that I don't precisely recall the name of. It was a heavily wooded area and very rural. We were surrounded by acres upon acres of forest. It was an eerie feeling, however, standing in that forest as every single tree was in a perfect line with the other as a grid. So when you stood in the forest, you could see for a few miles in each direction. This is very much the opposite of how every forest I'd ever seen up to this point was. I asked about it and found out it was the site of an industrial accident many years before. As such, it'd been replanted. The reason for this anecdote is of course to illustrate that it's important to add variety and asymmetry to your forests. Having the same pattern of the same type of tree going on a single line endlessly is not a very convincing forest.

Forests and Performance

It's important to reiterate that forests can perform very poorly in this game engine. It's an extremely tricky task to make them work right as the angles necessary for visual optimization are very irregular, and it's difficult to know how much (as an engine) to show or not show. So if you are going to make a forest, understand there is going to very likely be a real performance hit to your game. I don't recommend forests beyond very sparing use; otherwise, you may find yourself with something that stutters along at ten or less frames per second on a top end rig. There are techniques to help mitigate this, as you will discover later, but even that is no guarantee. Until the game engine specifically has special provisions to deal with the problem of massive amounts of trees, we will be trying to "hack" our way through this by convincing a square peg that it truly can fit through a circle hole if it really tries.

So with that, let's get started making our forest and making it look good. We'll worry about the details of optimization in later chapters and even come back to this segment. For now, we're going to focus on making it good without killing your system.

Step one: Don't use flat terrain.

With a forest, the most important thing to remember is that flat terrain is boring terrain. You're going to want terrain that starts low and ends up high, which will give it a sense of depth. Also, most paths tend to be lower than the surrounding forest unless they are on the side of a hill. So what I often do is use the heightmap import tool (see page x) to pick some variable terrain. In this case, I used a section of mountains from Tennessee that offered some fairly big changes in elevation.

After I imported the heightmap into GameGuru, I began work on it.

This is not, of course, completely necessary. If you are working from the mountain walkthrough I gave earlier, you already know how to make convincing mountains. The method here is very similar. You are going to make your hills and then add the detail as we did before, using larger and smaller circles. It's important to choose a proper terrain for this type of environment. Most forests I've been in do not actually have a significant amount of grass on their floor; they are often dirt or leaf-covered. This may not be the case in every part of the world, but in the forests I've visited in the United States and Canada, it is the case. This means your ground floor is often a brown color, which is a stark contrast to say a meadow with purple flowers. Your ground level contrast will be in use by the vegetation system or other foliage if the vegetation system isn't available (more on this later).

Step two: Use lots of source/reference pictures.

As with the mountain building, it's important to have a solid frame of reference. From this standpoint, having a good image search (take your pick: Bing, Google, Pinterest, Tumblr, etc.) of "alien mushroom forests" or something of the like will drastically help your visual picture.

The primary objective here is to get a variety; there's a lot of forests all over the world, so try to narrow down what kind you are looking for. Often it bases around what kind of biome you are going for. So how hot is your location? What kind of trees are there? Are there trees that retain their foliage all year (coniferous), or are they the type that drop their leaves (deciduous)? Each of these has a different feel. Are there glowing crystals, floating spores, or perhaps eerily lit vine-covered temples?

Tropical rain forests consist of a combination of ferns and deciduous vegetation. The trees are often fairly large and very frequently have vines and moss in their midst. They may also butt up against a beach, which is very different from any other biome.

Coniferous forests are generally reserved for colder regions due to the tolerance toward that type of environment that those plants have. They reserve their leaves (which are often needles or very small) all year long. Some of the more common trees of this type are the cedars, pines, firs, and aspens.

Deciduous forests are the more common trees you see in temperate climates, such as in my part of the world. In our area, it's the Appalachian forests that form this type and consist of several varieties of maples, ashes, oaks, and sumacs. Deciduous trees are the ones that lose their leaves in the fall (or rain, in tropical regions) and as such they cover a large part of the earth.

Other good ones I like to use are "alien forests" or "fantasy forests."

Of course, there's other foliage in forests as well, such as vines, mosses, small plants, bushes, and shrubs. You want to try to build a basic idea of the "type" of trees and vegetation you want to include. It doesn't have to be extremely exact, a basic idea should do. From there, it's mostly down to your own aesthetic preferences.

Now in the case of my example, I ended up choosing something very offbeat: fungal forests. These are often relegated to the realm of science fiction or fantasy. So this becomes a bit of a challenge, but I took my same rules (as you will see in the following section) and applied them to various mushroom models I had.

Step three: Don't overdo it. Be mindful of your poly count.

Our primary method for making a functional forest is going to be gratuitous use of the spray tool in GameGuru. This spray tool is ideal for creating the randomization necessary by applying objects to terrain features at rotations and angles that would take you hours to do by hand.

When spraying our trees, we generally want to conform to several rules:

Use an 80/15/4/1 sort of breakdown. We are going to have a "very common" 80 percent of the trees be one type, a "somewhat uncommon" group that's about 15 percent of the remainder, with another rarer and then a "very rare" type that are your four and one percent, respectively. This method of laying down objects is something we will use time and again.

We will also make extensive use of the spray tool, so we want to spray vegetation that contrasts well against whatever terrain you ended up choosing. I have included several terrains with this tool and suggest the forest type. It has a brown texture that works well for outdoor forests.

When spraying your forest, be aware that a significant amount will likely be clipped off after a certain point. This means rendering that forest is pointless as the engine will limit you. Therefore, why waste the resources? For instance, no one is ever going to see the backside of your mountains. These areas will just eat memory and CPU unnecessarily.

When you hit tab-tab, you will see the technical information on the left. If you look at the number of polygons, you will get an enormous amount of them, especially in a forest. Hundreds of thousands alone will be used by the terrain, with many millions more used by forests. The trick here is to optimize our occlusion settings (see Chapter 21 on optimization for details on this) to clip the unseen forest items to help minimize the polygons being rendered at any given time.

One of my favorite tricks is to use a flat two-dimensional "forest wall" at the border of the forest instead of drawing more models. This is a vastly faster way of rendering a forest at the expense of visual quality. This is, of course, unimportant if the player never gets close enough to notice. So often we want to pen in the player with fences and rails to keep them on a path running through our beautiful forest. This way they only see the really nice foreground elements but never get a chance to see how we simply put up a "painting" in the background for the deeper forest.

Fog is also extremely helpful here, helping limit the players' overall visibility while at the same time establishing a sense of atmosphere (see Chapter 10 on adding ambience).

There's also some ways we can "cheat" the system to get vastly more "trees" if, for example, you are creating a nearby backdrop of a HIGHLY forested hill. This is a near impossibility to reproduce using models. The solution is to use the vegetation spray tool!

The vegetation spray tool is optimized for thousands of "small plants," but with a little tweaking and the right model, we can create a forest with it.

Enclosed in this chapter's included media are some examples of this. They go in your files\vegbank folder and will allow you to "spray" trees. This spray tree system will not have any collision but works great for creating massive forests with ease. Unfortunately, it takes away your ability to use the vegetation tool for actual vegetation, but you can spray in small plants with the regular i-key spray tool. This gives us a very effective method of building very dense forests that can also carpet hills or mountains.

Another trick we can use is code adjustment to make these trees we use "clip themselves" from view. While code is not the optimal method, on edge cases, it may make all the difference.

While we're talking about clipping, one thing I haven't covered yet is the FPE file. The FPE file, of course, contains all of the data of the model involved, and there are two settings that are relevant here—notably, the "occluder" and "occludee" settings. These control whether the "tree" can prevent objects behind it from being seen.

We want to make sure both of these are enabled so that the in-game occluder can properly clip the unnecessary entities. This will improve frame rate and performance.

Lastly, we want to make sure the forest, to put it bluntly, isn't too large. If you populate the entire map with a dense network of tree models, you will have a hurricane of bad performance on your hand. I recommend breaking large forest maps into multimap chunks that are easily managed.

Step four: Lighting carries much more weight in the woods.

Now that we've got our beautiful forest fleshed out, it's time to build the lighting the way we want. It's important to remember this isn't the city. There aren't going to be neon street lights and massive amounts of "light pollution" everywhere. Actual forests tend to soak up the light to a frightening degree at night. When a real light is placed, they are often very intense but have a quick falloff. It also is immensely more visible at a distance. This is because there isn't any other light around, making it far more noticeable. As such, you want to be very sparing with your use of lights in the forest unless of course it's got a fantasy or alien feel to it. A good example of this would be Ark®: Aberration, which has significant amounts of underground forests with bioluminescent trees. The trees, plant life, and even the animals all glow to some extent. This creates an eerie yet beautiful feel, but only shows itself when there's not any actual light present. It's possible to create something like that in GameGuru, though specialty methods like this are technically challenging. Thankfully, through the process of this book, you'll see ways and means of getting those objects done if you are clever.

Making a City

One of the most common battlegrounds you will find yourself in is a city, at least with modern FPS games. It's something familiar and common to the human landscape and really requires a special touch to create something that is not only meaningful but memorable. Cities are living, organic entities that often grow just like a real forest. Calling it the urban jungle isn't that far off, I'd say.

As with all of our previous works, we will be extensively checking reference materials so as to have a clear idea of exactly what we are trying to reach as a goal. Before we can do that, we need to have some idea of what kind of cities there ARE. Image searches are your friend here, truly. The variety of cities in the world is mostly distilled into a few groups, but within those groups are enormous differences. It's up to you to find references that meet your criteria to work with.

Now there's some debate over this but we can basically, for our purposes, break it down into four separate types of cities. There's the big (large) grid, the small grid, curvilinear, and the mosaic type, as shown in Figure 5.16.

It's up to you to choose what kind of city you feel suits your game best.

Each city has various "districts" within it, something that helps define a particular section. You might have a dock district with lots of shipyards and fish markets. There's almost always a city center that has large financial buildings, city employees, and the like. You can add residential areas, factory districts, office parks… the options are limitless. Just try to remember that most cities have these

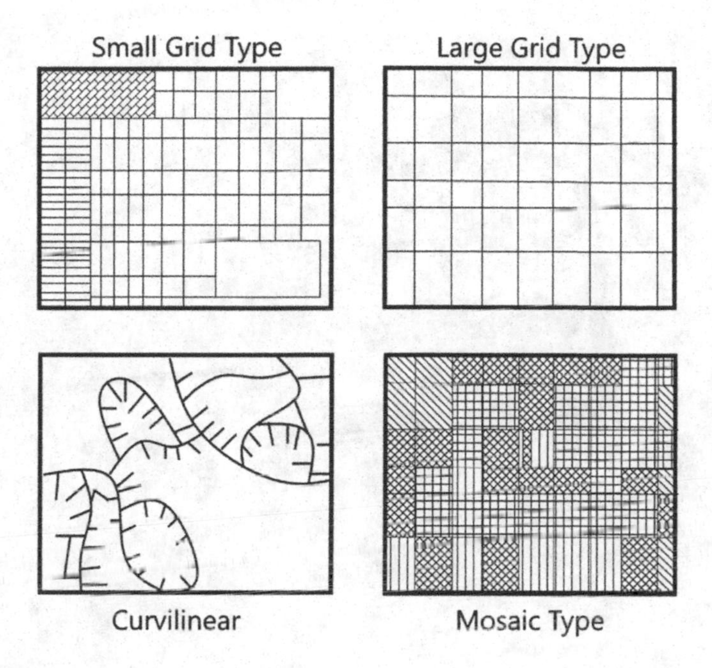

Figure 5.16

The four basic city designs of the world.

areas in clumps for zoning reasons. This keeps you from placing things all over the city chaotically. There are exceptions to this, of course, as we'll discuss. Try to outline the basic district types you will have. Remember, we're telling a story here: it doesn't have to be grandiose, but you want your locations to have some form of identity.

Is this a port city with a huge failing industrial district? Is this a steelworkers' town that folded once the mining cartel went under? Perhaps it's a financial district with lots of upscale restaurants. Have a vision of what you want the city to be so you understand how it will lay out. Once we have some concept, we then move on to actually putting together the city itself.

Big (Large) Grid Cities

First we have the "big grid" style of city, along the lines of New York City. These big grid cities are often large, simple grids that are easy to lay out and follow. When someone says "one block up" they literally mean one block on the grid. It's hard to misunderstand that, right? These types of cities typically have large, wide streets with intersecting back alleys or side streets that form a near-perfect perpendicular grid. An example would be from a game I made where I was doing an homage to another game that shall remain nameless (Figure 5.17).

At a player level, these cities are easy to navigate and easier still to understand. The wide avenues and large buildings generally tend to provide you with a sense

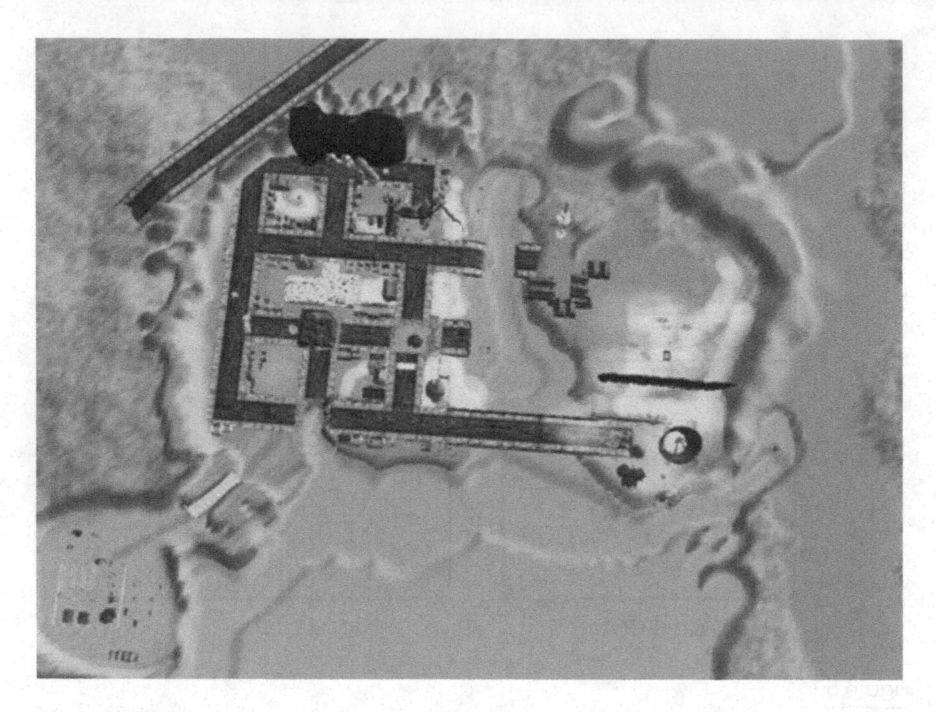

Figure 5.17

A simple large grid city made in GameGuru.

of "immense scale." They do, however, have the side effect of being exceptionally simple to navigate while at the same time being remarkably droll in terms of design. It can be difficult as well to set up barriers that are believable to the player. One great example of this was the game "the last of us," which used extreme drops, fallen skyscrapers, cracks in the ground, and killer fungal plants to help guide the player to their goal.

Small Grid Cities

Next up would be the small grid type, which is often more of your "old-world city," such as Paris. These cities are often not perfect perpendicular grids but rather a series of roads with small intersections all over. This is due to their existence over many centuries and the growth that accompanied that. The city planners were not considering the growth the city would have past perhaps a few decades. So it sort of kept a lot of the older roads and instead made major roads an accommodation that was supplanted by the older small roads. This is why driving in some of those cities in a larger car can be a tricky mess, for instance. Many of the older American cities on the East Coast have a similar design; they often had several major "spoke" roads running out of a main hub, then a crisscross of smaller side roads.

Building types should vary between modern and "old-world" architecture. The older buildings are smaller, generally two to three stories high, and are almost invariably made of stone. These older buildings will comprise large portions of the city's real estate and will typically have stores with housing above them. It's often a patchwork quilt with some general areas lumped together but is far less rigid than the grid-style city planning with it's neat little squares dedicated to different zoning. Often the historical significance of the older stone infrastructure is the underlying design of the city's growth.

These cities require some problem-solving to guide the player but often can be a good balance in terms of game design and giving them many avenues to explore. They often have large city centers with moderate-sized skyscrapers or buildings that quickly fall off to various districts with smaller building types.

Curvilinear Cities

A more modern design is the "grid with loops and patterns," which is a more organic design. What happens is the city starts with a fairly basic grid that has room for growth built into it. During that time, side streets, loops, alleys, and the like are added into the city by city planners in a way that will ensure that growth doesn't impact the flow of the city.

What's great about this design is you can have entire subsections of the city that are sort of cut off and isolated, allowing you to pen in the player for side quests or as a means of exploration. It allows you to get extremely creative with your level design, allowing your obstacles and barriers to seem more natural instead of poorly placed ways of stopping the player.

The buildings can be a wide series of modern types as their arrangement is more based on the logical values of geography and utility. It's a much more recent style that seems to be gaining traction going forward as cities explore ways to better use their urban space.

A good example of this type of city is New Orleans, which as far as cities goes is fairly interesting on its own by having the unusual trait of being also lower than sea level. As always, our cities are telling a story, and it's your job as the environmental designer to capture and portray that. For instance, if I were making a "New Orleans" game, I'd probably have it be a much wetter environment, possibly even half flooded, to help exaggerate and underscore the theme.

Mosaic Cities

The last type of city is a mosaic style. A common example of this would be the city of Mogadishu. It's your typical shantytown with a very chaotic pattern of small, tight streets that seem to make no sense and lead in no specific direction. It's a twisting maze of insanity and is a tricky proposition to build. That said, you can create some fantastic vistas for this type of setup. It conveys a sense of poverty very well, something that is difficult to bring across properly in other city types. The jagged street designs and mosaic-style building locations means this is an excellent location for hostile factions in close proximity as well.

The buildings are the smallest of all of the types and tend to be in exceptionally bad condition. You can even layer them as floors of a mega-skyscraper, like what was done in "Deus Ex: Mankind Divided®." I'm referring to the Útulek Complex, aka the Golem City Complex. This location was a study in verticality while at the same time giving the same fractured sense of soul to the city. These are chaotic locations that can have market districts inside of districts while everything is insanely cramped.

With these cities, there are often several fixtures due to the low income of the region typically portrayed; for example, in one case, there's going to almost always be an open-air market of some sort.

These markets frequently have lots of local products or produce. They're covered by tents as well; so plan for this end of things. There's often some run-down industrial areas that have been commandeered by homeless residents and, in some cases, a shantytown may have emerged. These cities often have few major landmarks, so make sure you provide enough geographically distant cues so that the player at least has a dim sense of in what direction they need to head.

Geographical queues can include things such as distant mountains, ivory towers, a radar dish, or maybe a dam holding back a nearby reservoir.

These faraway icons will serve as distant reminders that subtly give a player both a sense of scale AND an obvious point from which to figure their location should they get lost.

Cities of this nature are inherently flat with no real large buildings to speak of, so they often are comprised of many small buildings layered chaotically on each other. This layering can really create some unique structures for you to play around with (Figure 5.18).

Figure 5.18

Repurposing palettes as siding, boxes, and barrels as conduit.

The way I do it is to find several buildings of relatively similar size and shape. They should be small but different. I then begin layering them at odd angles to give an unnatural "built-on" feel. Adding wires, barrels, boxes as part of the building can also create a very interesting effect as well as providing the "rundown look" we are going after.

So we've got some sense of what KIND of cities there are. How do we go about making a believable one?

I'm going to assume you've at least seen the venerable TheGameCreators City Pack, a fairly robust series of city-related models produced for the GameGuru engine. This pack is frequently sold at a discount and can give you an excellent jump start into the world of city design. It's also been recently updated with improved models and PBR textures.

The components of this pack consist of buildings, streets, sidewalks, and extra components. The extra components are your traditional "fixtures" of city life such as odd monuments, fire extinguishers, rubbish bins, and just trash in general.

It's a pretty good starting point, though it isn't necessary for our purposes. Buildings are among the most familiar and thus common elements you'll find in a game engine's community. They're also extremely simplistic to model for a beginning modeler, and as such, you will probably be up to your ears in free buildings—not counting what I've included as assets with this book.

You will always need these components with a city, though there's a lot of flexibility in terms of what else you add. Try to figure out the story your city is telling. Is it a city clogged with traffic and overpopulation? What kind of vehicles are there going to be? Is this a futuristic city or a medieval hub with horses and carts? What types of supports will those vehicles need? Will they use gasoline, a blacksmith for horseshoes, or a futuristic charging station?

These questions are the fundamentals of story building and environment building. You don't have to have an obsessive amount of detail, but you want some sort of structure for what your city looks like and who lives in it. The latter is an exceptionally important question as cities, more than any other biome, are heavily populated. This means that it's very likely the people in your city will form as much of the ecosystem as the buildings themselves.

You generally are going to have several brackets of people that you will work around. This again will depend on what you're planning—for instance, if your enemies are part of this group or not.

Once you've got your scene, it's time to build it!

Building It

We now have some idea of what we're building. For our example purposes, we're picking a type 2 city. These city types are very simple but offer increasing granularity as we are building due to the number of side streets. The first thing we need are the main roads and any major terrain features.

Terrain features to consider are: A park or woodland area, a waterfront, hills on the outskirts, large bridges, and any landmark buildings.

These are focal points or subzones of a specific city that can vary from location to location. These elements may not necessarily be more than a set piece or may have intrinsic value for your level design.

With all of these city builds, I tend to place at least markers for where I want these things to go first. The way I do this is by spraying with the terrain spray tool the general "shape" of the city, using the darker colors for roads, greener colors for building placement, and yellows for other items such as special areas.

Going Vertical

With GameGuru, it is entirely too easy to build a flat city that has no depth of terrain at all. However, most cities are not like this at all, and as such, I'd recommend adding in several more planes of varying height with ramps between them. Another way to achieve this is to not start with a "new flat level" but instead use a "new random level" and then use the flattener tool at varying locations. Then from that point you can drag the ramp tool from site to site to create your "hill roads."

Many city environments take this tack, such as the cities in Half-Life 2™ with their narrow walkways and gangplanks on top of buildings. If you prefer to go more extreme, you could try to emulate the parkour-style antics of a game such as Mirror's Edge™. If you provide a big environment, many players will often try to find ways to utilize it. I personally like the methods of the Deus Ex games with their mostly flat streets that feature alleys, rooftops, and buildings to explore.

Whenever you're making a game, there really isn't such a thing as "not enough reference material." Feel free to stop what you're doing and find pictures to suit your needs or play a game to inspire you. Soon you'll find yourself walking down the streets of your own small town or big city looking at its design, wondering how you can incorporate your own world into something you are making. Rooftops are a strange place with any number of odd elements. Common elements range from air conditioners to power conduits, but odd elements could possibly include anything from a swimming pool to a golf course or open air garden! It allows some truly interesting choices and really gives you a bigger world to open a player up to versus just running around on the ground.

With this verticality comes some difficulty but also some wonderful bonuses in terms of adding perspective to your level. It's important that your background elements be low polygon count. You also generally want them excluded from the occluder (which is found in the FPE file, as you will see in Chapter 21 on optimization). This way they can be seen from an extreme distance but, due to their distance, won't do more than act as a background. The low amount of polygons will reduce the stress significantly that the user's system will have. There's simply no point to use high-quality models on something the player will only see at ranges that render those details void (see, for example, the cars in Figure 5.19).

It is possible to use models that have a "level of detail" setting, which allows the same model to have different polygon counts and levels of quality to the texture map. This is something that can be a huge boon if used properly as you can

Figure 5.19

Demonstrating the various LOD levels in GameGuru.

then use those same models intermittently up close and far away, thus reducing the number of unique models you need for your map. The downside of course is that you can, in turn, make your level look fairly monotonous.

There's also the issue of "going up." I mention this because cities are not just large swathes of buildings and streets but also have enormous vertical space as well. Some buildings can often act as their own level as well, which can even further exaggerate the distortion felt if the level is just too flat.

People innately pick up on sameness in their surroundings. Their eyes naturally perceive sameness as being unnatural, so you want to add that level of asymmetry to help facilitate the believability of your environment. Remember, here we're building a biome, a human biome, but a biome nonetheless. These biomes require some care to make them appear in a way that doesn't ring false to people.

This human biome is built over a natural environment. So we need to start with that natural feel and then add the human feel to it. This is why using the randomizer, a heightmap import, or even if you are doing it totally by hand then having hills, are important. These variations in terrain really add a sense of depth that can't be found on a single flat map.

Adding Environmentals

Without getting too in depth into the actual atmospherics of a level, I did want to at least give some basic guidelines here with respect to building a map that has a realistic atmosphere to it. Cities are interesting when building your lighting and environmentals in that they often have a significant degree of atmospheric haze. Consider the picture in Figure 5.20 with no haze.

Haze creates a sense of realism that can be found in virtually every major city in the world. This is often the result of pollutants but typically ends up looking

Figure 5.20

A fairly generic town with no haze.

like a thin fog that is ever present, reducing viewable distance and blurring far away structures.

Consider the difference shown in Figure 5.21. Which image seems more believable to you? To me, adding the fog makes it all the more realistic. You don't want to lay it on too thick, unless you are building a "polluted industrial

Figure 5.21

The same town with atmospheric haze.

city," for instance. In the vast majority of cases, it'll be a moderate setting, something that has a nice feel without going too overkill. I recommend these settings:

Fog start 4 (4%)
Fog end 16 (16%)
Color: 255(100%)/255(100%)/255(100%) (or 192(75%)/192(75%)/192(75%))
Intensity 25–50%

With these, you can achieve the same sort of effect as what I've done in my previous picture (Figure 5.21). Now, obviously, there are other things to consider here as well. For example, if you are in a city at night, you'll want to use darker colors than the max white/gray values. You will likely drag down to zero all of these numbers for fog color and then use a series of static and dynamic lights to provide significant depth to the scene. Given the limitations of the GameGuru lighting engine, this can prove to be a difficult task, though not impossible.

Often you'll find yourself relying on illumination mapped entities and large dynamic lights that apply light over a broad series of signs. An example of this would be that several "red light" district locations could potentially be mapped by a mere one to three dynamic lights of red, instead of one for each individual sign. The more color-diverse an area is going to be, the more difficult this task is going to be as you are truly limited on the number of lights active in a scene at any given time. The trick here can be to break up the city into light zones, trying to minimize the chaos caused by using multiple dynamic lights. Instead, focus on using static lights and a broad single color light as a "light strengthener" for the other lights in the scene.

The reason we're relying heavily on dynamic lights is that, unfortunately, static lights are always significantly weaker in terms of intensity and also in terms of how they show over distance. They tend to disappear into the night rather quickly without the assistance of a dynamic light for night scenes.

Little Pieces Matter

With a city, there are more than large buildings. There's a significant amount of secondary objects such as shipping containers, shrubs, overgrown weeds, benches, curbs, street lines, and other objects.

When placing city objects, try to snap objects together at first and then add variation from there. If you are using something like the TheGameCreators city pack, you will have a wide selection of secondary assets to choose from.

Let's start with streets and their details. The streets are a primary area for your player—a wide avenue for them to walk and interact on. Often streets are made as flat entities that you place, which is extremely limiting. I recommend only using those for flat areas; for the rest of them, I use a terrain that is included with this book that allows me to "draw" roads using the terrain spray tool. This way I can naturally follow curves, flow up mountains, and have roads that are slightly

Figure 5.22
Blending terrain onto flat surfaces.

curved. All of this contributes toward a realistic feel but takes a little more work than plunking down some snap-together streets.

While I do use this method for back roads and occasionally primary roads, I do like the consistency and feel of a high-quality "road" entity. So feel free to intermingle the two. Make sure you underlay any snap-together road with the terrain and blend it (Figure 5.22) with the terrain tool.

When placing your sidewalks, don't worry about placing them everywhere. Stick with high traffic areas and locations where the player will directly see a sidewalk or need to see it. Try to manually lower it so as to provide that all-important sense of depth to the player. We just use a subtle dash of asymmetry to really help things "pop" for the player.

Place your set elements such as benches, boxes, crates, barrels, trash skips, and trash itself in ways that don't just seem cluttered for the sake of cluttered but rather add to a scene. It's easy to go too heavy handed on this stuff. A light touch is all that's needed. When placing objects, use the rotation tool (with the shift key) to micro-adjust pieces so they are slightly off from each other, such as those in Figure 5.23. This gives the impression that it's more natural than just a series of boxes all on top of each other perfectly aligned.

Other really great elements to make use of are electrical switch boxes and wires on the backs or sides of buildings. These sort of represent "sprawling plant life" of the city, crawling over the sides of our buildings in small or large amounts. Again, try to paint them in such a way as your city demands. If you add too many wires, it gives it a feeling of a third-world country with haphazard wiring.

Figure 5.23

Using a slight offset to create a more natural shape.

Plant life in the city is fairly sparse but often takes the form of weeds such as dandelions or chicory growing near fences, in old parking lots, and cracks in the pavement. Make sure you use your vegetation spray tool in a logical fashion. Attempt to model and mimic what you see in both real life and your own reference photos.

Making a Desert

There is often some misconception about what type of biome a "desert" encompasses. I've always been a bit of a survivalist geek, so I have a healthy respect about how dangerous a desert truly is. Part of this is the fact that it's often insanely hot during the day but also bone-chillingly cold at night for the same reasons. Heat comes and goes in the desert areas, vegetation is sparse, wild edibles are rare, and water is a difficult resource to locate.

So if I asked you how many deserts you thought there were, what would you say? Did you know there are four primary types of desert? There's the traditional "hot and dry" desert, the semiarid desert, the coastal desert, and the cold (think of the great white north) desert. I'll bet the latter isn't surprising but isn't one you thought of. The same problems exist in all of these biomes: resource scarcity, weak vegetation, and generally hostile wildlife. Desert is any region that receives less than 50 centimeters per year of rainfall and covers large swaths of the earth. On top of that, a significant amount of GameGuru assets are oriented toward it, including the stock engine buildings. Let's not also forget the aptly named "Death Valley" DLC. For these reasons, we're going to cover this particular biome in detail to make sure you can make the most of it!

Each of these regions has their own details, so we'll go over each one in depth so you can get a better idea of how they differ. There are some common elements, however, so don't be afraid to intermingle.

The "Hot and Dry" Desert

This desert is characterized by slow sloping, low hills, and huge dunes of dead sand with little to no vegetation, even by a desert's standard. It's probably the first one people think of when they hear the word desert and rightfully so. These are cruel and punishing locations renowned for their extreme heat and dryness, some regularly reaching ~120 degrees F (49 degrees C) during a late summer day and 69 degrees F (20.5 degrees C) at night. Winter temperatures are much lower and often just as variable, with temperatures in the day of 50 degrees F (10 degrees C) to 32 degrees F (0 degrees C) at night.

They are often battered by heavy winds and sand erosion, leading to very small, sloped hills of sand. Sand, of course, is little more than pulverized rock. As such, one of the best tools we have for making a realistic desert is the "new random level" option! It produces a perfect series of "dune-like" hills that, when repainted with a sand texture, become extremely convincing as a desert.

Terrain will have a significant amount of rocks and gravel as they are on their way to becoming like the sand that envelops them. These rocks will sometimes form large outcroppings and alcoves, which provide ideal shade zones for predators to hide in. Predators are very common in this biome due to the sparse vegetation leading to few active herbivores. They do tend to be nocturnal, however. Insects and reptiles are the order of the day as well since they are ideally suited for the extreme heat. That said, there are significant concentrations of mammals, birds, and arachnids as well. Virtually all will have adaptations that will lend toward their survival in extreme heat.

Vegetation will almost always concentrate in these shade spots or in low points where the sparse amounts of water will accumulate. So try to make sure it sits in low gullies and dried riverbeds; locations where perhaps there is just a hint of water showing will often have a huge outcropping of vegetation. Please note the vegetation in this type of environment is almost always incredibly small, stunted by the lack of resources. The typical "tree" will only be scarcely larger than what would qualify as a shrub in more temperate areas.

For instance, the Mojave Desert is fairly featureless in terms of vegetation but is dominated by one specific type of "tree," the Joshua tree. The already Spartan landscape is sparsely dotted with these tough trees.

So really, when it boils down to it, you're not looking at too many set elements in this type of location—a few rocks along with some dry and stunted vegetation.

Ok, this isn't completely accurate. For instance, what about a car? What if there's a vehicle in the desert, rotting away under the hot sun? So this is worth mentioning. You have to imagine how intense the sand is there when it blows. Try to envision the pure, constant heat of the sun baking anything into oblivion. This is why we have "bleached white bones" in the desert, and old vehicles rust

Figure 5.24
A simple hot and dry desert.

away rapidly once their paint is stripped off by the unforgiving sun and sand. So feel perfectly free to add a half-submerged rusty car, some old bones from a dead cow… maybe some broken-down buildings here and there. Overall, though, even those items are going to be few and far between. They will, however, give you sufficient variety for the landscape you're doing (Figure 5.24).

For environmentals, I recommend using fog at a long distance as you will often be able to see in the desert for extreme distances. The downside of this is it should be hazy at long range for this type of desert to help approximate the "heat" effect without the use of any special shaders. These are the settings I use for this type of terrain:

Fog: far away, around 50 for start
55 for end
Color orange-red
Intensity 80

These settings will give you a suitably realistic long-distance haze that will leave close-range visuals unimpeded by the fog effect. It will also add a tint to the distance that won't be applied up close and will add to the "heat mirage" effect. Optimally, if you can get a third-party shader or effect that can properly imitate a real heat effect, that's the best choice. If not, then always opt for a creative solution!

Bloom post-effects in the desert can be tricky as you want to optimize the amount of blur you get from bloom while at the same time reducing the amount of oversaturation you get on nearby textures. I tend to stick between 50 and 60 for my values on desert maps, with hotter regions on the higher end of the spectrum.

The "SemiArid" Desert

The second type of desert is the type you see in the American West such as in Montana or at the Great Basin's sagebrush expanses in Utah. These deserts are MUCH cooler than the "hot dry" type of desert that comes to mind for most people. The summer months have very little rainfall, and the nights and winters can be extremely cold. This type of biome features vegetation that is often very hostile, such as cacti with spikes or poisonous plants. There's a significant degree more wildlife as well, with a lot more animals and predators in this type of desert. So here, we'll probably opt for a less harsh "heat effect" style fog and aim for one that better exemplifies the clear air and visibility you can have at long ranges (as shown in Figure 5.25).

Our level design will be roughly similar, relying on the randomizer to create realistic hills. In this case, however, we'll be utilizing a lot more rock materials to help exaggerate this terrain, as well as the terrain modification tools to create sharp cliffs and drops that are more characteristic of this region.

Vegetation can be sprayed down significantly more, but you still want to aggregate the bulk of your vegetation in logical locations at the bottom of hills and valleys where the water accumulates. You will, as mentioned, have access to a lot more vegetation if you have the models for it, so don't be afraid to use

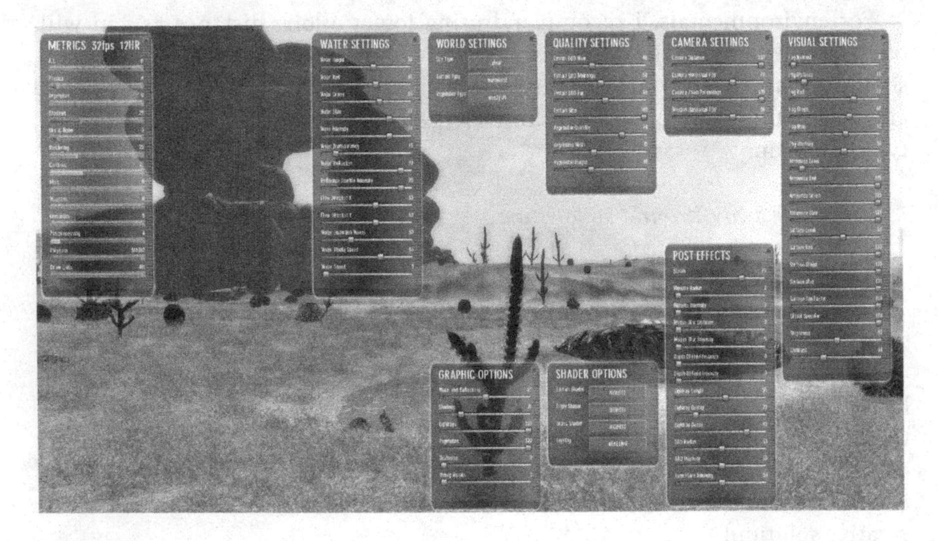

Figure 5.25

The semi-arid desert type settings.

Figure 5.26

The final product for a semi-arid desert.

significantly more to get your point across. Cacti, sagebrush, tumbleweeds, you name it (Figure 5.26).

The soil here is sandy and fine and less rocky than other locations save for the few regions where we will use rocks to exaggerate things.

Remember, also, if you are doing a game with a day/night cycle that this period of time at night has a huge temperature swing and can go from the high temperature days (100 degrees F/38 degrees C) to the very low temperature nights (50 degrees F, 10 degrees C)!

This will result in frost, and if you have some advanced scripting, perhaps a significant obstacle with temperature regulation for the player. Maybe they'll need a hot fire to stay warm or thick blankets to avoid losing HP.

Also bear in mind that the air is very clear in these locations, so you are going to want more above-average skybox quality, if possible. Your skies should look exemplary, with great detail and lots of realistic color. Drab and gray is not going to fly in these locations. Look for lots of oranges and blues. Alternately, if you have a nighttime scene here, you want a sky with a significant quantity of stars and very clear skies that have a minimum of cloud cover.

If you do have nighttime cloud cover, try to make sure the stars shine through without difficulty. This way it helps exaggerate the sense of open space that this type of terrain often represents. This area of the world is far more livable than the truly hot and dry deserts of the world, which is why you'll often see ghost towns or old towns in the American West. Granted, there's not going to be a massive quantity of people there, but it's entirely viable that a small settlement is doing just fine on this edge of the world.

Coastal Deserts

This is the one you will LEAST likely use and as such we'll spend the least time on it. Regardless, you should have some idea of what goes into this type of desert should you ever desire the type. It might make a suitable "deep space settlement" for a sci-fi game, for instance.

These are neotropical or "neartic," which puts them down as fairly cold deserts with temperatures ranging from 68 degrees F (20 degrees C) to 23 degrees F (–5 degrees C).

The soil will be remarkably similar to the semiarid desert with very fine and pulverized sand as its top layer of soil. Being close to the coast, they receive more rain than their other desert cousins. This allows for some deep-rooted plant life that is fairly robust.

In these regions, you will not find significant trees, however, but rather will find mostly grasses, shrubs, and bushes. Cacti are not necessarily something a person would see here. The terrain is characterized by flat expanses of totally bare mountains or hills. The valleys and hills are often packed with vegetation, but sometimes as you get further in, it is utterly devoid of life. It truly is a strange locale. One of the more famous ones is the Atacama Desert in South America. Long plains are often packed with grasses that measure a scant few inches in height.

The animal life is heavy with insects, mammals, reptiles, and predatory birds. There are some frogs, but they are specially adapted to life in those regions, often with modifications to help them survive the long droughts. This is, however, a fairly desolate location, and it's highly unlikely players will encounter significant amounts of living contact beyond the grasses and shrubs comprising the flora and fauna.

The terrain is probably best made by hand on top of a randomized underlayment with huge rock formations that have massive sheer cliffs. The mountains rise like juggernauts over the barren landscape and represent formidable terrain obstacles for those who challenge them.

Make sure you present towering, distant volcanoes with a little haze on them as the range goes out to really illustrate the atmospheric scattering from huge expanses of dead space. We'll get into atmospheric haze in detail later in Chapter 10 on "Adding Ambience."

Cold Deserts

The cold desert is possibly one of the most challenging environments on earth. Temperatures in the summer match those of the coastal desert type. In the winter, however, everything changes to stark and brutal 24-degree F (–4 degree C) days and even colder nights, often going deeply negative.

They stand out in this respect, often representing the "great white north" described by many. This area has titanic amounts of snowfall in the winter, almost cataclysmic levels. This is in stark contrast to the nearly precipitation-free summers.

This extra-heavy winter precipitation means the soil stands out here as very spongy and dense, allowing it to soak up as much water as possible for the remainder of the year. Plants are virtually nonexistent even compared to other deserts, resulting in huge swaths of snow-covered terrain in winter and, at best, a light dusting of small plants and grasses during summer. Due to the heavy precipitation, there's a fair amount of mosses and fungi here, which allows for a slightly more interesting diversity of living creatures.

Animal life is primarily mammalian here, meaning there are almost no insects or reptiles compared to other regions.

One nice thing about these locations is that they are fairly open to interpretation from a terrain standpoint, allowing you to use the randomizer to build dunes of snow, or you can build enormous mountainous terrain by hand. You could also use a heightmap importer for this as well.

With a snow environment, you're looking at a higher light level due to the reflectivity of the terrain itself. You'll want to maximize several values such as the surface sun value, global specularity, and surface level(s). These values are really powerful tools for any, but try the settings in Figure 5.27 for optimal results.

The fog can either be set for a long-distance haze like in the semi-arid deserts or up close if the weather is more inclement. The one exception here is you'll want to change the colors used to be more of a stark white, which is done by setting the fog sliders as follows:

Fog near: 0 (0%)
Fog distant: 2(2%) to 4(4%), depending on preference
Red/Green/Blue: All at 100%
Intensity: 90–100%

Figure 5.27

The settings for a cold desert or winter biome type.

This gives us the whiteness we're looking for while helping to apply that coloration to other items in the scene that aren't necessarily perhaps showing the snow-covered look as much. This is because fog is applied as a global layer over the existing color scheme.

So with that, and really in any scene, fog is one of the more powerful tools for "unifying" a color palette. This is most noticeable on outdoor scenes where there's a lot of a single color—like oranges, yellows, and browns for deserts. In this case, though, it'd be white or gray to apply that to everything in the vicinity. This can help create a sense of parity among elements that may be just a touch off. I have often noticed in particular with whites that they can often look very different when placed next to one another. A proper fog can help cover this. Famous examples of use of heavy fog were the original Silent Hill® games that actually used a dense white fog to obscure further details from players to help render times.

It is the simple tricks that save the day here, and fog is by far one of the most powerful simple tricks we can use for this type of thing.

Common Techniques

With desert biomes more than others, it can be difficult to "drive" the player toward a specific goal or location. You will need to carefully manage your use of impassible terrain to keep the player boxed into where you want them to go. Take, for instance, the game "Fallout: New Vegas™." This game specifically used large rock walls, cliff faces, outdoor buildings, and enclosures to limit the player. Beyond that don't go too ham-fisted with it as deserts in their very nature are fairly stark. This lack of any points of interest actually will acutely exaggerate the points of interest in your game. Essentially, it's the same as if you have a giant white canvas and paint a small black dot on it. This dot will stand out and people will immediately be drawn to it. The same is true when you are sitting in a vast expanse of relatively featureless terrain and suddenly you see a water tower rising in the distance as you crest a sand dune; you are going to immediately begin heading to that location to check it out.

There's also another simple solution: Paths can be used to guide the more astute players with even a moderate change in color or texture. Animal trails are often found in the wild where animals will regularly use the same logical route to various destinations. Over time, these paths form worn areas in the terrain that can be followed by players. This happens as well with humans who consistently set out over an area as well. Let's not forget old dirt roads either. All of these are easily implemented with the terrain spray tool and the terrain shaping tools. People are smart enough to follow most roads and know to expect a side road will often contain a house, which means supplies. Use this to your advantage!

In a desert, there's a lack of everything so all entities such as lights, buildings, signs of life, and trails are all more pronounced by a wide degree. It's one of the few areas where a little goes a long way.

Making Waterways

Making waterways can be a tremendous chore unless you're up for the task. Try to remember that water always flows downhill. You're not going to have random puddles of water in the sky, after all. If you are using the elevation tool, all you have to do is use shift-click to lower the terrain past water's plane. This will show the water on your maps. However... just going across the terrain in this manner is time consuming. Moreover, it will also result in high/low spots that, unfortunately, can have the unintended effect of allowing a player to pass through an area that was otherwise meant as an obstacle.

Given our new water controls, we have more flexibility here through Lua, but if we're not scripting, how do we provide a consistent experience for our users? The answer is the flattening tool again. If we create a spot of the depth we desire for our water, then by using the terrain flattening tool on it, we can literally click and drag to create massive lakes, pools, rivers, and tributaries. It's incredibly easy. I usually start with the large circle (+) and create the outline of my basic shape for the waterways. I then use smaller circles in half or minimum size diameters to ensure that there is sufficient detail.

Once I've done that, I use the blend tool on the edges to help blend it. I then paint the terrain using the terrain paint tool to touch up the beaches (Figure 5.28).

Bear in mind that in the current iteration of GameGuru, there are really only two modes of water-traveling. You can either have it shallow enough to walk across (creating ripples and sound effects) or deep enough to drown in. As such,

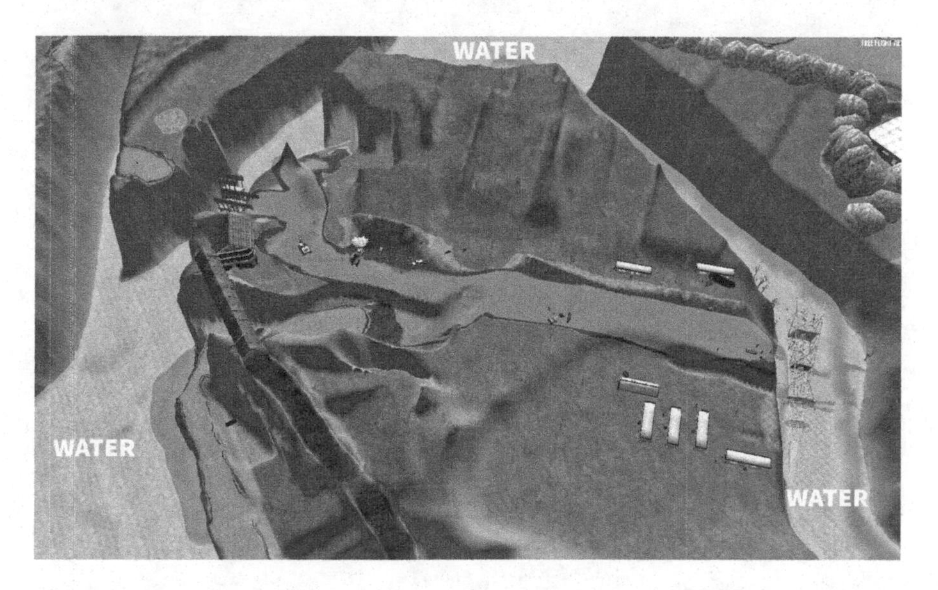

Figure 5.28

Using water as a barrier.

reserve your creation of waterways for those two tasks—creating a shallow bridge to walk on, preferably with a texture that indicates this (such as a sandy beach or rocky outcrop) or a barrier that cannot be passed (deep water that kills the player). You want to make sure the player can easily tell which is which if you are interposing the two. Try to make sure to put rocks and objects (perhaps a wrecked boat) if you have a sandbar they can walk across as a sort of land bridge. I typically use the mountainous pattern for the terrain for deep water to sort of help darken the area even more than it already will be. Generally speaking, if it looks light blue in the editor, it will be the right height for walking across. Dark blue will generally kill the player.

6

Adding Simple Functionality

GameGuru is billed as an easy game maker and a sort of everyman's game-making tool. In a lot of ways, it meets that criteria, if you know where to look. There is a lot of preconfigured functionality that can be used just from the editor itself. Where the editor ends, however, the coding begins. Beginners typically tend to shy away from code, though of course we'll be delving into it in much greater depth later. However, for the time being, there are some preconfigured functions that we can use to add some really necessary function to our game. These are easy to plug and play for even the most vehement non-coder.

Lights

The first function is still within the editor. This is the lighting system. The lighting that you see initially is dynamic lighting. This is a sort of "live" lighting that is happening in the engine directly. During the course of this writing, it underwent a huge revamp. Previously, we only had access to three active lights at any given time. This number was massively increased to 38… per entity! So you can literally have on the order of hundreds of functioning lights per level. They also have the ability to be configured as spotlights, which helps us focus where the light is

Figure 6.1

Light positioning is demonstrated with a colored circle radius.

going to be versus just a pure radius. This matters because dynamic lighting goes through walls, so positioning can be very important.

Usage is simple, as with most things in GameGuru. All one has to do is click on the marker's tab on the action column on the left (Figure 6.1) and scroll down to find a suitable light color you want to place. For our example, we're using a red light. Position your mouse pointer where you want to see the light in this level and position it. From here on out, that light will emit radiant light that will also illuminate entities. If we click on the light again and go to properties, we get a simple properties panel (Figure 6.2).

⊟ **General**	
Name	Light
Static Mode	No
⊟ **AI System**	
Main	light1.lua
⊟ **Light**	
Light Range	500
Light Color	77c8fd
Spot Lighting	Yes

Figure 6.2

The light properties panel.

For now, the only two configuration items you want to focus on are color and size. Dynamic lights tend to be large by default (500 units!), and so we're going to carve that down substantially to produce the best quality possible. So let's set this value to 100 units.

We'll place our red light in the logical location of being near the large red neon sign. In our reference picture (Figure 6.3) you can see this represented at the top of the picture with the cluster of lights.

Now run your test map and... Oh no! It's too washed out. The entire area looks red. We were hoping for just a slight glow, but instead we have a deep red hue that is heavily affecting everything in the nearby area.

TIP: The basic colors in GameGuru are almost always the wrong choice.

At this point, we have to correct the coloration. Let's bring up the properties pane again on the light and select something more suitable. I've enclosed a table in the Appendix for just this occasion. In this case, I'd like to use the equivalent red/green/blue (RGB) value of a high-pressure sodium bulb. We're going to select that by clicking on the color and modifying it using the chart provided.

The way lighting works is by effectively "painting" an opaque layer over a texture. So when we select this, try to think of it as a filter that will be applied over top of an existing object. So when we choose a bright red color, it tends to utterly overwhelm anything that's in its vicinity. Using a mellower orange color nearer to pure white will allow it to mask in a cleaner fashion and provide a much better overall effect.

Figure 6.3

The cluster of lights at the top ensures full illumination.

Recently, a "spotlight" feature was added. How this works is it creates a cone-shaped light that allows you to create some really interesting visual characteristics if you want a much more controlled display. You control the orientation of the spotlight with the entity rotate widget.

There are several included scripts as well that come with GameGuru that will perform specific functionality for you.

Light1.lua: This is your basic "light" script. This light script does nothing at all. It's literally meant as a starting point for future scripts of your own.

Light2.lua: This is a basic light script you will use if you want to create a light that operates via a switch. This switching system works by setting the default script of the light entity (which must be a dynamic light) as "light2.lua." You then must have the actual "switch" entity use the following script: "lightswitch.lua." Make a note of the name you use for your light. I'd recommend using "mainswitchlight" or anything along those lines. This way you can remember which light is being activated. You can also activate multiple lights from one switch if you use the same name for several lights.

Lightswitch.lua: This is your actual switch script, which works by connecting it to an object set as "static=no" and "default=lightswitch.lua." After you do that, go to the "ifused" field and type in the name of your light that is using the light2.lua script. This will make it so that when you hit the switch, the light toggles on or off.

These three scripts allow you to do some very basic light effects; later on, we will get into much greater detail on lighting in general several times throughout this book. I've also included my "lightkit" set of scripts, which will even further improve your ability to do impressive lighting effects without needing to do much or any coding!

Of special note is a fourth script called "lightzone.lua," which does not work how you would expect it to. It does not activate lights when you are in a specific zone but instead sets environmental effects using Lua so you can add fog, surface ambient colors, and other slide bars from the player stepping into a zone. It can be fun to experiment with, but bear in mind that once you step into the zone, it will permanently set your sliders to the new values for that specific map file.

Doors

The functionality for doors has mercifully been included with the game engine. It allows you to create realistic rooms that have doors that only open with a key and others that open by walking up and pressing a button. All one needs to do is select an appropriate door-compatible object, namely one that has the right animations, and choose door.lua as its script type. This will handle both doors with keys and doors without as the script by default reads the "ifused" field to see if a key is required (Figure 6.4).

So to configure a door, you must put information into the "use key" field for it to know what key to use. Whatever you place in there should match the name you choose for the entity serving as your key. This, of course, means any object with

Figure 6.4

The properties panel of a door.

the right Lua file attached will act as a key, which can provide some interesting opportunities as I will illustrate in the next section. Getting back to the doors themselves, it's important to remember that doors must be set as static=no for the properties; otherwise, they will not function. You also want to make sure physics are disabled on the doors; otherwise, you can get some unpredictable effects.

An interesting proposition is you can set a door as explodable if you want to allow the player to blow the door open, but the downside is that, currently the game doesn't recognize a specific type of damage. So if you do set that, they can then be killed by any type of weapon. Your best choice is to set it to a high value such as 10,000 and then modify an explosive weapon to do that much damage.

Keys for Doors

Likewise, keys for doors have their own code included called key.lua; this will make the name of the object a unique key that is stored with the player. This key will then be available for use with specific doors that are looking for that key name in their "ifused" field. Interestingly, you can configure virtually any object as a key, which allows us to do some cool objects for keys. Boxes, bottles, canisters, wallets—whatever you want can be turned into a key without incident. Some mild changes might be required.

As you can see in the previous image (Figure 6.5) we have an item that looks like a key, however it must be configured to be a key first before it works as one. Once we change this object to be a dynamic entity with key.lua as the script type, it makes it a sufficient item for pickup, which will then be used for a door with the corresponding entry in it.

Figure 6.5

The properties panel of a key.

Switches for Objects

Switches are a staple of many games, allowing secrets, sliding walls, doors to open, or any number of possibilities. We've already covered light switches and their ability to remotely operate one or several dynamic lights. There's also been a discussion of keys that in a sense act as a switch for a door that requires a specific component. However, there are some specific "door" switches that can be configured as a tether for the door itself. This door switch will open a door when a player presses a switch; it's a common function that you will use regularly.

Switchmain.lua acts as a common switching system for external objects such as doors and the like.

Here again, if you point it using the ifused field in the properties, it will activate any special remote code for "activation" in the Lua code. So even not knowing the slightest bit of code, you can run these scripts fairly efficiently. All you need to do is have an activator (the switch) and a recipient (the door). Then put the right codes in the right places, set up the ifused field, and you're off!

Adding Simple Enemies

Adding enemies is fairly simple for starters. Most of them, especially the base ones, come with the scripts already attached that they require to function. Your basic combat script is ai_combat.lua, which will handle a typical ranged enemy with a gun. For now, we won't get into more advanced configuration of our enemies. We want to place them in an open area and position them in a fashion that will allow us to perform the basic task of attacking our player with them.

There's three different types of enemies you need to be concerned with here.

- A ranged type. This uses a hit-scan system, similar to ray casting. It shoots a line out from itself near-instantly and, if it intersects with the player, then a hit is registered.
- A ranged "projectile" type. This is your basic rocket propelled grenade (RPG) soldier who shoots rockets at the player. The hits are not instant and so they will only register if the projectile strikes the player or the subsequent explosion causes player damage.
- Last is a melee type, which will seek to close the distance and attack when within range. This operates the same as the ranged hit-scan enemy as well, though it has a distance check on it to limit the maximum effective range to "melee" physical attack distance.

When you click on an enemy, you'll see a fairly simplistic properties screen, as shown in Figure 6.6.

So as you can see, there's a lot of basic properties here that give us a fair amount of control over the AI entity. Let's go over these.

Name is an arbitrary name of the entity. Don't use any special characters here.

Specular is how "reflective" the entity is. It's typically 1–100%, but you can go well past this (as you can for the specular field of all entities). You can go up

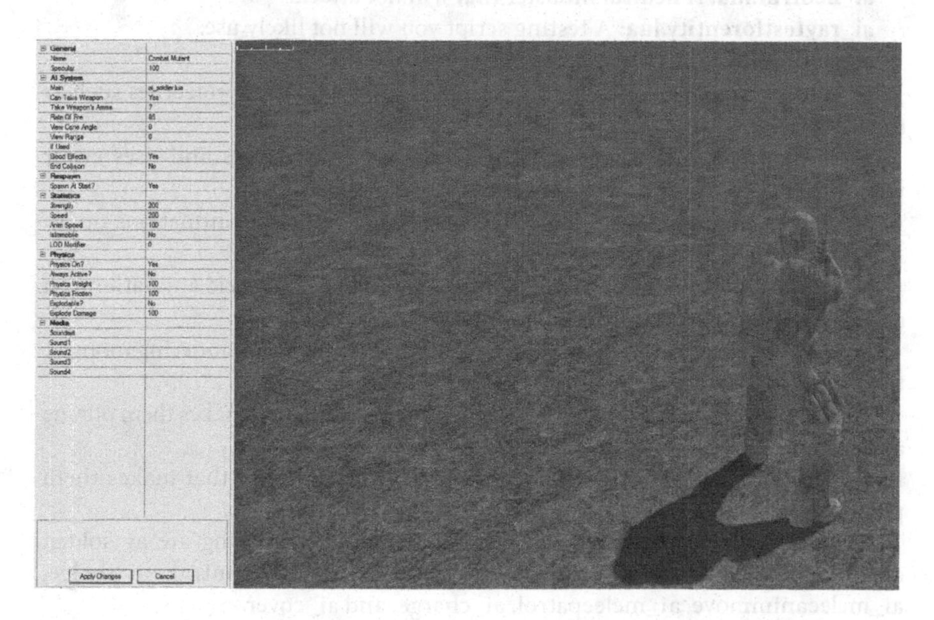

Figure 6.6

The properties panel of an AI entity.

several thousand percent to make the model exceptionally shiny; this is especially useful for metal enemies.

Main is the main script being called. By default, it's almost always going to be ai_soldier.lua: this is our basic ranged soldier script. It will handle movement, shooting, visibility, dying, and all associated basic functions for the enemy. There are other AI scripts as well in the scriptbank folder.

ai_charge.lua: Enemy will charge the player.

ai_cover.lua: Enemy will attempt to use cover zones (see Chapter 14 on advanced AI tricks).

ai_dance.lua: Enemy will dance at the player!

ai_demon.lua: AI script specifically for the flying "demon" entity included with the fantasy pack.

ai_dragon.lua: A fairly advanced script specific to the free "dragon" model that comes with GameGuru.

ai_fantasycharacter.lua: A fantasy pack melee script for enemies.

ai_fantasycreature.lua: For melee fantasy pack creatures.

ai_fastzombie.lua: This is a legacy zombie chase script that makes them pursue a player and melee.

ai_melee.lua: A basic melee attack script that they will not patrol.

ai_melee_animmove.lua: A basic melee attack script with animated movement.

ai_meleepatrol.lua: A melee monster that will patrol.

ai_neutral.lua: A neutral monster that will not attack.

ai_raytestforentity.lua: A testing script you will not likely use.

ai_soldier.lua: Your basic ranged attacker.

ai_soldier_rpg.lua: A patrolling ranged attacker who uses projectiles such as the RPG.

ai_soldier_rpg_guard.lua: A ranged attacker who guards and uses cover with the RPG.

ai_viewanimations.lua: A simple script to help you cycle animations on an AI. AI will rotate to face the player.

ai_viewanimationstatic.lua: A simple script to help you cycle animations on an AI. Will not rotate to face the player.

ai_wanderer.lua: A variation on ai_soldier that results in a wandering monster that cannot shoot.

ai_zombiewalk.lua: This is a legacy zombie chase script that makes them pursue a player and melee.

ai_zombiewalk3.lua: This is a legacy zombie chase script that makes them pursue a player and melee.

Of these scripts, of course, the primary ones we'll be using are ai_solder, ai_soldier_rpg, ai_soldier_rpg_guard, ai_wanderer, ai_neutral, ai_melee, ai_meleeanimmove, ai_meleepatrol, ai_charge, and ai_cover.

Next, we have several weapon-related attributes: can take weapon, take weapon's ammo, and rate of fire. These are fairly straightforward. The first is a yes or no that shows whether it will drop a weapon upon the death of the AI entity. The second is how much ammo that weapon will contain, which by default will be one "bullet" unless you specify otherwise here. Lastly, we have the rate of fire; this one can easily make a game unplayable as the GameGuru engine can often fire far faster than a player will respond and by default almost never misses. I recommend a 50 or lower for a standard difficulty and 80 through 120 for higher difficulty levels.

View cone angle and view range are fairly simple but have fairly long-reaching effects. Essentially, they dictate whether the enemy will "spot" the player. Now if you shoot the enemy, it will always activate the combat portion of the code. When it is walking around, though, it will be looking constantly for the player and will use these settings to determine if it can see them. A setting for the view cone of 0 is actually a 360-degree cone, and view range is in standard FPSC units, which are about 2–3 feet per unit in game. So really any setting under 1000 is probably best here, depending on the type of enemy you are using. The view cone extends out of the front of the entity and represents their field of view forward of their position vertically; so even if it's set to 45 degrees and the player is above them but directly in front, it will see them.

As a new user, these are probably the most relevant settings you will encounter in your initial usage of GameGuru. They directly control how your enemy will interact upon initial contact with the player, so take some time to get a handle on how they work. Bear in mind also that the facing of the enemy becomes very important: If you have them facing the player at the beginning, they will spot them immediately instead of patrolling.

You can skip "If Used" for now as that is solely restricted to Lua code.

Blood effects configures whether the blood decals will show when they are struck.

End collision is particularly useful if your enemy is going to potentially die in an area where they might "block" the player with their bounding box. What this does is disable collision after they die so that they can't, for instance, block a doorway with their body.

Spawn at start determines whether the game will start with the enemy loaded or whether it will wait for a "spawn command" from a Lua script or from an ifused field on a trigger zone.

Strength is the raw hit point pool of the enemy. In most games, the general rule is a weak enemy should have about one-third to one-fifth the amount of HP as the player. A middle-tier enemy will have 50 to 100% of the player's health, and a boss will be several multiples higher than the player based on how hard you want them to be.

Speed is the actual movement speed of the AI entity when it traverses, which in my opinion can be rather slow by default. Don't be afraid to play with this one to get to a point where you feel comfortable with the speed at which it moves toward the player.

Anim speed is how fast the frames of animation cycle on an action. Where this REALLY shows is if you set this value too high while having a low movement speed; they will look cartoonish as they move their legs in a whirlwind of speed but only move a few inches in game. I recommend a value between 75 and 95 for most entities.

Is immobile should always be set to be No.

LOD modifier controls the level of detail modifier, which is an advanced setting only accessible by models with level of detail settings configured into them.

Physics on enables ragdoll upon death. The various secondary physics settings operate as normal as well, functioning upon the death of the enemy and how the corpse will interact with the world.

Always active bears some special consideration. The AI in GameGuru can be a fairly CPU intensive process. If you set this to "always active yes" it will turn on the AI permanently, which can eat CPU cycles unnecessarily. Ideally, you want this on "no," which will limit the function of it to 3000 units. While this is still an enormous distance, it will still help shave precious CPU cycles when AI isn't turned on. It does NOT disable them after the player continues out of this range, though, so bear in mind if the player triggers an enemy, it will toggle it to "always active yes."

Explodable is the same as non-AI entities in that when it dies, it will explode if you set this to yes. It is particularly useful for enemies such as robots like the types in the Fallout series of games. Explode damage obviously controls the level of damage for the explosion. Unfortunately, the radius for this explosion is not tunable as of this writing.

Of particular interest are the "sound" settings. You'll note that AI entities have a significant body of options here that you may not see elsewhere. Soundset specifically points to a folder of all the sounds the AI might use such as alert noises, death gurgles, etc. This means different enemies can play different sounds. The individual sound1, Sound2, Sound3, and Sound4 are used by Lua calls for specific secondary sounds that can be played under various circumstances.

You don't need to know much here to start, only that the soldier does have a view cone that tells it how much and how far it can see. Play with them if you like, but for the moment, we're going to use elementary positioning techniques to set up the game in such a way that the enemies can be both hostile and passive at the start.

Our method for this will be to have their back turned on the player with a 90-degree view cone. If their back is turned, they cannot see the player: easy right?

Play around with it a bit. Simple enemies are easy to position, easy to use. They don't take much work to make function and can be added with minimal effort. Later on, we'll get into much more detailed use of them by adding waypoints, floor zones, custom AI code, and the like.

7

Adding Sounds and Music

The sound system in GameGuru is a complex and fairly sophisticated one for what is a very simple game engine. It allows a lot of flexibility and is divided into both sounds as a system and music as a secondary system. These two systems have to be approached individually in order to be able to be used properly.

We'll start with the sound system. First of all, you should know a little about sound before we begin. There are several types of sounds in the computer world. There's MPEG audio layer 3 (MP3) files, Waveform audio format (WAV) files, Ogg Vorbis compressed audio (OGG) files, MPEG audio layer 4 (MP4) files, Music Instrument Digital Interface (MIDI) files, and other types of "music" and "sound."

A Brief History of Sound in Computing

Computer sound systems were often a source of pain for gamers in the early years. This was because in a lot of ways these were the most restrictive systems on a computer. Sound cards were often vaunted and sought as highly desirable, in much the same way that a modern 3D graphics processor is. This is because they actually operated in much the same way—a second CPU that allowed dedicated processing of sound and music.

Most computers (from the early '80s through the mid '90s) were equipped with the most miserable of all sound equipment: the PC speaker. If you were like me, coming from the relatively rich sound system that was built into a system as old as the Nintendo Entertainment System® (NES) to the PC was a rude awakening. The PC speaker simply put was limited to only square waves. For those who never had a music theory class, let me explain this to you.

Sounds essentially come in four forms that sound differently. So, using a little onomatopoeia, I'll try to convey what they are to you.

Square waves are either at a maximum high or maximum low and sound like "beeps and boops." There is no transitioning the sound in any way.

Sine waves are rounded waves that alternate in a gradually scaling pattern, peak, and then go the other way in a gradually scaling pattern. They make little "hills" when visualizing them—like what you see on an oscilloscope. This results in a sound similar to a "wee woo wee woo" seesawing back and forth.

Triangle waves are triangle-shaped waves that gradually build, peak, and then fall off gradually. This type of sound is often like the previous wee-woo sound but is much sharper in transitioning.

Sawtooth waves (grows to pitch then drops abruptly) are triangle waves that have half of the triangle cut off. This means it acts as a halfway point between a square wave and a triangular wave by immediately dropping from the maximum high to the maximum low sound before gradually transitioning upward to maximum high again.

These four types of waves control the level of output the speaker receives and in what way.

My son recently asked me, "What is sound?" The answer to this is strikingly simple. Sound is the vibration made through air that is received by your ear and converted to signals by your brain. These vibrations from a modern speaker come from a thin membrane that wiggles when electricity is applied to it.

Well, the PC speaker is the same kind of "equipment," but the actual output on the motherboard was a pure square wave output: This means all you got were beeps, boops, or no noise at all. This embarrassingly simple kludge meant games lacked good sound, let alone music (PC speaker games notoriously had zero music).

That said, there were solutions. My old IBM PC XT (yes, I had one) was fully kitted out with an eight-bit sound card. This eight-bit sound card was tremendously limited by modern standards and yet was vastly more than the PC speaker could handle. These sound cards used a form of FM (frequency modulation) synthesis that allowed them to "emulate" real sound over a standard digital sound output to some speakers.

The Holy Grail at the time, often at a massive multihundred dollar investment, was an MIDI (music instrument digital interface) capable card such as the Roland MT-32, which had a launch price of $695 in 1987! Games often featured true MIDI sound as an option, but few people actually had the equipment capable of playing it. MIDI wouldn't even synthesize on early cards, with later cards offering first exceptionally poor synthesis that later evolved into higher quality sound that we take for granted today. This is an exceptionally long topic that I'm kind of blitzing through, yet I feel it's important to understand. I will personally never forget what it was like to upgrade from a SoundBlaster Pro to an "AWE 32" with full MIDI wavetable synthesis. Nowadays, we almost all use onboard chips that provide quality far superior to anything we saw in those days for a tiny fraction of our CPU power.

Key Concepts in Sounds for Video Games

In video games, there's a few important things to understand. First let's begin with several different elements of sound types so you know what you're working with.

There are uncompressed sound files such as .WAV files. These files are raw data, completely uncompressed, and while they offer the best possible sound fidelity, they also take up more space than any other format available. These files are often used in short, rapid sound effects such as gunshots or player noises.

Next are formats that are compressed; those come in two flavors: lossless and lossy. Lossless compression is exactly as it sounds—compression that doesn't lose data once it's compressed. These are typically not used due to processing time involved. Lossy compression is something more familiar to people; it's the realm of MP3 files and other common formats. These operate by compressing the data in a more simplistic fashion that does result in some data loss but is vastly faster to process. As the compression bitrate lowers so does the file size and quality. In GameGuru, the supported lossy compression format is .OGG, which while not very common easily converts to or from MP3.

Sound quality is often expressed as a combination of bitrate and sample rate. The bitrate is a simple measure of how "good" the audio stream's quality is. It's measured in kilobits per second, kbps, or just "k." In the early days, these sounds were recorded as 24 kilobits per second (24 k), though current hardware is frequently in the range of 64–128 kbps for sound quality. You can, as always, go higher, but the advantage may be lost as you are squeezing blood from a stone in that regard. This is, of course, unless you use extremely high-end production equipment.

Sample rate is the number of audio samples taken per unit time. This is done via a cycle rate (hertz) and a depth (bit depth such as 8 bit, 16 bit, 24 bit, etc.). Traditionally, games operate at 16 bit/44.1 kHz (kilohertz) sound very well. This is a common format and one I'd recommend you use if you are unsure of what to select. Bear in mind the human ear can only hear certain sound ranges so often it's not advantageous to go beyond certain recording levels as it will only be minimally impactful for the listener.

So to simplify this: high bitrate with high sample rate = higher quality audio. Higher quality audio has higher storage requirements. Many options exist but, in general, you can't go wrong with 128 kbps audio recorded 16 bit at 44.1 kHz.

Sound in games operates in "channels." These channels are pathways for sound that can play simultaneously. In early games, it was often a single (mono) or double (stereo) channel card and that was considered impressive. Eventually, "quadraphonic sound" with four channels showed up only to be eclipsed by the ever-impressive Dolby 5.1 sound and successive iterations. A little side note, the 5 means "5 channels" and the .1 means "and one subwoofer."

Sound in GameGuru

The sound system in GameGuru is broken into two components, sound and music, as mentioned. This is because sound is operated in "channels" as mentioned previously. GameGuru supports a number of simultaneous channels, but during the development cycle, it was decided that it would be best to break music into a dedicated channel with sounds on the remainder.

Music and sounds are both stored in a folder under your base GameGuru installation folder at this location:

<GameGuru base install location>\files\audiobank

These files are usually organized by folder. I like to make a folder for each project, which keeps my audio self-contained in the case that I need to use modified versions of sounds for a different project.

So let's start with the sound channels. Sound channels can readily be found on the properties of any object.

As you see at the bottom of Figure 7.1, there are several potential channel banks for this object. You can assign different sounds to each one and call them via Lua code simultaneously or individually.

Sounds may also be assigned via Lua code as well, which we will cover later.

For now, let's go ahead and use some sample code with a simple object.

With a "sound" slot, we can use two types of files: uncompressed (WAV) files or (OGG) files. Please note that when a sound recorded as "stereo" is placed in GameGuru, it will only be given one channel (making it mono), so it's best to ONLY record as mono to ensure it plays properly.

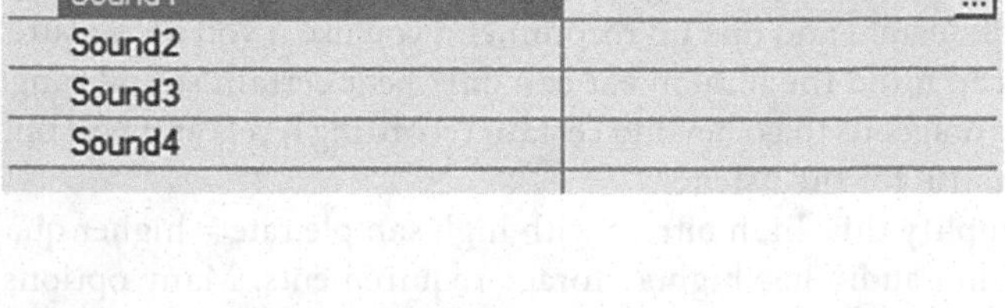

Figure 7.1

The properties subpanel for an entity's sound controls.

If an object makes use of the "sound" property, then you will need to make sure that you set "static=no" as well to ensure that it functions correctly. Your entity index number is how we reference it in Lua.

This allows us to call it as "entity X, sound 0/1/2/etc."

Another important thing you will want to bear in mind is that the sound volume system in GameGuru operates in decibels (a standard unit of sound volume). That said, though, despite the fact that it's a 0–100 scale, anything below 60–70 decibels is inaudible. This means you can only use 70–100 as your values for low to high.

Sounds can also be configured as a 3D sound, which changes the volume of the sound based on how far away the player is from the sound source. Please note this is a highly simplistic 3D system as it doesn't use positional audio with the speakers to produce a "true" 3D sound experience. It is, however, fairly effective unless the person is an audiophile. They can also be configured as non-3D sounds, which will just play the sound at the same volume regardless of where the player is in relation to it. This ensures that the player always hears it at the same volume, which is useful for things such as player actions.

The easiest way to add sound to your game is to add a "sound zone," place it, select the properties for it, and configure a sound in one of the banks. Once you've done that, as soon as the player steps into it, it will play the sound for them! Unfortunately, this is a highly simple process and you might need significantly more, which is why they include other pieces of code as well!

GameGuru also includes several other useful scripts that can be used regularly with your games with minimal coding. Those are:

Soundatplayer.lua: This will play a single sound as a "non-3D" sound while the player is in the zone; it is useful for perhaps sending things like an alert at the player or something that would be area-wide (such as a siren). It will play only one time while the player is in the zone.

Soundinzone.lua: This Lua file will play a sound specified in the properties screen in GameGuru's soundbank for a sound zone or trigger zone. The sound it plays will only play once while the player is in the zone. Sound emanates from the central location of the zone.

Non3Dsoundinzone.lua: This Lua file operates the same as the previous one but does it at maximum volume, ensuring the player hears it equally throughout the zone. So, in essence, it works the same as soundatplayer with one crucial difference: the code in this file is SPECIFICALLY set up to loop at the player. This is a very good way of playing a looping audio bit at maximum volume such as an alarm klaxon or even to use it as a cheap way of playing music (assuming you don't want to monkey with the music system listed separately in the next section).

Movewithsound.lua: Moves an entity forward 300 units and loops a sound.

Now as you can see, even with only a minor amount of work, huge gains can be found within GameGuru's sound system. Of course, many hobbyist game-making engines proudly proclaim "no code required" in their descriptions, but the truth is that if you don't learn to code even just a little, you will not get much further than the few scripts listed previously.

Granted, you could always buy them on the store, but when we get to the chapter introducing Lua (Chapter 11), you will see how exceptionally easy it is to control the sound system any way you choose. For now though, feel free to test with these sound files and see what you come up with!

Music in GameGuru

Lee Bamber coined the name for the music system as the "interactive dynamic music system." This particular system is fairly well fleshed out, and it would definitely behoove you to delve into some of the inner workings.

As mentioned previously, the music system in GameGuru is its own channel, which allows you to play it continuously without it having to queue in line with the other sounds that the system is playing. This allows it to play seamlessly and thus provide a great experience for the player.

For a long time, I've been very interested in music despite my utter lack of talent for it. In particular, I've always had an interest in music in movies and games. This music is often referred to as "ambient" music, which means it plays as part of the background. This music is frequently manipulated to evoke certain emotional responses from players or viewers. Think of say a scary horror movie, how it always builds the music up to a peak right before the sudden attack of an enemy. This type of buildup is a simple enough thing to do but is a very effective way to build tension where there might not be any. To test this, go watch that same scene with the sound off. Notice how it's completely flat now? All of the best games and movies I've ever seen often came with a fantastic soundtrack. While this may not be within your reach as an artist (my case), there are plenty of qualified artists, some even on the TheGameCreators store website, whose music you can purchase for use in your game. So make sure you find something good!

Now, with respect to how GameGuru handles music, it allows you to preload several .OGG files as music and call them in various fashions. There are five total "music slots" ranging from 0 to 4. Slot 0 is no music and the default. Slots 1–4 have various names, but really it doesn't matter so long as you call them at the appropriate times. These calls can be done with something as simple as a "music zone" that plays the music when the player steps in it.

What's really interesting is that the music system is configured to allow fading from one track to another, thus giving you some really high-quality transitions that sound pretty seamless. This allows for some very high-end music use if you're feeling particularly ambitious.

The tracks for music are specified in "files\scriptbank\music.lua." This file contains several lines that clearly show which tracks are being called.

-MUSIC_TRACK1 = "audiobank\\atmospheric\\assylumatmos.ogg";
MUSIC_TRACK1 = "";

The top item with the double dashes is commented out. You can both remove the dashes and put them on the secondary line (MUSIC_TRACK= "";) or you can modify the line MUSIC_TRACK1 to reflect an .ogg file in the same fashion as the example. Please note that your MUSIC_TRACK#s can only have one line that is active at a time. This means you cannot have something like this:

MUSIC_TRACK1 = "audiobank\\atmospheric\\assylumatmos.ogg";
MUSIC_TRACK1 = "audiobank\\atmospheric\\mynewmusic.ogg";

Instead it must have one of the two commented or deleted to function.

Example

-MUSIC_TRACK1 = "audiobank\\atmospheric\\assylumatmos.ogg";
MUSIC_TRACK1 = "audiobank\\atmospheric\\mynewmusic.ogg";

For us to change this, we need to modify the file to reflect the music we will be playing for our game. Please note, since this file is shared among all of your projects, I'd highly recommend making a backup for each game. I usually call mine music_gamename.lua with obviously the game name being whatever title I'm working on.

Keeping a copy like this allows me to swap the file as I am working; thus, when I go to make a standalone, I can either copy and rename the correct one or it will copy the one I have if I'm already set up right. Perhaps in the future the developers will attach this to the map file instead of storing it here.

Default Scripts

The default scripts cover a significant spread for you to work with. Most of them are fairly simple, but it bears covering so you know what you are working with.

Music.lua is your primary handler for music in GameGuru; it configures all of the major components of your four tracks of music. These four tracks are not only specified in terms of name but also length and fade interval. The tracks by default are listed as MUSIC_TRACK# with # being a 1–4. These tracks initially show as "", which is an empty value. Above it, in the stock GameGuru files, there are several commented out lines that have full pathnames to real files included with GameGuru. If you uncomment those lines by removing the double dashes from the front and place those double dashes in front of the line with the "" it will enable the default music tracks! You may also obviously modify those paths to point to your existing music tracks that you have saved in the files\audiobank folder.

Musicinzone.lua is a simple script that will allow you to set the music track you want to play in the properties and then call it via the player stepping into the zone.

Musicplaytrack1-4.lua are various Lua files that will play music when placed in a music zone or trigger zone. The music played will correspond with the track # listed referenced in music.lua: these files are fairly easy to use and are going to be the easy go-to choice for most people looking to add music to their games.

Unfortunately, despite these premade segments I'd like to say again that it will really help you to work with the Lua code on this one. It's simply not within the GUI interface in a meaningful fashion to work with the music system, which makes it significantly more difficult if you don't have some kind of foundation in Lua. Thankfully, I have a chapter or two later on that will help you get your feet wet with Lua. Once we get you into it, I'm sure you'll dive deep: Lua's elegant simplicity combined with the robustness of the Lua support for sound control will give you all of the tools you need!

Adding Effective Enemies

When people see the letters "AI" they think of fantastic killer robots, advanced computers destroying entire civilizations, or at least a computer-controlled character that serves as an actor in a game they play.

In almost every situation, they think of AI almost as a black box, something that is impenetrable and unknowable. It just works or it doesn't. The same applies for most people's understanding of the GameGuru engine's AI.

A great many years ago, I got my start with game modification delving into QuakeC and the AI bot code that someone else had built, which in turn had been rigged from the Quake monster code.

It was instructive as often times going through someone else's code can teach you quite a lot. Between that and some casual reading (notably "The Black Art of 3D Game Programming" by André Lamothe, Sams, 1995), I learned quite a lot about not only what AI is, but what it was capable of. More importantly, what it wasn't capable of.

AI as we know it generally tends to be exceptionally simplistic. It relies on a combination of something called a "finite state machine" and "fuzzy logic." We'll get into these more later in this chapter.

These two, combined, build our AI combat code. Thankfully, GameGuru ships with some bare-bones AI that usually suffices and has some interesting capabilities out of the box. As with all things GameGuru, it tends to have more power than you might immediately realize.

For the purposes of this chapter, we're going to stick with some relatively basic modification of the enemies as they come within GameGuru. This means using very elementary systems and modification of the properties panel as shown in Figure 8.1.

As I'm sure you're aware, it's important to know the limitations of any system. AI is no exception. If you want to make a good game, then you want to maximize what you have available to you. The only way to do that is to expand your knowledge.

First, a small anecdote. When I was a teenager in the '90s, I picked up a fantastic book by the now venerable author André LaMothe (Sams, 1995). Now André was a fantastic programmer in the early days, a pioneer who generously passed on his code and talents to those who shelled out the money for his books. It was worth it. I owned around three or four of his books. By now, he's a writer of some renown, and the fact is if you are reading game development books, you will eventually find one of his. I'm going to say outright the man taught me things I would have never learned otherwise. In particular, I own a book called "Tricks of the Game Programming Gurus" (André LaMothe et al., Sams, 1994). Now while some of this is dedicated to building your own ray casting engine, what's particular impressive is the information he provides on AI.

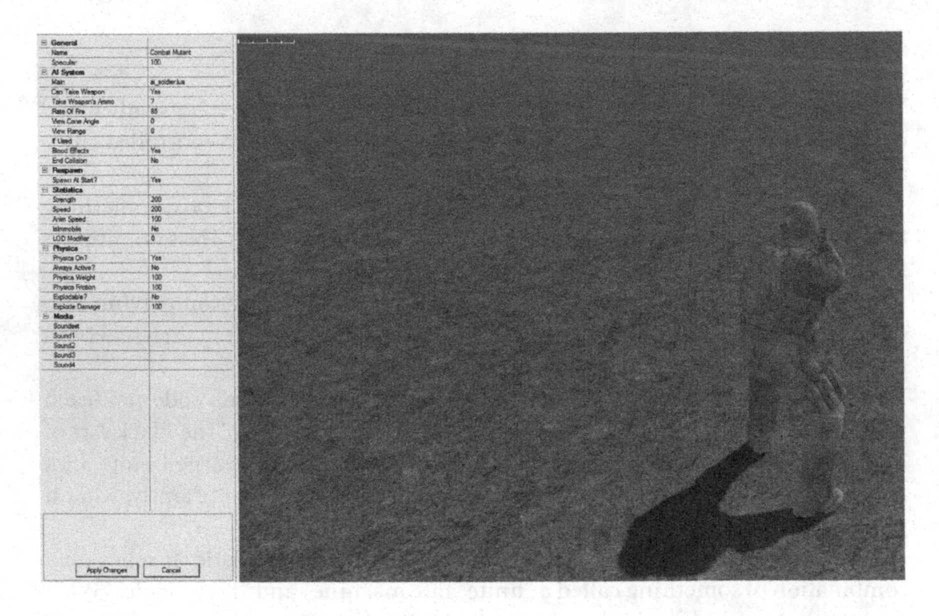

Figure 8.1

The properties panel for an enemy.

So let's go back to the mid to late '90s. I had several of his books I'd been pouring over and happened across several things all at once. First, Quake 1 had recently been released, and I was playing it like it was going out of style. I had discovered a Quake C decompiler (which was in French!) called "Deacc and Reacc." This opened up a whole world of modification to me I had not previously been privy to. I never understood the whole BSP tree thing at the time, so Doom mods never became my thing. C language code, however, I knew from my programming classes.

I also didn't have Internet but had a lot of bulletin board system (BBS) access. That meant no online gaming and made me very bored since I could play at school in the lab during lunch. When I got my hands on a bot called Darkbot, I was very excited—until I found it didn't work. It ran into walls, wouldn't leave rooms, stood aimlessly waiting for players, and was generally just bad.

That's when it all came together. I decompiled it and started digging into the code for it. Soon I had repaired the errors, improved the pathing algorithms, and added my own custom fuzzy logic.

The result was now somewhat infamous. I had created the first (to my knowledge) cooperative Quake1 bot called "Coopbot." Later, it was called Teambot and followed with the final version TeambotX. Over the years, other modders grabbed my code, rehashed it, and it ended up distorted. Eventually, some pieces of it made it into the reaper bot code, which I've always been particularly proud of.

I couldn't have done any of it without the C coding I'd just recently learned, the decompiler, Quake 1, a broken mod, a book by André LaMothe, and a lot of boredom.

How AI Works

When you think of "AI," what do you think of? Is it of fantastic machines performing human-like tasks? Is it video game enemies who seem to know your every move?

What about those bad instances of AI where it fails or is just outright bad? Those times when you are playing a game and an enemy is literally just standing there waiting to get shot in the head? How about those games where the game literally reads your controller input and responds to you before you even complete your move?

Do those ring a bell at all?

AI is generally not as complex as it might seem. In fact, it's actually rather simple. That simplicity is often the core problem with it, causing anything from gaps in the logic to slowness in processing by over-utilizing certain states. In fact, AI really is all about pretending to be intelligent instead of actually being intelligent.

So AI typically can be divided into two separate groups of AI. The first is the "fuzzy logic" type. This type uses a series of conditional rules to determine what

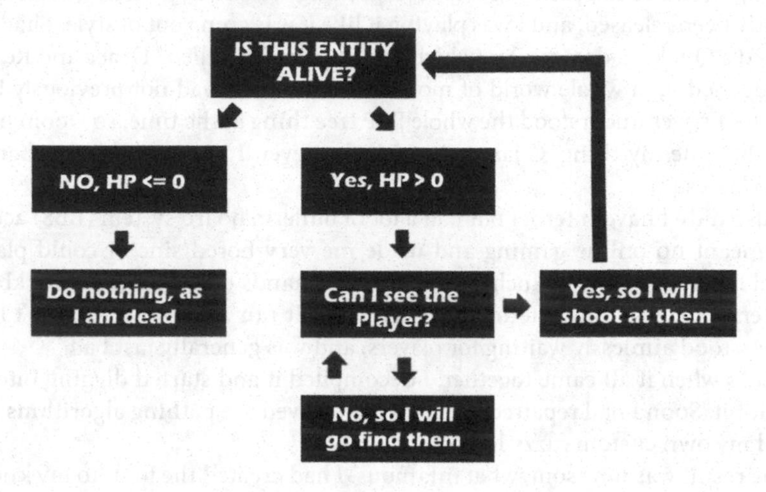

Figure 8.2

A simple fuzzy logic flowchart.

the AI is going to do. This allows you to build an AI that seems intelligent but really isn't.

Fuzzy logic can really produce some incredible effects by emulating specific conditions very precisely. The problem is that if there is anything outside of those conditions (see Figure 8.2) it either responds completely incorrectly, or worse, not at all.

The other type of AI is something called a state machine. State machines are fairly comprehensive and the better choice overall but lack the nuance of fuzzy logic as they operate in a series of "states." These states are often defined as shown in Figure 8.3.

What happens then is that there are specific conditions built in for a "state" that the AI resides in and acts a certain way. For instance, if their idle state is to lean against a wall and smoke a cigarette until the player shows, they will. However, as soon as the proper conditions for an idle state expire and a new state's conditions are met, it will then perform the actions of that specific state instead. The advantage of this system is that the AI is generally going to be doing something useful.

Most AIs are built with at least a fairly basic state machine and some fuzzy logic to simulate certain behaviors within the various states. This way you can provide logic inside of the state loop for the various states that helps provide a bit of realism to the AI entity.

GameGuru operates in this fashion, using several states to control the AI until death occurs. These states vary from AI to AI but typically follow the

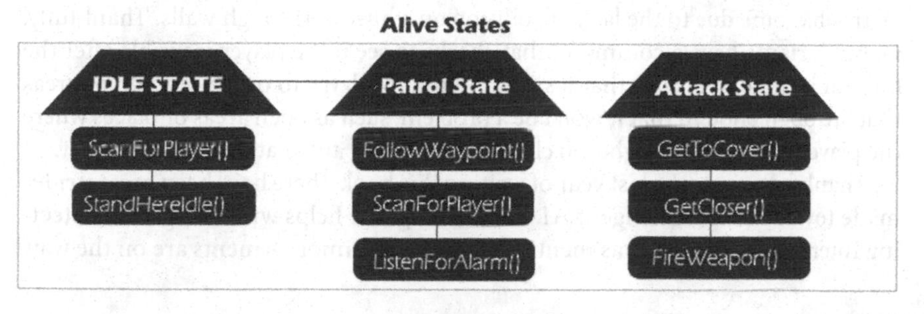

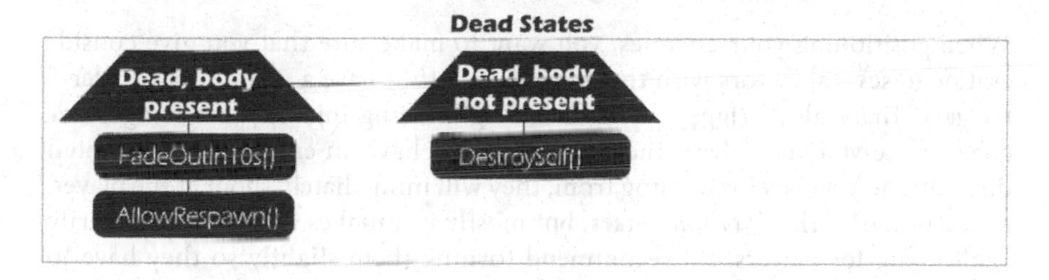

Figure 8.3

A simple state machine flowchart.

aforementioned model in some capacity. There are, of course, ways to get vastly more sophisticated with it, but at the end of the day, this is the core of what you are working with. Understanding these states is critical to your success, so let's get started!

Built-in Enemy Types

The built-in enemies consist of several different categories. In a lot of ways it depends on what you have with respect to DLCs and download packs.

The base kit consists of several ranged "modern" combatants featuring everything from Uzis to RPGs. This means we have two separate types of ranged attacks. The first is one that uses a ray cast from the AI entity as a "check" to see if it hit the player. If it did, it deals damage. This is referred to as "hit scanning." The other type is one that launches a physical object (in this case, an RPG round), which then has a collision box of its own. Once that collides with an object, it then causes an effect like damage or an explosion. One important factor to consider is that hitscan is never going to miss unless you add some code in the AI that gives it a possibility of missing. Projectile-based weapons have a flight time and as such can be dodged by the player with varying degrees of ease.

Fantasy and sci-fi DLCs add a few other functional types, most notably ones that use melee attacks. Melee is really handled through a "short range" hitscan. This can be troublesome due to the lack of collision on a hitscan through walls. Thankfully, newer variants have a command that checks to see if the player is visible after the hitscan is done to ensure that it's a "valid hit." Still, try to only use them in areas that are open enough that it won't be a problem, such as open areas or places where the player will not be caught too close to a wall with an AI attacking through it.

Thankfully, over the last year of writing this book, there have been great strides made toward more intelligent AI. This intelligence helps with things like detecting intervening obstacles as mentioned, and more improvements are on the way.

Placement and Positioning Enemies

When positioning your enemies, you want to make sure that you give consideration to several factors with them; one is that they have a certain set of "alert" triggers. These alert triggers range from sight, being injured, to having other enemies see you and "alert" them. Often, if you have an enemy that is pointed directly where a player is coming from, they will immediately shoot at the player, rather unfairly. This has some uses, but mostly just makes things unnecessarily challenging for players. I'd recommend turning them slightly so they have to adjust to the player before firing. This gives a slight delay that can be used to help give the player time to make their own preparations and adjustments. We'll get into this more in Chapter 14 "Adding Advanced AI." For now, just be aware that they have this functionality.

Placement of your enemies should be considered in a sense of how hard the encounter will be for the player. Enemies in GameGuru can actually be fairly ruthless if not tuned, and so it can turn ugly very quickly. Alternately, if you set them up a kilometer away in the open, standing outside while waiting idle for the player, they will get sniped unceremoniously.

Figure 8.4 illustrates this in several stages. The first stage is a wide-open enemy with no cover for himself to use. The second stage is an enemy placed behind

Figure 8.4

Demonstrating various ways to place enemies.

cover that it begins behind but won't use past that. The final stage is an enemy actually in a pit, using a floor zone, with sandbags as cover, and using a cover zone marker to ensure the AI properly uses it. Each of these is successively more complex than the previous.

The balance here is to hold your cards until you are ready to show them, so to speak. Get your enemies in a position where they can both be a threat to the player as well as be managed by the player. Use of things like corners, doors, and new rooms should all be a good opportunity for their placement.

When playtesting your level, try to see how easy the encounter is. If the entire thing can be managed without even a modicum of threat to the player, then work on making the entities better concealed or with a better view range. If the game kills all of your playtesters within 30 seconds, then consider dialing back the difficulty.

Bear in mind also the head does a massive damage increase due to a headshot check in the AI code, so if you are leaving the enemy's head exposed for that make sure it's what you want.

The example in Figure 8.5 shows that the head is exposed, allowing the player to kill the enemy instantly. In this case, it is not desirable for our game. So we changed the position of the enemy to behind a partial wall, which allows a body shot on the enemy. This allows the player to get the jump on the enemy without killing them outright. So as you can see, enemy placement is critically important!

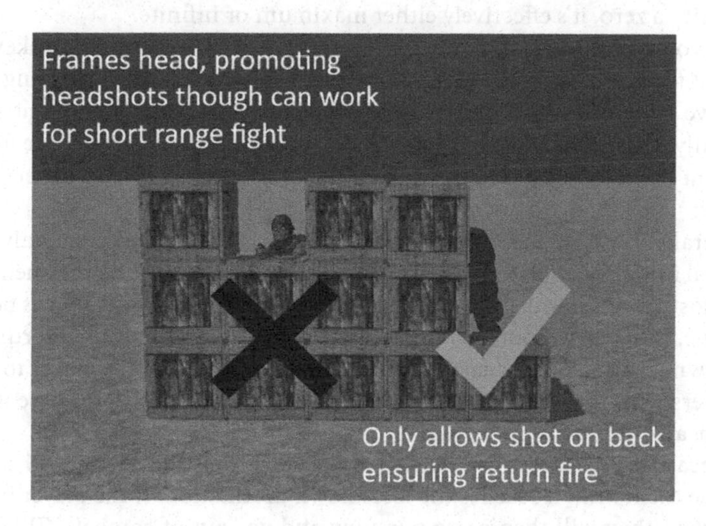

Figure 8.5

On the left, an easy headshot. On the right, the head is concealed.

Figure 8.6

Demonstrating the enemy view cone and range parameters.

Configuring AI Entities

Typically, as you rotate the object, you are, in effect, aiming them. They have a view cone and range that controls their reaction to the player (Figure 8.6). When you are maneuvering them, you have to pay careful mind to their configuration here. The default settings are an 85-degree cone and infinite view range. Anytime you specify a zero, it's effectively either maximum or infinite.

So if you use a 0-degree cone, it's the same as a 360-view cone. Likewise, if you want to seriously restrict the enemy's viewing angle, use something like 10 or 20. I've gone as low as a one to ensure that an enemy has virtually no chance of actually seeing the player. This is good if they're on a patrol route and you only want them to be alerted by other enemies who are acting as observers, for instance.

Generally, I use a cone ranging from 45 to 70 degrees. This cone only affects the actual initial location of the player. Once the player is fighting the enemy, they will almost always stay oriented toward them. This means they'll always be in the view cone. If the player outruns the view distance of the enemy, it will run to the last known location of the player and stop there. This allows the player to "reset" encounters with the enemy. At that point, it will then either stay where it's at or go to a nearby waypoint node.

To recap: If the player runs outside of the view cone, the enemy will continue to pursue them until it reaches the last known destination. If the player is STILL not in view, they will then cease pursuing and go "out of combat." This can be used for hide-and-seek style games if you like, allowing you to have enemies that the player must outrun to survive instead of shooting.

While there's a host of other settings we can modify for our enemies, let's start with these to get a solid grasp on the fundamentals for the enemies.

Custom Enemies with the Character Creator

One of the most simplistic ways to add an enemy is with the Character Creator. You can mix and match, then put your pieces together and get a fairly interesting derivative enemy. You are never going to have something completely unique from here, but it's often enough to create a bit of variety to differentiate you from the stock assets (Figure 8.7).

This level of subtle differentiation should be just enough to get you through if you lack the modeling skills to make your own.

I've included several unique pieces of additional components for the Character Creator that will allow you to even further set yourself apart.

Figure 8.7

A fairly generic enemy with a unique face from the Character Creator.

You can also edit the FPE file to modify the weapon used to non-standard weaponry. In the following example (Figure 8.8), we will use one of our custom weapons on the enemy from the Character Creator.

As you can see, you only have to change the one line, save it, and you'll have a weapon that's outside of what the Character Creator is limited to.

Once you place them in the level, they respond as any normal enemy would with view cones, nodes, and the like.

Later, in Chapter 14 ("Adding advanced AI"), we will cover additional AI-specific topics to help fine-tune your AI using GameGuru's built-in settings.

```
1  ;header
2  desc            = Combat Mutant
3
4  ;visualinfo
5  textured        = combat_mutant_D.dds
6  effect          = effectbank\reloaded\character_basic.fx
7  castshadow      = 0
8
9  ;ai
10 aimain          = ai_soldier.lua
11
12 ;orientation
13 model           = masked soldier.X
14 offx            = 0
15 offy            = 0
16 offz            = 0
17 rotx            = 0
18 roty            = 0
19 rotz            = 0
20 defaultstatic = 0
21 materialindex = 0
22
23 ;identity details
24 ischaracter     = 1
25 hasweapon       = modern\colt1911
26 isobjective     = 0
27 cantakeweapon = 1
28 ragdoll         = 1
29 endcollision    = 0
30 speed           = 200
31
32 ;headlimbs
33 headlimbs       = 32,54
34
35 ;statistics
36 strength        = 200
37 explodable      = 0
38 debrisshape     = 0
```

Figure 8.8

The FPE file of an enemy entity.

9

Advanced Lighting

In Chapter 4, we discussed several keys you've probably been wondering about until now. Those keys are the lightmapper function keys, Shift + F1–F4. For the most part, you will only be using one key: F3. That is because the bulk of these keys don't provide an actual lightmap! Most of them are either much-stripped-down functions (F1 and F2) or redundant (F4). F4 is noteworthy as a waste because it currently uses an out-of-date system, notably the decommissioned manual occluder. As such, we have a key that does nothing for now (F4) that can just be outright ignored as it acts the same functionally as F3.

The reason I am devoting an entire chapter to this subject material is because it is the one thing that can either make or break your game's ability to look like your game has a professional feel to it.

One important thing to remember is that every game engine has limitations. This extends, universally, across all engines: even the big fancy ones like Unreal or CryEngine. GameGuru is no exception.

In fact, you may see people talk about how limited GameGuru is, but the truth is that's almost always due to limits in both their understanding and their abilities.

In order to work with something, you must understand the fullness of its limitations. Limitations are not usually as hard a limit as people would like to believe; they often can be circumvented or worked around.

As mentioned, GameGuru is a primarily outdoor engine. The sun, currently, is a hardcoded entity. This means it's going to be at the same location, casting approximately a 6 p.m. shadow when the shadows slider is configured. These shadows can be disabled via the shadows slider. The sun's influence can also be disabled via the sun factor slider. Light rays emanating from the sun can be controlled or tuned for that as well. As such, indoor levels are a viable prospect but require a firm hand in working with the controls to obtain the results desired.

So how do we get lighting effects that can produce AAA quality graphics?

The answer is to understand our limits—and work around them.

Let me give you one really great example about working around your limits with dynamic lights. One dynamic light I failed to mention was the muzzle flash. It basically is an intermittent dynamic light that operates based off the gun's gunspec.txt file. This rapid flash of light is a small sphere of illumination that emanates from the player's position when a gun is fired (and the gunspec.txt file says to do so). One developer had the "bright" idea of making an in-game torch. He achieved this by making a torch model as a weapon, then causing it to fire frequently enough to use the muzzle flash as a torch effect. Clearly, this is not what the weapon system was designed for but, with a bit of cleverness, one can achieve uncommon results!

Static Versus Dynamic

Static lights and dynamic lights are two separate types that exist within GameGuru. Dynamic lights are the ones you will first encounter; they plunk down rapidly straight from the GUI and make a very noticeable impression on the game world you've created. However, as you keep setting them down, you'll notice some distinct limitations. Notable is the fact that you can only have 38 functioning at any one time. Please note that this is per mesh, so you can actually now have several hundred. If more than that function, they become unpredictable and sporadic. The dynamic light provided by these lights is reasonably good; it has a few drawbacks, however, that bear mentioning.

- The light radius specified as a default is almost always entirely too large. There's some residual backscatter out past the visible periphery, and it will almost always reflect on your other objects in other rooms.
- The first issue also affects this one as well. There's nothing to stop the dynamic lights once they go through a wall; they will continue to illuminate what is behind the wall!
- The colors that GameGuru defaults to are, in a word, unacceptable. There's a major level of rework required to make these colors functional.
- They are entirely too bright in many cases, often requiring very precise placement.
- Dynamic lights take very little memory but are more CPU intensive.

So there you have it. Now despite these limitations, there are ways around this. We have to turn our disadvantages into strengths. That's how we make not just good games, but great games.

The solutions here are fairly simple. First, cut the default size in the properties pane of the light down to 250 or less. The minimum size is 100, so you're stuck with that as your smallest light value, but in many cases, it's enough for a small 10 by-10-foot room. The default colors are easily rectified; we will edit them manually and select more appropriate colors for the type of lighting we're using. I've included a table of common light values in the Appendix to help guide you along. Each one has been tested and matches known real-world light bulb values to be fairly similar in GameGuru.

The brightness as a limitation is actually fairly easy to work around; we'll be confining our use to only dealing with bright objects. Be it a lamp, sign, or flare ... anything that has a significant brightness will be the subject of our use of dynamic lighting. The performance issue is something that must be carefully monitored as you build your level. For now, build it as best you can and optimize it later.

Another interesting component about dynamic lights is they can be manipulated while in-game, live—while the player is functioning in a map. There isn't a large amount of variation: usually just an on or off switch ... but this allows us via code to manipulate these lights in interesting ways. In the lightkit scripts I've included, I have some examples of this such as sequential lights, repeating lights, strobes, and alternating strobes like police lights.

What about the rest of the time?

Obviously, we can't rely on a sun that never moves and dynamic lights that are limited to three active simultaneously to do our work. We need more flexibility than that. That's where static lighting, also known as pre-baked lighting, comes in. Pre-baked lighting has a lot of positive benefits: it's limitless in terms of quantity of lights, is pre-rendered to minimize CPU usage, is stopped by walls, and will cast shadows independent of the sun. There are, as with dynamic lights, several drawbacks worth mentioning.

- Static lights don't impact specular mapping (more on this later in this chapter).
- Static lighting is weaker in intensity overall compared to dynamic lights.
- Static lights require a long bake cycle, which only gets worse the bigger your level is.
- Static lights are more memory intensive than dynamic: This is due to the fact they create a large graphic overlay that is stored in memory to be placed over the textures. So while it provides a really flexible system for creating lights, it can also easily destroy what little resources are available if you get too out of hand with it.

Once again, it's not about what the limitations are but rather how to work around them. Placing static lights requires a different methodology than dynamic lights. For one, they can be placed en masse. This allows us considerable flexibility with respect to positioning and creating blended effects. There are some important caveats to these lights that bear consideration. The first one is that they are a sort of color texture "mask" that is applied to a surface. As such, using a pure white light (255,255,255) will result in very little discernable difference to the texture beyond some brightening of it.

Also, because they are generally weaker, we either need to increase the size of the light to 1000 or add more lights around the room. I have used values up to around 2500 depending on the size of the room. Typically, you want to use the color value chart I've provided as well (in the Appendix), though it may take some toying with to get the right color and tone for your application. Now with respect to using large sizes, these do not shine through walls, so it is totally safe to use large sizes with static lights.

The next big hurdle will be the lack of specularity; this can only be resolved by adding a dynamic light into a room with static lights if you are looking to get that extra "shininess" to pop on your textures. Given our limits on dynamic lights, it is important to combine static and dynamic lighting in places where this will have the most impact.

Textures and Lighting

Textures in GameGuru are defined using a .dds or .png file. These files have their own drawbacks and benefits. The .dds (short for DirectDraw surface) file is the most common of the two, and you should definitely get the tools you need to work on them as being able to even do minor modifications of textures will have a huge impact on your final product.

I personally use a free tool called paint.net®: it's readily available at the website www.paint.net (imagine that!) along with a plug-in for it that allows me to modify DDS files. There are other great plug-ins available as well, including one that generates normals (another type of texture file) and alpha mask plug-ins (that control transparency).

When saving files in paint.net as a DDS, it will ask you what type of DDS to save. It's important to note that most DDS files can get very large in size if you aren't careful. This, in turn, eats your memory in ever-increasing bites. Typically, you will use the standard DirectX texture type 1 (DXT1) format unless you are saving transparencies, in which case you'll use a DirectX texture type 5 (DXT5). We go into this more in the "retexturing assets" portion of this book (see Chapter 16).

GameGuru supports a wide variety of texture types. If you recall from the "history of FPS" chapter (Chapter 2), textures are graphics that are stretched over a 3D object. Originally, this consisted of just a picture over a shape. Things have progressed a long way since then and, as such, we have a number of different types of texture files. These are denoted by the name of the file, an underscore, and then a designator, followed by the graphical extension (in our following example, it will be a DDS file).

Texture types supported by GameGuru are divided into two categories: DNIS and PBR:

Filename_D.DDS: The diffuse file, or the actual image itself being mapped over the 3D model itself.

Filename_N.DDS: The normal file, aka the surface normal. This provides a faked 3D micro surface on the texture. This is optional but recommended.

Filename_I.DDS: The self-illumination mapping file, detail to be found later in this chapter. Optional but recommended for signs, lights, and things of that nature.

Filename_S.DDS: The specular map file, effectively a "how shiny is this pixel" map. Optional but recommended for surfaces receiving a lot of attention. Also optional but recommended for metallic or wet surfaces as well as anything else. This only interacts with dynamic lights but, when paired together, can create a spectacular effect.

Filename_CUBE.dds: A cube mapping file. This is a mirror-style reflection of the environment around the object. It's used to approximate reflections for glass, metal, smooth surfaces like ceramics, and water puddles. It uses a six-sided cube that is mapped spherically on the object to generate the reflection. In the scenery folder, there's an object called "shiny skull" as a demonstration. This object is set up with six layers in it that each have a corresponding side of the cube mapping, such as top, bottom, left, right, back, and forward. This false reflection is not actually the reflection of the local environment but instead a premade one inside the file.

For a long time, these four were the extent of it. Now, with the addition of PBR textures, we have a much broader group as well. These files use a slightly different format. Specifically, they are listed as filename, underscore, PBR, underscore, type, and extension (again, DDS).

Filename_PBR_color: This is your base color map and diffuse texture.

Filename_PBR_ao: Ambient occlusion is a special map that creates false shadows on the object that act separately from the lighting.

Filename_PBR_illumination: This also works the same as the illumination map for the DNIS type. It works as emissive lighting overlay on the surface.

Filename_PBR_cube: This works the same as the cube mapping from the DNIS mapping.

Filename_PBR_gloss: This is where things get a little confusing if you're familiar with PBR mapping. In this case, GameGuru treats gloss as a roughness map, which is a simple black and white image indicating how smooth a surface is. It's inverted from typical gloss mapping so gray is not glossy, white is glossy. This does interact with dynamic lights.

Filename_PBR_height: Height mapping is a nonfunctional form of artificially creating depth to a surface. This is currently in an experimental test phase and may get added in the future.

Filename_PBR_metalness: This defines how metallic a surface is, a further extension over specularity, standard metallic texture. White will make this a metallic texture, giving it additional shine. Black is nonmetal and thus will be dulled. This gets affected by dynamic light.

Filename_PBR_normal: A PBR normal texture. Please note that normals on PBR use an inverted green channel, so you will need to use a third-party painter to modify this, in most cases, if you are using your own textures. If you bake your heightmap into the normal, it will really make your textures pop!

Filename_PBR_detail: The detail map is a powerful addition that allows you to add fine, detailed, scaled, and tiled across the model.

PBR adds a significant amount of realism to a model at the cost of much higher memory being used, as well as rendering costs with the CPU and GPU. I don't recommend building entire environments out of PBR unless you are building a repeating texture file over and over with models that all reference the same texture. That is dangerous, though, as it will likely create a situation where the texture becomes overused and unimpressive. That said, at least it will be a PBR texture! So it will look great, even if it is repetitive.

Alternately, you can build with high-quality background pieces and use the PBR assets strictly as sort of "high end improvers" for foreground objects. This way, pipes, tables, characters, player weapons—all the things they interact with regularly—have a nice look to them. This follows our rules of trying to build around a "low quality for unimportant or background objects to high quality for important foreground objects." Other games have used this same methodology when dealing with limited resources. A good example recently is "Deus Ex: Mankind Divided." Prior to writing this book, I wrote a fairly extensive review with a specific focus on lessons that could be derived from it for GameGuru developers. I sent the information to the senior technical designer at Eidos Montreal: Sylvain Douce. He was able to validate my estimations. So, thankfully, I can boil that down for you here: that game specifically used a lot of PBR textures but only in places where it mattered to save resource space.

What is a Self-Illumination Map?

What about the rest of the time, with say a well-lit street that has lots of windows, neon signs, bright lights, and vehicles? How do we provide a level of lighting that will make these objects illuminate as they are intended? The answer is with something called a "self-illumination map." This is a type of graphics file that effectively "lights up" portions of the texture automatically. These lights do not cast on any other surfaces; they are completely confined to the model itself. This way, we can simulate lit areas by creating another graphics file that will define what portions of the texture are not lit and which ones are lit. The game engine will handle the rest.

Take for instance the image of a sign in Figure 9.1. On the left, we have the base texture. On the right, we have the illumination map for it. What this ends up doing is making the letters on the sign light up. This simple but effective way of adding lights to your level is exceptionally low in footprint, meaning you can

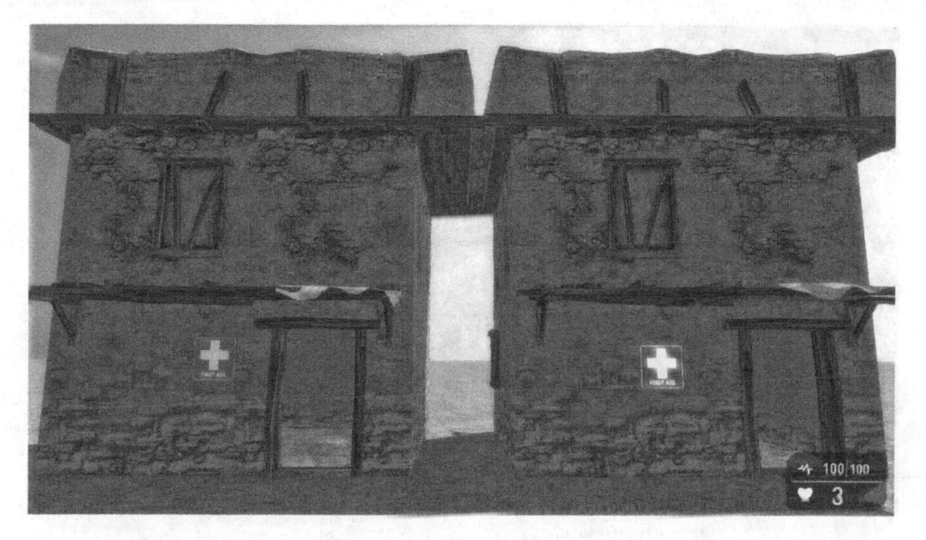

Figure 9.1

On the left, standard DNIS. On the right, an emissive illumination map.

use it over and over again. It's strikingly effective, too. You can use it to light up dozens of textures that normally would seem flat and uninteresting. LCD panels suddenly have realistic-looking touch screens. Buildings have slightly drawn curtains with light peeking out. Offices have a late-night worker or two. It's astonishing once you open the flower of possibility how much you can add in there.

What is Specularity?

Specularity is a system of adding yet another layer of graphical complexity to a seemingly basic thing as a texture. Specularity applies a level of reflection to a texture, thus allowing us to more clearly define edges and even provide a metallic look to objects.

Thankfully, we can achieve a really shiny texture without having to resort to PBR. A specularity map on its own isn't going to eat a meaningful amount of memory and will add a lot of variety to our surfaces. This texture type will reflect two different types of lights: dynamic lights and sunlight.

This level of "shininess" is controlled by the specular value of the entity in the FPE file and the actual specular map itself (Figure 9.2).

Detailed Information on PBR Textures

PBR is physically based rendering, which we touched on a bit earlier. This PBR mapping interacts with your environment more dynamically than standard DNIS mapping at the cost of increased overhead for the engine. It does, however, have the capability to add really impressive-looking models to your game if you are judicious with their usage.

Figure 9.2

Demonstrating various specularity settings.

Reflection mapping inside of GameGuru is done based off the ground and sky. However, you can create local maps by taking screenshots of a room and creating a cube-map instead, or you can use a generic cube map if you have one.

Color: Raw color with no lighting information. Small amount of ambient occlusion can be baked in if using it for micro-surface occlusion. The color range for dark values should stay within 30–50 RGB. Never have dark values below 30 RGB. The brightest color value should not go above 240 RGB.

Roughness: This describes the micro surface of the object. White 1.0 is rough, and black 0.0 is smooth. The micro surface, if rough, can cause the light rays to scatter and make the highlight appear dimmer and broader. The same amount of light energy is reflected going out as coming into the surface. This map has the most artistic freedom. There is no wrong answer here. This map gives the asset the most character as it truly describes the surface (e.g., scratches, fingerprints, smudges, grime, etc.).

Normal: The normal map is the same as any other though, as mentioned previously, the channel for green is inverted.

Metallic: The metalness texture determines if something is metal or not. Pure white is "raw metal," and black is a nonmetallic surface. Transitional grays can cover the spread of less shiny surfaces such as dull metals, woods, and the like. Also, according to one user (Belidos at https://forum.game-guru.com/thread/220065), the following is worth mentioning:

> With metals and roughness, the areas indicated as metal in the metallic map have a corresponding metal reflectance value in the base color map. The metal reflectance value in the base color needs to be a measured real-world value. Transitional areas

in the metal map (not raw metal 1.0 white) need to have the metal reflectance value lowered to indicate that its reflectance value is not raw metal.

Also, with metal/rough, you only have control over metal reflectance values. The dielectric values are set to 0.04 or 4%, which is most dielectric materials. The dielectric is hard-coded by the shader and you don't need to set it in Substance. Some shaders add a specular control that allows you to change the Fresnel reflectance value at 0 degrees.

That's quite a mouthful. If you are a high-end texture artist, you will undoubtedly find this information incredibly useful. For the rest of us, I have a much more easy-to-digest explanation in later chapters.

Diffuse: The diffuse texture is a color map with no lighting information; ranges for dark values should be between 30 and 50 RGB. Here again, don't go below 30 or above 240 RGB if you want your results looking right.

Glossiness: Glossiness is an inverted roughness map with pure white being smooth and black being rough. It's done on a micro-surface level, and roughness will affect how the light rays scatter. This can have the result of making highlights appear broader and dimmer. According to the user Belidos, this map has "the most artistic freedom" and there are "no wrong answers." It allows you to give lots of interesting information to a surface such as smudges, scratches, and the like.

Specular: The specular map is, as mentioned previously, a shininess map that controls how shiny (specular) a light is on it. Obviously, this has a significant impact on how the model will react in the world when confronted with dynamic lighting. Remember that "clean" models generally reflect very well, while "dirty" models will be duller and less shiny. Here again, the mapping is done with a range of white to black, with white being "very shiny" and black being "not shiny."

TIP: Use custom textures whenever possible.

It's one thing to buy a product on the store and use it. However, anyone else who has used the item will also have it in their game. Often what I will do once I decide to use a product for a project is I will make a copy of it from the files\entitybank\purchased\<asset> folder to a separate folder named for my specific project. So it would look like this: files\entitybank\<projectname>\<asset> … after moving that to the separate folder I then modify the textures (notably the _D.dds file) using a free program such as paint.net.

Now when I say I modify it, there are a wide variety of techniques I employ. Some are as simple as applying a slight change to the colors; other times I will actually build a new layer and compress it down. If nothing else, though, just applying a filter to it can often make the difference. A good place to start in paint.net is the color histogram (Figure 9.3), which has several lines you can click and drag to modify the colors used in the image.

This, in turn, can provide some pretty wild results. Especially when you realize that you can limit it by using the selection tool to modify said colors.

The end result provides a simple but effective variation that shows just that extra bit of effort to players in the know but also helps you get that extra edge

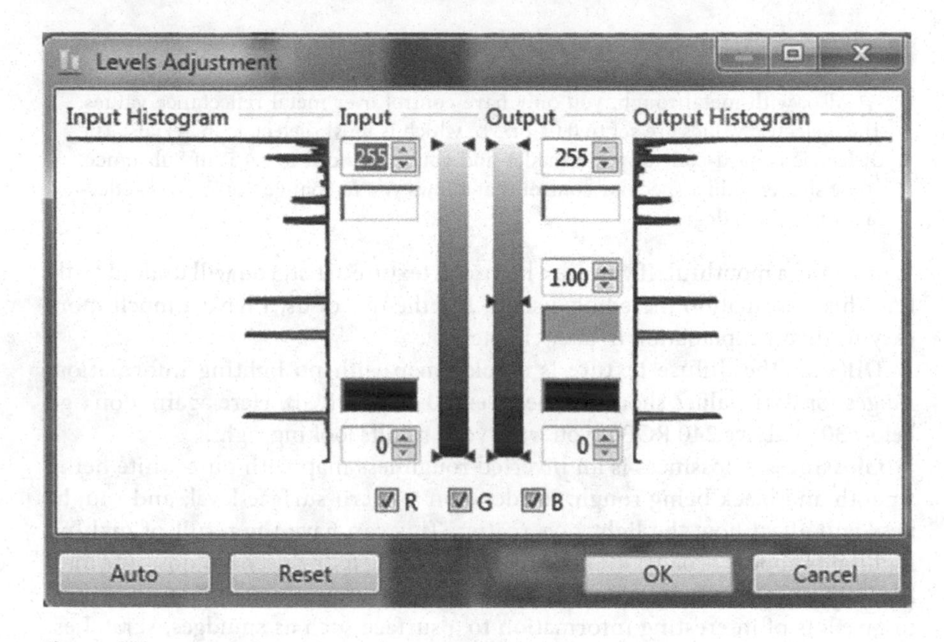

Figure 9.3

The color levels for an image.

toward your game's world-immersion. This is especially true if you have a specific color palette you are building toward.

In the '90s, many video cards were limited to very strict color palettes, often as low as 256 colors. This meant that game developers had to carefully select relevant colors to provide the right experience for their users. While this is no longer a concern in the 16+ million color palettes we have now, there is still a good reason for providing similar colors throughout a game. Think of being in a forest. In the forest, there's a lot of greens and browns. You're not going to find neon pink there in most cases. Even if you do, the reflection of ambient green light from nearby trees and plants will tint it slightly toward a green color. This type of ambience helps keep the player from falling into a state of disbelief about their environment.

Optimally, you'll be making your own textures from scratch, but this can be a difficult process at best. Tools like Normalizator help simplify this, though, so don't be afraid to experiment!

I go into much greater detail on this in Chapter 16 on retexturing assets.

Static Light Mapping

Static lights are an essential component of getting a great looking level out of GameGuru. While they cannot do everything, they provide a very capable level detail to a level by mapping over textures with colors and hues that are only feasible

PROs	CONs
"Infinite" lights	Dimmer than dynamic
Low CPU/GPU cost	Increased memory cost
Colors blend well	Doesn't affect specular
Doesn't go through walls	Only affects static objects
Quickly rendered	Long compile time

Figure 9.4
The pros and cons of static lights.

when the object is lit. Static implies they do not change, and this is very accurate. There are some significant advantages to static lights, as well as some heavy offsets. We covered a bit of this earlier, but let's just show the pros and cons again (Figure 9.4).

So, to be fair, there are some drawbacks. However, as with all things GameGuru, clever use of this tool will allow you some fairly impressive results. I'm here to ensure that you are able to achieve them.

Let's quickly review the list.

First, you can have an infinite amount of static lights. This is a hugely important feature and allows you to quickly set a light, configure it, extract it, and then shift-click tens or hundreds of duplicates. Of course, each light will impact compilation time (see following sections). They are, of course, dimmer than dynamic lighting, which means that you want to typically use brighter spectrums of colors or a higher surface slider value. It also is helpful to use a larger radius value, as mentioned earlier.

Next, we have the CPU, GPU, and memory costs. While your central processing unit (CPU) and graphics processing unit (GPU) will have only a minimal hit to their performance, the mapping for the static lights will eat a significant portion of memory depending on the size of your level. This can translate to several hundred megabytes of data or more. Given our limit of 2.5 GB (due to GameGuru's being a 32-bit engine), this can be painful. It's important to back up regularly to ensure that if you do accidentally get overzealous with a light map that you can return to a previous state where the game is stable.

Now we see that I have it listed as colors blending well but not affecting specular. Specularity, as mentioned, is a special texture map that affects how shiny something is. You will need to integrate dynamic lights in order for this to work.

Static lights will also not go through walls, which is a known side effect of dynamic lights. This error can be rather frustrating, causing lighting artifacts to appear in places where you don't want light showing. It's the primary problem with dynamic lights beyond the quantity issue. This means you can safely use static light for interiors with fairly wild abandon without worrying about it showing in the room next to the one you are in.

The dynamic lights issue, while annoying, can be cleverly dealt with by adding a false light source on the offending wall. Obviously, we can't fix it otherwise. You can also try reducing the size of the light source, though due to the way dynamic lights scatter, it can often prove difficult. This is remedied by using spot lighting to direct the light.

Of course, the compile time for building static lights can reach into the multiple-hour range if it's a very large and complex map. So be aware of this, and maybe set it at a time when you feel you can safely do it without impacting your work on a level (such as when you are sleeping).

One negative of static lights that needs going over is that they only work on static objects. This means that if you place a group of static lights in a room with an enemy, the only things that will be mapped are objects that are expressly set as static! Objects that move or change such as enemies, push-able boxes with physics, exploding barrels, and the like, will not receive any light from a static source. You will need to add a similarly colored dynamic light in the area to receive the right effect.

So, for these reasons, we have the following understandings with static lights:

We can and should use as many as we think are appropriate with a larger size of about 2–4× default.

We can and should mix them when necessary with dynamic lights to achieve realistic lighting.

We should make a backup of a working map before static lightmapping, then test accordingly.

Setting static lights is a fairly simple proposition. Go to the properties on a light and change it to static = yes on the object properties. Voila, you have a static light! You will know at a glance if a light is static as when highlighted, it will have a red circle not a green one. This way you don't need to consistently go into the properties to find out if it's a static light or not. You'll find little tricks like this tend to pay dividends when you are performing a repetitive task a few hundred times.

Another good way to set up your lights is to configure one light the way you like as static and set up the range, color, and other settings (such as physical height and position). After you've done this, click extract, hold shift, and click. Then, continue holding shift and clicking to place more duplicate lights. This way if you are, for example, doing a hallway, you can place the lights at the same height with the same settings over and over to give the maximum realistic feel.

One little hack that is worth mentioning here is that there is a setup.ini file change you can use to get rid of the sunlight altogether if you don't want it affecting your static light mapping.

In setup.ini find the line that says lightmappingdeactivatedirectionallight and change its value from 0 to 1:

lightmappingdeactivatedirectionallight=1

This setting is normally set to 0; if you change it to 1 as listed previously, this will disable the sun's directional lighting, which will allow you to use purely static and dynamic lights in-game. This way you can make sure the lighting is precisely how you desire. Worst case, you make an enormous maximum size dynamic light as a "stand-in" for the sun. Again, it's not optimal, but until we have at least a creative workaround, this is what game design is all about!

On Lighting Temperature and Color

Lights are measured in a color scale called the Kelvin scale, as shown in Figure 9.5. This scale shows how "hot" the light is.

The default RGB choices for GameGuru are less than ideal. They tend to be far too drastic and wash out your textures. They can, however, be useful for neon colors. Beyond that, though, the white, yellow, cyan, red, green, blue, and magenta palette used for the colors is unfortunately all wrong for regular everyday lighting. I've included in the Appendix a list of common colors and their respective "real-world light" color equivalents.

So there are a few important facts here that you should be aware of. First of all, white colors do not make textures white. In fact, the closer to white you get, the more it affects the transparency (or alpha mask) of the light mapping. So pure white only brightens textures! It doesn't actually make the room look like it has a light in most cases. So, generally speaking, what you want is a color that's close to white but has a tint of blue, orange, or what have you that makes it seem realistic. Again, the exception here is if you are using something like a neon light or something you want to be deliberately overwhelming.

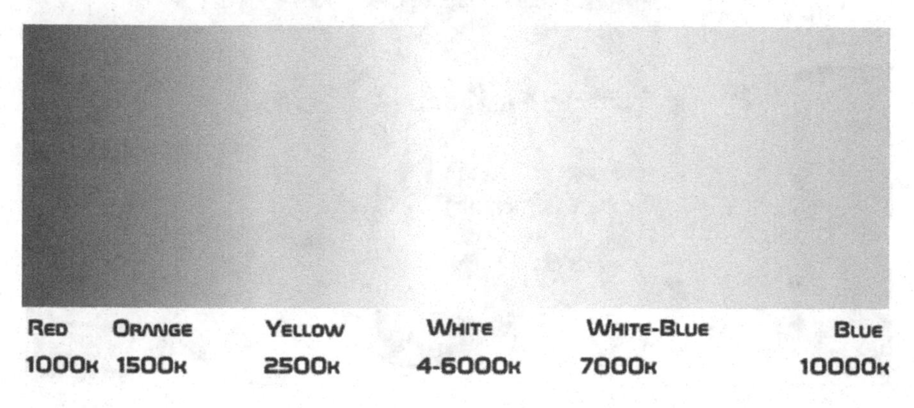

Figure 9.5

The Kelvin scale for light color.

If you recall, earlier I had mentioned that the light radius is different when going from dynamic to static. I typically find that it works best if you multiply whatever value you find works best in dynamic by about 2.5–3. So a light of 500 in dynamic mode would be better served around 1250–1500 in static mode. Likewise, a size of 100 for dynamic lights does best around 300 for static. It takes some practice.

You may also find the lights simply aren't showing brightly enough. Often this can be traced to your surface level slider on your "tab-tab" settings screen. The surface level slider directly affects how bright the lightmap is on the surface of your textures.

Tips and Tricks

There are times when casting shadows is actually problematic. See the picture in Figure 9.6.

Notice how behind the light there's a massive black shadow? This is caused by the placement of the static light, which is directly in front of the barrel. We don't want this, so one answer is to remove the barrel, compile the lights, and then place the barrel again. This will remove the black shadow we're seeing. Alternately, you can try repositioning the actual light itself.

TIP: Mixing colors provides great results.

Ever notice how when you're looking at a sunset or sunrise, you get spectacular color spectrums that are extremely difficult to emulate with an artistic palette? This is because the blending used for those colors is extremely complex. Often, systems that allow interactions of simple colors in a direct way (such as sunrises and sunsets) can produce better results than what we could do intentionally. Some

Figure 9.6

Poorly placed lights result in errant shadows.

call it serendipity or a happy accident. I like to try to reproduce those accidents by periodically trying combinations of static light colors in the same space. Often you can get dramatic color changes that aren't possible with normal in-game texturing.

TIP: Mixing dynamic and static provides AAA quality results.

Another great technique when building your lighting is to mix dynamic lights with static. Now personally, I try not to abuse dynamic lights. I find that the 38-light limit for dynamic lights can result in some glitches. The good news is it used to be worse when there were only THREE lights available for use in a dynamic sense, but at least that translated to good discipline in later projects! So try to stick these lights in places where they will have enormous impact, such as large open spaces or areas where there's a very significant event occurring. This way you can ensure that the lighting system is able to handle your work correctly. By placing these lights in areas with a lot of static lighting, you can really abuse specularity in ways that will provide a level of detail not typically found in GameGuru games. This goes double if you are using PBR textures.

TIP: Use lighting as a navigational aide.

One commonly taught method in level building is to place lights where you want a player to go. This is because as humans we tend to notice lights due to our advanced optical system, which allows us to see in vast, sweeping colors. Because of that, we tend to focus on bright areas as areas of importance. Use this on the player to help guide them where you want them to go or to direct them to a secret.

You'll see in Figure 9.7 that we have a long corridor and above it is a single light, which is making it very clear where we intend for the player to go.

As mentioned previously, we can use this as a navigational aide.

Figure 9.7

Using lights can attract players like moths to a flame.

Light placement is hugely important and can be summed up as something that should seem realistic whenever you use it. All lights have a source and a direction. We'll get into this more as we build our atmosphere in Chapter 10 on "adding ambience." For now, just try to make sure your light sources have an object they come from, even if the object is a texture on the wall that looks like a light.

Illuminated Objects and Ambient Lighting

Secondarily, you can add illuminated local objects to really help out the ambience of a scene. Imagine, for instance, dark corridors flanked by rows of glowing lights on mainframes as you stalk from aisle to aisle. An abandoned store's sign is illuminated as "open." Glowing lines on the floor indicate your direction, mushrooms lighting up a dark corner of a cave—the possibilities are limitless for adding ambience through lighting. Illumination mapping is chiefly of importance here, but try to plan your static and dynamic lights around this to really help a scene pop.

Lighting is tricky business, but there are a lot of "little tricks" that are well-known throughout the level designing communities across platforms. The first trick is that a light is always coming from somewhere. You don't just want light for the sake of light. Light is a purposeful thing that emanates from a location (called a source). Next, you want to make sure you are layering your lights but also using a bit of variety with them in terms of color and type by mixing dynamic and static.

Ambient lighting is the soft, regular light we have throughout a scene. It's important to remember this comes from somewhere too. If it's the sun, then make the color match the time of day and scene. I divide my outdoor lighting into several "chunks" based on real-world observations and what I know about photography.

We have nighttime, which is easy. Nighttime is dark, though how dark depends on the weather, environment, and moon phase. Typically, I will use these settings for night:

Fog near: 0, fog distant: 2, RGB = 0%, intensity 90%

Note that the fog is used to actually make the whole scene seem black, giving a more true impression of it being nighttime.

Then we have the "morning twilight," which is in several phases. It starts off as a sort of "lighter nighttime" and then moves to a pale blue, then a pale purple, then a rosy orange color. These phases of sunrise are difficult to duplicate but, thankfully, I've done the work for you. The settings can be found along with all the others in the "light value" section of the Appendix.

Now the first phase, known as "astronomical twilight," is at best put as a "lighter nighttime" as mentioned. This means the sky will be slightly more visible and it will be about 20% brighter than nighttime.

The second phase is far more noticeable and is known as "nautical twilight." This period of time is before the sun breaks the horizon, but the colors are beginning to change. The skyline will have the reddish-orange glow that precedes the actual sunrise, and stars may still be visible. The sky should be a dark blue, bordering on black, depending on the time of day it is.

The third phase, known as "civil twilight," is the one most people associate with just before a sunrise. At this point, the sky comes alive in a flare of vivid purples, oranges, and blues. This period of time is generally very brief and, as the sun rises, you see a striking display of colors.

Around this time are two of the most famous periods in photography or art that are known as the "blue hour" and the "golden hour." Civil twilight is famous for the blue hour, which is when the sky is overwhelmingly blue and generally calm as it transitions from the deep blue of nautical twilight to civil twilight.

The golden hour is that wonderful period of time where the sky goes from red to orange to gold and has a gentle and dim color. The sun is low in the sky, and it gives great visibility at a distance. It comes after the sun rises and after the riot of color that occurs during the actual sunrise itself tends to settle into deep red tones that eventually become softer and more golden (hence the name).

After this, the gold color becomes rosy blue and then transforms into the white-blue that daytime represents. From here, it just gets whiter and brighter as the day goes on until the entire process repeats in reverse for sunset.

Twilight sunset starts with the golden hour, then sunset, then civil twilight, then nautical twilight, then astronomical twilight, and finally to nighttime. As such, you can reuse the same settings for each "time of day" to achieve the result you want for your scene.

This, of course, doesn't factor in things such as inclement weather or other variables such as being on an alien planet. That said, this can likely get you close to where you are trying to be.

One thing I cannot stress enough is regardless of what you choose for your time of day, try to make sure your level's static and dynamic lights are not the same. Moreover, you want to choose complimentary colors from the CMY (cyan, magenta, and yellow) wheel. Complementary colors are colors opposite those on the color wheel you use. Now this is a fairly heated and involved topic, but I can at least give you some elementary ideas to get started.

In computing, PCs use red, green, and blue due to the way colors are combined by the computer to produce output. Cyan, magenta, and yellow are traditional artists' colors used to determine what is considered a "hot color" or a "cool color." The idea is to then pick complements that match aesthetically. Some feel the best complements follow the RGB wheel that, for instance, says that the proper compliment to red is green. With the CMY wheel, however, a more natural complement to red comes back as yellow. It's important when lighting your level to choose complementary colors. If, for instance, your level is a dim blue, you want to pick a brighter orange or yellow as your complementary choice for static lights. This gives a much more pleasant feel to the players.

Adding Ambience

When I say ambience, I mean more than just ambient lighting. Ambience consists of the little details that help us build our mood or feeling that players will associate with the game. They are the sum total components that build the experience and create a believable environment for the players.

Many games have static lighting, enemies, a good level design, story, and some basic functions… but how do we make it feel real? How do we give it that extra shove toward the end goal of making this game something beyond your bargain basement "corridor shooter"?

One piece of advice I take to heart is that if I want to be good at something, I immerse myself in it. I myself like to immerse myself not so much in games but in mods, or modifications. There are huge communities of gamers who modify already good games and add loads of features. The reason, usually, is to fill a void that they perceive with the game itself. Often it's something simple, something that the developer could have easily done to help really improve the quality of the game for the player.

By delving through these mods, I get a good sense of what users want or don't want. What is popular? Why? Are they adding story? Are they adding characters or objects? How can I implement these same changes in my own work?

What I see time and again in many games is players adding ambience to their gaming experience.

Ambience is that subtle noise, those background sounds or pictures that help your mind construct an entire immersive experience.

Now that we've added all of our core components, we can go back and work on fine-tuning the experience a bit for better ambience. Take for example our rather generic street in Figure 10.1.

We've added some clutter and trash to give it a sort of dirtier feel, but it still feels too "new" to really give you that sense of immersion you are looking for as a player.

Furthermore, you can see for miles in the distance.

Lastly, there's nothing better for really tying a scene together like proper "ambient sound." This means two different types of sound. First are noises that are relative or triggered by specific objects to add meaning to a scene. The "psssh" of a steam vent that gets louder is one way to introduce ambience for the player. The familiar sound of vehicles and bustle of people as a gentle undercurrent the entire time you are in an area is another common method. In fact, there are many ways to create good ambience:

- Atmospheric haze
- Ambient trigger noises that are 3D/scalar
- Constant ambient noise
- Ambient or theme appropriate music
- Zone-specific clutter (graffiti/posters/objects relative to area)

These simple components will allow us to build a truly believable environment.

Figure 10.1

A typical city scene made in GameGuru.

Atmospheric Haze

Have you ever looked outside on a clear day and noticed that despite the clarity of your view, you can really only see a few miles before things start to get a little fuzzy? Atmospheric haze is the reason for this lack of visibility. No matter how clear the air is, it always retains some level of light-absorbing molecules that slowly reduce at range the amount of light that you can see. The further away from you, the less light makes it to you and vice versa. The simple answer to this is to add a light fog that increases in-game the further from the player you are. Try to color it in a fashion that relates to your current time of day.

The example from Chapter 5, adding environmentals, is a good model to reference for this.

There are many different types of haze that we can utilize. We can have fogs for daytime, nighttime, toxic gas, deserts, foggy morning, and the like. Many of these are included in the light value chart in the Appendix.

Ambient Trigger Noises

If you've ever played Fallout 4®, you know there are a lot of crows around throughout the game. There's a story-driven reason for this, it's rather insidious (spoiler alert): The institute uses them as their eyes and ears of the commonwealth. That said, though, the crows have the potential for really driving a huge sense of immersion but tend to be a bit underwhelming.

One of the more interesting modifications I saw to Fallout 4 made it "spookier" and a big part of that was use of the crow sound in louder volumes than they were originally using. It tended to startle me more that way, which helped break up the monotony of performing a repetitive task. In this case, the task was playing Fallout itself. To clarify, many games have become repetitive and monotonous tasks. The key to making a fun game is finding clever ways to disrupt that monotony that aren't obnoxious or annoying. This sort of "resets" the fun meter people have internally.

A good way to do that is a simple 3D sound that plays when a certain trigger occurs. I say 3D sound because it will vary the volume based on how close or far away you are from it. This is important because GameGuru has a tendency to make sounds too loud by default. So if you play a crow's cawing with the standard PlaySound function in Lua, it will blast the player with a very unrealistic crowing noise.

Instead, we want something more subtle. Take some time to play with the volume levels of your respective sounds and try to initiate lots of little triggers to help add to the ambience of a level.

In our example, we'll be adding some growls, some crowing, and some machinery noises.

In this scene, as you approach the pipe, a hissing sound will gradually increase as you draw closer. This gives a real sense of depth to the otherwise boring pipe and helps weave the story for the player. They know that the pipes are leaky now and make noises. I've even gone the extra mile and added a hurt zone script to injure the player if they get too close.

These types of on-demand noises are an important part of your world building; be sure not to neglect them!

Another type of on-demand noise is the jump scare. This type of horror scare is the rapid, fast scare that makes you "jump" out of your seat. These are frequently accompanied by loud noises that jolt you, causing an involuntary reaction. It's important to not abuse these but rather to keep them varied and off pace so the player can't adjust—if you're using them at all.

Constant Ambient Noise

Examples are constant subtle hum of electric lines, whirring of vehicles, people chattering in the backdrop. Use distant screams as ambient sound for horror-themed games.

I want you to stop for a moment and think about where you are. Just sit for a moment, close your eyes, and absorb the world around you.

What did you hear? Was it the thrum of your computer's fan? Were your children playing down the hall? Are you in a house with creaks and groans? A facet of everyday life is that we are bombarded by noise to the point where being somewhere quiet is almost always a sign of a problem.

It's quiet... too quiet.

You've heard this line a thousand times before in movie upon movie. People recognize silence more than they do a regular steady noise.

In this case, background noise is called ambient noise. A regular, steady ambient noise track for your zone will really help draw each area together. Take some of these examples:

Nature: Birds, leaves rustling, and wind blowing

Abandoned spaceship: Creaking metal, humming, and perhaps some electrical popping

Computer room: Electronic fans, keys typing, and more electrical humming

City: Faint sounds of people walking, talking, and cars driving by

Horror: Faint screams, thumps, and growls

Each of these sound themes goes with an area's feel, helping to enhance its immersive qualities. Imagine going into a war zone without any gunshots or distant explosions going off: It'd feel unnatural. Every environment requires its own feel and must be accounted for.

Ambient Background Music

Going back to the previously mentioned horror movies, one will notice that the backdrop music will increase in intensity as things slowly amp up and then rise to a frightening crescendo as the enemy shows up. It helps build tension and elicit a response from the viewer. It's a careful or sometimes ham-fisted strategy on the behalf of the director.

You, being the director of your own product, will be in charge of having appropriate music for your game to help set the tone and mood. Are you doing a futuristic game? We want lots of electronica and synth sounds. Is this a gruesome horror game? Perhaps some haunting violin. What about fantasy games? Acoustic-style guitar may work best. Here again, subject material is your best friend. See what others have done in similar situations and emulate as best as you can.

Sometimes quiet areas can be their own music, causing a player to be extra alert as mentioned previously. This can be used to introduce tension for a player in a foreboding fashion by helping them "gear up" mentally for a coming struggle. Using our previous example of the war zone with bullets whizzing by, now imagine it suddenly going quiet. That sudden shift in ambient tempo will cause an instant reaction in the player's senses.

Building Sound in Layers

Sounds are layers; layers that are heard at multiple times have to be planned to some degree or they will overwhelm and be confusing.

I tend to work on my sounds in the following order:

- Background ambient track first.
- Environmental ambience triggers next.
- Music after this, though it can be held until later if necessary.
- Jump scares and other more abrupt and loud sounds.
- In-game sounds like players, monsters, etc.

Thankfully, the store has a significant amount of these assets available at extremely low cost. There are also numerous sites on the Internet that will allow you to use their sounds as long as you follow the licensing requirements for them. (For more information on licensing, reference Chapter 22 on "Laws, licensing, marketing, and selling."

Zone-Specific Clutter

While you may have clutter laid down in the form of objects such as trash, plants, or other miscellany, it may just feel very overwhelmingly generic. This is where using zone-specific clutter comes into play. Generally, my rule is about 15–20% zone-specific clutter to about 75–80% generic clutter. This way, I can ensure the "flavor" of each zone is unique in some capacity.

- Graffiti.
- Signs and posters.

- Objects unique to an area such as specific equipment for a group or faction, an example being Fallout 4 and use of the "institute" equipment in institute-only areas.
- Story-specific hints or indicators, maps, etc.

These objects will really help give each zone a sense of both unity with the game and also a significant enough variation to make it unique.

Cutting Back on the Garbage

Too often we tend to kludge our way through a scene. Try to go back and reevaluate what you think is necessary and relevant. Cut down on the clutter, ironically. This type of scene optimization is not uncommon. Too many people go crazy with tons of junk everywhere, making it look like a scrapyard. The truth is, in most cases, there's a fine line between too little and too much. Invariably that's up to the eye of the beholder, but you want to capture as many eyes as possible in your view so as to increase your chances of being a hit game!

However, it really depends on where you are and what you are doing. Mostly try to strip out irrelevant clutter items that aren't useful to your scene. For instance, if you are in a computer processing center, you may not need a spilled milk carton or a pile of food in a corner. It's not useful for the scene unless you are displaying an IT person's bad hygiene. Wires, however, or maybe some conduit do make sense. Try to keep things as relevant as possible to the scene without going overboard on secondary assets that aren't necessary. Quality and quantity should be equally balanced. You might find that you have too many wires and need to pare back on them, so be sure to prune as needed. The chapter on optimization (Chapter 21) covers this pruning in greater detail. For now, just try to keep it in your mind as you build your scenes.

Lua Code Introduction

What is Lua?

Lua is the core scripting language used in GameGuru and, first, it's spelled Lua, not LUA. This is because it means the word "moon" in Portuguese, as it was designed by Brazilians Roberto Lerusalimschy, Waldemar Celes, and Luiz Henrique de Figueiredo. This simple, easy to use language has found broad acceptance in a number of applications.

The name moon comes from one of Lua's progenitor languages known as "Simple Object Language" or SOL, which also means sun. Lua is fast, portable, and easy to learn.

If you thought you shouldn't have to learn code, I am sorry to say that while that is technically correct, it's critical to your success as a game developer. The reason for this is that without learning even a shred of code, you will be utterly limited in what you can do. Other game development engines often use an intermediary system of "events" to get around the lack of desire most have for coding.

Plans have been in place for GameGuru to have a similar system, but it's never truly been implemented.

As such, you are either relegating yourself to only ever using the available "free" scripts that came with it or purchased scripts you will never understand. This, of course, is only true if you don't take the time to learn how to code. I can promise you a few things: It's not impossible to learn. Lua code is simple enough that even basic modifications are possible for anyone.

So let's discuss some features of Lua:

- Simplicity: This was literally designed as a language to allow programming by nonprogrammers. It's literally one of the best possible choices when presented with the myriad of options out there.
- Efficiency: Some Lua applications outperform native compilers.
- Portability: The code is usable on a number of systems.
- Extensible: Usable with extra extensions to add functionality.
- No memory management commands—meaning none of C's pointer and reference woes.
- Dynamic typing: Allows easy configuration of variable data types.
- Built-in text processing commands.
- A lightweight, stack-based virtual machine (VM) core that doesn't eat into in-game resources.
- Easily embedded into other applications (i.e., GameGuru).
- Support for procedural, object-oriented, functional, and data-driven programming

How is it Implemented?

Lua code is presented as a base language with some extensions that are GameGuru specific for utility purposes. This gives us a wide range of functionality from file control via built-in commands all the way up to GameGuru specific commands that control lighting on an incremental basis. It's implemented as a core feature within the GameGuru engine. It handles many of the "day to day" functions that occur within your game(s). When GameGuru initially was created, it used something called FPSC Programming Interface (FPI) scripting. This was a holdover from the old FPS Creator days and was considered a simple but functional scripting system.

However, early on in GameGuru's development cycle, it was decided to convert it to Lua coding. Now up to this point, I had no experience with FPI, and my scripting experience was primarily in the realm of C-like scripting or java-style scripting. Lua was an easy match. It has some odd caveats, however, that are somewhat unfamiliar for those who have used other languages; as such, it takes a little bit of a reorganization to understand it. We'll get to that later.

As it is, Lua has a compact, highly efficient core that operates within the GameGuru engine continually. Since it is such a crucial component, it's important to write solid code; otherwise, you might encounter situations that can cause Lua code to crash your entire game!

Simple Programs, Building Upward

A number of programs are included with GameGuru, or rather scripts are. They provide a fundamental backbone for you to work from. That said, you should understand some of the underlying basics of how to configure your own Lua programs. These scripts vary from opening doors to collecting ammo. They exist as either scripts that are operated when a player touches a "trigger zone," when the code is run manually via another process, or if it's attached to an entity.

Let's start with some of the most simplistic code possible. Implementing code in GameGuru is about as simple as anything I've ever done before. You will want a capable editor to start. I recommend using Notepad++, a free program available on the Internet. This program has some added functionality you can use to improve it, notably the Lua extensible markup language (XML) application programming interface (API), which I developed to help coding.

Installing the Lua XML API couldn't be easier. Now copy the .xml file into the plugins folder for your Notepad++ installation and restart the program. At this point, when you open a Lua file, it will auto-fill functions in for you and provide suggestions as well as a small bit of information about the actual function you are using yourself!

Before We Begin

Before we begin, it's important to understand a few fundamental principles of scripting or programming. These principles are very simple. First of all, scripting is a series of commands that make another program DO something. In this case, that other program is GameGuru.

Inside of a script, there are several common components to virtually any scripting language.

There are types of data such as strings, characters, numbers, integers, fractional (real) numbers, etc.

There are also variables: A name that can contain a certain type of value that is stored by the script or program. For example, a variable named "x-number-variable" could perhaps be configured to hold only numbers. It by default, however, is empty, unless you initialize it with a number. Try to name your variables something useful so that if you look at your code in six months, you'll know what these variables actually do! Variables come in two flavors: local and global. A local variable is one where it can only run inside of the code block you are working on. A global variable can be used anywhere. There are some performance considerations to both (see Chapter 21 on optimization for more details).

This is called "scoping," which determines how visible something is to the rest of the engine. There is a "global scope," which means all scripts can see it throughout GameGuru, and "local scope," which means it's only for this one particular program or function. This is useful if you are using something called "mytimer" as a variable in three or four different pieces of code but don't want them stepping on each other's feet. In that respect, you make them local by declaring them in this fashion:

Let's say you have a variable called "var_smallcup" with a value of "coffee" assigned to it.

As a global, it'd be declared as:

```
var_smallcup="Coffee"
```

For a local variable, you'd do it within the block of the actual function you are using it in and declare it as:

```
local var_smallcup="Coffee"
```

Now imagine that the function we are using is a desk; if we want EVERY desk to have coffee in their "var_smallcup" then we declare it globally. If we want to have only this one desk to have it, we declare it locally. Simple, right?

Now check this out: You can assign variables to variables!

Let's say we make a variable called "var_liquid1" and another called "var_liquid2" and we want to assign coffee to var_liquid1 (as we all know it's the more important of the two liquids) and water to var_liquid2, globally:

```
var_liquid1="Coffee"
var_liquid2="Water"
```

Now what if we have a series of local variables called "var_mycup" for several functions and they are to be assigned various liquids? It would then look something like this (note, this is called pseudocode and is not intended to be precise but instead a rough approximation):

```
function function1_main()
        local var_mycup=var_liquid1
end
function function2_main()
        local var_mycup=var_liquid2
end
function function3_main()
        local var_mycup=var_liquid1
end
```

This allows us to easily change several locations by modifying the earlier variable. So let's assume we want to change everyone who is drinking liquid1 to be "gourmet coffee." Instead of having to modify each version of the variable, we modify the original variable var_liquid1.

Lua's implementation makes variables extremely powerful due to the dynamic typing built into it. This means virtually everything (including functions) can be addressed as a variable or held in one. It allows you to literally build variables that are functions and other complex structures, which can make for some very creative code.

Variables are, in short, the lifeblood of virtually everything you do. The ability to store information, manipulate and use it is of paramount importance to scripting.

Constants are like variables, but in this case, they are names that have a value that never changes. For instance, if I set a constant to "mood" to "grumpy" then mood will always be grumpy. Please note Lua does not "per se" have constants included. Virtually everything you'd consider a "constant" is actually a variable in Lua. Mostly, it is in how you choose to use them—in that you will set a variable and never change it. The value in doing this is that you can call a variable and in doing so perhaps it makes it easier to understand. For instance, if you assign the variable v_green to 0, v_red to 1, and several other colors, then you can call them by their name instead of by a number, which can be somewhat confusing otherwise.

There are also functions: Functions are pieces of code that can be called directly, so that you don't have to rewrite the same code over and over again. For instance, a function might be called "eat_spaghetti()" and perhaps another function is called "put_spaghetti_onfork()." These would be called every time you performed those actions in code. Groups of functions are called "function libraries." GameGuru comes with a very comprehensive function library on top of the original Lua functions central to Lua itself.

Operators are the same as a mathematical operator; they do some kind of work between two things. For instance, if you add variable "number1_var" to "number2_var" in Lua and want to put it in a third variable, it would look like this:

```
Number3_var = number1_var + number2_var
```

Please note that in some scripting languages, at the end of every line, you need something like a ";" to show the end of a line, this is not necessary in Lua.

Now in GameGuru's implementation of Lua, there's a number of Lua scripts included with the engine. In all of these, there are several common functions that can be used. First is the "init" function. This happens before the main block of code is run and ONLY runs one time at the moment the program loads. This is useful for initializing variables, for instance.

Then there is the _main function. The _main function is your primary block of code, and it is run over and over again by the program. For efficiencies' sake, you are going to want to put something in there that prevents it from running unnecessarily—a check of sorts to make sure that it's not going to eat up precious CPU time trying to do something it doesn't need to. This function will run until the object is destroyed or code tells it to stop.

Lastly, there's the "exit" function. This function happens when the _main function ends, say perhaps on the termination of an AI entity. It's a lot like the init function in that it only runs one time, only in this case after main is all done. It's completely optional but can be used to perform one-time actions as the entity is being removed, allowing things such as respawning.

One last type of function bears mentioning and that's the "generic" function; this doesn't require any special designator but instead is just a second block of code that follows the convention for naming a function for Lua. This allows you to build your own functions for your script.

You might be wondering what I meant by "special designator" in the previous statement. To that end, when you make a piece of code, for example, let's just make one called "test_program.lua," this program's main and init components will look like this:

```
function test_program_init()
       mood_var = "happy"
end
function test_program_main(e)
       mood_var = change_mood(mood_var)
       if mood_var=="happy" then
              mood_var="sad"
       end
end
function change_mood(myvar)
       return "unsure" -- this generic function will return a new
         mood_var value
end
```

Now what this program does is start with a mood of "happy" and then change it to a mood of "sad." That said, there's no actual value to the mood variable. It's a string of characters, like writing a note on a piece of paper. We know this because of the quotations around the words, which designate them as characters. In the previous example, we use a generic function called change_mood to set it to "unsure" which will not pass the sniff test used by the conditional if statement.

That all aside let's get back to the topic at hand. You'll notice particularly that the init and main functions were preceded by the name of the Lua file and an underscore. This is the convention, or accepted method, in Lua of calling those functions. It is case sensitive so make sure you have the name correctly set! I have had numerous times where I modified code, changed the name of a file, or made some other minor mistake, and had the code not even run. It will literally cease to function if you don't get the name exactly as it is in Windows.

TIP: The version of Lua running with GameGuru requires that all Lua script file names be in all lowercase letters or in numbers. For example, NamE.lua is incorrect and name.lua is correct.

Another important factor here is that the code you include in a level, unless it is destroyed, will run over and over again. This means that effectively ALL code is looping and should be considered in a permanent loop state. We can use this to do some very interesting things, and also it keeps us from having to do redundant code like writing a second loop when one is already perfectly fine.

Basic Lua Commands

Now obviously this book can only introduce you to programming in Lua if you aren't familiar. That said, there are some really simple commands that can help you get started. Most of the commands in GameGuru (found in the Lua command reference in the Appendix) are fairly straightforward and easy to use.

The object here is for you to know what some common functions are and have some idea of what you are looking at so you can modify it.

It's actually fairly simple, but let's go over some of the easier ones very quickly.

Prompt

First of all, and probably the most simplistic of any commands is Prompt. Prompt places a blurb of text at the bottom of the screen for as long as it's being told to. If you aren't persistently telling it to use Prompt in your code, it will simply flash on the screen for the briefest of instants and be gone. The way around this is if you are only calling it once but want to see it for an extended period, use "PromptDuration," which allows you to specify not only a message to display but a period of time to display it. One important consideration here is that there is only one small area to display text for Prompt and as such you cannot use it for every single message you want to convey unless you accept that previous messages will get lost when you do. Coincidentally, this is the same command used by the 'text zone' now built into the newest versions of GameGuru.

For getting started, however, it's a great way to learn how to display information.

With Prompt, you can display all sorts of sensitive information and comment it out later. This is how I frequently "debug" my programs. Debugging, of course, refers to the process of removing problems from your code but ironically comes from an actual moth being found in a piece of early computing equipment that used vacuum tubes.

The following is a simple pseudocode example of a test_debug.

```
--test_debug=1
if test_debug==0 then
do_nothing()
else
run_debug()
end
```

Note in the aforementioned, I have a "comment"—this is an "unused line" of code that can be used for documentation and for rapid switches of code. In Lua, there are two types of comments. There's a "single line comment," denoted by two minus signs. This will comment a single line of code, as you may imagine. The other type is a "block style" comment that will do a huge block of text and is useful for writing long paragraphs about your product(s) or even to remove whole sections of code. It's done in this fashion:

```
--[[
This is a comment block.
Everything in between the brackets up top and below will be
  considered a comment.
]]--
```

Note that in this particular example, there's a massive block of code. If you do not "close" the block with the corresponding ending bracket and minus signs, it will comment out all of your Lua code. Now going back to our original example, you can see the "Prompt" command is commented out. This command is located inside of the loop and is called every time the player stands in the trigger zone that is running the script.

Just remove the two minus signs and now every time the player stands in that zone, they will trigger a check on whether they are in it. That check will pass and at the bottom of the screen a line with your Prompt message will display.

There's a significant value in being able to display text on screen, so correspondingly there's a lot of powerful control functions you will find later in the command reference. These range from positioned text, colored text, and even to things like loading your own font!

(e) is for entity

One very unique concept in GameGuru is the "entity" value, which is a unique number given to every entity and is called "e." This value has a local value inside of every single object in the game of "e." So this means that if you ever see somewhere that a bit of code calls for a variable called "e" then it will use that entity's entity id. This means you can self-reference an entity by calling "e" directly.

While this may seem confusing, I can assure you it isn't.

Think about the English language. When you talk about yourself, you say "I." It's the same thing here. Whenever an entity has Lua code, if it's talking about itself, it says "e." For example, let's say we want our entity to produce a prompt that says "hello" at the bottom of the screen. This code will be for a typewriter named "typewriter." The Lua code will be named "typewriter.lua"

```
typewriter_init()
end
typewriter_main(e)
local how_far = GetPlayerDistance(e) -- how far is the player from
  this entity?
      if how_far < 150 then
              Prompt("Hello, I am a talking typewriter!")
      end
end
```

The aforementioned code is very simple. It first loads itself, then creates a local variable that can't be read by any other code other than this code called "how_far." This "how_far" variable then runs the function "GetPlayerDistance," using the current entity running the code (e) to run a distance check to the player.

If that distance is less than 150 units, then it will display text saying "Hello, I am a talking typewriter!"

Easy, right?

There is one additional caveat bearing mentioning here. That is that sometimes you will see (especially if you peruse the Lua command reference in the Appendix) that a function can take an "e" as a value.

This means you cannot only self-reference an entity by using "e," but you can also call an entity directly if you know its entity ID!

For example, let's say we have a box in a hallway that when the player approaches causes an object down the hall to play a sound. For us to do this, we need to know the entity id of the object down the hall; so we have to mouse over the object in the editor, and you will see the entity id on the bottom expressed as {# | #####}. The entity id is the one on the left. Our test code looks like this:

```
boxtrigger_init()
end
boxtrigger_main(e)
local how_far = GetPlayerDistance(e) -- get distance of player from
  current entity and store in how_far
        if how_far < 200 then
                PlaySound(2,1) -- play entity #2's sound #1.
        end
end
```

As you can see the previous code is again very simple; this allows us to set up interesting events such as the one here, which allows an NPC to whisper to the player from afar, "Hey, come over here kid."

Timer

In every game engine, there is a timing cycle running, which allows the game to coordinate events. This timing cycle is probably one of the single most critical things running invisibly in a game engine. It gives a precise way to control when something happens. GameGuru's engine is built around simplification of this timing system to ensure that you are always able to know exactly how much time passed and where.

With GameGuru, there are a few basic timer commands as well as some advanced ones. We will focus for the time being on the very basic ones, notably "StartTimer (e)" and "GetTimer (e)."

StartTimer creates a timer relative to the entity (e) that will basically start counting seconds passed of difference between it and the "game time." So this allows us to create a timer for individual entities that can be used to trigger events. The timer is measured in milliseconds.

GetTimer returns the current value of the entity (e) and the associated relative timer. So let's use our previous example of the box triggering a man talking. This time we're going to have it trigger only after three 3 seconds, and it will only run one time. We'll call this script "boxtrigger2.lua."

```
boxtrigger2_init()
       bt2_hasrun = 0 -- a means to remember if this is the first
         time running or not.
end
boxtrigger2_main(e)
local how_far = GetPlayerDistance(e) -- get distance of player from
  current entity and store in how_far
     if bt2_hasrun == 0 then
           StartTimer(e)
           bt2_hasrun = 1
     end
local bt2Timer=GetTimer(e) -- store the current timer value for
  this entity into bt2Timer.
     if how_far < 200 and bt2Timer > 3000 then
           PlaySound(2,2) -- play entity #2's sound #2.
     end
end
```

In this case, entity 2's sound #2 is "How long are you going to stare at that box, kid?"

You may have noticed I like to "tab" my conditional checks, this is common practice to help make code more readable.

PlaySound

From our previous example, we learned a new command, the PlaySound command. PlaySound seems fairly self-explanatory but does require a bit of intelligence to use. It won't just play a sound without any context. If you recall earlier, the properties pane in the editor has a little area at the bottom for sounds. Each of the various entities have their own set of sounds. This is, of course, cleverly referred to as a SoundSet. These typically are arranged by number from zero to four. The official "PlaySound" function usage is PlaySound(e,v). So we already know e is the entity we want to use, but what is v? V doesn't have any special in-GameGuru function other than it signifies a "value." So in that respect, "v" is almost always something completely variable and unique to the function.

So in this case, value represents the specific "SoundSet" slot that you will be using, which corresponds with a configured .wav or .ogg file that can be played by GameGuru. It also plays it "from" the entity, meaning it tries to scale the sound's volume in proportion to the distance the player is from the entity. This gives it a slightly more realistic 3D feel. The sound system obviously has a significantly more in-depth code structure, but this will get you started.

Math Functions

Math is a massively important element of Lua, as well as virtually every other computer language created. As such, it's important you understand the sheer depth of math functions available. The following is just what comes with Lua, not even counting the custom ones developed just for use within GameGuru:

> *math.abs math.acos math.asin math.atan math.atan2 math.ceil math.cos math.deg math.exp math.ceil math.floor math.log math.log10 math.max math.min math.mod math.pow math.rad math.sin math.sqrt math.tan math.frexp math.ldexp math.random math.randomseed*

As you can see, there's a whole HOST of math-related functions that can really empower your work. Most of these are traditional math functions you'd find on any scientific calculator, and so you can find an explanation of them anywhere. There are a few that require a bit of discussion, however, as they are fairly unique to programming and not math in general.

Math.random is a massively useful function that will return a random value between two values. It's written like this: *variable = math.random(1,3000) – returns a value between 1 and 3000 and stores it in variable.*

Seems simple, but it can also return any number in between, which can be problematic if you get say "2996.000" followed by "2996.994." Sure, both of these are random, but you're more likely just looking for 2996 in both cases. This is where the next one becomes important.

The second is the Lua function "math.floor and math.ceil," which allows you to set a floor or ceiling on your math values so as to prevent the number from ever exceeding a potential maximum or minimum. It also forces the value to be an integer, which means you can always ensure you're getting a whole number that's above or below a minimum value (depending on which function you use). Floor will give you the integer above the "floor" you specify and ceiling will do the opposite.

Let's say you want to transform a number to an integer that never exceeds 255. This is useful if you're doing calculations that are say affecting a slider every second or so and incrementing one of the color sliders. The pseudocode would look like this:

```
function genericfunction_init()
        gfRunonce = 0 --gf stands for generic function
end
function genericfunction_main(e)
        if gfRunonce == 0 then
                StartTimer(e)
                gfRunonce = 1
        end
        local gfTimer = GetTimer(e)
        if gfTimer >= 1000 then -- every 1 second do the following:
                local randNum=math.floor(math.random(1,255)) -- choose
                  a random integer between 0 and 255.
SetAmbienceRed(randNum) -- Set the current screen ambience "red"
  color to whatever randNum is.
                StartTimer(e) -- restart the timer.
end
```

Now if you've never worked with code before, hopefully by now, you're starting to see it crystalize in your mind. There's a whole slew of Lua-related functions you can find detailed information at www.lua.org in the latest user manual. The previously mentioned "math.floor (math.rand (1,255))" and other similar variants will be something you find yourself doing very frequently if you are intending to randomize anything. You'll also notice that our function called another function. This type of function calling is completely legal and valid in Lua and is done in the order of "last in, first out." This means the first one done is the last one read, or in this case, the math.rand function is run before the math.floor function.

If Then...Else

Conditional logic such as "if, then, else" is found in virtually every single language in some form or another. It's a staple of coding, and I'm willing to bet you've probably at least been exposed to it in some form or another in the past. It goes like this:

```
if condition meets certain criteria then
	do some things
elseif another condition meets another certain criteria, then
	do another thing
else
	do something for anything leftover.
end
```

We can use this to make some fairly heavy-duty decision trees for anything from AI to weather control. Conditional logic is the core of virtually every decision made by a script.

We can even "nest" those decision trees to provide even further control of the conditions being used. For example, let's modify the previous example so that the second condition actually triggers another if statement.

```
if condition meets certain criteria then
	do some things
elseif another condition meets another certain criteria, then
	if condition2 is greater than condition, then
		do the first possibility
	else
		do the second possibility.
	end
else
	do something for anything leftover.
end
```

So in this example, you can see that it first executes a check on a "condition" and if that fails, then it executes another check on the condition. Assuming that matches, then it launches a new conditional check against an all new condition. This can go on virtually forever with enormous checks that span pages of code. It's important therefore to "tab" your code out each time you add a new if statement. Note, only do this for if statements, not elseif. This way you can ensure that you always know what layer of the conditional logic you are on.

Now in the case of many other languages, there's often other codes you can run to do even more complex tasks such as "switch…case." However, in Lua, it's distilled down to only using if, then, else. While this does result in some very ugly logic trees, it does at least keep it relatively simple since you only have a very limited number of choices to use for your code. It also ensures that anyone even remotely familiar with if…then…else statements can read your code.

This means in order to do something similar to a "switch…case" statement, you really just have to do a number of "elseifs." So it will look much like this:

```
if condition meets certain criteria then
        do some things
elseif another condition meets another certain criteria, then
        do another thing
elseif yet another condition meets certain criteria, then
        do yet another thing
elseif ....
        You get the idea...
else
        do something for anything leftover.
end
```

While not very sophisticated, it does allow us to do a nearly identical work to the common "switch…case" statements used in other languages.

Another thing that needs mentioning here is the use of logical and relational operators. These operators are basically comparisons done mathematically in Lua that have to follow strict rules.

Relational operators look like this:

== *"Are the operands equal?"*
~= *"Are the operands not equal?"*
< *"Is the operand less than the other operand?"*
> *"Is the operand greater than the other operand?"*
<= *"Is the operand less than or equal to the other operand?"*
>= *"Is the operand greater than or equal to the other operand?"*

As you can see, just from that alone we have a great deal of comparisons we can perform. Logical operands are "and," "or," and "not." This allows us to say "if comparisonA *and* comparisonB then…" to see if both comparisons match in a single if statement. We can also go with situations where only one or the other works, hence the use of "or." Lastly, of course, we have "not," which says to only accept it if the comparisons don't match at all.

All of this works within parentheses as well so you can order your comparisons by using parentheses to ensure that certain comparisons are done first before others. An example would be if you had three comparisons as follows:

if comparisonA or comparisonB and comparisonC then …

In this case, it will check to see if comparisonA works at all or if B and C match.

However, by reordering it with parentheses, we can get a completely different result:

if (comparisonA or comparisonB) and comparisonC then ...

In the latter example, what this will do is first compare A and B and then if either of those match as well as the third one, it will work. A simple restructuring with parentheses is all it takes to completely change the statement!

String Manipulation

Strings are another highly essential component of your programming in line with math. They allow you to store data without regard for what they contains beyond their being an alphanumeric series. This means you can store text and codes in a way that can then be manipulated by various functions to whatever end you desire.

Much like in math, Lua has a very extensive string function library. This allows you to do all methods of transformations, changes, and checks on strings stored in variables. Lua allows access to advanced string manipulation functions such as:

string.byte, string.char, string.dump, string.find, string.len, string.lower, string.rep, string.sub, string.upp, stirng.format, string.gfind, and string.gsub.

All of these are documented extensively within the manual you can find at www.lua.org and should probably have bookmarked by now!

Let's return to our example "if…then…else" code from earlier. We're going to use it to illustrate some of the more simplistic but still very useful string functions.

```
textchecker_init()
        textvariable="PerfEct"
end
textchecker_main(e)
        if textvariable == "perfect" then
                Prompt("Success, no changes!")
        elseif string.lower(textvariable)== "perfect" then
                Prompt("Success, but had to lowercase the string!")
        else
                Prompt("No success.")
        end
end
```

You'll notice here that we barely scraped the surface of the available commands for string manipulation. It's a long road with a lot of options, but be aware that if there's some way you need to manipulate text, someone has likely already done it. Plenty of examples exist around the web. Some of these string functions aren't all that intuitive, like string.find, which returns the position values and not what it finds. This is useful, but other times what you want is something like "string.match," which will search and display text found according to a pattern you specify.

Now that you've got a fairly decent foundation for working with Lua, feel free to take a look at the free scripts included with GameGuru. I'm sure, by now, you will see them with renewed understanding. Keep your questions for later, though; we'll have much more to cover in the advanced Lua chapter (Chapter 13).

12

3D Math ... Made Easier

I realize that GameGuru is billed as an "anyone can do it" engine and, to a great degree, this is very true. However, there are some complex things you will benefit from knowing—rudimentary mathematical principles that, in turn, will provide you a great foundation to work from. I'll be the first to admit I use a fairly unconventional approach to math. I tend to try to provide a simplistic understanding of complex materials because, in general, I find that math as a whole tends to overcomplicate things as a result of its layered approach to learning. I do, however, highly recommend taking some of the free courses (if you need them, of course) available at sites such as: https://math.mit.edu/academics/online/index.php or https://www.khanacademy.org/math

You know how growing up, you would see people talk about how useless learning all that fancy math in algebra and calculus was?

"I don't need this to count my groceries!"

Well... with computers, that type of learning is actually highly useful and something you can put to very good use. With 3D graphics, having a strong math background will help you significantly. In the interim, however, I think I can at least give you your "sea legs."

Cartesian Coordinates

The first of these foundations is the subject of Cartesian coordinates. This system should at least look familiar to most of you.

The simple grid in Figure 12.1 illustrates a positive X grid, a negative X grid, a positive Y grid, and a negative Y grid. This provides a very easy way to map two-dimensional coordinates. It provides a backbone for pretty much all things computer graphics and gaming related. This, however, only gets us part of the way.

To break it down further, positive X is up, negative X is down. Positive Y is right and negative y is left. This method was used for development of 3D style games that were actually two-dimensional such as "Doom" or, more notably, "Wolfenstein." A common technique with ray-casting engines is to translate a two-dimensional Cartesian grid into a functional 3D image using a technique called "ray casting." Ray casting works by taking fake "rays of light" and casting them out from the camera source (the player).

Where those rays intersect, they then create a vertical strip that has its size determined by the distance it has from the actual "ray caster."

This, in turn, creates an image like that shown in Figure 12.2.

Now this is obviously a very simplistic method of 3D world building and has long since been discarded as there are far more effective methods available. I do,

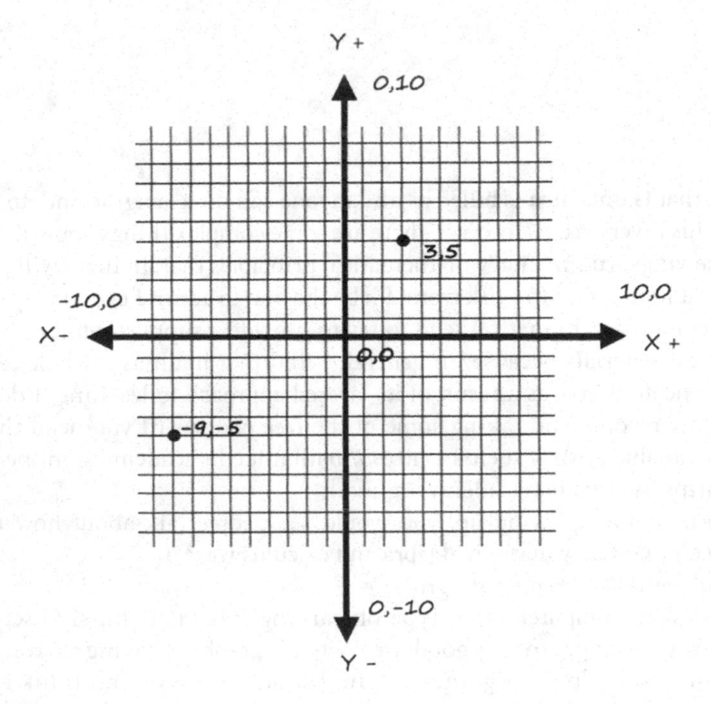

Figure 12.1

A demonstration of Cartesian coordinates.

Figure 12.2

A demonstration of a simple raycasting engine.

however, believe you will benefit from understanding it as ray casting is still in use in today's engines. Most notably when you use it in GameGuru, it will be from a Lua script to do what's called "hit scanning" for weapon hit detection; also some scripts use this to determine if you are looking at a specific location or object.

Furthermore, another common use of Cartesian coordinates is what's called texture mapping. As you can see in Figure 12.3, the difference when texture mapping is added is considerable. Now if you've built your own 3D models before, you can likely skip this section. If not, however, you should understand that, in our previous example, we took a two-dimensional grid and mapped that out using ray casting to create an image. However, you

Figure 12.3

A demonstration raycasting with texture mapping and lighting applied.

should have noticed the image was entirely solid-colored. I did this on purpose. One of the earliest users of the ray-casting method on a PC was "Hovertank 3D," as previously mentioned. This particular game has flat colored panels that were either light or dark colored based on their NS/EW orientation. So depending on what plane (the geometric flat surface, not the flying object) you looked at, you got a different shade of color. As computer graphics technology increased, so did the possibilities. One of these techniques was called "texture mapping." Used prominently in "Wolfenstein 3D," it took a two-dimensional bit-mapped image (a computer picture) and read the coordinates from the Cartesian map in the 2D picture. It then applied them to the strips it was drawing on each "wall" surface.

This technique of "mapping" a texture, of course, is still in use but is actually referred to now as "uv mapping" whereas the x/y of a picture is now u/v. We'll get to that later, but in effect you can now take a 2D picture and wrap it around extremely complex objects like the image in Figure 12.4.

So, you see? Understanding something as simple as a two-dimensional Cartesian grid allows us to do very complex tasks within game engines. We're not working with an old-style ray caster, however. We're in a fully 3D system, which means we need to use 3D coordinates, aka 3D Cartesian coordinates!

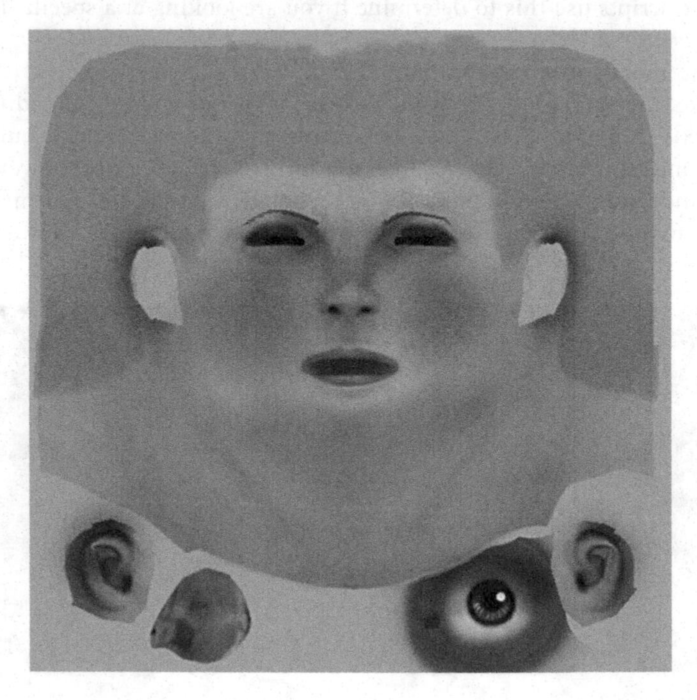

Figure 12.4

The graphic used for a face has to wrap around very complex shapes.

In a nutshell, 3D coordinates are a lot like 2D coordinates, only with a third axis (a line in which a curve or figure is drawn/measured/rotated/etc.) called positive z and negative z.

This positive z represents a forward of zero, and negative z represents a backward of zero. Now if for some reason math is tough for you, which is understandable, don't feel bad. This concept is something that can grow on you simply by doing. My son has learned about X/Y/Z axes (pronounced ax-ease) simply by using GameGuru at a very young age and so can you! Just try to keep it somewhere in the back of your head so when you start working with the 3D systems, it makes more sense to you.

This "Z" axis movement allows us to effectively define the depth of an object, which now gives us a real ability to create incredibly robust 3D objects and render them in real-time. It is of course wholly dependent on system hardware and architecture, but we've come a long way since the late '90s and "Quake" running on a Voodoo II card with 12 mb of RAM.

Euclidean Vectors

Euclidean vectors are a mathematical principle that effectively shows a direction a 3D object is moving. Seems simple, right? Of course, once you see it on paper it's often very confusing.

However, if you put aside the bad math teachers and their relative inability to dumb down concepts, it's actually fairly simple to understand. First, you have your starting position and object represented by X/Y/Z on a 3D Cartesian coordinate grid (don't you feel smart just saying that?). Now we want a means to say "this object, located at X/Y/Z is moving to this location X/Y/Z along this path." The direction it takes is commonly referred to as the 3D or Euclidean vector. It has two properties to it:

A magnitude (how far?)
And a direction (which way?)

Now vectors are actually tremendously important in 3D math, and there are entire collegiate curriculums dedicated to teaching you all about them. All I expect you to understand is when I say "this is a vector" that I'm talking about the magnitude and direction a 3D object is taking in a 3D space.

You can do a lot of really cool stuff with vectors. You can determine the velocity and acceleration from it; you can use it to plot direction, move objects, find the distance between objects, and a great host of other very valuable uses.

Normals

No, I don't mean "normal people" but rather a normal vector, which is a type of vector (you remember, magnitude and duration?). These vectors represent a perpendicular vector starting from a surface and perpendicular to a point. Sure, that is easy, right? I mean we all remember calculus... Don't we? I wonder how many of you had to go search "perpendicular" because you don't use it enough in your normal daily nomenclature (you searched that one too, didn't you?).

Fancy two-dollar words aside, this type of vector is especially useful in our hobby. This specific mathematical principle is used when you need to move a small amount toward a distant point in a 3D space. For instance, let's say you have a character who is standing in a field.

In that field, in the distance, is a gateway. You want to walk your character to that gateway. You cannot simply go directly to the barrel with a vector. Otherwise, you will instantly be there because you'll omit all the little incremental moves that take place along that vector to get you to that location. Instead, you make that journey in a series of steps. Those steps are obtained by "normalizing" the vector. So what you are in effect doing is taking the vector to that barrel and reducing its direction to a length of 1. This will give you a smaller and more specific unit you can use to multiply by to obtain the movement amount. Let's say you want to make that distance 50 steps. You would then multiply the "normal vector" by 50 and that'd give you your total amount of movement for ONE step.

Normal vectors also allow you to describe which way a plane (or flat surface) is facing as it can be a vector perpendicular to the plane itself.

Dot products are a comparison-based math operation done on two vectors that will give you a very simple result as to what direction these two vectors face. For instance, it will tell you in one single number (a –1, 0, or 1) whether the two vectors face the same direction, perpendicular directions, or opposite directions. It's one of those "fast and dirty" math operations designed for bulk operations without really complex formulas.

The "cross product" is a math operation on two vectors that results in a third vector. The order in which these vectors are put in matters significantly. A good example here is for collision detection and movement. That said, it's a bit outside the scope of what you'll ever find yourself using inside of GameGuru unless you're really into math. There are entire libraries of articles dedicated to these topics. My goal at this point has simply been to get you just thinking about them. By planting that seed, you can expand your own mental toolbox to build bigger and better games!

A Brief Note on Quaternions

This is going to be my last topic in math. I am saving it as it's the most complicated and also one of the most useful. Aside from being a highly funny little word, this complex mathematical function has a really simplistic usage. It allows you to rotate a three-dimensional object without actually killing yourself—or the computer—with unnecessary math with things like Euler angles or rotation matrices.

Basically, what a quaternion does is allow you to basically pick a point in 3D space (using our Euclidean vectors, as mentioned) and treat that as the axis of a spinning object via an angle represented by θ. So in effect, you have three separate components. You have your 3D vector (X/Y/Z), your fixed 3D axis of rotation (I/J/K), and your angle of rotation around the axis…

I'll be honest, it's all a bit heady at this point. Bottom line though is they allow you to rotate objects very smoothly with minimal CPU power. It's something that is supremely useful if you want to rotate a 3D object off-angle while having it follow a trajectory of some kind, like a spaceship. Thankfully, AmenMoses, a GameGuru forum community member, has made a completely free quaternion function library for us that allows us to use these functions easily and quickly to rotate objects in a 3D space using quaternions.

13

Lua Code, Advanced

Now we're going to get into the nuts and bolts of making custom code with GameGuru. With respect to Lua, one could write an entire book on that alone. So I cannot possibly go over every single command and the usage in detail, respectively. I can, however, go over some of the more complex functions and help walk you through them to jump-start you toward more complex tasks.

There is a massive store of commands available to you, most of which are fairly self-explanatory. That said, there's some very sophisticated usage you can perform with even the most basic commands. Do you remember the first command we covered?

Prompt Revisited

If you recall, in previous iterations you could easily display text, but what if you wanted to display variables? What about if you wanted to combine types of data and display them for the purpose of debugging your code? Well, all of that can be done if you use the right procedures.

As you know, you can pass text by placing it in quotes, which is fairly simple. We've done this before.

```
Prompt("Hi")
```

This, of course, isn't particularly interesting. How about if we have a variable display?

```
simplevar="Hi"
Prompt(simplevar)
```

This, of course, works for the most part without incident. If you use a number, however, it makes the most sense to cover your bases by using a function to convert it to a string first. This function is just called tostring and is used in this fashion:

```
simplevar=5
Prompt(tostring(simplevar))
```

As you see, you can nest functions to achieve a desired result. You can even do sophisticated methods like this:

```
Prompt(tostring(math.floor(math.random(1,10))))
```

In this case, what is specifically happening is everything is going from right to left as the nested functions unroll in this order:

```
math.random(1,10): Chooses a random number between 1 and 10.
math.floor -- Turns the random number into an integer.
tostring -- Converts the number to a string.
prompt -- Displays the now-converted string in the GameGuru test
  game mode.
```

So as you can see, this allows us a fair amount of flexibility, and it bears mentioning this can be done with virtually every function in Lua!

You can also merge values to format the display with a combination of text and numbers. The following example will give you a better sense of how to accomplish this.

```
simplevar=5
simpletextvar=" is "
prompt("The value for simplevar" .. simpletextvar ..
  tostring(simplevar))
```

This is because the double period in Lua is a special operator that concatenates strings together and thus allows us to build entire statements out of disjointed pieces of logic and code. Remember, this isn't something that is only done with Prompt but extends throughout Lua as a whole and can be done rather easily once you get the hang of it. The important thing is to close all of the functions with their requisite parenthesis, to convert numbers to strings, and also to not forget to include things such as the ..”” for concatenation.

Tables and Arrays

If you have any experience with other programming languages, you're probably familiar with something called an array. Arrays, for the uninitiated, are lists of stored values that can be recalled for later use. For instance, a typical array in the common language C would look like this:

```
int numarray[5]={2,4,6,8,10};
```

This particular example says "create a list of five integers: this list will contain a specified number at positions corresponding between zero and four." Please note that C arrays start at position 0, so it's not "1–5" but "0–4."

So for instance, if you were going to store the second number in the array (shown as 1) to the variable "x" it would look like this:

```
x=numarray[2];
```

We are, mercifully, not here to learn C code today. We're here to learn how arrays work in Lua. Arrays, being a tremendously powerful data manipulation tool, are hugely important for many different reasons.

So how do we create arrays in Lua?

The answer to this is simple: We don't.

Lua, believe it or not, doesn't use arrays… at least in the conventional sense. It uses something called tables instead. Tables are a special data construct with a huge amount of flexibility and very little sense of order to them. They present a whole series of new potentials and unconventional methods that can take a little getting used to.

First, and possibly most importantly, tables are dynamically typed. This means that they can store any type of data in Lua, which means you can have tables holding strings, numbers, functions, or even other tables!

That's right. You can make tables containing tables to create multidimensional data sets. This flexibility in data sets allow you to create incredibly complex programming structures.

We start by "initializing" the table. Typically, this is done in the _init function for an entity's code so that it's not called multiple times but instead is only done once upon loading the program.

Initializing a table is done by simple using this format:

```
tabletest={}
```

The table here, called tabletest, is now initialized. It's empty, of course, but can hold any type of data as mentioned. At this point, tabletest can now be accessed by a key, which also can be whatever you want.

The access method is similar to how an array is accessed in C. However, since it's completely dynamic, this means keys are literally created as you define them.

So let's say, for example, you want to assign a string with a value of "hello" to the first key in the table.

So we use this method of assignment:

```
tabletest[1]="Hello"
```

Seems easy enough, right? What if I told you that you could also use a string as a key? Let's demonstrate:

```
tabletest["two"]="World"
```

So… that's a little weird, right? I mean, how does it know what is what? Well, it does order them in a sense, but they are essentially stored as a giant slush pile. This allows the completely dynamic typing that allows us to contain combinations of data. So let's say we want to sequentially navigate this array; this can be exceptionally tricky since Lua stores them as keys, not as an ordered array. This means in many cases its unordered, despite perhaps if you were to make an array using sequential positions.

There are ways to access these data in a reasonable fashion, but we'll return to that later. There's lots of functions and codes that can be manipulated to provide us with a means to easily manipulate these data.

If, for instance, you store everything with a sequential integer value, you can access it fairly easily. While it's technically not actually in sequence, your keys are numerical and thus easily accessed in numerical order. So what do you do when you want to add to the "maximum" known number? Just use the symbol #, which represents the "largest" value of a table. For instance, if you have a table set up in this fashion:

```
newtable={}
newtable[1]= "hello"
newtable[2]= "world"
newtable[3]= "dudes"
```

Then, if you access newtable[#newtable], you will get "dudes" as your output. Similarly, we can add more data to the end of the stack by using:

```
newtable[#newtable+1]="and gals"
```

This code would now be equivalent to newtable[4]= "and gals," simply put.

Where this becomes valuable is when you are automating certain functions without a clear idea of what order they will be added in.

For Loops

Now up to this point, we've been using our built-in game loop, which I tend to prefer for performance efficiency's sake. There are, however, times where you absolutely need to go through a preordained loop. This is often done for loading variables or performing repetitive actions such as reading a file.

So, loops are fairly traditional and follow a standard format:

```
for starting_value, min_or_max value, increment_value
do
        stuff()
end
```

So how this works is there are three values we have to feed to the loop. This starts with an initial value that says where the loop begins. We then say we're only going to do it until a certain condition is met, specifically a minimum or maximum value. Finally, we say how much each loop will increment our loop counter for each iteration of the loop.

A practical example is as follows:

```
local x_var="0"
for local i=1, 10, 1
do
        x_var=x_var .. tostring(i)
        prompt(x_var)
end
```

So what this loop does is first assign an empty string variable named "x_var." It then loops through using a local index variable called "i" 10 times (starting at 1, adding 1 each iteration until it reaches the maximum of 10). In the process of that loop, it takes the current value of x_var and converts the current value of the loop index "i" to a string, then concatenates it with x_var. Now this happens very fast, so if you test it in game, you will only see the final output, but if you slowed it down significantly, you'd see it show output like this:

0
01
012
0123
01234

And so on until it reached the final value of 012345678910. Simple, right? Please note that loops are to be used with great care as they can cause the system to lock up indefinitely as Lua will dedicate all of its resources to completing the loop. If the loop is too big, it will cause a long pause in the game's processing as everything stops while Lua finishes the loop.

Now personally, like I said previously, I don't like to use these types of loops. That performance hit isn't worth it when there are more efficient ways to use the main game loop. There are a few particularly notable exceptions, however.

Do you remember the previous section on tables? Well, turns out there are a series of Lua-specific commands that you can use for loops to help you figure out what your tables hold. This is particularly useful for having a solid list of data with which to work from. Before we can do that, we need to know two new functions. The first is called "pairs" and the other is called "ipairs." These two commands allow us to iterate, using a for loop, through our tables and come up with all the juicy bits it has.

The best way to do this is to use this format:

```
for k, v in pairs(newtable)
do
        tempvar = tempvar .. "| ." tostring(k) .. "." tostring(v)
        prompt(tempvar)
end
```

So first, the k stands for key (like a table key) and v stands for "value," as in a table value. You'll notice the format of this for loop is different. When it is used in this way, Lua assumes that it will step through the loop one increment at a time. What this code does is go through every single key in the table and gathers its key and value. This way we know both the position of the table entry and its corresponding value. We then do a similar method of concatenation as we did previously, only this time adding in a "|" and a blank space to help make the output more readable.

I bet now you realize why this chapter is called advanced Lua, right? This is fairly complex stuff that honestly took me quite a while to wrap my head around, and I've been programming in various languages since I was a kid almost 25 years ago. That doesn't even count my many years of actual professional experience doing programming or my schooling! If you feel lost, just take your time and try to work through it a piece at a time until it makes a bit more sense.

So before, I mentioned "pairs" and "ipairs." You may be wondering what the difference is. It's a fairly substantial difference, so pay attention! The ipairs () function will go through each numerical key entry ONLY, and it will stop as soon as it hits a nil or empty value. Pairs will go through all keys, numerical or otherwise, but there's no assurance it will do them in any particular order. This is often useful for getting the output for later sorting if you are using something akin to a sparse table that has missing entries in it.

Another exceptionally valuable way to use a for loop inside of Lua is to read a file! Before we do that though, we need to go over some of the core functions that Lua can perform, notably the "io" and "os" functions. These functions allow you a terrific amount of control over a user's system, so take care with them!

The "io" functions are as they sound: input and output functions. A few of the primary ones are:

io.open, io.close, io.flush, io.input, io.lines, io.output..., etc. There's an entire section of the handbook on Lua.org that details these functions and their precise usage. I mostly just want you to understand as the reader that you CAN use these functions inside of GameGuru! This allows us some fairly exciting prospects such as writing data files or save states if you are so interested! You could also use it to do things such as read text from files for NPC output. File accesses obviously should not be done unless necessary as they are significantly slower than reading data from memory. That said, it still allows a broad range of potential for the user(s) and can really provide you with some fantastic utility.

Before we begin with actual code, you need to understand the basics of how file usage occurs within Lua. It's handled in this fashion:

> First, a file is opened. A method of opening is specified: either read, write, append, read+ (all previous data are preserved), write+ (all previous data are erased), or append+ (all previous data are preserved and all writes are written to the end of the file). You may also specify to use the file in binary format instead of standard American Standard Code for Information Interchange (ASCII) format.
>
> Next, things are done with that file—either items are read if it's open for read access or written if it's open to being written/appended to.
>
> After we are done, we close the file and save any data we want to write to it, if we are writing to it.

This process MUST be followed in this fashion or you will encounter errors. Virtually every single error you get from opening a file will be a result of you not following the process, skipping a step or command, or trying to do something too many times (such as repeatedly opening the same file).

With respect to how we will handle this in Lua, we're going to assign the file opened to a special file object that can then have special methods called descriptors used on it to perform tasks such as writing.

So now that we understand the basics, let's test it out. First, we'll make some very simple code to open a file for use, then write output to it. Then afterward, we will load that same output into a numerically sequenced table using a for loop.

```
—— code start
local file = io.open("test.txt", "w") -- open our file for writing.
filetest_init()
       redamb_var = GetAmbienceRed() -- grabs the color values for
         ambience
       blueamb_var = GetAmbienceBlue() -- of red, blue, green and
         stores them in
       greenamb_var = GetAmbienceGreen() -- global variables
       ft_haswritten = 0 -- a simple flag to show if the write
         occurred yet
end
filetest_main()
       if ft_haswritten == 0 then
              file:write("Red Ambient|" . tostring(redamb_var))
              file:write("Blue Ambient|" . tostring(blueamb_var))
              file:write("Green Ambient|" . tostring(greenamb_var))
              ft_haswritten==1 -- we're done, it's written
       elseif ft_haswritten ==1 then
              file:flush() -- save the file
              file:close() -- close the file
              ft_haswritten = 2
       elseif ft_haswritten == 2 then
              prompt("File successfully written!")
       else
              prompt("Something went seriously wrong if you are
                seeing this!")
end
```

Now in the previously example, you'll notice things like "file:write," "file:flush" and "file:close."

This is a method of using functions that apply to specific objects. Since our file object is literally called "file," we are saying "I want test.txt assigned to the object variable named file to write three variables to it, then save itself and close. After that we display a success or failure message."

Simple stuff, I'm telling you. This is really easy if you don't let it bully you into feeling intimidated!

Now the reason we're using the descriptor method is if we have several files, we can do things to many of them. For example:

```
local file = io.open("test.txt", "w") -- open our file for writing
local file2 = io.open("notatest.txt", "r") -- open a second file
  for reading
file:write("blah blah blah")
local x = file2:read() -- reads a single line from file 2, stores
  in local x
```

This is an overly simplified demonstration that should give you some idea of how multiple files are handled using descriptors.

Now you'll notice that the read() command only reads a single line.

The answer to this is to use a for loop for reading our data.

Example

```
	—— code start
	local file = io.open("test.txt", "r") -- open our file
	  for reading
	filetest2_init()
		ft_hasread = 0 -- a simple flag to show if the
		  write occurred yet
	end
	filetest2_main()
		if not file then break end -- if file is empty/not
		  there, then exit filetest function
		if ft_hasread == 0 then
			local lines = {} -- create a table called
			  lines
			local tempvar = "" -- initialize this for
			  later
			for line in io.lines(file) do
				lines[#lines + 1] = line
			end
			ft_hasread==1 -- we're done, it's written
		elseif ft_hasread ==1 then
			file:close() -- close the file
			ft_hasread = 2
		elseif ft_hasread == 2 then
			for k, v in pairs(lines)
				do
```

```
                        tempvar = tempvar .. "| ."
                          tostring(k) .. "." tostring(v)
                End
                ft_hasread =3
        elseif ft_hasread == 3 then
                prompt(tempvar) -- display final results
                  of file read, shòwing contents of file
        clse
                prompt("Something went seriously wrong if
                  you are seeing this!")
end
```

So in a nutshell, what this does is open the file and then test to see if it's there. If it IS there, then it will continue; otherwise, it will stop processing this code via the break command. As it continues through, it will set up some variables for holding data along with an empty table. It will then go and read our file, populating a separate item of the table with a correspondingly sequenced line from the file it reads. It then joins that information together as a string and displays it. You may have noticed, if you were paying attention, that both the reading and writing codes were simple state machines like that mentioned in the "adding effective enemies" chapter (Chapter 8)!

So as you can see, we've steadily built your skillset up from simple code that uses nothing more than a prompt to display all the way into the realm of file reads and table population. It doesn't stop there, either. Lua code is tremendously flexible, and there are hundreds or even thousands of commands available in GameGuru that can allow you massive flexibility in whatever you choose to attempt!

14 Adding Advanced AI

So by now you can place, position, and use your AI in a reasonably effective fashion. It's time now to really open up the potential of the GameGuru engine by using all of the little tricks and shortcuts available to you. Surprisingly, there's a well of really interesting techniques if you stick within what's available to the engine itself, regardless of whether you use Lua or not. Using Lua adds more function than you can imagine, to the point of literally writing your own AI from scratch if you prefer.

Waypoints and Nodes

A significant amount of players rely on how immersive the game is to keep them "in it." This ability to suspend reality hinges heavily on constructing a believable simulation for the player. Few things are immersion-breaking as AI that is simply standing there, waiting. This idle state, while totally natural to the AI, is probably the least desirable way to operate your AI. You want them moving around, patrolling, and actively performing tasks as their "idle." Often the big name AAA developers have something called a "sandbox" mode for important AIs that allows them to interact with the environment. Now while we don't have a sandbox mode, we do have a way to make the AI seem like they are doing something while they are in the game. The way we can do this is with something called waypoints.

Before we begin, let's do a quick discussion on how AI navigates terrain.

As mentioned previously, we have our state machines and fuzzy logic. What happens is when the AI is in a navigation mode, such as chase or attack, it will attempt to "read" the terrain so it knows what the local area looks like and then navigate around obstacles toward the player. The AI's goal will be to constantly move toward the player in most cases as this is just simple math to find a player's position and head toward it (Figure 14.1).

So while a "chase" algorithm is super simple, it's also prone to problems if there are obstacles. For that reason, provisions need to be added so the AI doesn't get stuck on everything in between.

For this reason, it will check for obstacles periodically, by scanning the local area for hitboxes. It then tries to navigate around them using logic.

The other method of navigation is a node-based form. Nodes are locations that act as a guide for the AI entity for movements that are chained together in some fashion. In GameGuru, these node chains are called "waypoints" (see Figure 14.2).

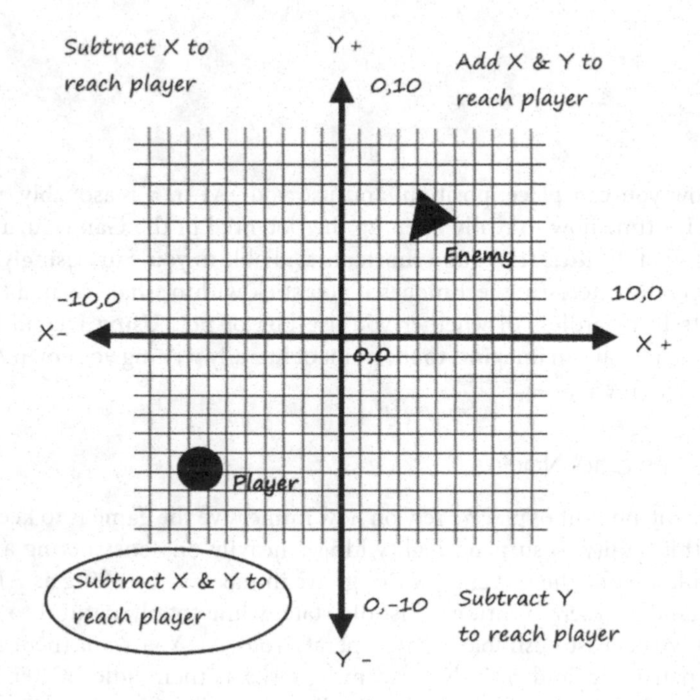

Figure 14.1

Using simple math to chase a player on a Cartesian grid.

Figure 14.2
A demonstration of waypoints in GameGuru.

Using Waypoints

If you recall, way back at the beginning of this book, we discussed the GUI. By now, that component seems fairly elementary to you, I'm sure. Looking back, however, you may remember we only glossed over the two buttons at the top for waypoints: notably "add waypoint" and "edit waypoints." These two are the bread and butter of our editing process for waypoints.

The way GameGuru works is that if an AI is near a waypoint, it will try to use that for navigation if it's idle. This way you can create paths that the AI will walk on, to appear as if they are performing functions such as patrolling or heading to a store.

Adding waypoints is a fairly painless process. When you first go to add one, you will get a little star-shaped icon with a yellow outline in the middle of your viewport. You can click and drag to position this little star as the primary start marker of your waypoint chain (Figure 14.3).

From here, if we shift-left click on the node, it will add another, which we can also drag. As we drag it, a line will be drawn indicating the path the waypoint will provide for the AIs navigating on it. These "secondary" waypoints are always subservient to the master waypoint created by the initial star of an "add waypoint" click. Using a shift-right click will remove a waypoint and reorient the chain's list.

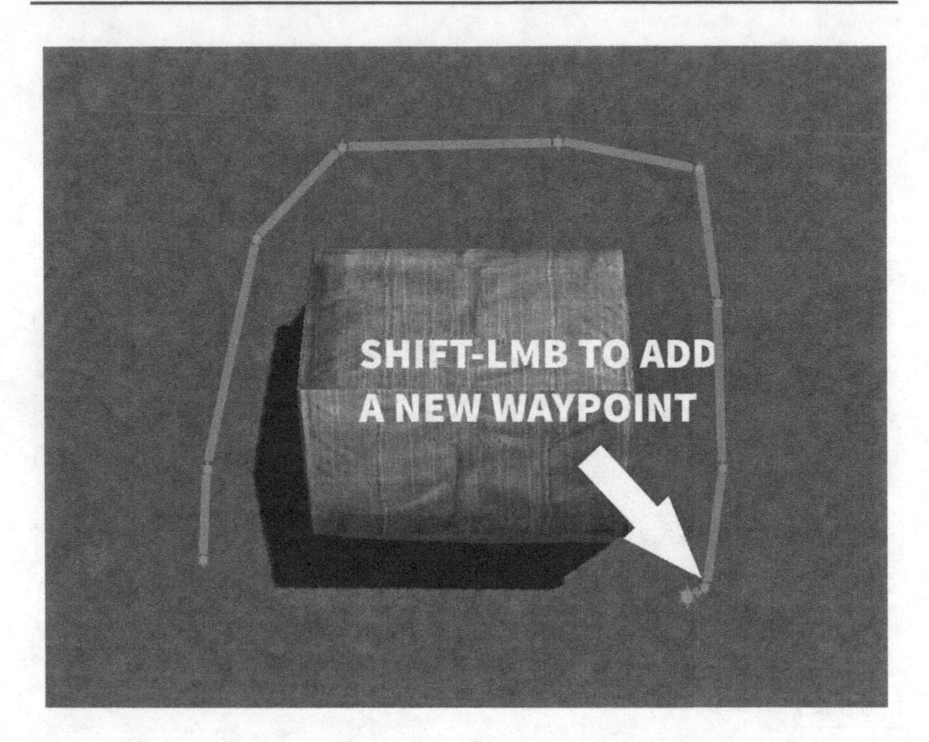
SHIFT-LMB TO ADD
A NEW WAYPOINT

Figure 14.3

Adding a waypoint in GameGuru.

This continues, indefinitely, until you add another waypoint. At which point, you begin a new node chain. You can have multiple, intersecting node chains for the AI to navigate. It will pick the nearest "start" node and use that chain to navigate. Bear in mind that these nodes are sequential, so they are numbered invisibly so that even if the AI starts on node 3, they will always follow the chain to the next one in a descending fashion.

AIs will generally try to find the nearest waypoint and walk along it if they are one of the included AI scripts. This means ones such as ai_soldier.lua will automatically seek out nearby nodes and use them, so there's no additional work there. That said, the range is relatively short, so you will need to either place it very close to the AI entity or move the AI entity onto the nodes. It needs to be within 200 "units," which is a fairly close distance in the editor.

If you are having trouble clicking the nodes to move them then your best option is to enter waypoint editing mode (Figure 14.4). This is done by clicking the waypoint mode button at the top or by clicking the M key on the keyboard. This will disable the editor's clicking of entities so you don't constantly get properties' popups when you're trying to access the waypoints.

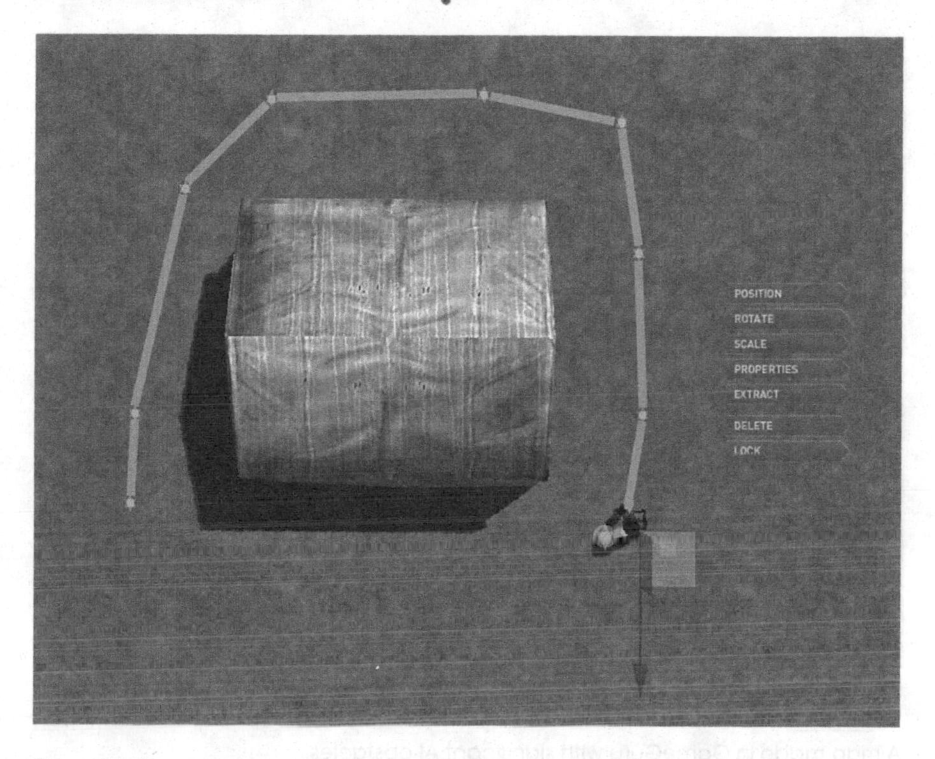

Figure 14.4

An entity must be placed within 50 units of a waypoint to use it.

Waypoint Tricks

Waypoints do not always have to act as a chain. In fact, if you have a highly complex terrain, you can actually use them in moderate numbers as a navigation mesh for when the AI is having trouble getting stuck on certain objects. Placing nodes nearby that help "reset" them when they drop out of combat is a really great way of ensuring that they assist the AI with pathing to the player if it gets stuck. Bear in mind this should only be done for extreme circumstances as typically when the level is built, there's a mesh built already. This mesh is typically during the phase where it says "creating AI obstacles."

This however, is not always perfect, as you will see.

Figure 14.5 is an absolute nightmare for the AI to navigate. There are too many physics objects in odd positions to easily calculate a path through the maze. Very frequently, the AI entities will get stuck on chairs or tables and stand there, waiting for the player to move somewhere so they can "unstick."

If an AI entity runs out of combat, however, they will either stand idle or move to a nearby node if you've placed one. This is where this method really shines.

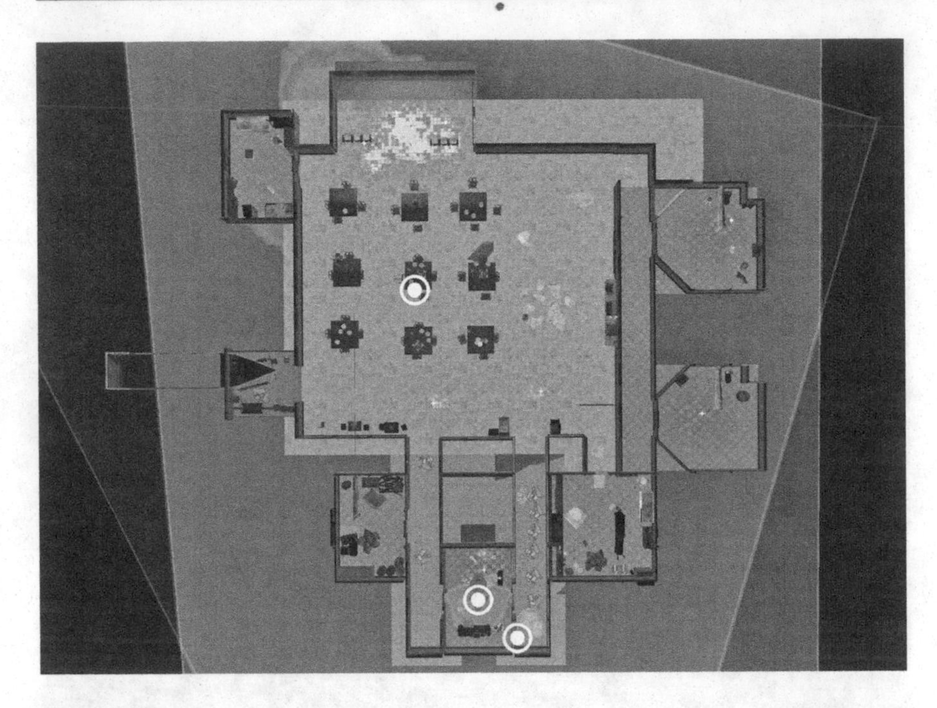

Figure 14.5

A map made in GameGuru with significant AI obstacles.

You'll notice I have only a few nodes that are actually lines, the rest are just starting points placed in between intersections of tables to help AI reset when it gets stuck (Figure 14.6). This is primarily because I kept encountering situations where the AI would literally just walk into a chair and not do anything until the player would angle correctly. This created a whole host of problems for navigation.

The solution came to me when I looked at the AI code. I realized that it would try to reset itself to a nearby node point so it could reorient. Obviously, you can make these node chains if you prefer, but the reality is that even just having the points placed created a horrifyingly difficult enemy to defeat. Anytime it would get stuck and the player would get away, it'd find a way out of the maze of chairs and tables to attack the player again.

Floor Zones

Floor zones are an important part of your AI's functionality. Normally, when the AI obstacles are built, they will work around a generic flat plane that is used for navigation. What happens, however, when you have a rooftop that you want them to be able to navigate to? How do you get the AI up there? With floor zones, we have a solution. A floor zone will give the AI a navigable plane that you can place

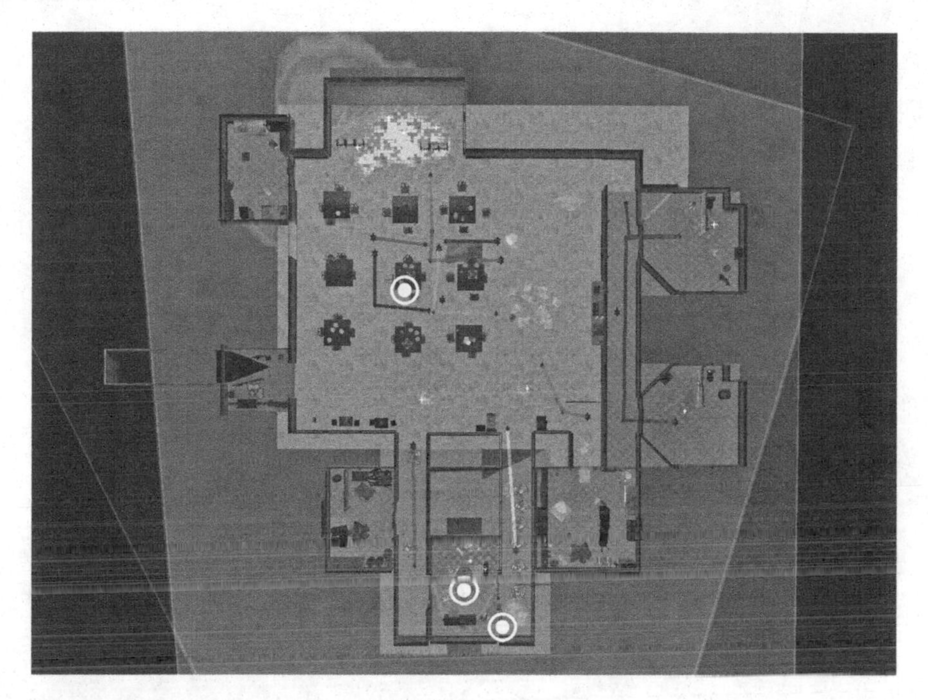

Figure 14.6
The same map, with waypoints to help the AI navigate.

at any height you want so that it can operate on multiple levels in the 3D space of your game.

If you go to the "Markers" tab on the left (as shown in Figure 14.7), you will see your list of various light markers and zones. The one we are looking for is of course titled a "floor zone." What this does is allow the AI to function on an area that is elevated or lowered in an unconventional way. When you choose a floor zone, you will see a blue square with several yellow stars on the corners.

The white circle in the middle is how you select the floor zone so you can position it. The yellow stars work much like waypoints, allowing you to click and drag the size to get the appropriate shape.

What's important here is after you set your floor plane, you need to connect it using a waypoint chain. This way the AI can traverse the terrain up to it via stairs or ramps. This also, of course, implies that you have a ramp or stairs available. Please note if you intend for your AI to only function on a rooftop, then you can skip this step.

There are also times where I have to place a floor zone for indoor areas because otherwise the AI will fall into the floor and stand there unable to figure out what it's doing. This, however, is more often the function of an incorrectly set FPE file. Either way, it's still a useful workaround if you cannot find a solution readily.

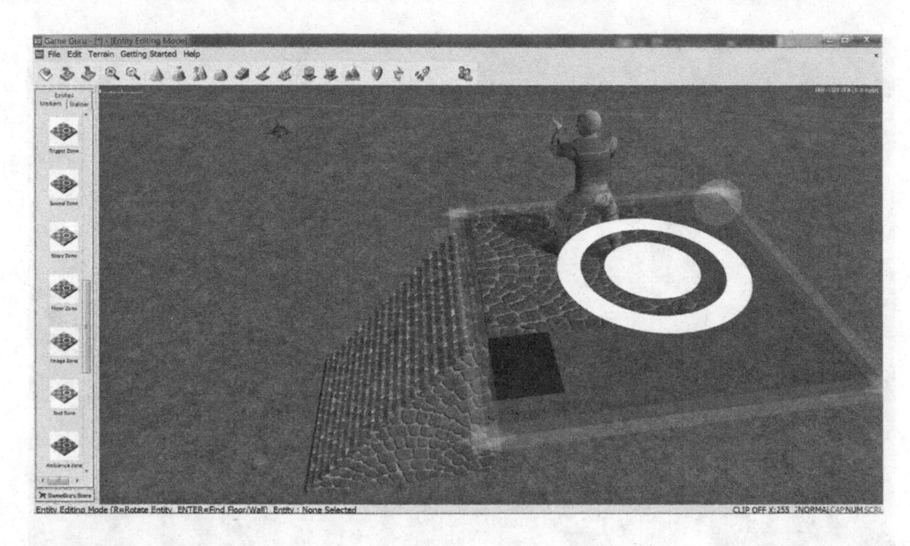

Figure 14.7

Using floor zones to place enemies above the terrain floor.

Cover Zones

Concealment isn't cover. This is a way of saying that just because you can't be seen doesn't necessarily make it a bullet stopper in the real world. Hiding behind drywall is marginally safer than standing in the open, for instance.

GameGuru doesn't have obstacle densities, thankfully. In the case of this game engine, any weapons that fire a hitscan "bullet" either hit or they don't. The AI can use cover to help protect itself by hiding behind obstacles that can give them some survivability. It does, however, require some help understanding what is considered cover and what isn't. We do this with special areas called cover zones.

Placing a cover zone is fairly simple. Once again, we're going to go to the "Markers" tab on the left. Once you go there, find cover zone in that list and place it on the map. You get an orange zone with yellow stars on each corner. These, as usual, adjust the size and shape of the zone. There's also an arrow for orientation that sets which direction they are going to take cover in. You want to rotate the arrow so that they are not hiding on the wrong side of objects.

When you set a cover zone over an area, the AI will attempt to hide behind any objects that are 40 units or higher or approximately half of a normal character's height. In this respect, it's important to make sure all of your objects they are trying to hide behind are of sufficient size; otherwise, they won't attempt to use them as cover (Figure 14.8).

Let's say you have a room with some barrels and boxes to provide protection. You want the enemies to use these to help increase the challenge to the player. We want to make sure we are creating difficult-to-hit enemies while at the same time trying to create a believable environment for them to be working from. Barrels

Figure 14.8

Demonstrating how enemies will use cover if it's properly sized.

and boxes, for instance, seem effective enough, but what about something like a store clothing rack? Should this be a place the enemy cowers behind to stay safe?

It's important to try to keep this in mind when working with cover zones.

Not all AI scripts support cover zones so use ai_soldier.lua or, if you want to be absolutely safe, use ai_defender.lua instead.

AI Tricks: Spawning

With AI, there are some clever implementations that we can do that don't really fall into their own individual category. For instance, how would you like to spawn an enemy when a player runs through a specific area? We can accomplish this by placing our AI entities, setting their spawn to no, and then setting a trigger zone with an IfUsed field matching the AI entity name! (See Figure 14.9.)

⊟ **General**	
Name	Trigger Zone
⊟ **AI System**	
Main	plrinzone.lua
If Used	Shotgun Soldier
⊟ **Media**	
Sound0	audiobank\misc\soundtrig...

Figure 14.9

How to spawn entities using the IfUsed field.

This is a great way to create surprise encounters, spawning enemies behind the player to catch them off guard. As you might expect, if you have several enemies with the same name, they will all spawn simultaneously as well.

AI Tricks: Respawning

Respawning is actually a fairly complicated feat in GameGuru. I've included some example AI, but it needs a lot of custom code to get it working. Regardless, it can be done. It requires a pretty detailed understanding of Lua for the time being. Feel free to check out ai_respawn.lua and the respawner.lua scripts if you're interested in accomplishing this.

Creating a Circuit with Waypoints

By default, a waypoint chain will cause the AI to walk from one end to the other in a back-and-forth pattern. If you want the waypoints to create a "chain" to link together, you can loop the AI in a circuit pattern.

On one hand, you need to know how to use Lua to modify the next bit.

On the other hand, it's an extremely easy bit of code, so we can do this with minimal work. The default waypoint "intelligence" is that it will walk on the chain back and forth going from one end to the other. If you create a circle or circuit with your chains that loop back onto each other, it will ignore this and continue to bounce back and forth. Unless, of course, you modify the code.

So, for example:

If there are five waypoint nodes, normally, it will go from one to two, two to three, etc., until it hits five. Once it hits five, it will reverse and go five to four, four to three, etc. Once it hits one again, it goes back up to five. In this case, we'll be modifying it to go from "one to five" and then restarting at one again. This way we can create a circular loop.

This is not supported by default but is fairly simple to do.

If you open "GameGuru\files\scriptbank\ai\module_combatcore.lua," you can find a few lines that look like this:

```
if ai_bot_pointdirection[e] == 1 then
        ai_bot_pointindex[e] = ai_bot_pointindex[e] + 1
if ai_bot_pointindex[e] > ai_bot_pointmax[e] then
        ai_bot_pointindex[e] = ai_bot_pointmax[e] -1
        ai_bot_pointdirection[e] = 0
end
else
       --some irrelevant code here.
end
```

So to make this loop, all we need to do is change this line:

```
ai_bot_pointindex[e] = ai_bot_pointmax[e] -1
```

To this:

```
ai_bot_pointindex[e] = 0 -- Reset the waypoint chain
```

And, voila! It will then loop on a circuit. I do recommend making a backup, as usual, or at least copying the line and commenting the old one out like this:

```
ai_bot_pointindex[e] = 1 --ai_bot_pointmax[e] -1
ai_bot_pointdirection[e] = 1 -0
```

It's important at this point to make sure that you set the end point and start point close to each other so it loops smoothly.

Indoor AI Fix

Over the years, there have been a number of issues with GameGuru's AI entities, notably on indoor areas. Most of these have to do with the way the node mesh is built for the entities as it generates the AI obstacles. Indoor entities sometimes are difficult to figure if it's an obstacle or if it's to be walked on. There's a workaround, however.

So for example, let's assume you are using a model that looks like the one shown in Figure 14.10.

In this picture, you can see that there's a floor and ceiling but nothing else. It is part of an old kit I have that allows you to rapidly snap together rooms. It often has issues, however, with AI and so you have to open the FPE file for it and find this line:

```
'forcesimpleobstacle=#'
```

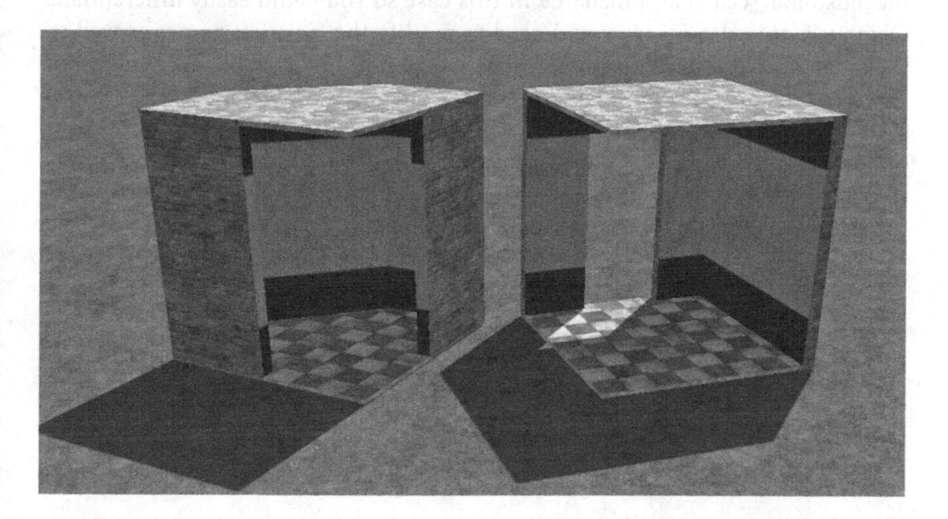

Figure 14.10

Snap-together levels can sometimes cause AI issues that require an FPE fix.

In this, what you want to do is modify the line to have a 3 instead of a –1 or 0 as it is likely to have. This will make it clear to the AI that it can walk on this object. Unfortunately, this is a full poly scan so it can be pretty impactful from a physics performance standpoint if there's a lot of odd geometry on your models. For elevated areas, you'll want to combine it with a floor zone to make sure the entire thing operates optimally, but it safely works with both in that respect. Some users do this by default to ensure maximum compatibility with their game though I prefer to make sure it's going to be necessary first so I don't have to eat unnecessary CPU cycles.

Lua, in AI

In the early days of FPSC Reloaded and GameGuru, Lua was something that was only barely supported. As the years ground on, however, we've had significant functionality added to the GameGuru layers that were previously hardcoded. One big improvement was with the AI system, which adds a wide range of features to the point where the entire AI code is built into Lua at this point in time. This means you can calculate anything from cover zone locations to waypoint nodes to the orientation of the player! There's literally no bounds to what you can do here, even going as far as writing your own AI if you so prefer!

I recommend going through the actual AI code directly to get a real good handle on it. The primary starting point will be something like ai_soldier.lua, which then has included files of "GameGuru\Files\scriptbank\ai\module_combatcore.lua." Your starting point would be to copy the module core files and rename their functions to their new names. I'd use something like module_customai_cc.lua as a filename in this case so you could easily differentiate. Obviously, this also means you'd need to modify the function names as well so they matched your new filename. After that, go nuts and try changing values for speeds or distances. Start small and work from there. Maybe modify the patrol systems to randomize their pattern a little bit instead of going linear. There's tons of books on the topic of AI and, admittedly, this would have to be an entirely separate book just to scratch the surface. For a full list of AI Lua commands, see the reference index in the Appendix of this book.

15

Advanced Engine Tricks

GameGuru is a fairly simplistic engine when you boil it down to its core components. It has a decent terrain system, a mid-range lighting system, some basic AI, a very basic character creator, and a host of other similarly set up features. The primary strength, of course, is that it's easy to use, specifically for people who are just getting started in game development. So when I say "advanced engine tricks," you very likely are scratching your head and wondering what specifically I'm referring to. There are a whole host of "hidden" settings that are never seen from the user interface (UI) perspective that allow you a significant degree of control over your game's output. There are also several undocumented "special" options that can give you an edge in your game's development.

Two files in particular provide an extreme degree of control over your GameGuru experience. The first is the "setup.ini" file, which has some many hundreds of settings you can toggle or configure. Some of these we will cover later specifically pertaining to performance, while others are useful for debugging. A few even open up possibilities for game makers to make games for virtual reality (VR)!

The other file is the settings.fx file, which controls your shaders and how they are configured on your system. This is an extremely powerful file with a great deal of highly complex settings in it that can produce some pretty amazing effects.

Setup.ini

The setup.ini file is a single resource of both mystery and great power. It's minimally documented but has a myriad of powerful functions that control everything from which video adapter is used to what keys are assigned. So much so that there's not enough room in this book to cover every single function. Thankfully, there are tools that have evolved over time to help simplify the modification and use of this file. As with all core game engine files, you will want to make a backup of the file before you begin.

There are a few settings here that demand specific attention; many will be covered later in Chapter 21 on optimization. In the meantime, we will cover the other pertinent settings. You can use either a text file editor like notepad or notepad++. You may also choose to use the free third-party setup.ini editor that I've included with our materials for this chapter.

Most of the settings in this file operate as a toggle, something you can either set to one or zero to configure whether it's on or off.

Some pertinent settings not used for optimization are:

fulldebugview=0: Setting this to one will give you drastically more debug information when the level is run, in case you are having some difficulty with your level.

terrainbrushmax=1000: Setting this higher or lower controls the maximum size your circle can be in the editor when hitting + or –. Bumping this up to 10,000 allows you to make enormous changes to terrain or with the "i-key" spray tool. This can be an advantage when working with large terrains.

defaultterrainheight=600: This controls the base height for the terrain in the game. It's helpful particularly when using a heightmap import tool so you can control where the terrain starts and ends. You can also set this height lower than your base water height (see as follows) to make a more watery map if you desire.

defaultwaterheight=500: This controls the base height for the water plane in the game. In years gone by, this was more important as it was the only means of controlling the height, but now we've got in-game sliders or Lua so it's really only useful now if you don't want to have to keep reconfiguring it each time you load.

forceloadtestgameshaders=0: Setting this to one will cause the GameGuru engine to recompile shaders each time, which is useful if you are modifying shaders or using settings.fx modifications (see the next section). If you don't set this to one, your settings.fx changes will never actually update the shaders! If you are using stock shaders, then you have nothing to worry about.

vsync=1: Set the monitor vsync to either off (zero) or on (one). If you set it to one, it will lock FPS at a maximum of 60, which is sometimes desirable for a consistent and smooth game experience.

Settings.fx

There's a lot of very comprehensive, powerful features we've worked with up to this point. Settings.fx takes it to another level. It allows you to directly modify the shaders of the engine in such a way that you can completely change the way they handle certain elements of rendering.

So what is a shader, exactly? A shader is an extremely powerful bit of code that performs a function on rendering, often for special effects or post-processing. Shaders were primarily driven by Pixar, who originally used them to "shade" surfaces. Since then, shaders have grown into a much bigger and more powerful system that is used to do anything from painting the reflection on water to providing bloom post-processing.

These extremely sophisticated bits of code allow you to perform near-miraculous changes to your game. Now assuming you aren't capable of writing your own shaders (like most of us), you might wonder what this has to do with you.

In the case of GameGuru, we have a very capable group of users, one of note being Preben Erikson. Preben's been writing shaders into GameGuru for a very long time. Many of them are exceptionally powerful but virtually all are disabled by default. This is to ensure stability with the engine, though we can readily dispense with that if we want to push the engine to the limit.

If you use Windows Explorer and navigate to your GameGuru folder, then files, then effectbank, you'll see a series of folders. The one we want is the "reloaded" folder. This folder has been there since FPSC Reloaded, GameGuru's previous iteration.

Inside of that folder is a file you can once again edit with a plain text editor like notepad or notepad++, the settings.fx file. This file has a lot of commenting and notation that is fairly self-explanatory. Comments are not like those in Lua; they use a C-language syntax so they use two // marks to indicate a comment. Enabling or disabling a shader is as simple as adding or removing commenting on ones you want to modify. So, for example, by default FXAA (a post processing anti-aliasing effect) is enabled.

For example, this line can be found in settings.fx:

```
#define FXAA//enable/disable FXAA
```

If you were to change it to this:

```
//#define FXAA//enable/disable FXAA
```

it will disable the FXAA post effect. Now, obviously, we probably want to leave this on to ensure graphic fidelity. However, if you are looking at the settings.fx file, and I hope you are, you will likely be getting some interesting ideas. For instance, you might be wondering what happens if you remove the two //s in front of one of the myriad of shaders that are disabled.

Some of particular note are:

```
//#define CARTOON//enable/disable cartoon (cel) shader.
```

Have you ever seen a modern game or video series where it's obviously 3D modeled but appears to be a cartoon? While it's entirely possible that someone could have hand made the thousand or so textures to make it look that way, the reality is it's much easier than that. What if it was simply a shader, changing textures according to a simple mathematical formula to produce that sort of output? Well, look no further. This is a very powerful shader that will impact your final framerate, but if you want to garner that look for your game, it's definitely worth investigating.

```
//#define NOCOLOREFFECT
```

This particular shader, when enabled, eliminates the "red screen" that is set up in GameGuru by default for when a player gets injured. Many users find this particular feature undesirable, so this was added as a means to modify that setting.

```
//#define ADDSKYBOXFOG//Add some fog to the skybox.
```

Keep fog colors below 94 if you use lens flare.

So this one is near and dear to my heart, specifically for my "advanced time of day and weather" system. If you enable this shader, it will allow your fog to creep up into the skybox. This will allow you to create exceptionally realistic twilight or night scenes and is a big part of the reason my time of day system was so effective.

```
#DEFINE FASTROCKTEXTURE
```

If you don't like how your textures are stretching for mountains, you can opt to take a slight performance hit and comment this line out with two // marks. This will give you better terrain mapping over high elevations.

Configuring Other View Modes

In GameGuru, it's very easy to make a game that fits the normal criteria for a first person shooter. This, however, is not all it is capable of. The game engine is capable of other "modes" of gameplay, however, primarily dictated by the player start marker. For instance, you can lock the camera at various angles of view to achieve: A top down game, possibly for racing or the like or a third-person isometric game, like a tunnel shooter. Doing this may require using specialized levels that have no rooftops. There are serious limitations to this type of game style, primarily in that you can only use one assigned weapon and have to pretty much code everything from scratch for the character's modeling and what not. However, for a very simplistic game type (say one type of gun), it works well enough.

A 2D-style side scrolling game: This is one of the more difficult ones as it has the same limitations as the previous game, and you run the risk of having ledges the player can accidentally fall off of. This means, of course, you need to create two transparent planes that the player can play between (invisible walls) to "hold them" in their flat little game that you make. It is, however, totally configurable.

All of these are done via the start marker's settings file. Third person is possibly the easiest to set up as you simply have to drag an entity onto the start marker to configure that. Enclosed are some examples with the materials of this book.

An Introduction to Custom Particles

Particles are a component of most modern game engines that allow you to create some fairly impressive graphical effects with more life than say your average sprite sheet. It's a fairly simple procedure, really. You take a graphic that is either a sprite sheet or a single picture and move it around. It is still a two-dimensional object, a flat pane of glass with a picture drawn on it, but it moves, lives, and dies.

I mean that literally, of course; it actually has a life cycle. This is typically referred to as it's "decay." So particles are born, go through whatever their life cycle is, then die.

Where they are born is called an "emitter." This is specified within the engine using Lua commands, specifically "ParticlesAddEmitterEx" and "ParticlesAddEmitter." The engine supports approximately 100 simultaneously emitters, though I don't recommend going nuts for performance reasons. Emitters are hidden entities inside of the engine. You cannot place them with the editor or GUI but can place them with code.

For future reference, both of these commands are functionally identical with one key difference: Ex allows you to bind a particle emitter to an entity whereas the latter command uses the player as a point of reference. This means for most situations, you will be using "ParticlesAddEmitterEx."

Now if you look in the Lua index later on in the Appendix, you'll see that these commands are among the most lengthy and difficult to use properly without some concept of what goes into them. Being that this is our primary initiator for an object to emit particles, we need to configure this properly to control most of what's going to happen as an effect.

Let's review this command quickly so you have some idea of what you're working with.

ParticlesAddEmitterEx: ParticlesAddEmitterEx(particleid, – create a particle emitter with the following parameters. animationSpeed, startsOffRandomAngle, offsetMinX, offsetMinY, offsetMinZ, offsetMaxX, offsetMaxY, offsetMaxZ, scale StartMin, scaleStartMax, scaleEndMin, scaleEndMax, movementSpeedMinX, movementSpeedMinY, movementSpeedMinZ, movementSpeedMaxX, movementSpeedMaxY, movementSpeedMaxZ, rotateSpeedMinZ, rotateSpeedMaxZ, lifeMin, lifeMax, alphaStartMin, alphaStartMax, alphaEndMin, alphaEndMax, frequency)

Wow! That is a LOT of commands.

Let's start with "particleid." Your particleid is a free emitter, which you obtain with a different command and assign to a variable. For your purposes, it's an entity ID pointing to an emitter that can spit out your sprite(s).

Next is the animation speed. This is how fast the animation for your sprite sheet is going to cycle. This, in turn, depends on how many actual frames are in your sprite sheet. It acts as a divisor or even multiplier based on how many FPS you want your particle to operate at. Let's say you have a simple eight-frame animation. To make it operate at 32 fps, you would need to set your "animationSpeed" value to four. Conversely, if you had a 64-frame sprite sheet, you'd set the value to .5: Whatever it takes to transform your sprite sheet # of frames to frames per second. If it's less, you multiply, and if it is more, then you divide! It's fairly simple once you get the basic concept.

startsOffRandomAngle is a setting that allows you to choose with a one or zero binary flag if the angle will be randomized on the generation of the particle.

The offset values allow you to set the position of the emitter in relation to the entity it is being placed on. This acts as a range, and so you have to specify a minimum and maximum.

The scale values will allow you to specify how much the object will "scale" or stretch through the life cycle of the particle. This also acts as a range.

Movement speed of the particle is also controlled as a range through a series of inputs here in a similar range as previous commands.

Rotation, you will notice, only has two inputs on one axis: the Z-axis. This is because it is a three-dimensional space but a two-dimensional object. There is no need for rotation on three axes.

Lifemin and lifemax are the range of how long these particles will "live" for in milliseconds.

Alpha values are the transparency values for the particle's life cycle again presented as two series of ranges. This allows for variability in the particles' transparencies to give a more realistic feel to some effects.

Frequency is a simple numeric value in milliseconds of how often a new particle will be generated.

So really in a nutshell, the process is this:

- Set an image to use.
- Get an emitter and assign it to a dynamic variable in Lua.
- Attach the emitter to an entity and have it start spitting out particles.

Obviously, there's more than that, but at the very core that bare minimum will get you started.

Please bear in mind when your emitter is done being used you will need to clean up your mess so if you do use a particle system. I recommend "freeing" emitters by using the ParticleEmitterDelete command to clear old emitters. Inside of Lua, we have a fairly extensive amount of support for sophisticated Lua functionality and control of particle systems.

A partial list of these commands includes: *ParticlesGetFreeEmitter, ParticlesAddEmitter, ParticlesAddEmitterEx, ParticlesDeleteEmitter, ParticlesLoadImage, ParticlesSetFrames, ParticlesSetSpeed, ParticlesSetAlpha, ParticlesSetAlpha, ParticlesSetRotation, ParticlesSetLife, ParticlesSetWindVector, ParticlesAddWaterLineEmitterEx,* and more. There's a lot of functionality as you can see, and, as you can imagine, there's a significant amount more than can be properly explained here. I highly recommend you check the enclosed samples for this chapter as well as the forums for a more detailed understanding. A link is included in the hyperlink reference Appendix.

An Introduction to Custom Physics

The physics subsystem in GameGuru is a very powerful mechanism that allows you to produce realistic effects entities and objects in GameGuru. This system, while somewhat intensive from a processing standpoint, can allow for very impressive experiences in what would otherwise be a perhaps very bland game. Physics-based games such as "Portal®" and "Portal 2®" allowed players a combat-free experience from an FPS perspective that was both challenging and unique.

There are several mechanisms that allow you control of your players' physics interaction in a game. They are:

- The FPE file settings.
- The property pane.
- Via Lua script commands.

The physics engine is one of the most deceptively simple systems in GameGuru. In fact, in many cases, it is right in front of you—you just never knew it. Remember the properties pane and its "physics" settings? Ever wonder exactly how that works?

On the pane shown in Figure 15.1, you'll see several properties that are directly modifiable via the editor.

First, we have the "physics on" property, which says whether it is actually something that actually uses physics. It has to be set to "yes" for physics to affect this object. Once this is configured, then at this point, the forces of the engine

⊟ **Physics**	
Physics On?	Yes
Always Active?	No
Physics Weight	100
Physics Friction	100
Explodable?	No
Explode Damage	100

Figure 15.1

The physics subpane on the properties panel.

will now be applied to this object. This means it'll be affected by gravity, explosions, and the player, among other things.

Now with that property, the first thing that will happen with this object is it will fall from wherever it is in the world down to the terrain.

The remaining properties here give you some measure of control over GameGuru's interaction with this object. First, there's the "physics weight." This value is computed from the volume of the physics collision box around the entity. In this case, the default value is always 100 as this is "100 percent" of the volume.

This is done so that the objects can all consistently be set at 100 but perhaps not respond the same way. For instance, you don't want an explosion knocking over a background element or building. Cars are larger than boxes so they should respond less to outside forces.

Using a setting of 100 will give you a decent baseline where the weight of the object will respond marginally to things such as gunshots or bombs. A good explosion will send it flying a moderate distance, and it will sink in water, based on the size of course.

Being that this value is a percentage, we can either increase it or decrease it to provide it with various effects. Please note the maximum "weight" in game is about 400 kg. Ironically, this is before it's converted to SI measurements since the "Bullet" physics engine that is used internally uses those values.

Now if you take this value and lower it to ten or less, it will mostly have the same weight as a small air-filled balloon. At sufficiently low enough weight, it becomes somewhat buoyant. This allows it to float in water, which can provide some really impressive results. In the other direction, if you raise the weight up to 1000 or higher, it weighs as much as a small motorcycle and will barely budge under the mightiest of forces. Obviously, these values require some playing with depending on the object receiving them.

Friction is another important value that will control how rapidly the speed of the object will degrade once it's in contact with a terrain surface. This can be useful for making large objects slow down rapidly or slide along an "ice-like" surface. Now it's a bit reversed from how it would be in the natural world; naturally speaking, friction is applied between the interactions of two objects, not necessarily as a blanket property on one side of things. Unfortunately, the friction level of the terrain surface is not something we can control, so you have to do everything from the entity side of things. It's also extremely important to note friction ONLY applies to the entity as it comes in contact with terrain. Due to limitations of the engine, two entities do not have friction between them.

These are your primary two "properties" that you can use from the editor. Regardless, they have a huge amount of potential if used properly.

Once you have a good baseline for what you like, then extract the object and shift-click it to copy it and the physics values for the remainder of that object in the level.

Now past this we have our FPE file settings. The FPE file has a wide amount of control that you need to edit it to obtain even more control of the object in the world. The primary value we are interested in is "collisionmode." This particular value in the FPE file for your object will allow you to configure what type of shell the object has with respect to physics. Up until recently, these settings didn't affect physics at all. Due to recent updates (as of this book's writing), you now have several very functional physics shapes available for you.

Collision mode can be set to zero for a default "box" shape, one provides polygon mapping that is only useful for collisions but still uses a box for physics. The other two shapes, however, are sphere and cylinder. These can be done by setting "collisionmode" to two for sphere and three for cylinder. The center of the cylinder for a model is computed along its y-axis in case you find it's not behaving quite as you like.

There's also a "no physics" and "no physics but can be shot with intersectall check" option (11 and 12, respectively). These will further allow you to have more control over the object's interactivity in the game world. The no physics option is fairly basic, but the other makes the object available to be hit by a ray-casting check by the players or enemies.

As mentioned previously, there is a significant amount of work that can be done with Lua as well. In fact, you can really say this is where the bulk of any really impressive physics will occur. If you're adept with Lua and feel like trying your hand at something really interesting, this is the way to go.

It turns out there's an entire supplementary physics library available as well as a few commands in the actual engine itself.

The engine's primary relevant command is "ForcePlayer," which will apply force on the player along the y-axis. This is very limited but can be fun to play with.

As you can see, the engine itself supports a few interesting commands that work a bit but don't do particularly much from a physics standpoint. For that reason, we'll be focusing on the included physics library instead.

The supplementary library is called "physlib.lua" and is included in your scriptbank folder. In order to add it to your current code, you need to call it inside of your Lua scripts like this (per the creator, AmenMoses):

```
local P = require "scriptbank\\physlib"
```

P represents a variable that can be any name you want.

In order to make sure the library is copied into any standalone created, add the following line to your scripts _init part:

```
Include ("physlib.lua")
```

So the first command you'll need is one that provides the dimensions of the physics capsule around the object in question. This command is called

"GetEntityDimensions." It will assign a series of properties to a variable as an object that you can then interact with. These properties will be:

w = Width of the object, i.e., the "x" dimension.
h = Height of the object, i.e., the "y" dimension.
l = Length of the object, i.e., the "z" dimension.
m = Mass of the object (internally GameGuru has a rather strange mass calculation that this mimics)
cx, cy, cz = The "center" offsets of the object, i.e., where the center of the object is relative to its origin.

Now I haven't really discussed properties, but this is a more advanced programming topic that goes hand in hand with something called "object oriented programming" or OOP. OOP allows you to create objects that are interactive and that can have subordinate variables assigned to them called properties.

An example would be:

```
local ball = {}
ball.color = "red"
ball.size = 5
```

So in this case, what will happen is you will assign a variable to "GetEntityDimensions," which in turn will make it into an object with properties as listed previously with all of the physics-related information for the entity for manipulation.

Example code

```
local dims = P.GetEntityDimensions (e)
Prompt ("height=" . dims.h)
```

Remember that "P" was what we used for our physlib "require" function. So this is saying to use the function from the physics library called "GetEntityDimensions" on entity "e" and return that information as an object called "dims" with the properties w, h, l, m, cx, cy, and cz. Then, make these properties accessible via dims.propertyname for future use.

From here, the sky is the limit. We have a lot of really fun functions in this library we can use that I'll try to detail to give you something to work with.

Here's a list of functions to whet your palette. I've included a full section in the Lua Appendix for them if you desire further detail. It's important to note though that physlib.lua has a significant amount of detail in it, which can be extremely helpful for determining use.

getPos3, getAng3, ObjectToEntity(obj), GetObjectDimensions (obj), AddEntityCollisionCheck(e), RemoveEntityCollisionCheck(e), GetEntityTerrainNumCollisions(e), GetTerrainCollisionDetails(obj), GetEntityTerrainCollisionDetails(e),

GetEntityObjectNumCollisions(e), GetObjectCollisionDetails (obj), GetEntity ObjectCollisionDetails(e), getHingeValues(dims,hingeName,spacing), getRealWorldYangle (), AddObjectSingleHinge (obj, hingeName, swingAng, offset, spacing, AddObjectDoubleHinge(objA, objB, hingeNameA, hingeNameB, spacing, noCols), AddEntityDoubleHinge(e1, e2, hingeName1, hingeName2, spacing, noCols), AddObjectSingleJoint (obj, jointName, spacing), AddEntitySingleJoint (e, jointName, spacing), AddObjectDoubleJoint (objA, objB, jointNameA, jointNameB, spacing, noCols), AddEntityDoubleJoint (e1, e2, jointNameA, jointNameB, spacing, noCols, RemoveEntityConstraints(e), RemoveEntityConstraintsIfDead(e), SetEntityDamping (e, damping, angle), GetViewVector(), and ObjectPlayerLookingAt (dist, force).

As you can see, there's quite a lot to work with, far more than we have time for in this tome but plenty to keep you busy. I'm also enclosing a link in the hyperlink reference for the physics library to AmenMoses's own tutorial on how to use this system.

16

Retexturing Assets

An important part of game development is the art that goes into your games. Unfortunately, some of us, myself included, are not professional artists. While you can certainly commission art for your projects, this can rapidly balloon your costs depending on from who you are obtaining your art. In many cases, if you want professional-grade work, you will be paying professional-grade prices. A large part of the reason for that is that, aside from the actual creative process, the tools themselves are often obscenely expensive.

Not being a professional artist has forced me to learn methods and techniques that skirt around my lack of expertise and experience. I am also always pushing the edge of what I can do with free-for-use programs instead of paying the latest license costs for Adobe Photoshop. While costs have become more manageable for artists using professional-grade tools through monthly subscriptions and specialty discounts for students, it still remains overwhelmingly expensive and adds much cost to the end product you pay for. When someone is shelling out hundreds of dollars a month for Mixamo®, Photoshop®, Maya®, Substance Painter®, and other AAA tools, it's not hard to understand why you often find yourself paying upward of a hundred dollars for a single good asset.

Figure 16.1

One of my first attempts to make a store item.

In my case, I found a combination of using free tools gave me sufficient access to create my own assets though, admittedly, the first few attempts were pretty ugly and outright rejected by the TheGameCreators store asset input system.

I literally drew a black splotch (Figure 16.1) that, admittedly, I was tremendously happy with for reasons that still escape me, and I said it was a scorch mark. I admit this to you because you have to realize that everyone starts somewhere, even if it's at the bottom.

For me, it was pretty close to the bottom. Thankfully, a little time and practice is all it takes to begin improving.

One of the easiest ways to get into making your own art is to simply modify art you already own! You'll only need a few simple tools: First, an image editor, second, some plugins or secondary tools to help further refine what you work on. In order to load images into GameGuru, it's crucial that you have the ability to output to a file type called a "DDS" file. This is specifically a "DirectDraw Surface" texture that is used by Microsoft's DirectX to load textures. GameGuru uses this image type almost exclusively for texturing models.

My preference for image manipulation is a free-for-use program called Paint.net, though many choose to use another called Gimp™. Gimp is not my forte, so I cannot tell you how to perform these same actions in that program. All of my instructions will be for how to perform simple manipulation in Paint.net.

Preparing Paint.net

Paint.net out of the box is a fairly complete program, but some extra work is required to get it functioning properly for GameGuru.

First of all, you can add special functionality to Paint.net with extra items called plugins. These plugins are crucial toward your success, and I highly recommend you investigate others out there once you are comfortable with our basic set.

The basic set consists of:

- DDS File type Plus for importing and exporting DDS files to GameGuru.
- NormalMapPlus for generating normal maps that function well with GameGuru.
- Alpha Mask plugin for working with transparencies in GameGuru.

This will get us the simplest framework to use for the purposes of doing our own work.

Most of the other tools are already built in—a series of important tools. These tools consist of blurs, color modification tools, layer modification and merging, and other various filters.

How UV Mapping Works

By now, you are more than familiar with the Cartesian coordinate system used by 3D modeling of X/Y/Z. What can be very confusing, however, is how a three-dimensional system can have a two-dimensional surface applied to it. This process is called UV mapping. No, this doesn't mean "ultraviolet!" It is an extension of "x, y, z" to "u, v, x, y, z."

The most simplistic 3D surface to work on is a square plane.

This simple two-dimensional rectangle is a straight 1:1 mapping if configured right. Thankfully, there are tons of examples for how this works, but I've included one for your reference in the relevant archive for this chapter.

For 3D objects, it's a bit more complicated but is best expressed as a series of surfaces. These surfaces are then extracted from a single 2D plane. You can also pack several textures onto one giant texture sheet called an atlas texture or decal sheet (Figure 16.2). This method can improve performance, but works mostly the same.

Let's imagine a three-dimensional pyramid. This 3D pyramid has equal-sized sides, so it's essentially equilateral. This gives us a total of four triangular surfaces and one square surface. Instead of having several separate files, a single image texture is used for all five surfaces.

In the map, there's a lot of dead space there, but that cannot be helped. Now per our previous discussions, you know there are other textures involved here to add additional detail. We won't be working with PBR just yet, for now we'll focus on modifying less difficult textures.

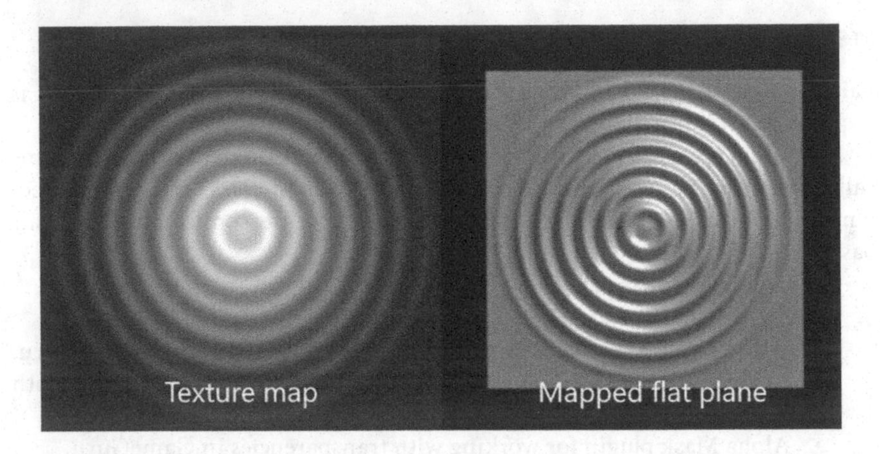

Figure 16.2

How texture mapping and normal mapping affects a plane.

That means our models will rely on the simple DNIS system.

D is for Detail map: This is your filename_d.dds file that contains the actual texture for the surface.

N is for Normal map: This is your filename_n.dds file that contains your normal map that makes a simplified bump map for your texture. Now, technically, you can get away with just these two maps as the bare minimum of what you need to retexture something. However, for additional detail, you can also have the following two maps as well.

I is for Illumination map: This is a simple full brightness map that will change the surface lighting on a model to the maximum. It's a very important and useful trick to make objects appear illuminated, hence the name. It does NOT emit lighting itself, however, so be aware you need to add a static or dynamic light to it. Again, the format is to use filename_i.dds when saving. In more recent versions of GameGuru, you can use variable levels to control how "strong" the illumination map comes across. This is to say the darker the RGB value of the white or gray color is, the darker the illumination map is. A full "white" color will be maximum value. Since this is just painted over the texture by the renderer, it allows some variability though appears to only take the highest value in the map as its reference. So you can't use multiple shades of gray for some spectacular lighting effects unless you put them on altogether separate models. In Figure 16.3, you can see what happens when the same model has several different FPE files with individual illumination map settings.

S is for Specular map: This map is similar to the detail map and, in many cases, may be unnecessary but does control a very simplistic "shine" effect, as I've mentioned before. This can be used to give a metallic effect to your surfaces by increasing how white the black-and-white map is. As you probably guessed, we just name it filename_s.dds when saving.

Figure 16.3

The illumination map can use any value from 0-255.

Using Paint.net to Modify

When you do go to save, make sure you choose DDS as your save as type (Figure 16.4). Once you do, you will get a second screen that asks you what information you want for your DDS file. This can be rather confusing at first, but don't worry too much about it. There's a good deal of information on these file types online, but let's simplify it further.

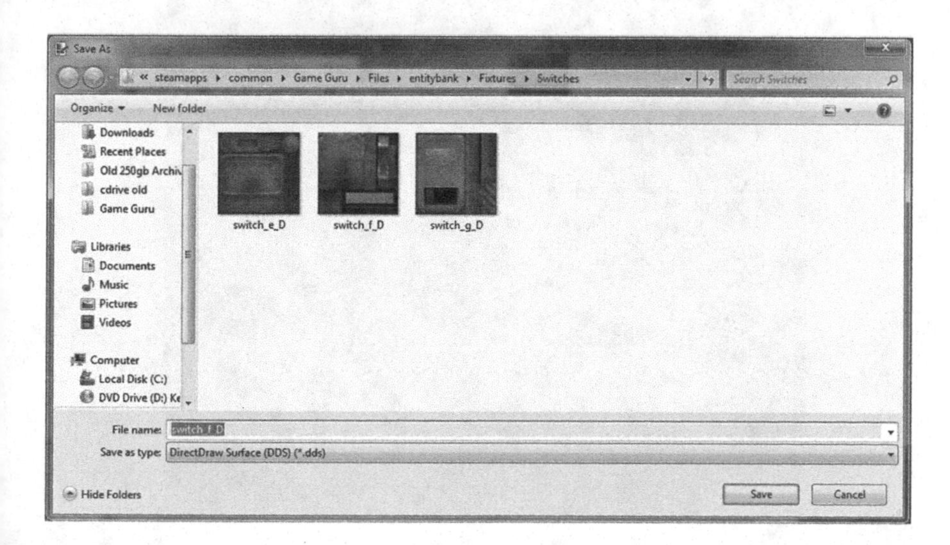

Figure 16.4

Saving as a .DDS file in Paint.net.

The setting you choose here will impact image quality and file size. If your picture doesn't have any sort of transparencies, then you want to use "DXT1," and I generally use "cluster fit" as the type. It seems to provide me the best results as DXT1 does compress the texture, which can result in some image fidelity issues.

DXT5 is what you will want to use with transparencies, though to save space, you'll want to also check off "save mipmaps" at the bottom. This configuration should result in marginally smaller files, though DXT5 is an order of magnitude larger than DXT1. So long as you aren't using a lot of transparencies, this won't be an issue, however.

Modifying a texture is something that is actually significantly easier than it might seem. The most simplistic way would be to draw on the texture directly.

This, however, doesn't always lend to the best results if you're not particularly artistic (Figure 16.5).

A more simplistic way to modify it would be to apply a filter, which is basically a computer algorithm that will modify each pixel you select in Paint.net in a certain way. By default, if nothing is selected, it applies it to the whole surface; however, if you start to get more advanced, you can use selection tools such as the rectangle or lasso select to choose specific areas to modify.

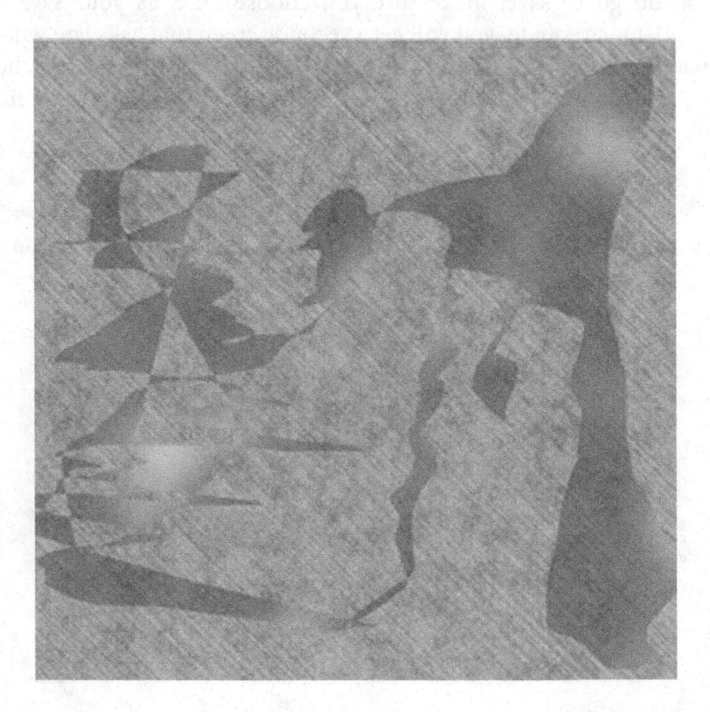

Figure 16.5

A poor attempt at weathering a texture.

I recommend experimenting with the filters on some test images to see how they work. Once you have tested things like blurs and embossing, you can then try them on actual surfaces for models and see how they look in game.

Creating a normal map is done with a filter. When using the NormalMapPlus filter, go to the filters menu, then stylize, and choose NormalMapPlus. Make sure that you have the entire picture selected when you perform this action. After you apply it to the same bad texture you get the image shown in Figure 16.6.

Make sure you save the second picture as the same filename as the detail file with a _n instead of a _d at the end! This will show GameGuru that this should be treated as a normal map.

The last tool we added was an alpha mask tool. This tool makes your textures more transparent and requires a little bit of figuring to learn but is fairly straightforward. If you hit CTRL-A, it will select all of your picture. If you then go to filters/special/alpha mask, you will then notice it turns part of the image clear. That part will becomes transparent. The parts with the light squares over them will become partially or fully see-through depending on if they were colored or if they had empty pixels in them.

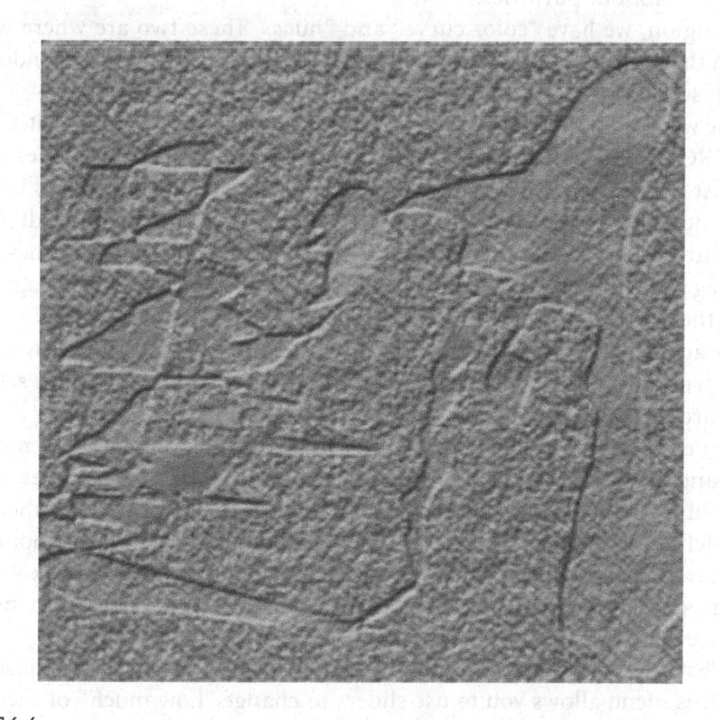

Figure 16.6

Using filters can help clean up even messy work.

Also, with this tool you can also select specific areas using the magic tool, lasso, and rectangle select tools. This allows you to choose specific areas to make transparent.

Changing Diffuse Textures

One of the easiest ways to modify a texture is to merely change the colors for the entire texture. This is done by opening the detail file and going to the Adjustments menu.

On this menu, you have several very useful tools you should familiarize yourself with.

The first is "auto-level," which will try to equalize the color values across the entire spectrum. This can provide some very unique results, and I always give it a whirl—though often it's too much for my tastes. As the saying goes, your miles may vary.

The next is "black and white," which does exactly what it says. It converts a texture to black and white, which turns all colors to grayscale. In most cases, we'll avoid this.

Brightness and contrast are two other controls that will act similar to how your TV handles those two values and, frankly, aren't going to adjust the color significantly for our purposes.

Moving on, we have "color curve" and "hues." These two are where we will perform the bulk of our color-changing operations. The color curve window will bring up something like Figure 16.7.

In the window at the top, you can see a bar that says "luminosity" in it. Change this to "RGB." This will allow us to move the red, green, and blue values for our image. At the bottom, there's a checkbox for each of the three colors. Uncheck all but one of the colors, then click up in the area with the lines and drag. This will modify that one color (in our case, red). Drag it around and then click again. Now drag some more, and you'll see there's another point it will work against to modify the color curve with.

Once again, play with it and see what you can find. It's often quite easy to make a white truck a different color by just modifying the color curve after selecting the textures on the UV map you want.

If you exit this menu with cancel, all changes will be reverted. For now, let's do that and try going to the hues menu instead. In this one, the two relevant bars are the saturation bar, which controls how "dense" the color is. The other is the hue, which is a cheap way to modify the color itself. This way, in my opinion, is a little easier although somewhat imprecise. Personally, I mostly stick with the color curve system to modify colors, but I recommend trying both of them to see which one works best for you.

One last way to modify colors is by using the "levels" option off the Adjustments menu. This menu allows you to use sliders to change "how much" of each color there is. Again, it's really down to preference here; all of them mostly produce the same results.

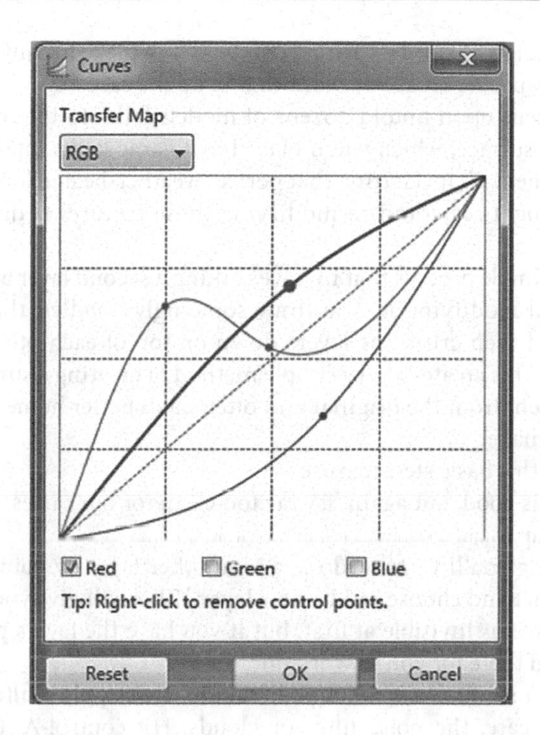

Figure 16.7

Adjusting the colors can be done through the curves panel.

The last three are invert colors, posterize, and sepia. These are common graphical tools that work as follows:

Invert colors reverses the color palette, providing a psychedelic effect.

Posterize controls how well the colors blend together.

The last one is sepia, which is sort of like the black-and-white coloring. In this case, it will turn everything to a brownish tone. It's often used as a photographic filter to give things a more pleasant antique look.

So now you should have a good handle on how to modify the colors of a project without actually redoing the texture from scratch. Try starting with a simple white texture and modifying that to get the results you want. I've included a simple white cube that you can try different colorations on for this chapter.

Weathering Textures

One specific technique I like to use is weathering a texture. This is the process of making a fresh and clean surface look worn, beaten, and rusty. Think about some of your favorite games. If you dwell on it, you'll recall that often surfaces are dingy and uglier in most cases. Often, when you have a perfectly clean surface, it gives the impression of sterility, which can be out of place for anything but doctor's offices and specific areas you want that to be the case on.

I've seen dozens upon untold dozens of models fall into the trap of having a perfectly sterile surface, which when placed in a game looks totally out of place for the environment it's in. Getting that perfect weather-beaten look is thankfully easier than it might seem and so modifying those textures is definitely within your reach!

It's a rather simple process that involves taking a second layer above your current texture and modifying it. You draw some ugly doodles, then make them transparent, and then crush the layers down on top of each other in a process called merging. This creates a very simple method of creating a surface that looks markedly different from the original and often has a better home in the types of games I like to make.

Let's start with a basic steel texture.

This texture is good, but again, it's far too clean for our tastes. We're going to have to scuff it up.

The first thing you'll want to do is add another layer by going to the layers menu in Paint.net and choose "add a new layer." This will give you a second surface that often seems invisible at first, but if you have the layers pane open, you can see it's listed there for you to work on.

Since you can see below it, what you want to do is apply a filter to the entire region—in this case, the noise filter or clouds. Hit control-A, then select the whole area, and apply the filter/special/alpha mask filter to it.

After doing this, go to the Layers menu, then layer properties. We want to change the blending mode to either multiply, color burn, overlay, or reflect. These will all provide slightly different effects to the way the layer is merged down. Bear in mind as with all of these, you can do it with a "selection tool" like all of the other filters. If you do it on a single layer with multiple selections, you can actually choose which areas of the texture receive the weathered look.

It really all depends on what you want. In our case, we're going to choose a few large blocks but avoid the edges to ensure that it's able to tile properly.

The last thing we will do is go to the Layers menu and choose "merge layer down." This will combine the two layers and produce your final texture! Now all you have to do is save it as a new detail file and you'll have a new texture. Bear in mind that if you modify the name, you will also need to edit the FPE file to reflect this.

17

Adding Advanced Design Elements

Your first maze, listed earlier, was probably incredibly simplistic. Upon play through, while enjoyable, perhaps you noticed how quickly you could go through it.

Mazes are interesting things; they provide a sense of satisfaction for completion and require intelligence to resolve. From the days of ancient Greek legends about Minos to modern movies about labyrinthine puzzles, it's clear we love mazes. They often represent the pinnacle of what we consider a form of primal thought: our higher order intelligence approaching a lower order problem. With that respect, go back and look at your maze. What you have is most likely a clear-cut "start to finish" level design with maybe an occasional twist or turn. To really give it its due, we need to give it a little bit of a finer touch.

We're going to take our demo map and add a few twists and turns by examining each component a piece at a time.

Level of Detail and Model Quality

One of the great advantages of GameGuru is an extremely well-priced asset store, along with its massive free asset library. Some of these are out-of-date, lower quality works that are perfectly suitable for regular use. Moreover, they generally tend to work exceptionally well as low-quality background objects that are usually not incredibly detailed anyway due to visibility issues.

GameGuru is a 32-bit engine. This limits the potential of games made by some respects in that you are limited to 4 GB total addressing space for memory. What that means for you is that, realistically, your application will have at most 2.5 GB available for textures, models, code, and other components. This means that we have to be extra judicious about how we handle our ultra-high-quality assets. Every time you add something using multiple levels of detail (LOD) or physically based rendering (PBR), it's going to eat into the available resource pool. This dwindling supply of approximately 2.5 GB of total RAM goes fast. In a lot of cases, you're looking at nearly a half a gig to a full gig for terrain by itself. Once you start adding in massive 2048 × 2048 skyboxes or 4-k resolution textures, it won't take long at all to completely consume the memory that is available. Once that happens, watch out! GameGuru's stability goes right out the window at that point. Level of detail models allow us to have multiple detail levels on a single model, thus saving resources.

Fit and Finish

The classic shareware release of "Quake" followed the same pattern as the original "Doom" release. The design process was one, however, of steady refinement, where drafts were created, then discarded, then added back in, then repurposed, and finally refined until, ultimately, they obtained their final state.

This type of flexible development combined with constant refinement follows one of the narrow paths to victory that can be duplicated by any developer.

Personally, when I'm writing a book or making a game, I always flesh it out in the same way. I start off with broad chunks—big things that really don't look that great at first. Then I proceed to flesh out the entire thing, start to finish, in that fashion. Once it's complete, I go back and add detail to it. I then go back one last time (three times total, usually) and put my polish on it. This way, I can start with a pretty rudimentary structure that then grows into something with a great measure of detail to it.

An example from my writing process would look like:

First pass: *A topic list of "talk about topic x, talk about topic y, and talk about topic z."*

Second pass: *A three-paragraph statement about x, a one-page talk about y, and a half page on z. Each one is expanded by a three- to four-point margin over what they already were, giving more body and substance.*

Third pass: *Cleaning up the language, fixing/editing each segment, adding better statements, and rewriting sentences. In most cases, this results in about a 10 or 20 percent refinement on each segment. There's a certain irony in that I literally did that exact process when writing this chapter.*

From a game development standpoint, it looks more like:

First pass: *Big empty room, maybe 1–3 pieces of objects used to signify better-looking objects.*

Second pass: *Empty room gets furniture added, enemies, maybe a few clutter objects. Looks like a real scene at this point and, in many cases, the average indie gamedev would probably wrap it up here. Some primitive lightmapping if you're trying to be doing better than average.*

Third pass: *Going over with a fine-toothed comb. Swapping objects that are going to be performance hogs or that will look out of place due to art style with better matching objects, adding more clutter, decals to the wall for effects like dirt or decay, etc. Lightmapping and dynamic lighting is finalized.*

This is what we are going to be doing with our game. We already have a functional level. At this point, we need to now expand on that level and really bring out the detail as best as possible. We are somewhat limited in our endeavor due to the use of stock assets, but there's a lot of really good stuff out there for free we can leverage for the purposes of creating a really sophisticated environment.

I should mention there are a few additional steps in game development that really aren't listed as part of my writing process, but that is peer review (beta testing) and optimization (page count reductions/additions). In this case, we will need to have other people, preferably on other hardware, test our levels and games. We will also need an optimization phase. There are, quite simply, going to be things we put in that will need to be culled for the sake of performance. It may be that you place an entity that looks great on every street corner that just destroys FPS on AMD® cards. Or it might be that there's an AI that is plodding along and needs a smoother AI Lua implementation. That phase will happen after your development cycle as a separate series of phases. This will be covered in significant detail later in Chapter 21, "Optimization."

Adding Cutscenes

A common storytelling method for any AAA game is the "cutscene." These movie-style sequences convey specific dialogue and sequences to the player that give them a better sense of immersion while they play. Indie gamedevs are typically not held to nearly as stringent standards with cutscenes being fairly well known as a lot of work for very little reward.

That said, it makes for a good "icing on the cake" if you can afford to learn it and, while it's generally not easy or fast, it will provide an extra layer of detail to your storytelling. As with all things, if you can obtain a level of proficiency with it, you can get a fairly efficient process. Even better, since it's generally considered something done above and beyond, even the most basic attempts can go a long way toward giving your game a little more credibility.

Generally speaking, there are three ways you can do a cutscene.

First, you can use actual character models and the in-game camera system, which is controlled completely by Lua. This is the most technically limiting method as it requires an extreme level of proficiency with both the engine and 3D modeling. This is likely not going to be your first go-to choice if you are reading this book, but it does bear mentioning. My camera kit set of scripts will get you started with some basic Lua control of the camera. Beyond that you're going to need to completely script the controls and models to achieve the result desired.

The second method is probably the most simplistic in that it doesn't require much work beyond playing a video in the game. GameGuru allows people to play videos with scripts using something called a "story zone" that will play a video when the player enters the zone. The video itself can be something as simple as something you recorded with your phone in the world. Imagine a scene where you want a car driving by and some dialogue over top of it. Go out onto your front lawn and record a car driving by! Then use one of the myriad of free video editing software packages available and narrate a voiceover. Is it amateurish? Sure, depending on your video skills. However, it's also the most cost-effective and simple method available. You can also use some interesting software (unrelated to GameGuru) that's relatively well-priced. It's called Atlantia animation and allows you to create easy animated scenes. As of the time of this writing, you can buy a copy for around $20 USD.

TIP: Story zones use videos that remain in memory for the duration of the level. So don't overload your game with story zones or else you'll use up all of your available memory!

The next method is one courtesy of "Len the Man." Now Len's cutscenes aren't going to win any awards but, through clever use of some in-game video, he was able to make some fairly convincing footage that looked like the first method but was accomplished by using the second method. Now granted, he did use some custom model movements, but the entire cutscene was done via recording in game footage and then editing it outside of the editor itself. He even modified the mouths to move by modifying a few select frames and drawing in some open mouths (as shown in Figure 17.1).

This method is a very effective way to use the available tools and skillset you have to maximum effect. It still takes time, it still takes effort, but it's worth it when you can produce reasonably decent scenes in GameGuru. In Len's case, he used Windows Movie Maker to import all of his recorded videos and join them into one contiguous piece. He even took it one step further and used actual screenshots that he then resized to fit into Windows Movie Maker and directly edited them with a paint program so he could make a "stop motion style movie" effect. The end result was worth it, with a very homebrew solution resulting in a respectable effort from an indie gamedev!

Once when I was very, very young, I had a school report due (seventh-grade English) and I decided to make a video home system or VHS (yes, it was that long ago) movie for it. However, I'd spent several months working with something

Figure 17.1
Adding cutscenes can be done with even simple tools.

called "Mario Paint" for the Super Nintendo Entertainment System. I made several animated scenes, recording them manually using the VHS. I even added custom music from "Mario Paint." For the ending, I simply recorded me spray-painting the words "the end" onto a canvas. I was particularly proud of that part. In retrospect, it was embarrassingly simple, but I can't fault the method at all. For the time, it was a fairly advanced method compared to my classmates. The same methods can be employed by you with some creativity and experimentation.

Decals

Decals, of course, aren't limited to static pictures displayed on walls and such. They also can be animated effects, which act as sprites that are animated. They are frequently used for things such as fires, smoke, torches, sparks, and the like. While these can add a really nice flair to your game, they lack the "cleanliness" of a true particle emitter.

Animated decals also come with a major drawback: Overuse of them in a scene will cause significant deterioration of performance. Granted, you have to REALLY overuse them if the hardware is even near the median level of modern equipment. It will still, however, have a measurable impact. This goes even further with the understanding that it's not just a single picture but a series of frames that are played in sequence. This means it will also have a fairly measurable impact on video memory utilized as well. Good examples of this are ones that come with my weather kit enclosed in the book's media. These decals look great but if used in any large quantity will flog a system fairly severely and also use around 40–60 mb of video memory! However, properly placed a good decal can provide a wealth of "ambience" to a scene.

Animated decals come in two different varieties—the kind that keep a fixed position and thus expose their 2D plane to the player as they move and the kind that face the player regardless of their position.

This is configured within the FPE file settings and also the property settings for the decal. Personally, I find it's very rare you're going to use anything but the type that adjusts its facing. The rare exceptions for me, personally, are where I am layering several to give a 3D effect. In the cases where I use one, I almost invariably will use the self-facing style. Interestingly, as you begin using them, you too will see them in other games and may begin to get ideas from ones you play commonly as it's a fairly regular tactic.

Animated decals can also be controlled to a limited extent by Lua scripts. These scripts are often limited to simple things such as hiding or showing the decal based on the entity ID but can also be combined with powerful scripts such as the user Amen Moses's physics library to "attach" decals to an object and use them for things such as jets that fire on a moon lander.

I highly recommend setting your decals up with either a range check via script or setting the "always on" property to no. This can help reduce the performance drain by such decals and prevents them from showing clearly at long distances (which is also a problem, especially in night scenes).

Decals on Surfaces

Proper use of decals is crucial to providing a believable scene. Decals give you a sense of realism by mapping over common areas (which if you recall, are virtually all repeating textures) with a two-dimensional picture. These pictures can be anything: oil slicks, trash, blood, and more. Some kits even have holes you can map, breaks in walls, anything you can imagine (see Figure 17.2).

It's important not to go overboard with them as they do tend to eat a lot of resources but, at the same time, they can really add a lot to a particular scene, giving it that much desired sense of realism. There are a few issues with using decals, however, such as if they aren't configured properly. One such issue with decals is sometimes they cast shadows and so you may find yourself doing some FPE editing to remove the "castshadows" by setting it to –1. There's also the issue of the object potentially being set accidentally as a dynamic entity with physics enabled. Not only is this unnecessarily CPU intensive, but it also is going to produce unpredictable effects such as having decals that can be "kicked" or will fall from walls and land on floors. So while you can produce some really great effects with decals, they require careful management.

Figure 17.2
Decals can add detail to even a bland location.

Clutter

Clutter is a topic of contention in the GameGuru community. On one hand, there are those who feel that clutter adds an element of realism to a scene and thus should be added on in quantities that are generally up to the beholder's personal view of an area.

On the other hand, there are the purists who believe that the area should be as clear as possible to ensure maximal framerate and thus performance in an engine that often struggles to achieve decent results on anything less than really good equipment.

As with all things, I believe the answer usually lies somewhere in the middle. Having a purist approach to clutter means your levels will often be bland and banal in color and design, despite the performance gains. Having too much clutter not only looks excessive but also hogs performance. Having just the right amount gives a clear sense of identity to a scene while only minimally robbing performance.

Clutter, in my opinion, is hugely important as indie game titles go. It can really make or break the way a scene is set. So what is clutter, precisely? Clutter objects are the small, useless pieces of the environment that give it both flavor and character.

Give each room or space its own miniature story. We're not talking something verbose, but perhaps "this person is a cat person that likes to be a nosy neighbor." I didn't just pull this out of thin air, mind you. I actually got the idea from "Deus Ex: Mankind Divided." In the opening area, the main character, Adam Jensen, explores his apartment complex. This area has several different neighbors that you can break into and use as a sort of side-distraction. They're not critical to gameplay but add flavor and intrigue to the story. They also provide the player with some goodies in the forms of secrets. One neighbor is an avid cat enthusiast. The windows are shuttered with steel blinds, except for one that has a telescope pointing at our protagonist's apartment door. All throughout the apartment are cat pictures, cat posters, cat food bowls, cat litter trays, and what have you.

This type of attention to detail is required for landmark rooms and everywhere else is a sort of "general story" that sets the environment for the player. You want to take your "generic apartment building" and really bring it to life. Even though in our previous example there are no AI objects involved. No cats, no people. It's literally a static room, but you get the impression of life from just the objects in the room.

It is, of course, only prudent to reuse clutter objects whenever applicable without overdoing it. This way you minimize the resources being used by the engine for more critical things such as high value assets like character models. It's a tricky balance but, typically, what I do is make similar areas *mostly* similar. I don't make carbon copy clones (that is just lazy and feels artificial), and I don't go all out with every single room having completely unique clutter objects. Instead, I use an 80/20 rule and generally keep approximately 80% similar and then change the remaining 20%.

Again, it doesn't have to be much, just a little here and there to provide distinction between areas that are similar (such as the aforementioned apartment complex rooms).

Positioning Objects

When you are designing a room in an interior space, try to have a theme you are working toward for each area. Position objects in such a way that it's believable. One easy method of doing this is to VERY slightly adjust each piece of furniture with the rotation tool or by using Shift-3. This gives each individual element a slight variance that makes it more passable to the human eye (Figure 17.3).

It's also important to pick familiar designs that give a sense of truth to a scene. For instance, if you are in a warehouse, you want to have shelves full of boxes. These are expected; the human eyes and mind will pick this up and then decipher their meaning. Each room tells a story, even if it's a small one. In the case of a warehouse, it may be a story of "this is a room for storing things, illicit things for bad people."

Try to work through the flow of the room; make sure it's not designed in an unintelligent fashion. You want something that causes the player to work their way through it, not walk from one end to the other.

The picture in Figure 17.4 shows an example of bad design. You can see clearly to the other end of the room, which means the player is going to run straight from one end to the other. This design ensures the player will tunnel directly to that door, without really checking anything else.

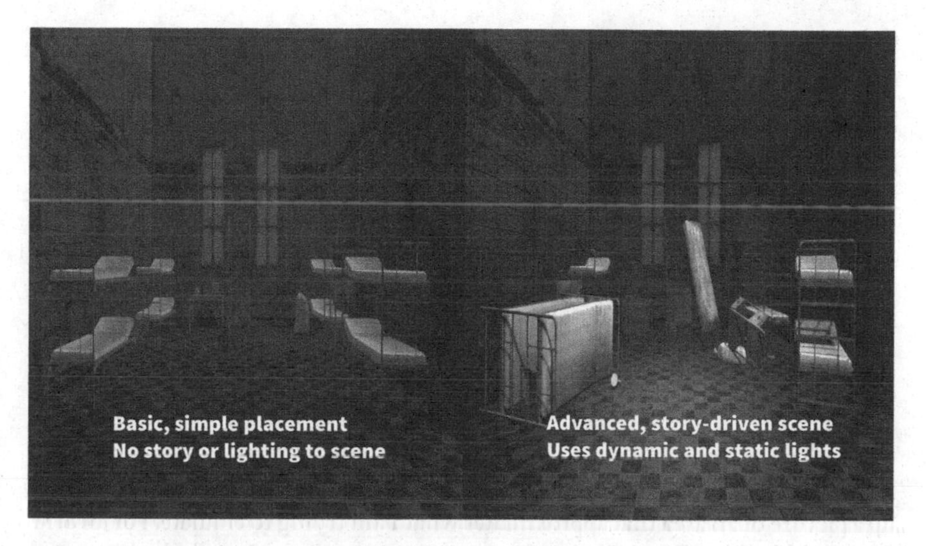

Figure 17.3

Scenes should try to tell a story.

You can, of course, use this to your advantage.

Maybe you place a secret in one of the offshoot areas or perhaps set up an ambush with enemies hiding in the blind corners. These types of maneuvers have to be used to make boring areas like the one in Figure 17.4 more interesting.

Figure 17.4

This room lacks an intelligent design.

Garbage Objects

Real life is generally fairly messy. People leave their dishes on counters, clothing on beds, and small bits of trash lying around. Garbage, in general, adds a sense of grimy reality to a scene that helps you, the world-builder, create more believable spaces for the player to roam through. Don't be afraid to add objects like empty bottles, food containers, bits of paper, and other scrap components.

I generally tend to pair up these components with their respective spaces. For instance, electronic parts in a computerized area, bits of food in employee spaces… trash in alleyways, and the like.

Vegetation

Giving personality to outdoor areas can be difficult. However, there are thankfully plenty of examples to draw from. Almost always what I'll do to start is load up a picture of an area that approximates what I am trying to emulate. For an arid desert, I'd look up Death Valley, for instance. Alternately, I might look at some Kansas farm country for a large flat plain filled with agribusinesses. So decide the type of area and terrain you want on a broad level, then decide on the scene of the place. Give it a little story and then decorate around it. Maybe one family fought valiantly against zombie hordes and there are corpses strewn in a path before they were finally overcome. Place some player-style corpses in the house and put a key card near them for their garage.

One important component of making your outdoor areas look good is using proper vegetation. It's important not to over- or under-spray vegetation; it's a powerful tool, and you want to use it as best as you can. I tend to place it in places like low points near ditches where water accumulates and also in places where an object might shear unnaturally against the terrain—most notably near trees and rocks to help hide the inconsistencies between the model and the terrain. While a few trees and rocks really go a long way to adding to a scene, they also can really seem out of place if there's no vegetation implemented.

Now the vegetation tool has been in GameGuru since the early days and was one of the first truly purpose-built pieces for GameGuru (then FPCS: R, if you recall). During that time, I remember extensive testing being done to optimize the framerate and function of the vegetation spray system. So, as a result, it's one of the best implemented and fastest components in the GameGuru engine. It will do great things like vary the direction, shape, size, and width of vegetation to provide a more realistic feel to it.

In the real world, there are places where vegetation tends to accumulate on a regular basis. These are on the edges of pathways, in fields, and near or away from trees. Now for those of you who didn't regularly frequent the pine forests of central Pennsylvania (it's not called "Penn's Woods" by accident), you may not know that the acidity of the pine needles actually creates a BARREN area near pine trees. It essentially stunts or kills all vegetation at the base of tree.

Figure 17.5
Different types of trees for forests.

It's important, as such, to know what kind of environment you're working around. When we are world-building, little things such as "does this tree have a lot of vegetation around it" do matter and should be respected (Figure 17.5).

There are other types of clutter, of course, that we can use to help create a more asymmetrical feel to our levels. It bears repeating: Asymmetry is what the human eye will see as natural. Symmetry is almost a key indicator that something is man-made.

There's a place in Pennsylvania you've probably never heard of called Milton. Many, many decades ago, there was an industrial accident there that caused massive deforestation and die-off of the forest. The decision was made to replant trees to rebuild the forest. I was visiting a friend of a friend out there and one of the most surreal things I've ever experienced was standing in the forest(s) of Milton.

The reason for this is that the trees are planted in perfect little rows. At first blush, you can tell you're in a forest, after all, you're surrounded by a variety of pine trees and other forest foliage. Something initially just "feels off," however. Then you realize you can literally stand in between the trees and look for miles in one direction without anything blocking your view. The trees are in a perfect row and are the same type, which creates a sense of the forest not being natural. Which is, of course, accurate—because it's not natural.

Moreover, it adds a sense of eeriness to the location. While this can be used to your advantage, on the by and whole, it's important to keep in mind that repetition is something human minds are keen on picking up on. Humans are excellent pattern parsers, simply put. We can see repeating patterns in natural or unnatural locations and immediately start to draw comprehensive conclusions from this. Sometimes when nature makes these patterns (such as basalt columns in a volcano, with their uncanny hexagonal shape), we infer that in a spiritual or religious sense. In other cases, we just know it is "fake" and don't accept it as being part of the environment.

Since this entire book is about creating a believable environment, it's important to know that we are making something that has to be modeled after the natural world. Therefore, tree types will be somewhat varied but mostly uniform. Figure about an 80/10/5/5 distribution on tree types for outdoor scenes. A good ratio is:

- 80% of your primary tree type
- 10% of another tree type
- 5% of two other tree types

This pattern of tree types will give you a very natural and fluid feel to your levels while not overburdening your level with TOO much variety. Too much variety can both tax the very limited resources of GameGuru and also look out of place. In a forest, you generally tend to have a few types of dominant trees and a few others that are part of the biome but not necessarily overwhelming in strength. There will be the occasional pocket of vegetation that is different from everything around it, sort of like an independent city-state enclosed by another nation.

The same pattern applies to your vegetation as well. When you are using the vegetation spray, as of this writing, you cannot change between different types of vegetation. You have to use the one type that you select on the TAB-TAB settings screen and spray. This system is highly efficient and will attempt to add artificial variety by varying height, size, and width with some level of intelligence. The problem is it will always be one type of vegetation. As such, you must go and use separate "foliage" models to spruce up (get it?) a level. There's a vegetation pack you can obtain for GameGuru that gives you many varieties of bushes, flowers, trees, and the like. This vegetation pack is something I use regularly, often choosing 2–4 varieties of bushes and flowers to help add a level of realism to a place. For tighter clusters of foliage, use the "I" key to select the sprayer tool and then use the minus key to make it very small. This will give you thin but heavy clumps of foliage. If you want to create the occasional sporadic flower or plant, pick your desired foliage and set the circle for the spray tool very wide by using the plus key. Then click intermittently or drag across an area.

This method can be repeated for other outdoor elements such as rocks and logs. When using this tool, however, be aware from time to time you may encounter sprayed elements that are completely out of place. This happens when the randomizer does something silly, like tilting a bush sideways or placing something completely irrationally. So make sure you give it a good once-over when completed so you can ensure that the level is not sitting with a glaring defect in it, such as a rock hovering in mid-air.

Going back to rocks and logs, these are two outdoor elements that are also crucial to making your level have a sense of realism. Rocks tend to be in this distribution:

- 10% very small rocks.
- 20% a rock field model, such as the one in the sci-fi kit. A rock field is a "spread" of small rocks so you can rapidly place many hundreds in a single area. This is also computationally more efficient.
- 35% medium-sized individual rocks, varied to 2–4 varieties.
- 15% large rocks.
- 25% extremely large rocks.

Obviously, this changes based on your terrain, but I find this is my usual distribution pattern. There are exceptions to this, however. Large rocks make excellent obstacles and as such are often used to block player passage beyond a specific location. They also, as previously mentioned, make fantastic navigational landmarks and should be placed in locations that create a memorable picture. This memorable picture has drawbacks, of course, as it will have increased attention, and if you are using a substandard or poorly mapped model, it will stand out like a sore thumb.

Bear in mind there's also the use of "negative space" to consider.

In the case of negative space, this is when an artist uses a LACK of something to create something. If you are in a forest, for instance, only to stumble across a clearing: Is that not out of the ordinary? This clearing in the middle of an otherwise heavily cluttered forest will stand out in the person's mind the same way a large rock outcropping will. They will remember the location and attempt to path to it. Most gamers will even expect something such as an item drop or enemy there as well. Make sure to use that to your advantage. We'll get to that more later on in the "secrets and lies" portion of this chapter.

For now, focus on making believable outdoor areas. Have your reference documents available and check them often. You remember those, right? Those pictures you have of your areas that you are attempting to emulate and capture in your scenes?

You should have these readily accessible so you can cross-reference what you've made versus what you are working toward.

So if you've been following our typical workflow, you've been working top down, large to small—painting your terrain, placing your major landmarks, then big set pieces (large rocks, trees, fallen logs, etc), repainting your terrain, placing mid-sized items, spraying vegetation, using the random sprayer to spray smaller objects, etc. This will give you a very realistic-feeling level that should look great!

Of course, there's other things I haven't mentioned to this point that are fairly obvious, but you'd be amazed how many people don't even consider—notably the actual quality of your models.

It is one thing to use the free models included and use them well. It's another to download someone's first attempt at modeling a rock that looks like it'd have been poor quality in the late '90s. You need to be discerning and selective about the things you choose. There is a great deal of free media out there, but if you are genuinely trying to make a game and make money on it, well … consider what you're using before you use it.

Even some paid media is low quality or overpriced. Caveat emptor: Let the buyer beware; and you as gamedev have to be equally aware of the materials and equipment you are using.

Better Enemies

Enemies in this game require some fine-tuning; out of the box, they are minimally capable and as such are something that you can really do a lot more with if you're willing to take the time. Little tuning tricks include modifying their view cone, range, and adding a distance checker.

More impressive things are cover zones, nodes, floor zones. While the previous chapters should prepare you for this, a good part of having a better enemy is also how they look and act. It's supremely important to the player's immersive experience that you provide something outside the norm. Don't be afraid to take chances to change models or purchase something truly outlandish.

Here again, though, purchasing is a buyer beware situation. Oftentimes you can't know the exact quality of what you are receiving, and most of the assets are in the bargain-level pricing region of five dollars per model or less. If you look around, even static assets for other engines typically start at double or triple that amount. So you often times don't know exactly how good the AI will be for a specific instance. This is doubly so because the AI is typically made from a modified Lua script found on a forum or from the stock scripts. Neither of these are particularly powerful. You can be assured that it will take some finagling to make even a high-priced creation function precisely right. This is the hazard, though, with any sort of "á la carte game builder" such as GameGuru. The consistency of assets on the store is typically wildly variable, so do the best you can and plan to work around problems.

TIP: Plan to work around problems instead of trying to push through them.

With artificial intelligence, it can be notoriously buggy. That said, if you've followed the rules laid down in previous chapters, yours should be functioning fairly well. The reason I'm mentioning it here is because, of course, nothing is perfect. In one example, I had a haunted house and there was a huge "lobby" room with a massive boss in it. The boss NPC was a savage brute with tentacles I'd purchased from the store. Normally, it tested well, but inside of a structure such as a house (which was actually a single model with an interior), it failed to understand position. It would sit down in the middle of the room and just sit there ineffectually. I had similar problems with "stock" models as well until I placed a floor zone at the right height. That eventually resolved it and allowed the creature to attack properly, but now it was hitting through walls and I needed to adjust the Lua code to only alert when the player opened the door to the room. This was accomplished with a simple series of changes to a custom door Lua code, which then set a global flag that was checked by the then modified AI code to the monster. This wasn't perfect, it still had glitches, but most of them were easily overlooked by the fact that the monster was enormous.

Things like this are simple adjustments once you feel comfortable adding a line or two of Lua code but can make all the difference with your custom objects or purchased assets. Sometimes, all it will takes is adding some pathing nodes with the waypoint editor. Don't be afraid to spend an hour or two experimenting with individual AI. AI is one of those items that can really make or break a user's perception of the game. Nothing breaks immersion quicker, I think, than watching an enemy or NPC do something truly stupid, like trying to walk through a wall.

Better Objects

I've mentioned already the importance of picking higher quality assets to work from. While this can cause a minor amount of selection issues in terms of limiting what's available to you, it does really improve the quality of your game. Now this is always a careful juggling act. If you are seriously attempting to make money on your game, you will likely be SPENDING money on it as well. It's highly unlikely free assets (barring ones you make yourself or are lucky enough to obtain that are of sufficient quality) will meet the stringent criteria necessary to help your game be a success.

That said, GameGuru's community has always been a fairly tight-knit group that understands the cost/value proposition of GameGuru.

That is to say, it's a relatively cheap game engine and so the assets (even the really good ones) are often very well priced. Don't balk at the fifteen dollar packs, though, even if you only bought GameGuru for that much on steam sale. Quality assets are always worth it. If you check around on the Internet at third-party sites, or even for other game engines such as Unity or Unreal, you will see the pricing is often four to ten times higher for similar styles of objects.

So in general, understand that you are going to be using things that may have some issues with them. Other times, you may find yourself pleasantly surprised by something that may have been a low-end purchase. It's really a mixed bag, however, as it's important to remember that you should be ready to work with potentially issue-laden objects. Thankfully, the store does have a ticketing system that allows you to submit issues, but there's no guarantee that will go anywhere for you. Most vendors in my experience are fairly decent about fixing problems, though, so it's always worth a shot if it's something you can't fix yourself.

Objects purchased from the store are fine, but it's important to make sure they match well and are utilized to the best of their ability. We want low-detail objects as background objects; foreground objects should be the highest detail applicable.

Hands and weapons are typically the very highest detail; environmental things are typically a mid-grade, with specific points like shiny pipes getting special attention to help provide a real sense of depth.

We've gone over this at length, but I repeat it endlessly since it's a process that needs to be drilled into everyone from a design standpoint. Have a clear sense of process and always verify the quality of the purchased assets you are using.

Mini-Games

When you're building your game, there's always the potential it will become not only monotonous but also the most dreaded thing possible: boring.

To combat this, modern games often use a "mini-game" within the game to help break up the relatively static gameplay with something completely different. This method and technique has been used for at least 20 years, with a home in virtually every single modern game in some respect having some kind of capacity for additional play within it.

This capacity for additional play often rewards the player with various components that allow them to either progress the story or level or to achieve enjoyment doing something else other than running and gunning.

Many of my favorite games of all time included mini-games within them. While GameGuru is a fairly static system of being a first person shooter creator FIRST, it also has secondary abilities to add things such as drivable vehicles, isometric third-person views, and other possibilities.

It's important to at least plan for something of this nature being in your game, which should in turn allow you to create a more enjoyable experience.

While these can be actual games in and of themselves, I would caution against making an entire game out of something that is already tricky to do in GameGuru. It's good to push the limits, as you've seen as you have read through this book, but pushing too far can often result in broken games and extreme frustration.

Mini-games don't need to be anything major. They can be something as simple as a script you purchase from the store that allows you to move some boxes to depress a button that opens a door. This sort of not-so-blatant homage to another game often goes over well with a player. In this example, it was a portal-style game. One example of this is a recent work by one of the forum mods (Synchromesh) called "Protascope." (See Figure 17.6.)

While he did make this an entire game in and of itself, it could easily be adapted to a mini-game on a separate level map.

Implementation is as simple as getting the player to another level that has a completely different configuration for the start marker. The trickiest component is saving the user's information as often with different game mechanics, you may need to use such things as Lua scripts to remove weapons and then to re-add them later. In one extreme case, someone actually used Lua code to launch a separate executable to run a mini-game to emulate an arcade!

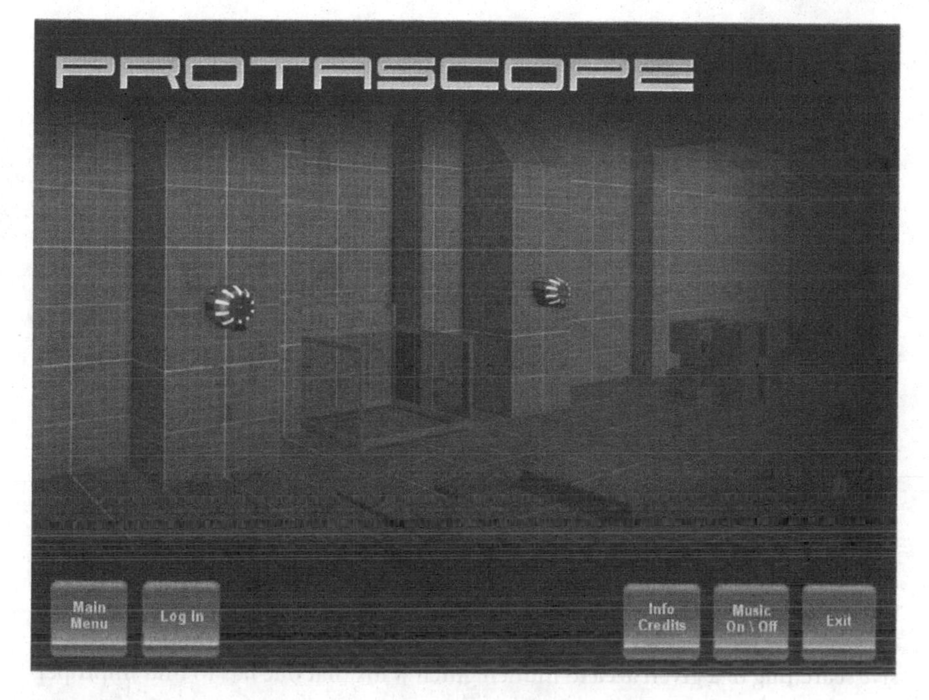

Figure 17.6
Protascope demonstrates many techniques for mini-games.

Secrets and Lies

Building secrets into games is another time-honored, or in some cases, time-lost tradition of keeping players interested in your product.

For example, imagine the following level design. It's a simple rectangular hallway, with one room on it. Does this excite you? Is this interesting in any way? Sure, you might have some fantastic set pieces, and it might look tremendously good, but from a simplified view as shown, is it something you'd spend a lot of time thinking about?

Of course not.

However, once you add a few secrets—a hidden wall here, a tunnel system going to another secret room, a secret ammo container—then you add a lot of interest where previously things were banal and plain.

So let's examine what this means by comparing against the pictures as we build on this area.

Hidden Areas

The first type of secret is a "hidden area." These areas are zones that are visually unable to be seen by normal means until a condition is met. Sometimes the condition is very simple, such as pressing a hidden switch. Other times it's a complicated set of events that have to occur that allows a player access to a door that would otherwise remain closed.

These areas are effective and simple methods of rewarding players directly for exploration of large areas, notably for doing hard searches for "that hidden doodad" that will trigger the secret. Oftentimes this acts as a mental exercise that provides the player a direct reward for taking a long look at your own extensive work of level design.

The way I add secrets is often to not start with them but instead to build my base level, with the regular design minus any secrets. During the testing and playthroughs, there are often dead areas that have no content. This includes things such as long hallways, large rooms, dead-end alleys, and other similar areas that have no redeeming value beyond providing a set dressing. This is a perfect time to introduce a secret for the player as a reward for exploration.

So once you've set up your main lines through the map, go through with a fine-toothed comb and try to add hidden spaces.

Hidden Items

Hidden items are probably the most basic of secret types, a simple way to directly reward a player for their game-playing. This can range from Doom 2016's method of placing secret-specific hidden objects in places that can only be found by extensive searching of a given area to hidden glitch walls that one has to find improper texturing to know they exist.

These sorts of rewards are often used in survival horror genre games where ammo is sparing and enemies can be difficult to take down. It means the players have to spend extra time to "beat" the game by looking to find the ammo, health, or other consumables they desperately need.

Use of this method should be somewhat sparing as well, however, because an overabundance of free objects detracts from the thrill of finding them. Generally, what I try to strive for is a solid idea of "this is the amount the player needs" but here is a little extra to help them along. It's also nice if you give them advanced weapons early to help reward players who play through a second time. This way they can more readily feel powerful at the beginning of the game without detracting from the new player's experiences.

I would recommend tiering your "hidden items'" style secrets in this fashion:

- **Tier 1:** Simple and abundant. These types of hidden items barely qualify as secrets but act more as rewards for more completely searching an area. An example would be extra ammo stuck far away from the actual exit of a room.
- **Tier 2:** Tucked away but available. These types are generally a higher order of power (i.e., more powerful weaponry or higher quantity of weapons) and feel more like a secret than the previous ones. It should not be a top-shelf piece of equipment, however, but instead like a weapon that appears one level ahead of a normal arrival of the equipment.

- **Tier 3:** Hidden and scarce. These secrets are the very obvious "secrets" of a game. They are difficult to obtain and often have a very deliberate sequence of events or location that's utterly hidden that has to be found just for the purpose of obtaining them but offer a massive reward to the player for doing so.
- **Tier 4:** Easter egg. Frequently, the most rare and elusive of secrets but rewarding in a sense of true accomplishment. An Easter egg is a special kind of secret, generally something unique and personal to the developer. They often take the form of a joke or hidden message. The first Easter egg was famously found in the video game "Adventure" from 1979 on the Atari console of that time. Easter eggs have taken many forms over the years, but they all have the hunt for the secret commonality to them and are often quite silly. You are well within your rights to put a few of those in your game as well; there are even benefits to doing such a thing, such as increased publicity if you advertise a contest around it. These secrets should be almost absurdly difficult to find and something that will make sense at least to the users and yourself once found.
- **Tier 5:** Cheat codes. These aren't so much secrets to find in games so much as secrets players use to change their game experience. I won't go into too much detail here, but I will mention sometimes these can enhance the player's experience by significantly modifying things in-game with larger heads, special weapons, modified game mechanics, and the like.

Game mechanic abuse is a rare, but interesting, method that requires some serious out-of-the-box thinking to configure for players. These are secrets that can only be found by abusing the game's faults in such a way as to obtain them. For instance, "requiring" the player to use a cheat code to unlock an Easter egg in the map. One particular example is in the original "Rise of the Triad" game, which literally required you to abuse a game feature simply to find the end of the game! There's also the "Super Smash Brothers Melee®" "name glitch" that required you to enter a very strange set of controller commands to play as the end boss.

Sometimes these are intentional (such as with "Rise of the Triad®"), and other times they are by accident.

In my own experience, I had once coded my "Quake" cooperative bot and had a bug; this bug involved the AI players sometimes telefragging themselves on the way in but not necessarily getting the death signal code. This resulted in the AI players becoming flying, disembodied heads that spewed blood as they flew. They also spat nails and were invincible. So I decided to re-add it, but you had to meet some pretty odd criteria to get it to happen. I then hinted at it in the changelog included with the updated files so people knew it was a secret, thus facilitating the "Easter egg hunt." Only one player ever found it, aside from myself, of course. So there is something to be said about having it be maybe not TOO well hidden. Some Easter eggs were found many years later! Occasionally, this is useful for rekindling interest in an old game. I often find Easter eggs being "found" right before a big re-release of an old title to be suspicious at best. That said, it's probably good marketing, so we can't really fault them for it, can we?

Techniques to Help Players Find Secrets

Off-color textures are a time-tested and proven way to show where a secret is. Human eyes are calibrated to look for variances in patterns (Figure 17.7). They seek and find things that are out of place; this likely traces back to our hunter-gatherer roots. The same tricks can be used for helping them find secrets, though I caution you against being too consistent with this method. If you use the same trick over and over, it becomes boring and repetitive. Try to mix it around and be creative about the application of it.

Another method is to use obvious piles that have something peeking out of them. This will catch the player's eye in the way a diamond in the rough will. They are then rewarded for paying extra attention to the environment and given additional resources for their quest, whatever that may be.

TIP: Have players search for a diamond in the rough, literally!

Using lights to draw players as a moth (or lack of) can be an attractive way to lure players, but again, you have to watch beating them over the head with it. If you do this too often, it will become rote for them. Instead, use "flickering lights" in one secret area, a solid off-color light in another… switch it around! Maybe even have a completely dark area that stands out for them.

TIP: Use lights or an obvious lack of light to draw players to a secret area.

Off-beat paths are rewarding, thus they should be treated as a special "flavor" reward for the player. Give them additional paths through a level and then let them discover the really hard-to-find ones have additional rewards for them. This will have the players spending inordinate amounts of time just searching for every little secret path. A good example of this is the "Deus Ex" series, with the structured approach the developers took to make sure there were 3–5 ways

THIS PANEL HAS NO COLLISION
OR PHYSICS ENABLED

Figure 17.7

A secret panel with no physics or collision is a simple method.

to do everything. While this is probably a bit more than the average independent developer can manage, it's still worth considering.

TIP: The lesson is—the road less traveled has more rewards.

There's often so much more depth lying just beneath what appears to be a very simplistic room design. Secrets are a valuable tool; use them to enhance and enrich the player experience.

Custom Elements

So you've polished your game and it really feels like an actual project, and yet... something just feels cheap about it. It still has a lot of that "asset flip" feel. Asset flipping is a much-derided practice where a game engine such as GameGuru, Unity, Unreal, or other similar engine is used with stock components to throw together a game and release it. This thrown-together game is, unfortunately, a poorly constructed mess and is designed just to generate a few dollars for the developer at the expense of any positive reputation or gameplay for the players. It's typically the lowest of the low by indie gamedev standards and thus is to be avoided whenever possible.

So how do we avoid that? Why does your game still feel like a cheap asset flip, even with your hundreds of hours of hard work?

The truth is because you are likely using a great many of the stock components and don't yet realize it. There are significantly common elements that you will want to go over with a fine-toothed comb before your product's release.

First, the sounds! The original sound system has some very generic and overwrought sounds—notably the death noise made by the final moan wav files. These sounds make the game easy to rapidly prototype but really should only be treated as placeholder assets. Not only that, whenever they are placed in a game, they stand out significantly as something that clearly shows a lack of effort on the part of you, the content creator. Think of the Wilhelm scream from the Warner Brothers sound library (thank you to my years in radio). It's an immediately recognizable sound that virtually everyone who has watched a movie is familiar with.

I don't know, personally, if there's anything worse to me than an obvious lack of effort. Call it a personal pet peeve that I cannot deal with a lack of effort in games. Sounds, however, are an often-overlooked element of GameGuru games that definitely speak of a lack of effort or thoroughness.

The default sounds can be found in your GameGuru Folder\Files\audiobank\voices\player folder. In this folder are files such as gaspforair.wav, hurt1.wav, and finalmoan.wav ...among many others.

Each of these initial sounds is likely going to need at least a common replacement or at least a basic swap with a less noticeable sound system. Couple that with the fact that the stock sounds have an awfully inconsistent volume to them. A prime example is the "zombie moan" that always comes through about three magnitudes higher in volume than anything else.

Now obviously, the simple answer here is to make your own sounds, right?

Wrong.

For those who have not spent any time actually working in an industry involving finely tuned sounds, you may not be aware of the incredible nuance that goes into making your own sounds. It's entirely possible you can do it with the right hardware (which seems to be coming down in price thanks to the thriving twitch/YouTube streaming industry) but be aware it's difficult.

I personally know a fairly prolific YouTube video game channel-maker and her setup is fairly extreme for what amounts to about 4000 subscribers' worth of work. She writes scripts, has a multi-hundred-dollar analog microphone running to a hundred-and-fifty-dollar sound processor. She then pumps that through multi-hundred-dollar recording software. You see where this is going.

In order for her to record, she has to turn her bedroom into a recording booth complete with sound deadening mats on the walls (she tells me she improvises by hanging blankets), turning off all electronics or background noises, and proceeds to drone out the world while she records. That's before she even edits out the pops, hisses, lip smacks, and other technical errors made during recording. I've done some guest recordings for her, and I can attest to how difficult getting even moderate quality sound is.

Now there is a simple answer here and that's to either purchase some sounds from the store that are made by people who already are competent with sound engineering. Alternately, you can always hire someone directly, and usually the rates for voice actors or sound creators are fairly reasonable. Not to mention there are a lot of "attribution free" (see Chapter 22 on licensing for information on this) sound effects out there that are quite sufficient.

Assuming you've replaced the sound library with one of your own for your project, my best recommendation is to get familiar with smoothing out the sound volumes to make them consistent. This is where a small amount of work will help you really seem far more professional in the long run.

While in the course of writing this book, I came across a YouTube review of one of our community member's projects. It was actually in a collage of other GameGuru games and was *supposed* to be a target of derision and ridicule. However, by the time they got to the community member in question's game, they were rather shocked at the quality of it. At one point, he says something along the line of "well, this was obviously made on their twenty-dollar headset, but they get points for making all their own sound effects."

Of course the game was polished and beautiful, which meant the guy spent a lot more time playing it than trying to make fun of it. Even when he did attempt to make fun, it felt flat because it was obvious he was having a good time and was looking for a filler for his video's format.

Replace the HUD

Another glaringly obvious "stock asset" that is often overlooked is the original heads up display (or HUD). While quite acceptable, it's a fairly simple matter to replace the image files involved to get a better heads-up display that's far more customized. This also gives you the advantage of having something unique, which many will subconsciously expect. These files are:

<GameGuru Base Install Path>\files\languagebank\neutral\gamecore\huds

In these folders are your various HUDs that are applied to EVERY GameGuru game you make. So if you choose to modify these directly, make sure you make appropriate backups not only of the originals but ALSO your modifications. The reason for this is because whenever GameGuru receives an update, it will check against what steam lists as the "proper" files. If it sees any changes, it will then delete your modifications and replace them with the defaults!

I, however, do not prefer to do these by hand but instead prefer to use the StyleGuru program to modify my HUD. It is a simple, clean way of making an effective interface for your users without all the mess of doing it by hand. You'll learn about that in Chapter 18 on "building a standalone."

Explosions

GameGuru is all about putting together something fast around rather specific limitations. One of these limitations is a fairly bland explosion system. While the physics are fleshed out, the actual decal sheet used for the explosion is not only repetitive but fairly subpar in terms of shape and design. Having a high-quality explosion can be costly, though there are answers out there in the form of premade sprite sheets that can be purchased or found for free. These sprite sheets will give you significant variety with respect to your potential colors. One major negative, however, is that there's only one explosion used by everything in the game. So short of some clever Lua coding, it's virtually ensured anything you use will become boring and flat over the course of your game (Figure 17.8). Thankfully, by this point, you should have some workarounds for it.

The texture sheet for explosions is a simple eight-by-eight sprite sheet stored in your GameGuruFolder\Files\effectbank\explosions under the file "explosion2.dds." By this point, I hope you were paying attention to Chapter 16 on retexturing assets as it described how you will use a free program called paint.net and a plug-in for it to save DDS files. If you skipped that section, I recommend you go back now and revisit it so you can make appropriate modifications in this portion.

Still with me? Good. If you have a decent set of eyes, you should have noticed there are several different explosions listed here. These explosions are for various secondary weapons like the fantasy weapon set or the fireball wand. The primary one we're worried about here is the default explosion, which is the explosion2 file. As always, I recommend backing up any changes you intend to make. Also, be aware that since these count as "core" files to GameGuru, you will want to back up your proposed changes as well. This is because steam will literally overwrite your modified files as soon as a new update comes through.

So you may be asking what a sprite sheet is. A sprite sheet is a series of images that will play in sequence. This sequence is similar to those old-style cartoons

Figure 17.8

The default GameGuru explosion is fairly basic.

where 20 or so frames loop endlessly. In the case of the explosion, this is usually a once-and-done affair, however. Sprite sheets are typically a series of frames that are all the same height/width and are on a specific pattern (specified by the shader or engine) in a single graphical file.

This single graphical file will sometimes use one long row of the images or a series of rows and columns that are in a set order (Figure 17.9).

This concept is used for everything from explosions to puffs of smoke. Now somewhat obviously, the more "frames" there are, the better detailed and smoother the animation will be. The downside of that, of course, is that these images are not being rendered but rather stored and displayed. This means more graphical memory is used than you might think, especially if it's exceptionally detailed.

These hardcoded explosions can be modified by using a new eight-by-eight sprite sheet that you put into that folder with the proper name. So if we, for instance, delete explosion2.dds, then copy explosion3.dds and rename the copy to explosion2.dds, we will replace the default explosion with the one from the fireball. While it doesn't quite fit our purposes, it does prove the point that it really is as simple as a file change.

Personally, I like to make my own explosions with one of the myriad of "explosion generators" on the Internet, though some fancier methods involve various plug-ins for higher-end tools like Adobe Photoshop. Whatever your method, the end result is that we have to copy the file into this folder as a DDS file type with the name "explosion2.dds." This particular "default" explosion controls all the normal bomb types such as exploding barrels or enemies or the various grenades.

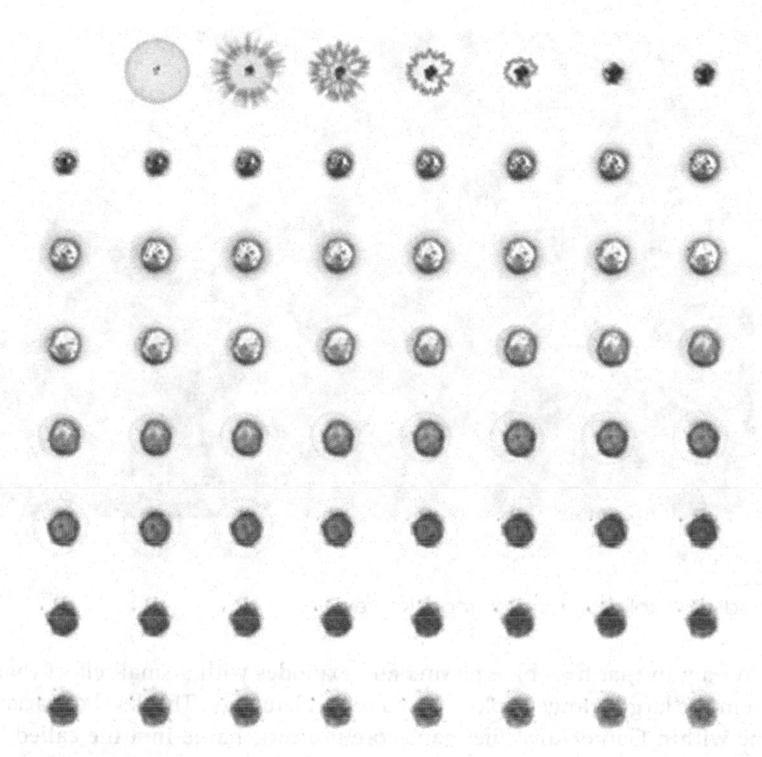

Figure 17.9
A simple 8 × 8 explosion sprite-sheet.

Improving this can result in a much better experience for your users, like the one shown in Figure 17.10.

I've enclosed a few examples of this so you can see what I mean in this chapter's folder of the media with the book.

Bottom line is that most of the basic explosions and effects in GameGuru follow this same formula and frankly aren't impressive from a graphical standpoint to begin with. So really it won't take much to improve. This will give you an edge over those who opted to use the lackluster stock graphic sprite sheets.

This can, of course, be applied to any of the files in the files/gamecore directory, such as the bullet splats and whatnot. While you may not feel you are a very competent artist, I assure you that given the low level of quality you are starting from, literally any changes will be immediately noticed by anyone who is familiar with GameGuru games. Most, I'd expect, will give you a nod for simply thinking to change such a commonly used object. Remember, it's the little details that matter in the finishing stage.

One interesting caveat to explosions is that you can specify sprite sheets for individual explosions for your various projectile weapons! This means that we

Figure 17.10

The modified explosion is much more impressive.

can have a gun that fires blue plasma and explodes with a small effect that differs from the large orange explosion of a rocket launcher. This level of variability is done within GameGuru\Files\gamecore\projectilename in a file called "projectilename.txt." By now, you should know this isn't 100% precise. GameGuru provides a lot of examples with it that you can use to modify or copy for testing. So in this case, we're going to copy the "modern" folder that includes your RPG weapon. So let's right-click on the folder, choose copy, then paste. Rename "copy of modern" to "ModernTest."

After you do that, go into the subfolder and rename the rpggrenade folder to newrpg. All of the subfiles in that folder should be renamed manually as well to newrpg to help avoid confusion inside of the GameGuru editor.

Your final result should look like this Figure 17.11.

There's a txt file in this folder that by now should be called newrpg.txt, and we're going to add two lines to it near the top. These two lines DO NOT exist

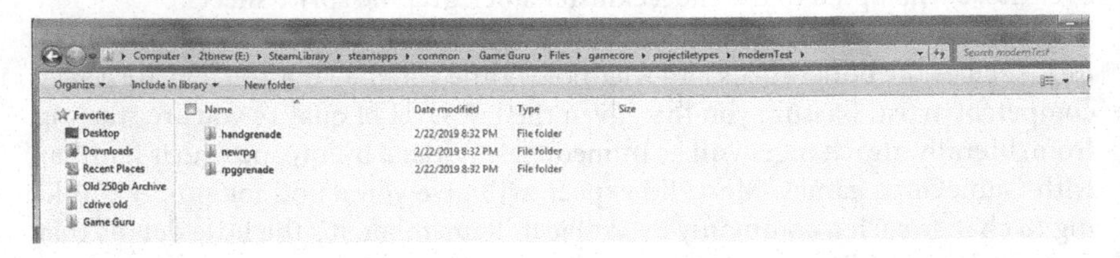

Figure 17.11

The projectiletypes folder has a very specific structure you must adhere to.

normally and need to be added but allow us to change the explosion to a new sprite sheet like the one I've included with this book.

```
explosionType = 99
explosionName = "8x8 sprite sheet of explosion.dds"
```

These explosions are found in the effectbank folder, so make sure you copy them into the proper location; otherwise, the engine won't know where to look. That, however, is it! After you modify that file, then you will have a second RPG available to the player start marker called newrpg that fires and uses the new projectiles. Unfortunately, you'll also have to make changes to other weapon-based files if you want a reload or the like by copying the ammo and weapon itself, but the same process applies there. Now copy the old one, rename it, and edit the FPE file to reflect the change. At that point, you're done!

What's wonderful about these "little details" is once you've done this for one of your GameGuru games, you can reuse your own assets for future games, thus cutting future development time. It's important to constantly work toward completing games and refining your toolkit. So you might find it takes you 15 hours to put together a really good sprite sheet your first time for an explosion. It then translates poorly in GameGuru but still looks better than the original.

However, you may come back three months later and try again, get it done in 30 minutes, and supersede the previous effort! This constant progress and momentum will drive you to success.

[illegible] and need to be added but they never change the explosion to a new [illegible] sheet like the one [illegible].

[illegible]

[illegible]

These explosions [illegible] you copy them into the [illegible] the engine won't know where to look. [illegible] and have a second DPL available to [illegible] new [illegible]. Unfortunately, [illegible] to make changes to other weapon-based [illegible] if you want [illegible] by copying the [illegible] and weapon [illegible] the same process [illegible]. Now copy the [illegible] and edit the DPL file [illegible] the change. At that point you're done [illegible].

What's wonderful about these little details is once you've done this for one of your [illegible] games, you can [illegible] your assets for future games, thus cutting future development time. It's important to constantly work toward [illegible] game and [illegible]. Soon [illegible] you'll [illegible] a really good [illegible] better than the original.

However, you may come back three months later and [illegible] again, [illegible] 30 minutes [illegible]. This constant progress and [illegible] to success.

18

Building a Standalone

So you're finally to the point where you feel like you can try pulling the trigger to export your game for a player to test. The export process is called "building a standalone" and can be tricky. What should be a fairly painless process of a single button click can often turn into a rage-induced stream of expletives. Sometimes it exports without incident and you're left scratching your head as to why this one level output correctly while the rest didn't.

How a Standalone is Built

The following is what happens with the process for GameGuru once you click the "Create Standalone" menu option:

First, it's going to output your level and all of the associated assets and scripts to your "my documents" folder in a "GameGuru Files" folder. Underneath that should be a new folder bearing the name of your level. You can rename this to whatever you like.

In this folder, a customized version of GameGuru will be exported that doesn't allow editing but instead just acts as a simplified player for your map. It also adds a custom menu system that has no additional customizations to it (Figure 18.1)

Figure 18.1

The default standalone's menu is very generic.

but can be easily changed with an image editor and Lua coding. The Lua scripts for the menu are all directly available within the export folder.

From here, GameGuru will then recursively go through your level and find other levels referenced by a winzone script. It will grab their secondary assets and copy those over as well. This continues forever until it finds a level no longer using those scripts and assumes you are completed.

The asset files are encrypted, ensuring that the average user cannot readily steal your assets by simply downloading your game.

This encryption process can sometimes be fairly lengthy, so the export process may seem like it is hanging as it's outputting these files. The best way to tell if the process is genuinely hung up is to check the file size of the output folder. This can be accomplished through Windows Explorer by right-clicking on the folder itself and choosing properties.

Upon completion, you can open that folder up and find an .exe file that has the same name as your first level. It will load and open as a real game now. This is where we find out just how much actually got translated over properly and how much will need to be repaired. Repairing is a fairly simple process, but it does have hurdles to watch for.

Custom Lua Standalone Menus

A few years back, the menu system was significantly overhauled to include complete Lua functionality. This functionality comes in the form of two separate folders that appear when you make a standalone in the standalone game's files subdirectory.

The two new directories will be savesgames and titlesbank. Savesgames contains a significant amount of useful files. By default, it will have only three: a readme.txt file, sounds.dat, and graphics.dat that all contain basic settings for sound and graphics. Other files that will be stored here are screenshots the player may take and also save game files, as you might imagine.

Titlesbank is where the magic happens. This contains all of your graphic images for backgrounds, menu sprites, cursor icons, and the like. It also has all of your Lua scripts that interact with the player and allow them to have a menu as well as run your game. While on the surface it appears a highly simplistic system, this is definitely a case of still waters running deep. I say this because the actual Lua system here is fully featured. You can literally run almost any command you would in regular GameGuru here. It's essentially a miniature level that has an image display overlaid on top of it. Let's review the Lua files briefly here so you know what they control:

Win.lua: This file details what will happen when a player completes your game. At bare minimum, you can easily configure this to display an image with perhaps a "you win" screen. On a more complex level, you could script cutscenes, scroll text, or even have it play a video!

Lose.lua: This file is, as you can imagine, the game over screen for the player. The same rules apply here, allowing you to configure customized game over screens that can have context sensitive death screens, for instance.

About.lua: This Lua file covers what happens when the player goes to "about" on the main page. The default is that it will display an image and a way to get back to the main menu. Obviously, all the same rules apply here.

Sounds.lua: Is a rather complex file that controls what sound files do what on your title screen and how they interact with the menu itself. This is not one I'd advocate messing with much as for the most part, there's not much you can do to add to it in a meaningful way.

Loading.lua: Now we get to a fun one. While the basic loading screen was already mentioned as being a tremendously slow chore that doesn't give meaningful input, you do have the ability to change the background image to something simple to provide utility to your users by providing backstory or instructions. Except, what if we did something even more interesting? What if we put a simple game, such as a Galaga-style game, on this screen? Wouldn't that be something? Well, that's all within the realm of possibility. The loading screen, for all of the torturous waiting times, can actually be an opportunity to give your players any kind of experience you want—so long as you can either code it yourself or hire a competent person to do it for you. Either way, at bare minimum, you're going to want to familiarize yourself with this one.

Gamemenu.lua: This is your "in game menu" Lua code that pops up when the player interrupts their game by hitting escape. It's customizable in many ways like the title screen Lua and, as a result, you can add all kinds of extras here. That said, this one is one you will likely leave alone as it's fairly complete from a user standpoint. It allows a return to the title screen, saving, and other generic features that you'd find in any other game engine.

Graphics.lua: On this file, we find the graphics settings are stored in graphics.dat and loaded from there as well. This configures the quality levels and resolution of the GameGuru system for the player to whatever their desktop is set to. This allows you to make sure you will always have the proper setting for a system, though it could cost the user some frames if their desktop is very large on a system with a very slow processor or GPU. As with all of these, it's completely customizable.

Loadgame.lua: This handles the loading of save game state files. If you have custom variables that need to be loaded, this is where you'll want to do that.

Savegame.lua: This handles the saving of save game state files. If you have custom variables that need to be stored, this is where you'll want to pass them.

title.lua: Your main game title screen. This highly customizable code can have menu options added, display a background, have a mini-game added, secrets, you name it. It's utterly flexible and, in that regard, you can build it out however you need to. If you want to reposition the title screen's menu to a corner, go for it. It's just a few X/Y values away!

Nextlevel.lua: The code contained in this is your "winzone" for when the game isn't over yet. This allows the game to configure loading the next map and continue the game.

Some important notes here. First of all is that sprites stay loaded indefinitely, unless they are manually unloaded. There's some examples of this in the Lua code where you will see a function called _free (example: title_free) and it deletes the sprites from memory. It's important to clean up after yourself to avoid unnecessary memory usage.

The display order is typically 3D, sprites, then text. However, there are some commands you can call to change this order—for instance, if you want to display sprites on the top layer so they aren't overwritten by text from Prompt and other Lua text commands:

The command "drawspritefirst" will put sprites before 3D, making it the top priority. You can also use:

The commands "setspritefirst" or "setspritelast" to set the place in the display.

Beyond all the aforementioned commands, your normal array of math, Lua, sprite, and other associated commands will work here allowing you significant flexibility with the menu and title system. Do bear mind that the sound system is NOT functioning here as it's technically not loaded yet, so it's reliant upon whatever is in the sounds.lua file.

I highly recommend watching the very informative podcast that was done by Lee Bamber, available on YouTube, titled "Broadcast #34, Customizing Your Standalone Game Menus." This podcast has a wealth of information about the structure and development of the menu system as it stood upon implementation.

StyleGuru

So you're probably staring at this wall of code and thinking "do what now?" right? This is not uncommon; the menu system is fairly well contained for the basic user and, at bare minimum, you really won't find much need to modify it. In most cases, you're just going to want some different background pictures, maybe some fancy buttons… right?

Well, look no further than StyleGuru. This program was made by a user years ago as a third-party attempt to control the menu system as easily as possible, and I have to say it's exactly as it was intended. It allows a massive amount of change to be made to the menu system without having any idea how to really do anything at all. You can modify fonts, change buttons, backgrounds, etc. It's an impressive piece of work that's as intuitive as it is essential.

It's a separate program, obviously, but when loaded gives you a very easy-to-use menu that allows you to build graphics any way you like for any screen you have. Granted, some of the graphics need work, but it's as easy to add your own as it is to use theirs. What is most important about it is how seamlessly it creates the secondary files and folder structure necessary for your standalones, removing the chore of having to manually edit dozens of files to cover every resolution setting in the game.

It's really a phenomenal tool that frankly should be integrated into GameGuru itself. In the meantime, it's completely free and included with our media. The original developer (a German user named "Sanguis") has since ceased development as he saw it as mostly complete. I agree with him, and I'm sure after you use this program, you will too!

When opening it, you'll come up to the screen shown in Figure 18.2 to start.

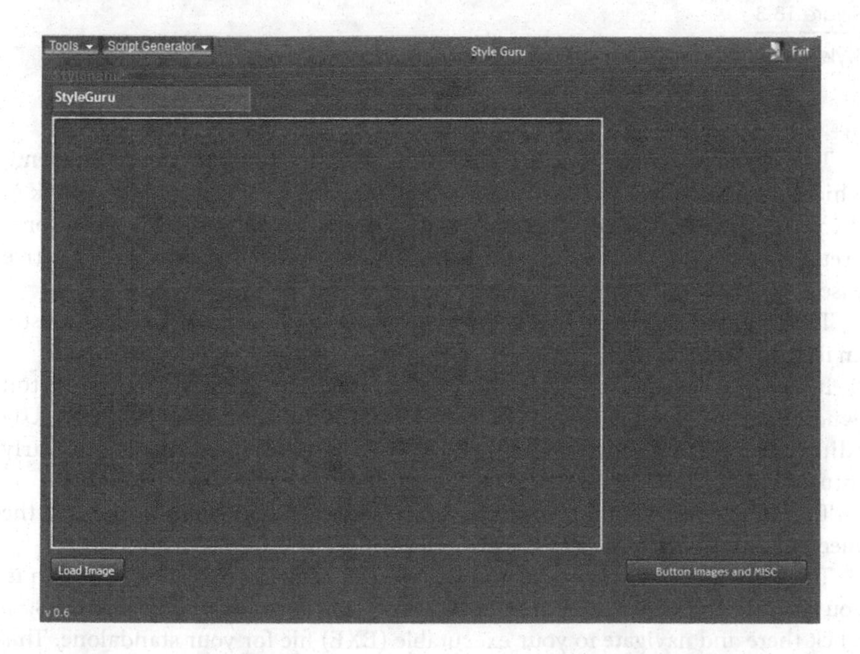

Figure 18.2

StyleGuru's main screen.

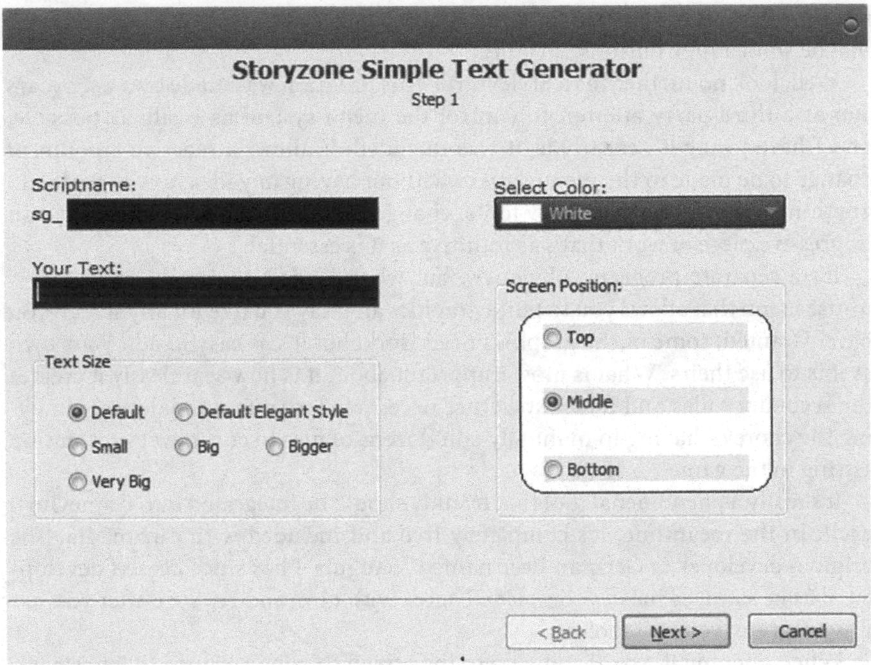

Figure 18.3

StyleGuru's story zone text generator is fairly straightforward.

This screen has a few important buttons. Up at the top is the tools menu, which has several useful functions we'll circle back to. For now, take a look at the script generator. This script generator is extremely limited but does some pretty useful things, allowing you to make story-related scripts with relative ease (Figure 18.3).

The Tools menu (Figure 18.4) allows you to use the "designer," which is mostly an image creator.

It also has an icon changer (for your standalone game's icon), a button generator that easily allows you to modify the in-menu buttons, an HUD editor, and a game cursor changer. All of these, as mentioned, are fairly intuitive.

The most overwhelming, frankly, is the designer—but that's just from the sheer volume of options. Let's go through each of these one at a time.

The icon changer is the most simplistic, so let's start here. When you open it, you get a very minimalistic screen that says "Load Game EXE File" (Figure 18.5). Click there and navigate to your executable (EXE) file for your standalone. This will then load the EXE and let you change the picture!

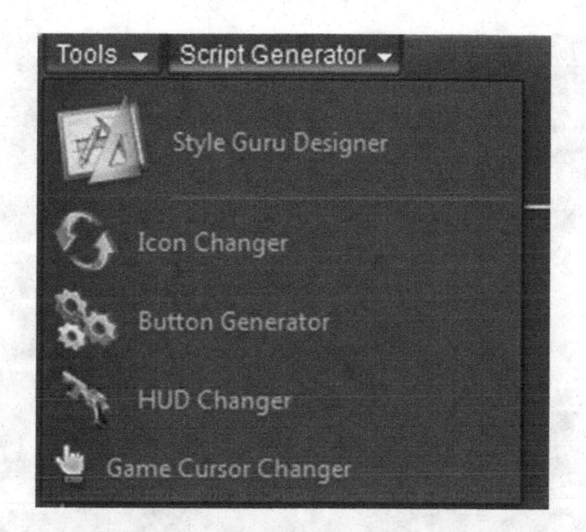

Figure 18.4

This is the Tools pulldown in StyleGuru.

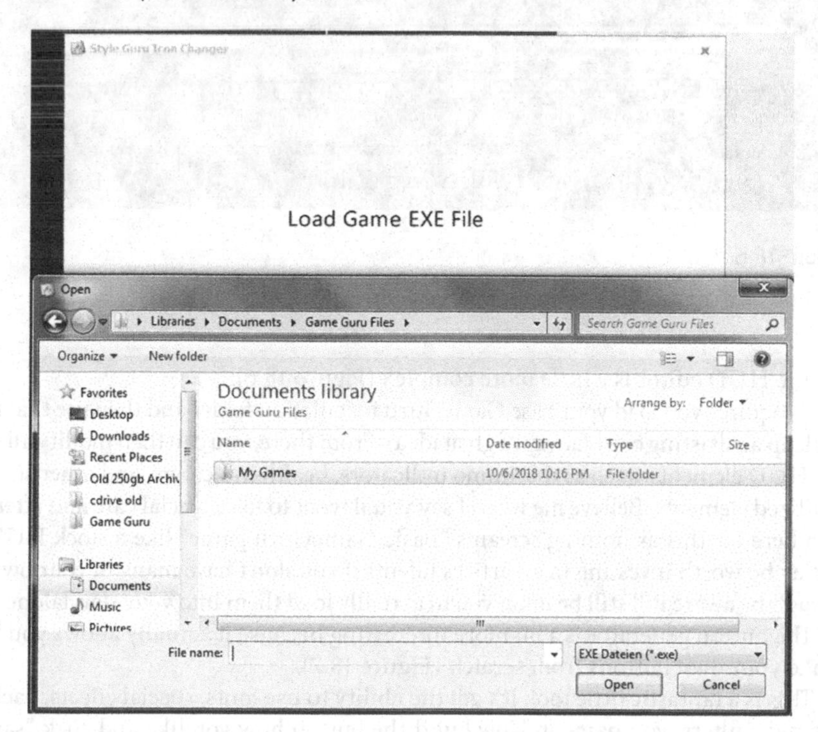

Figure 18.5

Demonstrating the icon changer of StyleGuru.

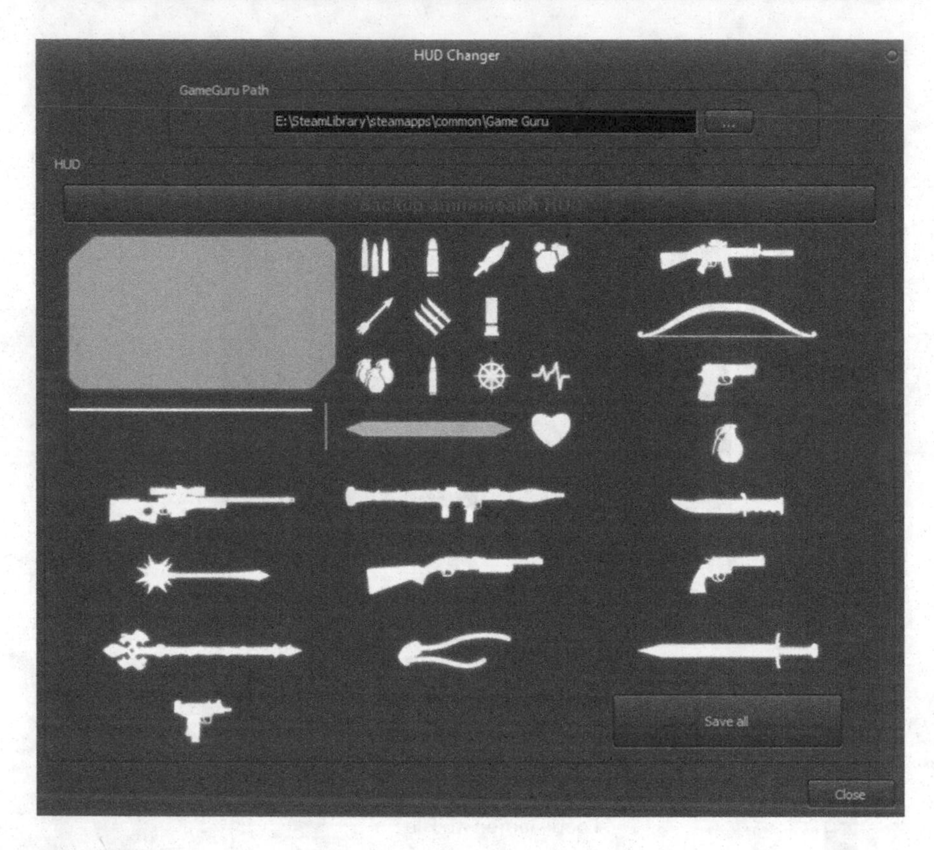

Figure 18.6

Demonstrating the HUD changer of StyleGuru.

The HUD editor is a little more complex (Figure 18.6).

It requires you load your base GameGuru installation folder and then use that to back up an existing copy (always a great idea). From there, you can then modify all of the HUD elements, such as the ammo indicators, health indicators, and other standardized elements. Believe me when I say you'll want to take special care and attention here for this as nothing screams "basic GameGuru game" like a stock HUD. It may be worth investing in an artist's talents if you don't have many of your own, though be aware it'll still be upon you to actually load them into your standalone.

The button generator is a bit more interesting because it actually allows you to make your own buttons from scratch (Figure 18.7).

This is a fantastic little tool. It's got the ability to use fonts, special effects, backgrounds, filters, you name it. Now build the button how you like and click "save button." It will then save it as a .png file on your machine. I recommend making two of them as you'll need them later. The second one should look larger or different in some capacity as it's going to be your "mouse over, selected item" menu

Figure 18.7

The button generator of StyleGuru has many options.

button. So you need to make two buttons for everyone: an idle one where it is just sitting and looking normal and a second one that indicates it's currently selected.

The designer allows you to make loading screens, backgrounds, you name it (Figure 18.8). It's got several different options at the top: background, graphic, and text. The background is your total background image. You can either import your own or use one of his ready-made ones.

The graphic portion is a simple graphic overlay system, allowing you to place ready-made graphics and position them. You can also drag the dots of their boxes to resize them; you can set a transparency level on the right with the "blend slider." It's an extremely simple process that's the epitome of "WYSIWIG" or "what you see is what you get." Once you feel satisfied with it, click save image and it will save it as a JPG file in a folder of your choice. You will then load this file later using StyleGuru. It's a very simple image editor with some clipart you can use. While this seems ridiculous, it's extremely good for as lightweight and simple as it is.

To use this art, go back to the main screen and click "load image" at the bottom. You will be presented with a screen like the one in Figure 18.9.

You'll notice a lot more information populates on this screen. It tells you the dimensions of the graphic image as well as asks you what kind of image it is. This

Figure 18.8

Creating screens with StyleGuru is very easy!

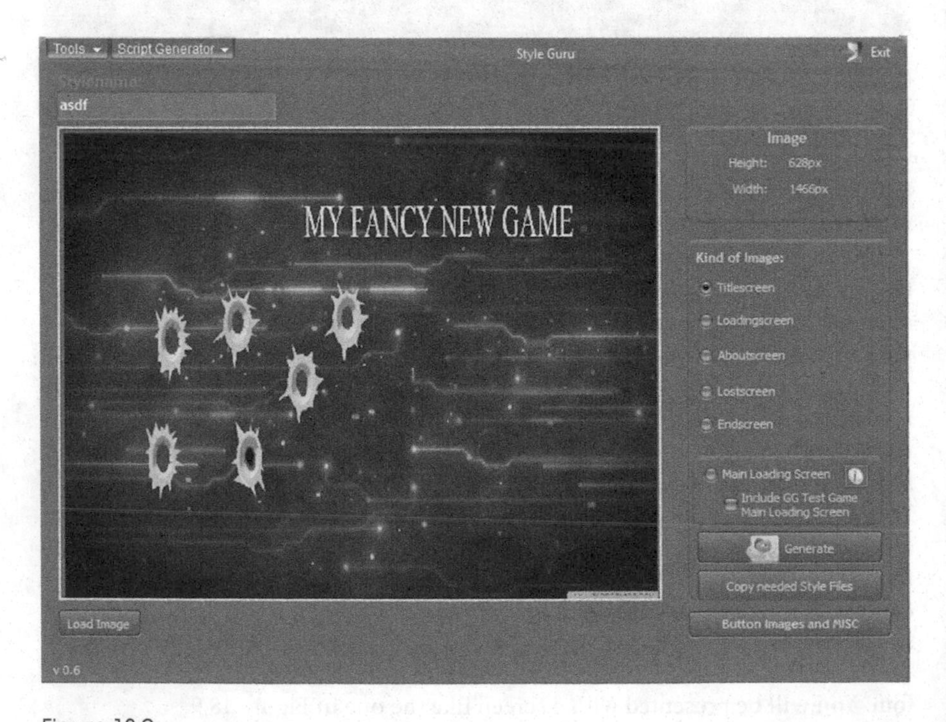

Figure 18.9

Before using your new screens, you must export them to your game.

is so you can specify where in your project you are going to place this. Will it be a loading screen or a title background? Click and it will configure it for you. When you're done setting up the name of your project (use your game's name), its buttons, and associated images, then hit the generate button to finish. It will prompt you for the output location and overwrite the files there with the ones specified in StyleGuru and... that's it! It's hard to imagine an easier way to get this done.

Packaging Your Game

Obviously, a fairly common method of packaging your game for transmission is to use a zip file or rar archive file. These file types allow you to compress the file easily, though with tools like 7zip you can break the file into multiple chunks for easier transmission.

Of course, each medium has a separate method of packaging. Steam®, for instance, uses the steam SDK. Other systems have similarly unique methods. If you're seriously marketing your game for release on these platforms, you will need to familiarize yourself with these distribution systems.

That said, what should you send?

Typically, when a game is configured initially it comes with an installer. It's all well and good to send a standalone as a simple zip file, but this does nothing to actually set up the program for the customer. You are often going to want to build an executable for them to run that's an "all in one" installer.

A frequent recommendation is a third-party utility called the ClickTeam® Install Creator. There are a few other options as well such as the free product "InstallForge." Lastly, there's also a third-party product called "Game Launcher Creator." GLC was not made specifically for GameGuru, but one of the older users did create it as a game launcher for many platforms. It does, however, seamlessly integrate access to GameGuru and offers a wide host of features such as a functional updater, server connections, media links, a simple system for generating menus, and the like. I asked a few users of it for their thoughts, and the general consensus was that it was very easy to use with the tutorials and worked great.

FPP Files

FPP files are special files that allow you to include a list of files that will come with your standalone once copied. This is especially useful if you are intending to copy specific secondary files such as scripts, music, entities, or models that are having difficulty getting moved over.

These files have to have the same name as your standalone export's map name with a file extension of .FPP at the end.

Inside of the file, there are two different headings to use:

[standalone add files]
entitybank\folder\file.ext

entitybank\folder\file2.ext
[standalone delete files]
entitybank\folder\file.ext
entitybank\folder\file2.ext

As you list the files underneath, do not use commas but instead put them on a separate line. The game engine will read these files and copy them over to your standalone if they are under [standalone add files]. If they are under [standalone delete files], then it will delete those files upon copying over. Please note the words and brackets for "[standalone add files]" need to be put into the FPP file for it to know what to do.

19

Finishing Touches

By this point, you've done a significant body of work on your level.

There's been work done and more work done. It goes on and on, doesn't it? When do you call it done? There's a certain level of finish you should be aiming for, depending on your product. It's exceptionally important to present a product that is clean and competent if you are vying for commercial success. No one is going to want to pay any kind of real money for a game that looks like something that didn't have any measure of effort put behind it. People don't just shell out 60 dollars for a new game title just because; they do it because it shows a level of quality that they feel brings them value in line with the game they are trying to play. Of course, one of the advantages of being an independent game-maker is your profit margins are much, much lower and, as a result, you can get more from less.

For example, you might not need photorealistic three-dimensional models. You might be able to get by with an eight-bit '80s' retro look that significantly reduces the strain on your art abilities and budget. The game, however, still will require refinement. The trick is not getting stuck in a loop of "refinement" where a game is really well finished, but you're making changes that impact it by .001%.

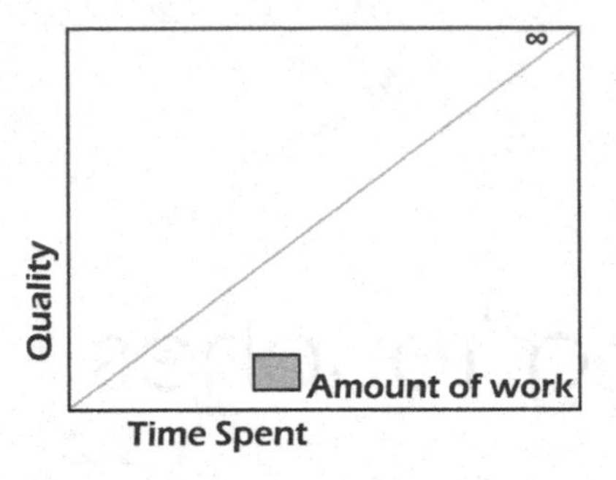

Figure 19.1

A simple work/time/effort graph.

Figure 19.1 is a greatly simplified work/time/quality chart. This chart represents how the level design and post-editing works. Post-editing is the editing that comes after you are done developing a product. It's used in movies, sound, game design, and a great deal of other industries. We are "in post" at this point. Your levels are designed, they are mostly put together and are lacking that final refinement. What you want to do here is smooth over the rough edges that remain without spending too much time sinking into finishing touches that cost you so much time that you miss your window for actually earning money back on this.

I recently (relatively speaking, to the time of me writing this) read a blog post talking about how a developer managed to put eight years of his life into developing his game. It was an interesting bit of text that really sank its teeth into common mistakes that people make in game development that really aren't listed.

These were boiled down to "work on irrelevant features"—in his case, making his own custom terrain engine and throwing 90% of it out, writing his own engine from scratch, and other features that were not crucial to the game's function. Thankfully, a lot of that heavy lifting is already done with GameGuru, but the same traps exist; it's very easy to get caught into a loop of predictable failure. A common loop, for instance, is to find yourself trying to fix a tiny issue that requires 20 hours of work but really only a tiny fraction of consumers may notice. An even smaller fraction will even care enough to complain about it.

This is why you see "obvious bugs" like rocks that disappear when people approach, and it seems like it should be an easy fix. Yet you find yourself wondering why <insert large multimillion dollar publisher's name here> left that obvious bug in. This is because at the end of the day, time is literally money—and there are times where you simply cannot afford to fix every single tiny error that comes up. That said, it's important you don't just leave glaring errors in the game or things that just look out of place. You want to offer a consistent level of quality while at the same time not miring yourself down in fixing every single tiny detail.

It's a bit like the difference between a mid-range sedan and a supercar. Sure, the supercar has an ultrafine level of detail—but it's selling for 10–30 times the cost of the standard sedan. In our case, the sedan is the standard you are up against. You can't make a supercar unless you either hire more people or spend more time.

Instead, what you are going to have to create will be along the lines of a "kit car"—something that trades areas of say interior refinement to give additional performance that the sedan might not have while at the same time trading away things you can't hope to match them on.

So how do we do this? Obviously, the later phases of playtesting will clean some of this up, but a significant amount of time should be spent doing the following:

Examining Major Scenes

Major scenes act as anchors for the player. They are common or memorable locales that will provide them a significant "base" for their understanding of the game. People tend to remember high and low points; they will likely not actively remember every little alley and corridor. So focus on areas that are large and important. Go over them with a fine-toothed comb, making sure to clean up any models or positioning that looks out of place. Really hammer those points home.

Most major points of interest will distill down to:

- One or two major geographical features (such as a mountain, a monument, a large neon sign, etc.).
- Lots of set pieces to help cement the scene (police cars, market stalls, obelisks, and other types of mid-level pieces). Remember to keep it consistent for this scene. Typically, a significant amount of nonplayer characters will be here as well.

One supremely telling "rookie mistake" is to have major graphical anomalies in areas that are of prime importance.

For instance, improper use of colors/hot and cold colors out of place or using models that don't match the scene. For example, no one wants to see a vivid green sign in the middle of a "cold blue winter" backdrop. It just looks out of place and weird. So consult the complimentary color wheel and hot/cold color wheels that follow.

Lighting

I've said it before and I'll just reiterate that your game is only going to look as good as the lighting you have in it. If you are using poorly chosen static lighting, badly placed dynamic lighting, bad atmospheric effects, lack of lighting, or any combination of those… then you are going to look exactly as you likely should: low quality. Low quality is something that begs people to not spend money on your project; it begs them to look at it as another low-quality project that someone threw at steam to try and make a quick buck. If you want to entice people, really spend the time to learn how lighting works. There's a lot of information out there ranging from industry talks by John Carmack (the man himself) to developers discussing how they used it in their games (Mirrors edge, for instance). Links for these will be included in the hyperlink reference list at the end of this book.

So yeah. After you've built your game, added your fancy PBR models, and gotten really good at making something bad look good, then check your lighting. Check it several times even. Make sure it looks stellar because it's going to need to be to compete. Lights should all have a good light source that should have a proper illumination map to really highlight how it is actually a functioning light.

By now you've probably got a good handle on lighting. However, this is the time when you want to really make sure that you've got that right shade of red. The default colors, if they were being used as placeholders, should be taken away and replaced with more scene-appropriate colors that don't cause too much of a jarring effect when overlaid. Remember, you want to harmonize the scene. An example of this that I find quite often is when new game developers use the default color yellow. This probably seems like the safest one to choose because after all, most light is yellow right? Wrong.

Hopefully, you've been paying attention because if you have, then you already know that most visible light that we use is a version of blue-white or yellow-white. Actual yellow light just seems unnatural and weird. Unless you are actually going for that look, avoid using that color!

TIP: Again—do not use any stock colors for lights! Always use a lighter version or a less harsh version.

This also goes for your light radiuses as well. In many cases, the default size is just too large—another fact you should be well aware of right now. However, at this point, we're assuming you already did that correctly, so the trick here is to go in and really rein in those numbers to a more precise value. This is not something you have to do for every scene.

Think of your game as an art gallery … the big scenes attract the most attention, so you should really spend a few hours just really going over it until you're satisfied with it. Don't be afraid to give these pieces a little extra love.

AI Behavior and Location

By now you're probably already able to predict what I'm going to say here, but we need to make sure that these scenes are airtight! Anything out of the ordinary in these areas will stick out like a sore thumb. This is especially true of AI. AI is tricky on a good day, but by now, you should be a seasoned pro at it. Even still, you want to really test these major scenes to their limits. As focal points, they will attract incredible ire if they are poorly constructed, and few things are more glaring than bad AI.

So, here some suggestions on how to improve your AI in these scenes:

- Adjust the capsules of the models so they don't jam up.
- Provide sufficient room for them to maneuver.
- Test multiple routes through the room so you can verify they are functioning correctly.
- Use a large mesh of nodes to ensure proper navigation even through difficult terrain.

One of my prouder moments was a personal game I made for my wife with my son. We built a Five Nights at Freddy's-style simulator for GameGuru. The AI had significant difficulty navigating the map, which made it a lot less scary than it could have been. I put nodes in many places, cleaned up the location of the tables and chairs, and this provided a horrifyingly good AI that hunted the player relentlessly. It's actually the same as the example I gave in the advanced AI chapter.

She both loved it and hated it. I remember her saying, "Wow that was incredibly scary, did you have to make it that hard?" Obviously, after that, I tuned the difficulty by modifying the AI's speed and HP, but the core lesson was that the AI's navigation was successful! This example, however, also underscores how important it is to have testers who are willing to tell you when something is outright too difficult for the player. Don't be afraid to tone it down a little, for the sake of gameplay.

Item Location

When you built your maps, hopefully you accounted for your item location. You probably spent a painstaking amount of time building your maps, placing the objects and power-ups, right? Even if you did, you will likely find that some are just... poorly placed. I liken this to a story I heard about a local college that built walkways. I arrived there to visit a friend and asked him about the oddly shaped walkways running interspersed through the grounds of the campus. They curved around trees, through courtyards, and the like.

I asked where the regular "rectangular" walkways were. He told me the story about how, for the first few years of the college's inception, they opted not to have any walkways. They did this because they figured that people would use the most efficient routes possible. He said they figured they'd have a lot of unused walkways and dead grass. As a result they waited a few years and then paved over the trails people were already using! These paths are called "desire paths" (Figure 19.2) and are rapidly coming into use in civil engineering to help design more natural and intelligent walkways.

You see, as game developers and designers, we tend to get tunnel vision on our levels. We know not only the design of the level but *how we expect the*

Figure 19.2
Demonstrating how desire paths work.

players to use it. Players, however, will often forego this in the name of their own efficiency. For this reason, it's important to have playtesters tell you what items they did or didn't obtain—so you can see how far out of the way your power-ups and gear might be. Imagine having an epic loot cave but no one knew how to get to it because it was inconveniently placed! That's the core of what we're trying to avoid here.

So try to clear your mind and treat your own levels like they are new and unknown. Go into each room and try to find your secrets or blow through it fast like you're racing to the end. How easy or hard was it to find your items? Do you need to add a flickering light to get their attention? How about moving some set pieces out of the way to provide better line of sight to it?

So first, isolate what items are being missed.

Then figure out how to get the player to it. This type of "forced guidance" is an essential component of trying to provide a good player experience.

Core Gameplay

This one is a tough one.

I'd hope, by now, that you've got a pretty clear sense of how you want your game to play and have been working toward that bit by bit. It's a critical component of your final game design so you have it where you want it by now, right? Or perhaps, just perhaps, you really don't.

A lot of games change core game design midstream because of limitations in engine design, changes in design philosophy, and/or changes in the game design itself. Sometimes you want a story-driven game and you find that it's better as a fast-paced shoot 'em up. Try not to look down on such things, often they can be happy accidents—for example, the aforementioned shoot 'em up was Doom! The original game had hundreds of features planned that were ultimately thrown out.

It's around this point you're going to go around with your virtual pruning shears and start removing extraneous elements. You will start removing things that may have been part of a grandiose design document but really have little use or function in your current game. Maybe save them for a future title. Nothing's ever a waste here. If your plans for a massively complex inventory management system end up being a lot more basic than you intended, simply work around that and save it for another title further down the road! Use the lessons of today to power your games of tomorrow.

Sounds

So you've built your scene, it's looking great, and the AI is functioning correctly. Everything is running smoothly and you're standing there in the middle of a living, organic space that really feels excellent. Then you hear it. The overwhelmingly loud and abrasive bird chirping from the hastily placed ambient sound zone triggering. You note it and think about how you need to modify the volume on that one. Then you realize you're far away from the trigger area and it's happening at full volume, indicating it's not handling 3D sound correctly. You write that one down, too. As you initiate combat with the local gang member NPCs you placed, you realize the enemy screams are canned and terrible … because they are the stock ones that came with the game engine.

This example is a very real-world one that should properly illustrate how important sound design is. No matter how good your game is, sound is really the "icing on the cake," as it were. The little components that exist within game design are so critical to producing a really good work versus a "decent rookie attempt."

Obviously, you are wearing a lot of hats at this point. It's difficult, of course, to manage all of these tasks and still be able to produce quickly. So, in many cases, you're going to have to budget your time. Take an hour or so and just give a quick run-through. Listen to the sounds and make simple adjustments to them as needed. Often just putting a filter on them with a freeware sound program or reducing their volume is sufficient to improve the sounds to a passable point.

Using Stock Components

You are using GameGuru and, as a result, have access to a huge amount of materials and assets. This includes official "vanilla" assets and TheGameCreators official DLC. These products, while helpful, often end up making your game have the unfortunate side effect of looking just like everyone else's.

As you can tell from previous sections, using "stock lighting," "stock sounds," and "stock AI" are almost always a recipe for a mediocre at best game.

I tend to only use those components for the purpose of being stand-ins for more effective third-party elements. That said, often times you can get away with these for obscure things like background elements or buildings. Foreground elements, however, will stick out like a sore thumb. Some final pruning should be done with respect to checking out the following:

- **HUD:** The stock heads-up display is a dead giveaway that it's a GameGuru game.
- **Decals:** Explosions, projectiles, etc. Even simple changes to these can have a lasting impact.
- **Weapons:** Using stock weapons is acceptable, though I recommend going and doing some image modification to them to help differentiate them. Even something as simple as putting a filter over something or changing the shading can be sufficient.
- **Textures:** If you are planning on using a stock game component such as a building or the like as a foreground element, try experimenting with an art program to modify the colors of it to help both differentiate it from other GameGuru games as well as unify it with your own game's color and tone. Adding blood splats, rust, or other touch-ups can go a long way toward user perception.
- **The title screen:** We touched on this earlier in Chapter 18 about making your own standalone game, but it really bears repeating that an aggressive and unique title screen will help you stand out.

Know When to Stop

One of the biggest considerations as a developer you will struggle with is knowing when to stop. Game developers are renowned for adding features upon features upon features. It's just so easy to add more when you get the itch, right? What's wrong with adding another new weapon? How about some really fancy code to replace your previously clunky code? This syndrome is referred to as "feature creep."

The thing is, you are likely working on this alone. With that, you are limited on how many hours you have available to spend, so budgeting your time is a critical ability that will keep you well served through your hopefully many projects.

TIP: Never add new features right before a release.

One of the biggest mistakes you can make is choosing to make major revisions right before a release. In one particular example I recall, a developer decided to make significant changes literally the night before debuting his game at the career-breaking E3 convention. It practically buried him as players became enormously frustrated with the barely functional copy. He was forced to literally debug it on the fly and try to fix what he could right there on the showroom floor. The most embarrassing part was he had a functional, stable copy ready to go before he decided to go monkeying with important pieces at the last minute.

There's also times where you decide the game just isn't good enough and needs more work. This is also a problem. While I don't think anyone can debate that there are times that games were released too early, it certainly doesn't mean you should spend seven years in pursuit of indie perfection. There's a great many developers out there who love solely to develop. They develop, endlessly pursuing that one game, releasing beautiful screenshots of a project that in seven or more years they are no closer to releasing than they were when they were started.

This is fine if you really are doing it for the love of your project, truly. I, myself, am a doer. I prefer to get things done rather than having works of art that span decades that will never actually reach completion. This can be a hard thing, letting go of a beloved thing. This does not come easily to anyone who truly loves what they're making. At some point, however, you need to be able to let go, to allow the project to stand on its own two feet. When you get great ideas, write them down! Keep those little gems for the next great project or the sequel to this game!

There's also the issue of money and, frankly, you're never going to make any by just perpetually rolling back releases. Personally, I see this as a lack of responsibility because if you never put yourself out there, you'll never find out just how bad your project really was.

That said, I've seen enormously bad GameGuru games make fairly significant money. Now I'm no advocate of producing garbage to make a quick buck, but I believe the answer lies somewhere in between. You can produce something that isn't absolutely perfect and blow the doors off those awful asset flips. Best yet, you'll be able to use the money you earn to provide even higher quality projects in the future.

Learn to love the little nuances of your game, the things that make it unique. Try to appreciate how a box that isn't perfectly placed actually makes the scene look and feel more alive.

Clean up what needs cleaned, add details where they need added, and try not to lose yourself in the minutiae. You are just one person after all and have to work within those reasonable limits.

Hopefully, you've cleaned up the graphics, sounds, AI, lighting and other miscellaneous components to provide a really great experience for your players. At the end of the day, though, the remainder—the pieces you leave in— are your flavor, your style. Little things you do differently than others will help define your game, and if they aren't impacting the game's performance or design negatively, then they are probably not worth obsessing about.

Probably.

On Crunch Time

In the industry, there's a period of very frenzied finalization that a game undergoes before publication; this is often referred to as "crunch time."

Crunch time is an extremely difficult period where friendships fray, connections wither, and divorces happen. Seriously. When I was writing this book and entered crunch time, it was an act of necessity. Long hours were spent preparing and then having several forcible rewrites due to the great morass of changes that had occurred over the year I'd written it. I knew exactly how much I needed to get done and how fast it needed to happen. It wasn't pretty. Thousands of words a week in a nearly obsessive fashion until it was completed. I was writing on lunch breaks, after work, late at night until it was done. As you can see, it is. You still have to take time to get the rest of your life done, though, so don't neglect those important to you. I still took time for my wife, my kids, and life in general.

Recently, there have been a large amount of exposes covering the 'crunch culture' that has burned out employees at many major AAA studios. This has resulted in botched products and failed launches.

Try not to kill yourself for your project. I realize that the overwhelming obsession that goes into making a creative project can be all consuming, but try to remember why you are doing what you're doing and spend some time with the people you care about, especially when you are most busy. It's easy to get mired down in the details. It's for exactly this reason that if you take some time away, clear your head, and spend some time with your family, you will be often better off for it. They can help save your sanity just like you can save your relationships.

20

Testing and Troubleshooting

So you know that immense amount of time you spent working on your game?

You're going to spend about that much here, too. The old adage is that the first 90% of development equals the last 10% of testing in terms of time. And while you've undoubtedly done some playtesting, here it bears mentioning that standalone games require even further testing because they are never 100% identical to what you built in GameGuru—not to mention the differences you might have added into the standalone system that could cause errors. The trick here is to leave no stone unturned.

The biggest issue we, as developers, encounter is that we already know our products. So as a result, we unintentionally avoid things we know are broken or automatically take the most efficient path through the level. While this is good for development, it's bad for testing. A good tester will take unusual paths and deliberately misuse things in order to expose vulnerabilities in design.

It often helps to have a second set of eyes. Alas, unless you are some sort of mythical creature, that is unlikely. The next best thing is to enlist the help of multiple testers. Using their eyes is far more reasonable, after all. Often times you are going to have them test, but if you do so, you may want to ask them for a trouble report. You'll want the information shown in Figure 20.1.

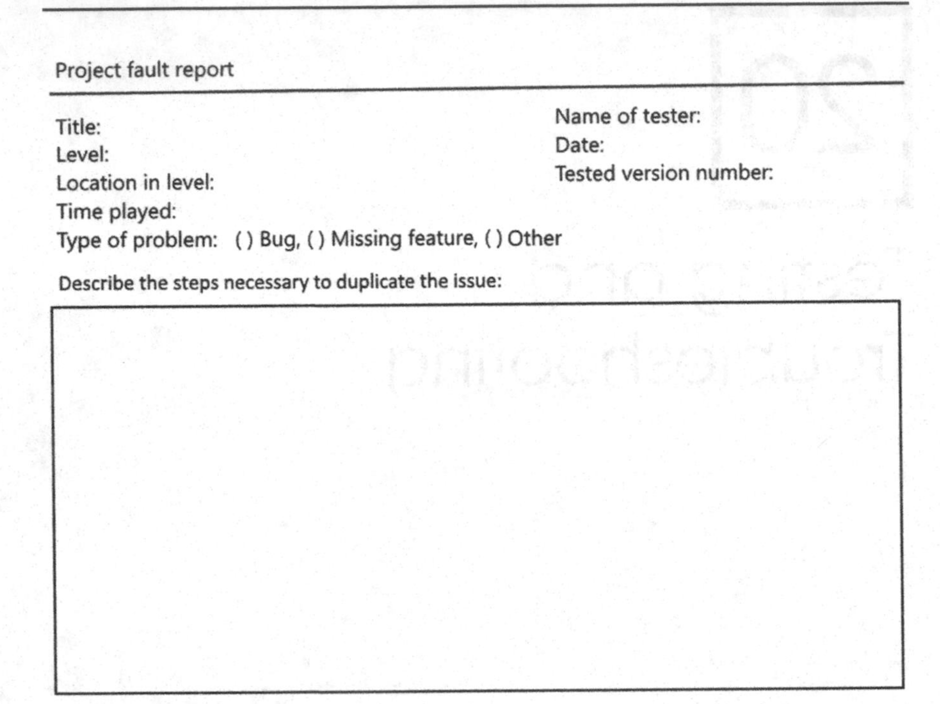
Project fault report

Title:
Level:
Location in level:
Time played:
Type of problem: ( ) Bug, ( ) Missing feature, ( ) Other

Name of tester:
Date:
Tested version number:

Describe the steps necessary to duplicate the issue:

Figure 20.1

An example of a fault report for beta testers.

It's important, when trying to find a problem to know how to duplicate it. Duplicating a problem means not only is it repeatable but that a specific chain of events lead to the ultimate failure in question. You want any details you can get so be ready to follow up with your testers if you cannot get sufficient information from their fault report.

Paperwork can be a lot to manage but can really help with the headaches. Alternately, if you prefer a freeware system that can do the same work via a web server, you can look into Bugzilla™, which is a free, open-source solution for bug reporting and bug tracking.

Testing

Once upon a time, I worked with a guy who wrote some really innovative programs for a job I was at. These were tech support tools and pretty much became required for anyone trying to fix a customer issue. The guy had a knack for really picking out things that needed tools and quickly putting together something in visual basic. He was having some difficulty with a program and asked me to check his code so I obliged. It was an absolute train wreck, the literal "spaghetti code" you've undoubtedly heard of. I eventually found a bug by tracing out some of the math in it.

That said, later on, I had my own program I needed help with and asked him to test it. I didn't expect what I got but I have to say in retrospect it was highly instructive. He came back to me several hours later with a veritable laundry list of errors. I was blown away; I had thought that my program was foolproof. I had intended to hoist it up as an example of how a *real* program was done. Pride and all that, of course, being what it is cost me a clear view of what was going on. Interestingly, he had not only a list but the ways he had come up with the errors were things I had never thought of—things like clicking on a button hundreds of times.

While this might seem really odd, it's important to note that developers often know their product so well they will innately avoid errors without realizing it. Something as simple as "I know the left side is not done so I will avoid it" or "I want players to go right here" quickly balloons out of control when put in the hands of a competent tester. A competent tester will do everything wrong. They will go backward in paths that are obviously forward, attempt to jump out non-functional windows, and fall in the lava just… because.

While this seems insane, it is exactly how testing should be conducted. You, as a game developer, will invariably be testing your own product. In that process, you need to remove your game developer hat and put on your tester hat. The tester hat is one that is deliberately trying to break your product. The tester hat doesn't give a hoot about how the game is supposed to be, only that it works.

Testers should also be looking at content issues, providing suggestions for missing details and areas where the FPS drops on their systems using different hardware types. This clearly is going to be limited in scope unless you've got enormous funds to work with but can be offset by using more testers for your product. Minimally, you want at least three or four good quality testers. Optimally, you'll have around ten or twenty. Testers will often work out of the goodness of their heart, to a point, or at bare minimum, for a free copy of a game. That's a reasonably fair trade if you are trying to avoid people pushing for refunds on a faulty product.

So take your game and tear it down. I've included a "broken level" for your purposes of testing. It features several examples of the following:

- FPS drains caused by unnecessary resource usage (like trees behind walls where they can't be seen).
- Erroneously aligned textures.
- Enemies that block paths when killed.
- Models with textures that are misspelled in the file, causing black surfaces.
- Lua code that fails and crashes the level.
- Objects with vastly incorrect physics properties.

And much, much more. This file will serve not only as a good example but a good practice to see if you can not only clean up the errors and make it functional!

The First Two Hours

When you begin playtesting your game, there will be a lot of work and time put in to making it clean and polished. One can tend to get distracted by minor errors dragging you down long rabbit holes and paths that make you waste precious hours that could be better spent elsewhere.

One of the plates you absolutely should spend significant amounts of time polishing your game is in the first two hours or so of game time. You need to absolutely hook players with a great story, environment, and gameplay right out of the gate. There's a pretty crucial reason for this, something you might not have considered: like steam. I mean, sure, we all want our players to actually enjoy our games, but there's a pretty strong reason to keep the player interested for two hours in particular. That is primarily because that's the guideline for how steam determines refunds.

> *Another point made by Gitelman was the importance of the first two hours of any game. Steam accepts free refunds of games so long as it hasn't been played for two hours, so it's supremely important to ensure the player is hooked in that amount of time. That's where McCain came in to explain that the opening tutorial and story mission were iteratively improved over many, many drafts.*
>
> – From an interview with Mitch Gitelmen by Sarna.net on the Hare-Brained Schemes® release of "BattleTech®" for PC at http://www.sarna.net/news/battletech-devs-talk-about-making-game-on-a-budget/.

This developer spent significant time and effort in making sure the initial player experience was not only enjoyable but engrossing enough that they would not even consider a refund for that time period. I realize it probably feels a bit bold of me to say that it's such an important consideration. The fact is that in a lot of ways, though, this is a big kick in the teeth to release a game and then suddenly have to pay out refunds because you released a game that was incomplete or simply bad.

You want your menus to be catchy, your loading screens to be short, your levels to play well, and your game to be interesting! Think about most of the games you play by a modern studio these days: Most of the real glitz, glamour, and beauty in the game is found right at the beginning. This is done to "hook" the player and get them invested in playing the game through at least to the midway point or completion. This means your story needs to come out of the gate strong along with the actual game itself being the best it can be.

To confirm, you will be spending a great deal of time playtesting those first few hours of the game to dial in the experience as much as you can for the player's benefit and your own.

Troubleshooting

Troubleshooting is a process—a method—that allows you to find and resolve your problems. I have spent many, many years as a professional troubleshooter for everything ranging from Internet connection problems to multimillion dollar virtual server hosts. All of these systems are essentially troubleshot the exact same way. Coincidentally, troubleshooting GameGuru can be done in precisely the same manner.

Troubleshooting is a process of exclusion; your primary goals should be to first replicate the issue, to then gather specific data pertaining to your issue, and finally to begin excluding things that it cannot possibly be. Your objective is to winnow down the problem to one or two possibilities and then begin addressing them accordingly.

So I usually start with a single question: "When did this start happening?"

The reason for this is because it's an open-ended question designed to elicit a response from the person reporting the problem. If it's myself, then I will answer it as if I were a user. From here, you can discern a lot of things: Is it happening when a certain item or condition occurs? Was it working before object X was added to the game but broken afterward?

Next, what we want to do is check the GameGuru log files. There are several vital sources of information here that will give you some concept of what is going on. In a standalone game's folder, there's the GameGuru.log file, which goes over an item-by-item analysis of what successfully loaded. This can give you some idea of what may have caused it if you know what the workflow is supposed to be. In the GUI editor, this file is called "guru-mapeditor.log" and contains roughly the same information. Of particular note is "guru-mapeditor-last.log," which is another file and is the log from a previously loaded level. The reason this can be more important is because often when there is an error with the editor, it will reload the level automatically. This inherently wipes out the data in guru-mapeditor.log, which means you almost always want to be looking at guru-mapeditor-last.log instead. This file has a similar structure but vastly more information than the one created for the standalone file. This is because it will also show you the editor's information as well. Often this is less useful for reasons we'll get into shortly.

So now that we know there's a problem and approximately when it began along with some rudimentary data about the game from the log file, we can begin trying to exclude irrelevant data.

Our final goal here is to figure out both what is causing this problem and what will fix it.

Once you have a good idea of some of the conditions involved with creating the problem, the next step is to recreate it. Recreating the problem ensures it's duplicable, which means it is solvable. Nothing is more frustrating from a troubleshooting standpoint than trying to fix an issue you can't even isolate!

Some other questions to ask yourself while you are working on this that will help speed you toward resolution:

First, is this happening both in the GUI editor and the standalone?

If the answer is yes, then you can stop using the standalone to troubleshoot. If it's happening in the editor, fix it in the editor, and it should resolve in the standalone.

If it's only in the standalone, then the problem is likely a difference between the two—almost always a missing file.

Second, is there an error message?

Error messages are supremely helpful. I've included an Appendix at the end of this book that has a list of known error messages produced by GameGuru along with the resultant codes on them. If there is an error message, can you do a search on the Internet for the exact error? Which brings us to our next question...

Third, has anyone else already fixed this problem?

Why should you need to reinvent the wheel? There are undoubtedly people out there who have already experienced this exact same problem, and if they have, you can leverage their solutions to your benefit. The growth of modern search engines means that you can save yourself significant time and energy by just checking around and seeing if someone is already in possession of a cure for your woes. This also can include spending time on the forums or discord. Checking with others can be the key to victory!

Common Problems and Resolutions

Objects Popping In and Out Visually

This is a fairly simple issue that can be traced back to the occlusion settings. It can be verified easily by disabling occlusion by using the slider and setting it to the lowest setting. If the issue resolves, then you know the objects involved are improperly configured for occlusion. You'll need to modify the FPE file occluder/occludee settings to resolve it.

Character Creator Buttons Not Visible

This is a fairly well-documented issue that can be traced to your Windows desktop font size being set to 150%. Reducing it to 125% or 100% should resolve this issue.

Slow Loading

It's a fact of life when opening and using the GameGuru editor, but when you open your game(s) you expect them to load quickly. The fact is that there can be times where this can be excruciatingly slow. There are several things that cause this slowness, but frequently this can be fixed in the optimization phase of your game development. In one of my particular projects, I had a level that literally took 15 minutes to load in an older version of GameGuru. Things have happily improved since then; however, it still takes a good solid five minutes to load. Worse yet, there's no indicator showing what the loader is doing during the process beyond a barely visible bar at the bottom that will stall at points for minutes at a time on complex levels.

The key here is to be patient and wait. If it fails, it will invariably provide you with an error message. If you can't wait that long, try to check the bar to see how far along it is when it dies.

In my experience, the two greatest delays are going to result from both calculating the physics and creating AI obstacles. The latter even more so than the former, though they both will result in enormous slowness. Both of these are covered in the next chapter (on optimization). One upside is that AI obstacles are calculated primarily on the first load. So, if you load it once and then load it again, the second time will take significantly less time.

Missing Scripts

GameGuru takes a good shot at trying to copy all of your relevant scripts over, but it's exceptionally common to have custom scripts not get properly copied over. This is unfortunate, but easily remedied, by copying the appropriate script to the matching location. The downside to this is while this WILL resolve the issue, it will also leave an unencrypted script that can be ripped off by the first enterprising user. As such, it's a risk we have to take, though you can try opening an issues ticket on GitHub for your specific issue to help get the scripts properly copied over. FPP files will also help get your missing files moved over as well

Missing MultiTexture Objects

Another known problem that purportedly has been fixed was the lack of ability for GameGuru to copy multiple textures for multitexture objects over properly. The fix is the same, to find the object that is failing and to copy the other textures over. This also results in a lack of proper encryption; so here again, if that's something that is going to be a problem for you, contact Lee Bamber and company about it.

Path Not Found Error

Sometimes this is caused by a missing object or a bad definition in an FPE file. If there's a path not found error, then check to see if the object in question is in the files folder. If it IS, then check the FPE file and verify that it looks correct. In one particular case, a user had to simply add a missing semicolon to the line to indicate a line ending in the file.

Video Memory Issues

The setup.ini file takes on a life of its own here with respect to standalones. The dividetexturesize=1 value, in particular, can be a real lifesaver if you modify this to a 2 instead of a 1. This change can cut video memory usage in half and works as a good shotgun fix for issues that seem to make little to no sense. That said, it can also break things, notably weapons, in game. It can, however, have big gains in both framerate and video memory, so it's worth noting here.

Memory Consumption

Light maps cause issues with memory usage; as such, you want to test often, test early, and avoid overloading the setup.ini file. Moreover, strategic reuse of objects is critical. Those objects often fill up more and more memory, so you want to make sure you are consistently using objects whenever possible. This includes stretching, scaling, and skewing them to any extent necessary to create variety. For instance, I will often use concrete blocks to make walls but also use them as interior design elements as well.

More often than not, you'll find yourself dealing with crashes caused by one of two things: either your Lua code will fail with a crash or you will consume too much memory. This, in turn, will cause either slowness or outright failure in the form of an error.

The simplest solution frequently can be found in simply restarting the client. Often, memory fragments may not be properly released and the most surefire way to manually release them is a restart of the GameGuru editor.

AI Issues

I cannot stress this enough—rigorously test your AI. AI, in this game engine, is highly reliant on a module from the "DarkAI" system that is a bit of a CPU and resource hog. Errors with monsters falling through floors are easily resolved by adding a floor zone. Navigational issues are resolved by adding navigation nodes. Testing to make sure this is playable and interesting is critical to the success of your game. No one likes an AI that is too good and no one likes one that is dumber than a box of rocks. Finding that balance is a critical component to your success!

Asset Management

If you've been following this guide, you probably have a good idea of how to structure your work. Indeed, it can be difficult given the lack of asset management within GameGuru. However, you can self-organize your files into separate subfolders to make things easier. You can also copy your work into separate GameGuru folders if you have enough space for multiple instances of GameGuru.

Other Errors

There are going to be times where you are going to have unfamiliar errors. These errors are almost always related to missing content and, thankfully, there's a file that's generated when a standalone is created that details all of the file copies that GameGuru does for the standalone export.

This file is found in the standalone game's base folder and is called "contents.txt." It details every single copy that was done during the operation of the game and also will show what failed in copying. Part of my process for building standalones includes always checking this file to verify that the files carried over correctly and to directly find any errors before I even load the level.

If you are not using the standalone, but load a map with missing models, these will be listed in a text file bearing the map's same name in the same folder in it. For example, if your map name is mybigmap, then the text file will be mybigmap.txt and it will be in the same folder.

This, of course, doesn't discount the other log files as well, which often can provide other clues as to what's going on. Remember, this is your product that you are working on so you will need to familiarize yourself with the inner workings as much as you possibly can. Don't let yourself be scared off by the concept of log files being technical jargon. Worst case, someone else on the forums or on discord can help interpret it for you.

Real-World Examples

Real-World Example #1: Len the Man's Cowboy Shooter

I frequently help other users within the GameGuru community and, in one particular example, a user had a game that was dying on the fourth level. It ran fine up to that point, but as soon as the fourth level loaded, wham, down it went. No error message, just a black screen and a dump back to the Windows desktop.

So we outright know "when does this happen" and the answer is when you hit the fourth level. So to further detail this, I asked him for more specifics. Is it as soon as it opens or… is it at a certain point in the fourth level? The answer of course was "as soon as it opens." We checked the log files and the last five lines showed the following:

1114153: begin loading LMO files S:0MB V: (1286,37)
1130820: loading LMO t.terrain files S:7MB V: (1294,126)
1145158: initialise final game variables S:46MB V: (1341,277)
1145774: immediate title settings applied S:0MB V: (1341,277)
1145919: main game loop begins S:0MB V: (1341,277)

What this shows us is that the game *loaded*. That's the important thing. It means it got past all the prerequisites of bringing up the engine and failed *after* loading the level.

So upon further questioning, we then find out it's not as soon as it opens but rather after walking around for 30 seconds to a minute. This is a big clue … remember that specifics matter here, and we now know that it's functionally loading the level without incident but instead is dying *after* you explore the level. This led me to believe that it probably was when a specific entity came into view or became active.

This was further compounded by him saying, "When I shoot the enemy characters it crashes." So now the original question of "when does this start happening" can be answered like this:

> After loading level four and walking around a bit, when I shoot an enemy character the game crashes.

So at this point, the next step in our exclusionary process is to make a backup and then reload the original. This way, we have a point we can return to if there's a problem with our troubleshooting. Once the original was reloaded,

I had him delete all of the offending characters and, unsurprisingly, the level worked just fine.

At this point, we know it's the enemy itself, and we can either try to fix the enemy character or use a different one. Since there were no Lua errors being thrown, I knew we could exclude the AI as a potential failure area. Instead, it likely was either a weird glitch with the model file or more likely the FPE file. I advised him to try going to the FPE file and comparing it against others. With FPE files, even a single out-of-place character can kill an entire entity, so it's extremely important to be very particular with them.

He did a line-by-line comparison of both a functional enemy NPC and the failing one and found this:

> I just checked the suspected NPC and the whole line about the weapon was missing. It should have been— hasweapon = modern\Magnum357.

This simple mistake caused a huge series of errors that, once corrected, fixed the entire system.

Real-World Example #2: A Personal FNAF Clone

In this example, I had a private "Five Nights at Freddy's" (FNAF) game I had made for my wife's birthday. This game consisted of the player avoiding several enemy entities until a timer for 5am was reached and they were able to begin the next day.

It worked great in testing with the editor so I was fairly saddened to see a major bug crop up during the last level of the game when in the standalone version. Since it was standalone only, I knew the problem had to be limited to that specific area.

One of the characters I included was a custom character that had information made from the Character Creator included in GameGuru (Figure 20.2).

This was supposed to be "Foxy," who typically was one of the more difficult antagonists in the "FNAF" series. I designed this one to be faster and with different AI than the other two. I should note that all of these had modified and custom AI.

The problem was when you loaded the last level where Foxy was, Foxy wasn't there! Not even a little. There was simply no sign of her. This made the game fairly disappointing when the culmination of the game could never be reached.

Since I wasn't getting any errors and it was only a missing model, I began checking the standalone game log file to see if anything telling showed there. It appeared perfectly fine!

I remembered, however, that there was a special file created for standalone games called "contents.txt." This file detailed all of the files copied over and if there were problems. I quickly isolated that some of the character creator models didn't copy over and, once added to the files\entitybank path, it resolved the issue!

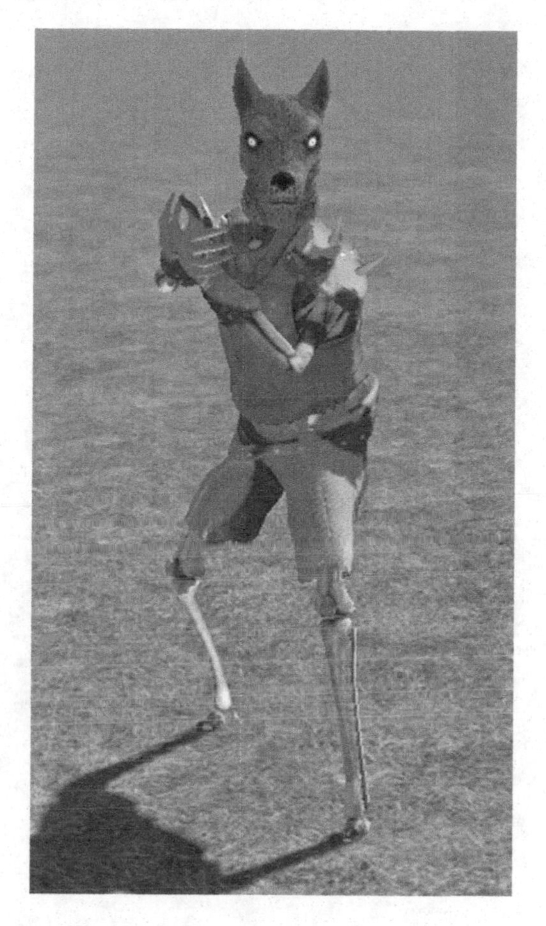

Figure 20.2

An extreme example of using the Character Creator.

Real-World Example #3: Duchenkuke's Soldiers

Duchenkuke sought help for an issue with one of his games where he had modified an FPE file to change the soldier's weapon that was being used. The problem wasn't that it was using the wrong weapon, however, it was that it was dropping the wrong weapon upon its subsequent demise! He tried deleting the FPE file, reconfiguring it, and re-adding it to the level. None of this worked.

Another user recommended he try deleting the .DBO file, which is the compiled model that is loaded by GameGuru. This fixed the issue after restarting the GameGuru engine. While the fix itself was a bit of a "voodoo fix," it was only possible through Duchenkuke reaching out to the community and finding another user who had already dealt with it himself once before.

21

Optimization (and More Testing)

Optimization is the process of reducing resources being used by a particular process or function that may be impacting the performance of a program. In this case, the program is your game; the resources are your textures, art, models, code, and associated assets.

Optimization is a fine art and, genuinely speaking, can make or break a game. Entire books have been dedicated to the subjects of optimizing models, code, and the like. Given my limited space, there's only so much I can do to get you there. That said, there are a lot of things that we take for granted and, in this phase, it'll be beholden upon you to stretch your brain and figure out very creative solutions for the issues your game encounters.

These days it's not uncommon to find gamers running massive, multithousand dollar gaming rigs that have overwhelming amounts of horsepower for running even the most rudimentary of games. In the case of GameGuru, believe me when I say a badly optimized game can choke even these sophisticated computers to a crawl.

Reading the Performance Statistics

Testing your frame rate and getting detailed diagnostic information is as simple as launching a map and hitting tab-tab in the editor. You'll see all the performance details on the left; this can be very helpful for isolating a hot spot of activity that's eating CPU. For instance, if the poly count jumps into the many millions, you can be sure it's a model or the terrain. Most of these statistics actually represent various CPU timers that, when they escalate to higher values, are bad for performance. A few represent direct, raw numbers that are supremely useful. Indeed, in the case of "polygons and draw calls," they are literally called "mainstatistic#" in the GameGuru core C++ code.

While there's a lot to look at in Figure 21.1, the primary values of import are the raw FPS, the polygons, and the draw calls. Those are your big three, but let's cover all of them from top to bottom to show you every single point of failure so you know what to look for.

The most important thing on this screen is in the upper left and that's simply your FPS reading. The FPS is your "frames per second" and will give you a one to one idea of what the performance of your game currently is.

Next to the FPS you will see a number followed by "HR." This might seem important, yet it is not. It's a legacy function from a time when GameGuru was planned to have a built-in day-to-night transitioning system that was removed. This day-to-night system had an hour or time of day and this number was to represent the "hour" of that time of day. Since the sun is essentially built in as a static 6 p.m. or 7 p.m. late-day sun, you can ignore this number.

A.I.: This is where you will see the impact your AI entities are having on the CPU. I can tell you outright that AI is a frame rate buster, so if too much is happening at once, it will absolutely devour the game's performance. As such, you want this bar to stay as low as possible. The following sections will detail how you can improve this particular statistic.

TIP: If you click on the A.I. bar, you get a hidden menu that will break down what AI components are actually slowing down the game directly. As in Figure 21.2, it will show you: Lua Engine, Entity Updates, Dark AI Control, Dark AI Update, Character Logic, and Attachments.

Physics: Physics is another high CPU intensity bar. If this is spiking, then you probably have too many physics objects interacting at any given time. It can also happen when you have a complex model with per-polygon collision activated instead of a more simplistic collision test like box-type. The amount of calculations required for this can be a tremendous drain on your system.

Vegetation: This one is fairly straightforward and only covers the GameGuru vegetation sprayer. In general, it is minimally impactful compared to other elements on this panel (Figure 21.1), though it can still cause problems if you are scraping for every ounce of frame rate.

Shadows: Unfortunately, a common point of pain for every game engine is shadow processing. The math involved with determining how light interacts and how shadows are cast has long been a point of contention with 3D games. There are various methods of handling this, but in GameGuru, it all boils down to a single slider for shadows that controls how the dynamic lighting system displays shadows.

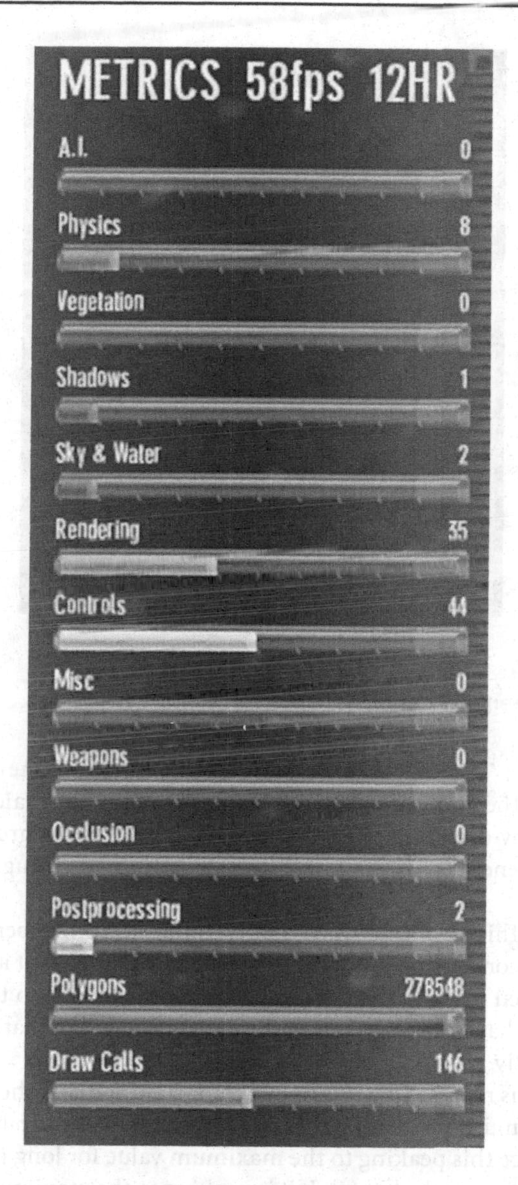

Figure 21.1

The tab performance settings house a wealth of data.

If you believe shadows are an issue, disable them by pulling the slider all the way over to the left. In general, this is a moderately impactful item that can cause a 2–4 frames per section drop on an average scene. Please note this does NOT impact static shadows, so you can still use static light mapping and have shadows cast in that respect.

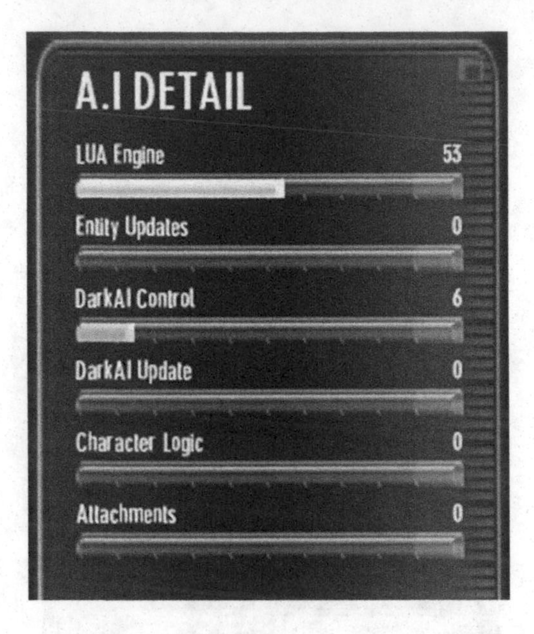

Figure 21.2

Clicking on A.I. performance gives detailed AI info.

Sky & Water: This is a consolidated tab, making it somewhat difficult to know which of the two is causing you the most pain. That said, it's fairly easy to test via Lua by disabling these two to see which has the greatest impact on frame rate. In general, this is a lower impact setting, resulting in a few frames lost in speed.

Rendering: This is a sync timer representing the time spent rendering the screen in milliseconds. This is a fairly useful statistic as you want it to be a relatively low value between five and thirty or so. If it starts getting into the hundred-plus range, you likely have a serious issue with your game's design that is slowing things down significantly.

Controls: This represents a minimally important statistic showing an approximation of how much processing time is being used by the input control system. Unless you notice this peaking to the maximum value for long periods of time, I wouldn't worry too much about it. If it is peaking to the maximum, you are likely dealing with a situation where there's a bad Lua script that has a loop checking input too often. This statistic frequently can run into the '50s and '80s without incident as input checking is actually a fairly intensive part of an engine's main game loop.

Misc: This is a complement to rendering because instead of actually counting the length of time of a render cycle, it's the actual count of how long it rests in-between renders. As far as being a useful performance statistic, it really isn't. As such, you can basically disregard this one. If, for some reason, this is producing any substantial number beyond 100 or so, you probably will want to contact Lee or TheGameCreators about a potential bug in the code.

Weapons: This will likely be one of the only sliders you will never particularly spend time looking at. It tracks some information about how much as a resource the weapons are costing the player, but the reality is it will only ever be a fraction of what other lower-hanging fruit will be. This can safely rest in the 50% range without ever impacting performance.

Occlusion: This is probably one of the least necessary sliders to worry about—this is because occlusion is actually beneficial for your frame rate! It cuts out unseen objects, reducing rendering cost. If this one is going high, it's likely due to a difficult calculation occurring on a specific object with odd geometry.

Post-Processing: This covers all of the special screen shaders and effects that are done after the screen is drawn and can result in a massive performance drain if not properly managed. Generally speaking, this should always be a very low value; if it starts to even go past a five or so, it's probably eating too much of the system resources. Tuning this requires disabling things such as light rays and bloom.

Polygons is a literal count of every polygon that is being held by GameGuru memory and effectively being displayed. This is a somewhat useful for determining when you have too many objects in a given area at one time. However, this isn't the whole picture (no pun intended) in this case. For one, the number for this is always high. This is because of the terrain and the four hundred thousand-plus polygons stored in memory. Note that this is still there even when you have terrain disabled.

Draw Calls represent at least one, possibly more, of every object being "drawn" on the screen. This is a highly important bit of info, likely the most important performance information statistic next to the raw FPS count. Draw calls should be around 250 with a top end of around 500. Once they go beyond those numbers, it will start to seriously drain performance on even top-end systems. The trick here is to run through your level and, if you see a place where it spikes, try to determine which objects can either be replaced or removed to kill the performance bottleneck. Please note that, officially, draw calls are actually each material of an object, so PBR objects significantly increase draw calls and can easily overwhelm a scene if you don't take careful steps to optimize object quantities and positions.

Quality not Quantity

There are a lot of times when we are developing that we just sort of "go overboard." By that, I mean we simply add too much of a thing that consumes resources. I had one specific situation where I had a massive map that had large amounts of very interactive enemies. This game slowed to a crawl after about two to three minutes and, eventually, I figured it must be the AIs causing the problem because as I killed them, the game would speed up!

If you recall, much earlier (in Chapter 5 on making a forest), I discussed how trees can just absolutely destroy a game's performance. This is for a number of factors—first, they have a lot of individual polygons that require lots of calculations to determine what can be seen and what cannot be seen.

They also are frequently set as physics objects. Now think about that for a moment ... physics objects with tons of branches, leaves, and trunks sticking off of them. This requires even more computational ability by your machine. These aren't even going to hit the GPU—this is purely a CPU-based activity as it tries to calculate the physics for this immense amount of trees.

So the first thing you need to ask yourself, before you get into any kind of fancy tricks, is do you really need all of these things that are causing you so much headache? Can you cut it down to save memory and processing power, thus improving frame rate?

Your goal in this phase of optimization is to remove unnecessary or redundant elements. Why use 30 static lights when only 12 will do the same thing? Look critically at your scene and decide what you can live without. Are you loading a high poly model that is only used for a single clutter object in a single room (such as in Figure 21.3)?

On the note of polygons, it's important to remember that there's an upper limit for many people on how many you can safely display. Generally speaking, less is more when it comes to performance figures regarding polygons. The safe way to play it is for highly important elements, or areas with a lot of player contact, to use higher quality and poly count assets.

Figure 21.3

Using high quality models requires careful placement.

Background elements should always be low poly count to ensure that they have a minimum impact on frame rate. Remember, the further away a player is from the object, the harder it is to see. Ultrahigh definition graphics mean nothing if the player is so far away it looks like a blur anyway.

The same applies to sky boxes and terrains. Using ultrahigh-definition (2048 × 2048 or higher resolution) textures on these might provide a marginal visual performance improvement, but most likely will only give you a slightly better look while costing you huge amounts of memory and processing time. Often, you are better served by a 512 × 512 or 1024 × 1024 texture resolution for these objects. That said, I personally don't mind using a 2048 × 2048 sky as I find as a player that I really love when a game uses a high-quality sky, but you will have to bear in mind that there are inevitably going to be performance trade-offs for such a choice.

Occlusion for Fun and Profit

Occlusion, in the context of GameGuru, is the act of removing elements that are behind an occluding object. The object removed thus increases overall performance as it's no longer being rendered. This doesn't remove other elements of the object, such as Lua code that might trigger or physics that need to be calculated, but it can really improve the performance significantly if done correctly.

The first thing to consider is what needs to be occluded. Often times, for close and mid-range elements, they will act as both occluder (has the ability to cull elements behind it) and also "occludee" (can be removed if out of view). There are, however, certain elements that should never be occluded, like background buildings. Nothing, in my opinion, looks worse than a low poly model suddenly disappearing and then reappearing in the background just because it was behind a nearby building.

These settings are found in the FPE file for your objects. They can also be found in the properties for some entities and amount to a simple yes or no value. The FPE file is the same, only in this case, it's a zero or one to represent the no or yes, respectively.

Please note that if you have the occlusion slider at zero, none of this will matter as occlusion will be turned off. While that's useful for troubleshooting objects "popping" into the scene (often caused by bad occlusion settings), it also causes a massive performance drain by disabling all engine-side occlusion. As a rule, you want your occlusion slider set all the way to the maximum value. The engine's occluder is really rather a smart bit of code, including fancy components like "predictive occlusion" that ensures that objects are less likely to pop into view when coming around a corner. As such, there's really very little value in turning it off aside from using it to troubleshoot (Figure 21.4).

Some users choose to make the bare minimum of models to maximize their performance. In our community, we've got a few notable users who stand out in this regard. First that comes to mind is a user named Bugsy that uses a fairly extreme method. His models are often simply flat planes that only have one side of the model with a texture on it (Figure 21.5). This is done to ensure that no

⊟ General	
Name	Broken Cinderblocks (Large)
Static Mode	No
Occluder	Yes
Occludee	Yes
Specular	100

Figure 21.4

Proper configuration of the occlusion settings greatly helps performance.

unnecessary textures are displayed, particularly from the back. This has the dual utility of reducing polygons and texture memory.

While this has practical benefits, we can achieve quasisimilar results by using the proper FPE file settings. What we are looking for is one to enable something called "backface culling." This method of performance optimization is done by the engine and the GPU, which will avoid drawing any unseen surfaces from the player's perspective.

In the FPE file, there are several settings that are relevant here. First off is "cullmode," which configures how the culling is set. Setting this to "0" says that the backface can be culled. If you have an object with cullmode set to "1," it will draw the backside of an object even if a player isn't looking at it. This means the best practice here is to use cullmode=0 whenever possible.

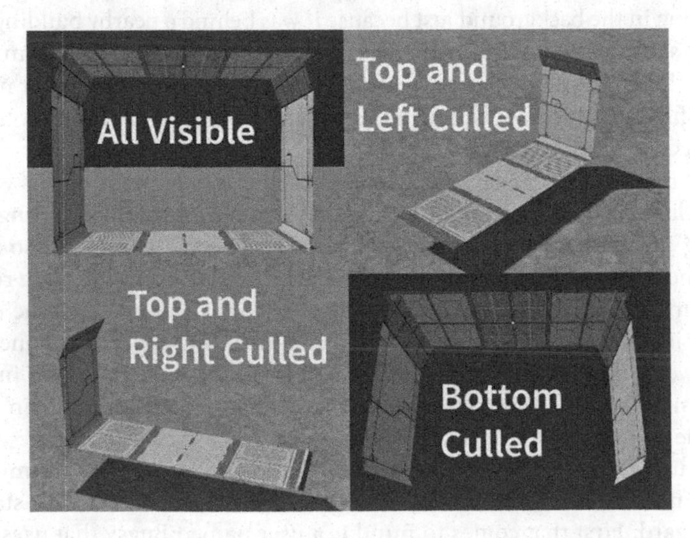

Figure 21.5

For maximum performance, manually cull your model's backfaces.

Tab Settings and Performance

This is where you are likely going to achieve the greatest gains in performance. Your tab-tab settings directly affect the performance of your game. If you recall from much earlier, there was some discussion on how to improve frame rate. There are a few that are always going to result in much larger gains than others: Notably the occlusion slider, the camera draw distance, and your post effects. All of these are configuration changes that will have massive impacts on the frame rate as it's delivered.

As mentioned, occlusion should almost always be enabled. This will greatly improve performance.

Camera draw distance is a little trickier. There are huge performance gains to be had by simply not drawing things, but the downside is that if you don't draw enough, the game looks awful. Lowering these sliders will cause an immediate and massive gain to your FPS but should be used with extreme caution, especially in scenes with elements that are further away. Once they are off the camera distance limit, they will not display, thus removing a lot of your creative possibilities. That said, it is likely to provide the largest gains for your ever-vital frame rate.

Beyond that, we've got our post-processing effects, and the bottom line is if performance is critical, you need to turn most of these off. The big hitters are bloom, light rays, and SSAO. These effects provide some graphical nicety but, in general, tend to eat a lot of frame rate—especially on lower performing machines.

TIP: If you disable bloom, it disables all other post-processing effects. This is useful for excluding whether post-processing is the source of a frame rate drain.

While the menu system for a standalone game has graphical settings that sort of emulate this, these settings are unfortunately hard-coded into the engine as three various configurations. What you CAN do is add a menu item to that menu for "ultralow" and "ultrahigh" settings. Ultrahigh would be highest quality settings, furthest camera distance, and all post-processing effects on. Ultralow would be your "very low camera view range," lowest quality settings, and no post-processing effects on.

So while we're here, I should mention that the title system's three "settings" are fairly basic for low, medium, and high. These settings are exceptionally basic; they don't take into account anything fancy. They ONLY manipulate the shader levels for the terrain, entity, and grass. These are set accordingly to low, medium, and high to correspond with their configured setting. The only other thing that is modified is the distance transition modifier, which on low and medium is set to 1 and on "high" is set to 10.

Every other setting has the slider value matching whatever is listed for the game's map itself. This is yet another reason why proper understanding of Lua and relevant functions is so critical. We can override the game engine's core code programming by extending functionality in the titles menu and by using the graphical Lua commands to extend the user's experience.

Debug Mode

If you recall, we spoke about using the tab-tab screen for performance information. Well there's another crucial key we need for actual performance testing. That's the F11 key (Figure 21.6).

F11 gives you vital information about the hardware but, more importantly, allows you to completely disable entire components of the engine. This means you can use it to blanket-test and exclude specific components you suspect might be causing slowness or latency. This allows you to begin excluding specific elements based off of what you find in the performance panel.

If you suspect physics are an issue, just press the corresponding F-key and disable it!

The options are fairly straightforward, as you will see.

The GPU-type version of DirectX it is operating, the refresh rate, the screen resolution size, and the following options:

1. Terrain toggles the terrain on and off. Being that this is one of the largest consumers of polygons, expect this to usually add a few FPS.
2. Water toggles the water plane on and off.
3. Gun toggles the weapon system on and off.
4. Light mapped object system (LMOS) toggles the lighting system on and off. This is a pretty useful one for determining whether you have a serious fault in your lighting setup.
5. Sky toggles the sky on and off.

Figure 21.6

Hitting F11 will put you into a very useful debug mode.

6. Physics is a supremely useful toggle that can quickly tell you if physics are causing major frame rate loss. It won't tell you WHICH physics, but it will give you a decent yes or no on it.
7. AI toggles all of the AI code on and off and is another very useful toggle to determine if there's a major slowdown caused by one of your AI entities.
8. Grass toggles the grass on and off, in case the vegetation system is causing slowness.
9. Entity enables or disables all entities on the map, which—while a bit heavy handed—can be useful for excluding whether it's a graphic setting or something wonky with another option. I usually start here and work downward.

Now that we know that, we can use that as part of our troubleshooting process, though please bear in mind it only works in the editor.

Another important diagnostic mode is, of course, debug mode, which is configured by using the tab-tab slider screen and moving the debug visuals slider over to maximum. Please note this doesn't mean you'll be "debugging visuals" but rather enabling debug visuals. It's a tiny, but important, distinction. What this will do is allow you to see the bounding box of every object, AI specific information such as view radius cones, AI vectors, and other important information. It can be helpful for determining if there's a glitch or bug, though in general, the most useful information you'll find here will be what you see on the collision box for the entities. Overly complex ones require more calculations, as we will get to later.

Removing the Bloat

Removing physics on objects that don't require them is a simple way to really speed up performance on maps with a significant amount of entities—notably forests and other complex environments. There is no reason to be doing collision checks and physics details on any object that isn't actually a part of the direct environment of the player. This means background objects and nonessential items are all things that can be disabled from a physics point of view. The optimum way to do this is to either control them via the FPE file itself or to modify the first one you place with "physics off" in the properties. We then spray that one instead of the default.

Another pieces of low-hanging fruit in the "cull unnecessary garbage" pile are your terrain, water, and skies! For instance, your game is taking place in a sewer level where you've generously raised the water level to intersect a tunnel that the player runs in. There is literally no way the player will see the sky or terrain so, using Lua, we can disable those components to speed up processing.

Likewise, if a player is in an enclosed building, you can disable terrain while they are indoors (assuming they aren't supposed to see the terrain) to help provide an FPS boost.

As I discussed before, more advanced users can take this even further by removing polys that aren't going to be seen and their corresponding textures on a per-model basis to free up additional resources. Some users take this to an extreme, maximizing their frame rate in inches. These tiny gains begin to add up, creating a snowball effect of optimization that can create a huge edge in performance if you are a skilled model editor.

Optimized Level Design

The worst kind of level is a large, flat level that goes on endlessly and is full of disparate elements placed haphazardly. Not only is it awful in gameplay, but it's also absolute hell on a processor, regardless of what engine you use.

A great example of a finely tuned level is actually included with GameGuru as an example level. That's the "morning mountain stroll" level, designed by the user "Wizard of Id" many years ago for a contest that they ran prior to the rebranding as GameGuru. This level handles a hundred or so AI entities by skillfully using the terrain to manage how much the player sees at any one given time.

Part of building your level is optimizing the set pieces. Hopefully, by this point in this book, you've gotten a good handle on designing a quality level. However, there are a few pitfalls you should specifically seek to avoid—long corridors, rooms full of enemies, areas packed with small physics objects, large open spaces, and maps with simply too many objects on them. Each of these is fairly self-explanatory but makes a huge impact on your level's design as a whole. Make sure that entities are static unless they are absolutely required to have dynamic features such as dynamic shadows or movement. Set them from "always active=yes" to "no" unless absolutely necessary. Your levels should only contain a handful of "always active" objects; otherwise, your CPU will constantly be trying to update things that likely aren't even near the player!

Optimizing AI is a difficult feat accomplished by using the following rules:

- Use small packs of enemies instead of large groups.
- Set them to "always active = no" to enforce a 3000-unit minimum range for activation.
- Place them around corners and out of sight if they are not in use. This way they will not impact graphics at all as it attempts to animate them in an idle state even if they are inactive.
- If possible, and the distances are tight enough, put a separate "distance check" in the Lua code for the AIs, which cuts the active distance down to a pittance. Alternately, use the view range to reduce their visibility so they aren't active beyond a certain point in combat.

In the game, there's the "always on" setting that can configure a distance check in the engine as to whether an object is active. However, there are other ways to do this that can provide meaningful benefits if you intend to use significant amounts of AI objects. This particular method adds a few lines to the AI code or object code that prevent it from running any code beyond a certain distance. By using this Lua-based method, you can create short, close combat situations that don't create a drain on CPU resources.

It will not be an effective method for long outdoor spaces, but if you are trying to create a rapid-fire, high-speed game, something with waves, or a labyrinthine fortress with tons of micro encounters, this is the way to do it.

The code is simple but looks like this:

```
local PlayerDist = GetPlayerDistance(e)
      if PlayerDist < 1500 and g_PlayerHealth > 0 then
            module_combatmelee.main(e,ai_combattype_
              bashmelee,ai_movetype_usespeed)
end
```

As you can see, this adds a second check on the AI, preventing it from becoming operational until the range check is met. If you understand your distances properly, you should be able to tune this easily. Personally, I prefer about 1000–1500, which is about half of the distance of the fairly large "always on" check. One downside of this system is that if you use it, any AI that isn't killed will continue to remain active. We could add a bit of code to further deactivate them, but the problem is that in order to do that, we'd have to literally kill the enemies after a certain range. It's up to you whether you want to add additional checks to reduce CPU cost.

Optimizing Your Set Pieces

Set pieces are among those things that can make or break a game. Background elements can be as low as a few dozen or a hundred polys. Foreground elements can range from a few thousand (say five thousand for a small object) and up to twenty thousand for very detailed elements. Realistically, most will vary between five and fifteen thousand polys per model. Optimizing these pieces is a rigorous process of removing backface textures and removing unnecessary polys through special processes in 3D modeling programs that reduce polys and optimize models. There are entire books on these subjects, but it's important to note a few basic tricks with respect to optimizing your models inside of GameGuru.

First, we need to consider the location of your scene. Using our build process for levels, we want to remove unnecessarily heavy poly objects from locations that don't require them. Imagine a highly photorealistic storefront with tables, chairs, silverware, and dishware.

While I'm all for photorealism, there's something to be said when you're getting only 1 FPS for a photorealistic screenshot. So let's see what we can do to clean this up. Start with the smallest objects first, like the small white cups on the table. While they are beautiful, they consist of significantly overrealistic models that simply have no value from a gamer's point of view. Consider this—the most they will do is possibly stop and admire that you spent so much time on a single cup. Would you rather they spend that time thinking about a cup or your game?

Another thing to consider here is texture depth. Foreground elements require high levels of detail, but within reason. There's no need to use 1024 × 1024 texture maps for such a simple cup either. You can easily get away with a much lower texture depth that is also going to have less of a render cost in terms of video memory and draw calls.

In this scene, we're using several different types of cups. While it's important to have variety, is it truly necessary to have five different types of glasses and cups? We need to simplify the scene down a bit, reducing it to one or at most two different types of cups. This alone will save huge on draw calls by eliminating the waste of resources in using too many different types of a simple object.

On the note of draw calls, there's more to consider here as well. Each "material" for an object is subject to their own draw call. These add up, costing precious render time, which reduces our most vital statistic—frames per second. So if we're using a standard "DNIS" map, then the most we can expect to use for a single object in terms of draw calls is about four. If our example cup, however, is a PBR textured cup, then we can expect the draw calls to be almost double.

In this respect, we need to make sure that we save PBR for textures that actually need it or will stand out in a very particular way. I tend to save it for shiny surfaces such as metal, crystal, or other objects that will have a more exaggerated effect. I've found that using it on duller surfaces such as brick or stone tends to end up looking almost identical to a standard DNIS style texture.

There are even more ways to optimize your draw call rates beyond just using smaller textures and avoiding PBR. Let's assume we're going to use a fairly optimized set of models. This set of models will consist of several textures that are used on several different models. The reuse of these textures means that if we want, we can comprise them all on something called a texture atlas. A texture atlas is a simple way of saying a texture that has a series of textures all on one sheet. This allows us to use ONE draw call for the whole sheet for every model that accesses it. Unfortunately, if you aren't familiar with UV wrapping and making your own, you will likely need to get an artist to do it for you. However inconvenient, this could very well be worth the cost of having someone remap your models to a texture atlas solely to save on draw calls and highly optimize your game.

Optimizing Your Lights

So we've talked about lights a lot. I hope you've gotten a good handle on how to place them and create beautiful environments for your games. Of course, by now you know that the lightmapper increases memory usage. This is because the way the lightmapper works is by calculating the way the light should look, then applying a special alpha mapped texture over top of the detail maps of the game.

This alpha mapped texture adds to your memory consumption. In fact, it is not uncommon on a large enough map to have a lightmap that actually breaks your level entirely by exceeding memory limits!

There are, of course, good practices and procedures to get around these limitations.

First, build your level in the center of the map. This way the lightmapper doesn't waste time lightmapping the outer layers of the map. Keep it small if possible, to avoid unnecessary sectors being lightmapped. For instance, if you have a sector of the map with a single misplaced object, it can result in the lightmapper adding mapping unnecessarily to that sector.

Second, less is more … as usual. This is one of those very simple concepts that helps you out significantly later on. The idea here is to use very large static lights (like size 1500+) in the minimum quantities necessary. This way we can optimize our build times and reduce the total size of the texture map as much as possible. Remember, you can use an infinite amount of static lights, but in many cases, this just creates additional overhead. So think about your light sources and their placement so you know you aren't increasing the strain on your engine.

With dynamic lights, the CPU is more impacted than memory since it's not doing it with a rendered texture layer. Regardless, they do impact a scene in terms of frame rate as they're calculated on the fly, so be judicious with the use of dynamic lights. We're essentially trying to balance two separate things here—first, the memory of a static light map, and second, the frame rate hit of a dynamic light.

Once you've done your level best to optimize the position and quantity of lights in your level, the next step is to optimize your setup.ini file settings to ensure that you are running trim and lean with your lightmapper configuration.

The two big settings here are lightmapping quality and texture size settings.

The setting "lightmappingquality=500" is the default, and this can be brought down significantly. It does impact how the actual lightmapper LOOKS when it's done, so it's a setting you'll have to play with and remap. I recommend starting with a value of 25 or 50 and working your way up in increments of 50 until you get close to what you want; then dial it in by increasing or decreasing it by 25. You will likely end up around 100—125; however, some users actually recommend going as low as 25 due to the unique look it gives the lights and shadows.

The setting "lightmappingsizeterrain=2048" is the size of bytes for the lightmapper on terrain, and it is vastly oversized. I recommend bringing this down at LEAST to 1024, though if you are going for performance optimization, a more realistic value is 256 or 512. Any lower than that can reduce the quality to a point where it is untenable. It will, however, significantly save on memory and reduce load times for the level by setting it to 256 or 512.

The setting "lightmappingsizeentity=1024" is the size of bytes per static object texture and, while this isn't as bad as the terrain texture settings, I definitely recommend cutting it down to 256 or 512 as well for the same reasons.

Bear in mind that every time you change the setup.ini file, you need to restart GameGuru. It also affects every level you use, so make sure to make a backup before you run it with the new settings.

I recommend setting up a simple map like the one included and doing your lighting tests from there. That way you can ensure that you have it dialed in exactly how you want it. Then once you actually lightmap, do some spot checking to ensure it's what you want in terms of quality.

Optimizing Your Post-Effects

Post-effects, in all of their screen enhancing glory, are performance hogs. Some are worse than others, but the fact is that they all will eat your frame rate up in bits and chunks. The various settings, while graphically beautiful, often can cause extreme slowness.

When in doubt, turn it all off.

No bloom, no lightrays, no SSAO, no motion blur, no vignettes, and no depth of field. All of these are, in varying forms, frame rate killers. Of course, as mentioned earlier in this book, if you disable bloom entirely, it will completely disable all other post-processing effects—so if you need a "nuke it from orbit" solution, that's the one to use!

That said, they do serve a function of making the game look and feel better. So it behooves us to find the best compromise that we can for our game's intended look. Many aren't necessary; I always disable lightrays and lens flares. I very frequently find myself using bloom because I enjoy the way it blends colors, giving a sort of poor man's anti-aliasing. SSAO is subpar in GameGuru and has been for a while so that can be disabled as well. There are alternate shaders available but, in general, you are going to want the minimum necessary. Having a significant portion of the various shaders tied into the bloom shader makes troubleshooting difficult at times if you intend to use that. Always start by disabling bloom if you're finding a performance dip you suspect is caused by post-processing effects. The best practice is to build your level and optimize it first, then add the post-processing effects afterward.

This goes double if you're using a third-party post-effects processor such as ReShade.

Optimizing Your Code

Code can be a huge source of drained resources if it's not properly managed. Unfortunately, many scripters and game developers simply lack the background to know how to write efficient code.

In that respect, the simple rule here is "do more with less, or better yet—do nothing at all." Generally speaking, code bloat is caused by authors who do things in a way that either takes too long or wasn't necessary in the first place.

Real coders in full-on Lua will typically use something called a profiler to check the performance of their code. This performance check can be done with debug functions in Lua and allows you to see how much memory your variables are consuming. This level of micromanagement is probably not necessary as it's very unlikely you've programmed anything carrying data of that size.

What we want to do with our system is optimize the code as much as possible by manually looking at it to see if there's anything that we can simplify or reduce.

The two main points of contention are conditional statements and loops. Loops, in particular, can be absolute CPU hogs that destroy the performance of a game. They should be used sparingly as you have to try to remember the game is always in a loop already! The "main game loop" runs constantly, polling every piece of code, so adding a secondary loop without piggybacking off that original loop is often wasteful.

What we don't want with a loop is the worst-case scenario, something called a runaway loop. These loops are cycles that never return to the "real world" and, as such, just become totally self-absorbed little monsters that use all of your processing power to perform their loop function.

Usually this results in a program "locking up" and represents the most extreme version of a greedy loop. What we want to do when using a loop is spend the minimum amount of time actually computing the loop. One method of doing this is using a process called "loop unrolling." Imagine this:

```
For I = 1 to 100
        Print I
End for
```

So this loop in a nutshell will print a number 100 times. Doesn't seem like much and, actually, given the relative cleanliness of the code, seems very efficient. Let's look in more detail, however… we have a minimum of 300 instructions going on every single time we run this. One for the loop, one for the print, and one for the end for. Consider if we were to do it this way instead:

```
For I = 1 to 10
        Print I; Print I+1; … Print I+9
End for
```

Now looking at this, it's not particularly pretty, but it does cut the processing down to nearly a third for the same code. While I can't teach you every trick to optimizing code, I do want to get you in the mindset of "saving instructions." Little bits add up, and you want to do everything you can to find the big drains in your custom code so you can clean them up.

Lua has a few common performance hot points that you will want to visit. So let's review them now.

Use local variables whenever possible. This is because local variables are significantly faster than global variables in Lua due to the nature of the way they are stored.

TIP: Always use local variables unless absolutely necessary!

I personally avoid "while" loops and for good reason—they're often three to five times slower than a comparable "for" loop.

Multiplication is significantly faster than division or exponents due to the way CPUs handle such things. Try to change math from this: x=x/2 to x=x*0.5 or x=x^3 to x=x*x*x. This might not look as pretty but saves in the back end where the CPU is doing real math and real work.

There are significantly more, but this is a good start to get you on your way. For further reading, I'd recommend "Lua Programming Gems."

Remember, it's about getting the maximum value for the minimum work from your code and CPU. Take a moment to turn unnecessary globals into locals, change your math to multiplication where you can, and clean up your loops. That alone will save a few dozen or even perhaps a few hundred percent of CPU cycles!

Performance Hacks and Tweaks

By this point, I'm going to assume you have a fairly good fix on optimizing your game. You, hopefully, have a clean level design, good placement of background objects, code that isn't eating your CPU alive, and a fantastic set of slider settings on the tab-tab screen to help keep things flowing smoothly. There are, however, a few "hacks" that allow us to take an axe to specific things that can help speed along our development time significantly. Some of these have already been covered, but it doesn't hurt to review.

Cullmode should be set to 0 in the FPE files whenever possible, occludee and occluder configured properly, and occlusion enabled in the tab-tab screen. This will ensure the unnecessary objects aren't being drawn.

Also in the FPE file is a setting called "collisionmode" that allows you to configure the specific collision box this mesh or model will have. Collision boxes by default will often be a zero for "box shaped," which is fairly efficient. However, less is more here, so if possible use 11 or 12 to disable physics (12 does disable physics with the ability to use the raycasting functions for detection). The least efficient shape is one, which is the "polygon shape." This method uses the actual model's mesh as a basis. That said, polygon is the optimal setting for surfaces a player will be walking on, so you may be stuck with it in some cases.

Also in the FPE file is a setting called "reducetexture" that allows us to literally divide a specific model's texture quality to save video memory and rendering cost. This is a great way to test the performance of a reduced texture by setting a divisor in here. So, for example, the default is one, which means a one to one value. If you set this to two, it will divide the texture in half. This means a 1024 by 1024 texture will now be a 512 by 512 texture. You can use this to see if there is stretching or unacceptable artifacts on the model this way. What I like to do is test it here, then actually modify the image itself. This way, there's no additional math being done by the engine beyond what's necessary.

Now while that handles FPE files, there are also a lot of little hacks you can do within the setup.ini file for your game. I've included a setup.ini editor in the materials for this book so you will be able to load that and check or uncheck what you like. Bear in mind that unless you are copying a custom setup.ini to your standalone game's folder, this will affect ALL of your projects. As such, make a backup of the original and try to use this as a last resort for your final standalone game's performance tweaks.

Remember earlier when I said that "long flat planes" are the worst kind of terrain because of their high poly count? Well there is a way around that if you absolutely must have a flat game (for example, if you are making a 2D top down shooter). If you toggle "superflatterrain," you will get a large flat plane that you cannot edit that also is comprised of considerably less polys.

There are also some "detail" settings you can change to help speed things up and reduce resource consumption. These are:

- **reflectionrendersize=512:** This is the size of the texture generated for your reflections. The bigger the number, the better the reflection, but the more resources used.
- **dividetexturesize=1:** Another texture divisor, this time applied globally across ALL textures. If you set this to two, you will cut your TOTAL texture size in half, but this can have drastic effects for your game. Primarily, it's useful if you are concerned about a game possibly using too much video memory.
- **lightmappingquality=500:** This setting will improve lightmapping quality if you increase it to a thousand, but it can really cause a high cost for rendering it. Likewise, reducing it improves render time and changes the quality. Lowering it will reduce the light map quality but significantly reduce the render time.
- **lightmappingsizeterrain=2048** can safely be cut in half to reduce the texture size used for the lightmap data for terrain. Generally speaking, this should equal whatever your terrain size is or larger; 2048 is the maximum you'd ever use for terrain size, and I've already cautioned against it. See the section on "optimizing lighting" for more details.
- **lightmappingsizeentity=1024** sets the texture size for the lightmapping texture on static entities. You can often safely reduce this by half to 512, but it may cause some chunkiness in the lightmap itself. It does, however, significantly reduce render time and reduce memory consumption. See the section on "optimizing lighting" for more details.

- **realshadowresolution=1024** is another one that can be cut in half, thus reducing the total cost of your shadows if you absolutely must have them from dynamic light sources such as the sun.

All of these settings impact the raw CPU and memory usage by GameGuru. What about optimizing the load times of the game though?

In that case, there are a few hacks around that as well:

- **skipobstaclecreation=0:** By default, GameGuru will generate obstacles for all entities for AI. This, however, can be skipped by toggling it to a one if you are comfortable with the result. It's generally not advisable but can significantly improve load times in the "generating AI obstacles" phase.
- **skipterrainobstaclecreation=0:** This does the same thing but only for the terrain itself. Here again, if you are using a "superflatterrain," there's no reason to ever have this set to zero. Alternately, if your AI will only ever operate in a flat area, this is also unnecessary and can be set to one to disable it.
- **forceloadtestgameshaders=1** causes the game engine to recompile the shaders each and every time you test a game run. While this is useful if you are modifying shaders, it is a waste of time and resources otherwise. In most cases, you'll want this set to zero to disable that so it just loads the existing shaders.

22

Laws, Licenses, Marketing, and Selling

So you finally built your game, tested it, and prepared it for release. What do you do now?

Put simply, you still have a lot of work ahead of you. If you've been smart, then you already at least started the preliminary steps of the plan I will present to you.

You'll need to:

- Prepare yourself legally.
- Market your game.
- Set up your distribution channels.
- Sell the game!
- Deal with customers.

Independent game development is rife with stories about the John Carmack and John Romero developers of the world, who make it big with blowout sales and enormous profit margins. Romero and Carmack's twin Italian sports cars became the sort of high-water mark that overly ambitious game developers would measure themselves by. During the '90s, it was a Wild West, with huge profits and huge losses for indie studios. Romero's rise with id Software was met with the fall that came with his own studio Ion Storm. Each of these failures accumulated into a sort of critical mass where stability was needed. This is where traditional publishing models stepped in. Once they did, however, this severely cut into individual development studios profits in return for a financial safety net. They provided studios with capital required to get games developed and ensure a consistent level of quality. Even they took regular beatings, however, on failed games, as evidenced by major studios like Rare®, Enix®, THQ®, Square®, Bullfrog®, and various divisions of Eidos® or EA®.

These failing studios then have a choice: get gobbled up, merge, or disappear. So they assume the logical conclusion and join another group who is larger… until they possibly fail, too. It's a vicious cycle in commercial video game publication. In fact, the budgets are often so large they need to sell millions of units just to break even. This is further compounded by the publisher's model that gives very slim profit margins to studios while the publisher reaps all the benefits. Often a studio may see as little as 1–2 dollars per game sold, and that's mostly due to the industry standard 10%–20% royalty on net profits—that means after the publisher pays taxes and other associated costs. This doesn't even factor in how the publisher doesn't sell the game for MSRP, but rather for a cut below that. So you have a game for $60 on the shelves, which perhaps sells to the store for around $40–$50 a copy. The store pockets $15 or less on the sale. The publisher then pays their taxes and fees (whatever they may be), and then the developer's royalty is pulled from that amount. After everything is said and done, the developer usually has to sell something on the order of 500,000 to a 1,000,000 copies just to break even (see Figure 22.1).

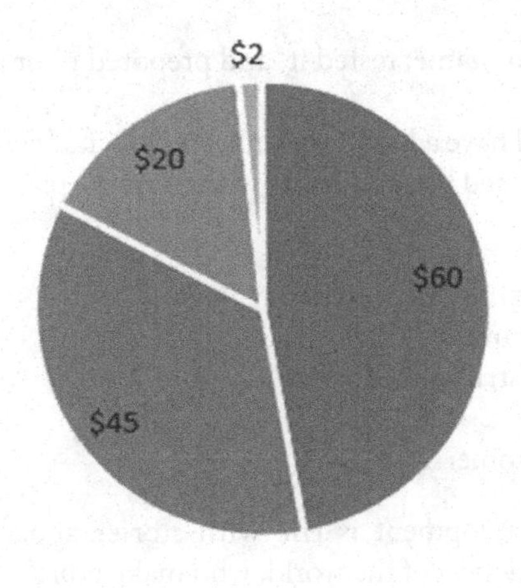

Figure 22.1

The tiny slice is what you would take out of a final sale.

Now imagine the game development studio has to pay their employees to make a game. This game requires salaries, equipment, software, and a host of other services they will need money for. So the publisher gives them money called an advance, often in the hundreds of thousands or millions of dollars. This is money that is in a sense owed to the publisher. The publisher will thus take all royalty payments until the advance is repaid. If the game is a failure, then the game developer isn't profitable; the publisher will often buy up the scraps of what's left and add them to their own internal studios. It's a constant roller-coaster ride for some developers who are forced to go from job to job just to follow their passion.

Failure in the video game community is common. Why am I bringing this up? It's important to understand that failure is something that can be as unavoidable as the tides. All developers experience some measure of failure. Unless you are some kind of insanely good game creator (in which case, why are you reading this book?), then you probably are going to at best achieve moderate success. That's with a ton of hard work, mind you. Successful games are built on the backs of their developers as they carry it through to fruition. Occasionally something sells itself, but this can often backfire when user expectations don't meet what's provided. It's a tightrope act and a difficult future to balance.

I'm sure by now, you feel a tinge of trepidation, a bit of fear in your gut. "What have I gotten into?" you ask... "How can I even hope to be successful?"

Well I'm here to say it's not only possible, but likely, if you have the right mindset. Success is, as with many things, a choice.

You have to choose to see the advantages while turning your weakness into strength.

But I'm only one person, making this game!

While you are usually but one person, you have a distinct advantage in that respect—one you must harness to the best of your ability if you want to be successful: You don't pay any salaries.

Most of these modern AAA games are massively bloated endeavors with multimillion-dollar budgets. A significant portion of that budget just goes into real estate and salaries. You already have your house. You already have a computer. You already have yourself. So you're ahead of the curve in that respect.

But what if sales are weak?

This is a distinct possibility, but you should know that when you are self-publishing, as most independent developers are, you are going to have significantly higher profit margins. So while you may only sell five thousand copies, you may actually pocket $5 per copy for a fairly good chunk of change!

On Limited Liability

I'm only going to touch on this topic briefly as I am not a lawyer and as such cannot provide legal advice. I can, however, give you some basic concept of what you are looking for so you can decide for yourself what you may or may not need. Please note I am only familiar with this topic from the standpoint of being a citizen of the United States; you will have to consult your local laws for specifics relative to your region. More on that later.

For now, let's discuss the topic of limited liability. This extremely important topic is the primary reason why corporations are such a fixture in modern culture. Typically, when you make a product, you make it by yourself as an independent game dev. From a legal context, this means you are the "sole proprietor." That means, in a nutshell, that you are the only owner of a product and the business that is selling it.

It also means that you are the one responsible for it if something goes wrong. So you are *personally liable* if someone incurs injury from your game. I know this sounds absurd. You're probably wondering how someone can incur injury from a video game, but the fact is that stranger things have happened. What happens when your innocuous game maliciously makes fun of a celebrity who then sues you not only for all the profits of your game but also for damages associated? Suddenly your little enterprise is costing you thousands or bankrupting you because you callously chose the wrong subject matter for your game.

Moreover, because you are personally liable, this means they can go after everything about you for repayment: your savings, your car, and your house, for example. They can literally destroy your life over what may have been just a simple jab at someone's credibility.

Of course, there are business insurance models that cover this that may totally be a good option for you. The real solution, however, is limited liability.

What is Limited Liability?

Limited liability is the legal term for several legal business entities that are independent of their owners. As such, the only assets that can be liable in a civil or criminal action are typically the assets of the business itself. Sure, your business might get destroyed; but your life will go on. Every single corporate entity is a limited liability entity. This is why members of the board for a corporation are typically not personally liable for their actions—no matter how destructive. Now there are ways to penetrate this shield, such as say an email trail proving your personal intent in performing such an action. So nothing is bulletproof here; you should always take a measure of caution in your work.

That said, there are numerous methods of limited liability that will provide you with at least some armor against legal claims. Some will advocate something called an "S-type" corporation. This is a small corporation ideal for a sole proprietor as it is limited to 75 shareholders maximum. It does require filing quarterly reports and other corporate-specific tasks as upkeep, however.

You can also look into creating an LLC or "limited liability company." This type of hybrid company is effectively a corporation without the hassle of filing paperwork (which I tend to loathe). So it has all the benefits of a sole proprietorship without the negatives of having full exposure to legal problems. It does, however, have a maximum life of 30 years, so you would need to make arrangements to have it carry over to a new organization at that time.

There are other types of limited liability arrangements as well, such as the limited liability partnership (LLP).

Each of these should be researched and evaluated for your region. For instance, I know in the UK they have similar configuration of companies such as corporations and private limited companies. A lawyer is of prime importance for this step and will be able to guide you to the best option.

Licensing

Similarly, licensing is also a consideration. With GameGuru, you have a fairly open license to use what comes with it virtually however you want. There are many times, however, people feel that should extend to everything they use in GameGuru as well, which is not true. Many times gamedevs may find "free art," "free models," or "free music and sounds" on the Internet and incorporate them into their game. If they fail to read the fine print, they may end up in a situation where they can be legally held liable for violating the licensing of said terms.

What's more is there are an incredible amount of licenses out there. Some will give you full reign over everything, allowing you complete dominion over a free product. It is, in essence, yours from that point forward. Some are strictly for personal use and not to be used in a commercial product. Others are only good if you provide attribution. That's a fancy way of saying "make sure you tell people who gave you this."

When I made my "Advanced Time of Day and Weather System" for GameGuru, I wanted to include a thunder sound for when lightning would go off during a rainstorm. I found a good one using something called "Creative Commons 3" that allowed me commercial rights to use it, but I had to provide attribution. Following this to the letter allows me to include content I wouldn't have the ability or time to create on my own but still avoid any legal trouble from the official intellectual property owner.

Licensing can encompass many different aspects of the actual development process. Sometimes you need a license for intellectual property (IP) such as a story or idea. Other times you may need to have a license for software, contracts, or if you're developing for a game console. At the time of this writing, GameGuru is not available on console so it's not something you have to worry about. Given some of the projects in the work, this is a very viable possibility in the future, though, so it behooves you to know it's out there. Licensing can encroach in a number of ways. It's another element to balance in your ever-expanding portfolio of things to balance.

Even worse, there's no one set of licenses for each of these things. There are general public licenses (GPL), creative commons (CC), historical permission notice and disclaimer (HPND), informal licenses, public domain (PD), and many… many more. It can be a lot to manage, so this is where taking some notes on where you get something "free" from along with the particular license type as part of your TDD will prove helpful in this stage. This doesn't even count the need to use licensed software for your game development. Some people think they can use pirated copies of software to make their games (pirating GameGuru or Adobe Photoshop, for instance) and then when caught can literally lose all of their earnings through legal proceedings.

There are ways around this of course. One example is something called fair use. When you have something that can be defined as a "derivative work," there's a certain amount of license by yourself that can be taken with respect to using them as the blueprint for your inspiration.

Fair use is effectively a way to mitigate liability by allowing certain cases where you are allowed unauthorized use of certain material protected by copyright. It is not, however, a catchall.

One particularly famous example is the "Mona Lisa with a Moustache." In 1919, a painter by the name of Marcel Duchamp made a very good copy of the Mona Lisa, albeit with a simple modification of a moustache and beard. This simple modification ended up allowing it to fit within the realm of fair use, and thus it became a legal derivative work with its own unique copyright.

You cannot create the next great game based off a TV series you didn't pay a license for the rights to. Sufficient modification would need to be made so that it could pass legally. You're probably better off at that point renaming every character and redesigning every distinct object to the point where it's going to be a different game anyway.

Licensing is a major concern to all game developers, large and small.

The rule of thumb here is to always stay on the right side of the law. Always avoid toeing the line. Worst case, if you find yourself in a situation where you think you might be infringing, make sure you take the necessary steps to stay legal. The extra inconvenience on the front end is worth avoiding the incredible legal hassle on the back end.

In fact, some AAA organizations allocate huge portions of their multimillion-dollar budget toward licensing. In one famous example, Atari spent $23 million USD securing the license rights to make the "ET®" game for the Atari console. It famously flopped, and extra copies were buried in a landfill.

More recently Crytek, of CryEngine fame, sued Cloud Imperium® alleging they broke the licensing agreement and infringed on their copyright. All this because CIG switched from CryEngine to Lumberyard®, which is the Amazon-owned fork of CryEngine.

Those legal waters look awful murky, don't they?

This brings me to my next point.

See a Lawyer

Sure, you can read documents or even this chapter and feel very equipped for what's to come. You might even have submitted your own paperwork on a legal website and registered your own LLC. Who's to say what impetus you've taken? My own experience, however, is that it's always best to consult with a lawyer.

Now in my case, I have had the fortune of growing up with a mother who spent many years as a legal secretary to a large law firm in a local city. As such, I had easy access to resources that I normally wouldn't have considered. That said, knowing what I know now, I'd have still paid the costs gladly. A good lawyer can save you an incredibly large headaches later. Having a lawyer write and file your paperwork for your LLC, verify your licensing meets requirements, and write your own licensing agreement will probably cost you hundreds or thousands of dollars.

In the end, though, you will be protected. Covered. Safe. Your life will not be ruined by people who are suing you because your game is too addictive (this happened to the developers of "FO4") or because you used a not-so-clever teen's catchphrase in a game (the lawsuit against Anonymous Games).

In the end, some legal issues are truly unavoidable. This is why you might also consider asking your lawyer their thoughts about professional insurance to cover the losses incurred by a lawsuit. A disclaimer here: For a brief stint, I was a licensed insurance agent in the state of Pennsylvania in the United States. Our training and testing was rigorous, so I did learn quite a lot. It wasn't the career for me though, and I got out—but not before getting a healthy appreciation for the actual value of insurance.

Put bluntly, insurance isn't about protecting what will happen (annual doctor visits, the occasional scrape) but about what could happen, catastrophically. It's absolutely worth getting yourself covered to protect all the angles. This is often called "professional indemnity insurance."

There are many types of limitations on losses, but overall coverage can be extended to losses of profit, claimant breaches on contracts, claims from external content providers (art, audio, and the like), from a breach in warranty or guarantee (to a point), commercial terms, and more.

Costs are usually paid annually for coverage often fifty or a hundred times more than what you paid for. So five hundred dollars a year may give you up to five hundred thousand dollars in coverage. This gives you enormous flexibility in the event of a legal claim. Again, as with the earlier sections of this chapter, I urge you to seek a qualified professional for the best, most current advice on how to obtain the right kind of insurance for your needs.

On Kickstarter and Crowdsourcing

These days there's an increasing desire to get "other people" to fund projects. It's a tempting thought, one I went through myself many moons ago. Back when I was much, much younger (with a significant amount more hair on my head!)

I had some really groundbreaking ideas for games. I also was intellectual property owner of a science fiction book I was working on. This gave me a great wealth of things to work from. I was, however, as I always have been, exceptionally thorough with covering my bases. If nothing else, I found I was a good planner. So I had some competent friends with me that were interested, had them sign NDAs (non-disclosure agreements), and set out to work on secure funding for our venture. This at the time consisted of writing up a 50-page business plan complete with budgets, projections, and lots of reference materials.

I found some investors, but the bottom line is they were asking for 60 percent ownership of a company for a meager fifty thousand dollars in startup monies. This was barely sufficient to get a game started with seven people, let alone several out the door. The experience burned me out, and I moved on to other professional opportunities later.

Nowadays people think the answer is Kickstarter. For the uninitiated, Kickstarter is a site where ideas are proposed and backers can pledge monies toward the successful completion of said idea. They help fund new projects for people making projects in an assorted array of communities including game development. Projects only receive monies when the objectives posted are met, and strict guidelines must be followed for when they are not. There are obligations by the project maker to achieve as well based on Kickstarter's contract and licenses. Occasionally, a scam makes its way through as well.

Kickstarter has been the home of a few famous game projects and failures. Some successes have been CIG's "Star Citizen" and HBS's "BattleTech." A notable failure was "Yogsventures®" and the inevitable ensuing scandal. Vital lessons can be learned from successes and failures in this context. Even TheGameCreators and GameGuru started with a Kickstarter attempt.

Public funding opens another can of worms, something that is not as easily closed. It is one thing to waste your own money, quite another to waste the money of several hundred (or thousand) others.

While it has proven to be a valuable tool for getting new ideas off the ground, it has also resulted in some rather spectacular failures. I'd caution any game developer against going to this as their first choice, at least until they've established a few successes under their belt.

Marketing

For this segment, I spoke at length with an acquaintance of mine, Johann "Ivan Ertlov" Ertl. Johann has worked on several AAA projects, notably the "Painkiller®" series. He has several interesting interviews on indiedb.com that paint a picture of someone who has seen the good, the bad, and the truly ugly of the indie game developer's world. At one point, he lost his house due to monies owed by a publisher that melted down while he was doing work for them as a developer.

Coincidentally, he also has the most commercially and critically successful GameGuru game: "Father's Island." He also used the preceding engine of FPS

Creator Classic to build another game a few years before called "Into the Dark," which was also a welcome success. He was able to give me some excellent information on the methods and processes he used to pave the way to success with his marketing efforts. He is essentially the highest standard we have in the GameGuru community for success and, as I learned many years ago, if you want to be successful: emulate success! Find someone who does what you want to do and do it the way they do it; it's a blueprint for winning. Some apologies here as English is not his primary language.

Ivan Ertlov Interview

MM: Tell me about your first game.

IE: My first game was released in Germany when I was 11: a text adventure for the C64, with ASCII graphics written in BASIC.

MM: How would you measure a GameGuru game's success?

IE: I would say, if you put a GameGuru game on steam, have at least a few thousand copies sold, and still more than 50% positive reviews... then you did something right.

MM: How did you market your games?

IE: For "Into the Dark" (FPSC), we started with the first marketing activities, which was the buildup of a decent Indie DB presence: http://www.indiedb.com/games/into-the-dark/

We fed it with regular updates, screenshots, interviews, in late 2011, which was one year before the German disc release, two years before the Desura release, and almost three years before the Steam Release of the "Ultimate Trash Edition."

A press tour to all major European gaming magazines was done in 2012 and 2014, both before the releases of the respective versions. We built a Facebook presence for the game, our studio, and the main character in early 2012 at these sites:

https://www.facebook.com/HomegrownGames/

https://www.facebook.com/intothedarkindiegame/

MM: How did you use Facebook as a marketing platform? What other advertising did you leverage?

IE: We used Facebook advertising with a custom-tailored target group centered around English-speaking fans of trash and gaming; basically, targeting people who had enjoyed "A Fistful of Boomstick" or "Deadly Premonition," as well as the combination "Trash movie fan + gamer." We mimicked the target group for Google ads, too, and had some ads/features in online magazines.

We had a significant bonus because we got additional press coverage for the fact we were allowed to have a swastika in the German version; this was an exceptional permit issued by the German authorities and picked up by the German gaming press.

MM: Do you feel that this normally "negative" press was beneficial for sales?

IE: I would say, the press coverage around that led to 300–500 additional copies sold on Steam. That is a significant share of direct sales, since most of our 40,000+ Steam Copies were purchased in sales or bundles. We also gained enthusiastic support from core gamers, which led us to winning the prestigious "Game of the Year 2014—Community Favorite" award from German GameStar Magazine, *outrunning both "Skyrim®" and Fallout in the final voting. That didn't hurt the sales either!*

We also actively supported Let's Players that were dedicated and masochistic enough to play through the entire game.

MM: What about for Father's Island? Did anything change?

IE: For Father's Island (made in GameGuru), we used a similar approach but had less of a marketing budget (due to the smaller scope of the game). However, the basics were the same. We opened our social media presence on several platforms:

http://store.steampowered.com/app/460940/Fathers_Island/

https://www.facebook.com/fathersisland/

http://www.indiedb.com/games/fathers-island

As said, it was much smaller in scope and basically our first, and so far last attempt to put something commercially viable out based on GameGuru.

However, the press reviews were far better than with "Into the Dark," and also the average user ratings are slightly better up to date.

We even won some minor GotY awards—and, despite the fact that I personally find "Hunted—One step too far" the better GG game on steam, "Father's Island" is the only BOTH commercial and critics-wise successful GG game on Steam so far.

We ran for all our games tests with marketing and advertising, here is a brief summary:

Facebook ads: Absolutely vital if you manage your target group and time schedules for advertising wisely, and if you create engaging content. If you optimize all that, you can get 1.5–2.5 dollars net revenue out of each dollar spent. You will burn cash until you are there, and the experiments will be burned money sometimes, but after you reach the sweet spot, your advertising is printing money at an average ROI of 200%.

Instagram: Forget it, not usable for proper conversion rates.

Twitter: Can be used carefully, wait for Indie gaming hashtags trending and jump aboard.

Pinterest: Never ever.

Google ads: Can be even more effective than Facebook ads but need a real pro. I sometimes manage to have successful campaigns, and the next one fails horribly without seeing any major difference. It is voodoo to me, so I recommend an expert.

As for distributors: Well, it depends.

If they don't agree on paying an upfront or minimum guarantee first, and just want to do a split revenue deal, I avoid it like the plague. That means they are not convinced enough to put in some real marketing effort.

As for part distributor-part publisher deals, they CAN be good, it's just very unlikely.

I published some articles regarding that here:

http://www.indiedb.com/games/into-the-dark/features/interview-dealing-with-publishers-from-indie-to-hired-and-back

http://www.indiedb.com/games/into-the-dark/features/insider-tipps-publishing-contracts-and-publishing-deals

Coincidentally, these articles were actually a clever form of marketing for "Into the Dark"!

As you can see from the articles, I am very skeptical regarding publisher/distributor deals.

MM: Thank you for your time, good luck on your future projects!

Distribution Channels

Things have come a long way since the late '90s. Now with Steam, GOG®, Humble Bundle®, and other distribution channels, there's a lot of fairly easy ways to get your games to their potential buyers. These channels are not without their own hang-ups, however. Each one has a separate pay structure and system for submission. Some of these have unique payment systems (Humble, for instance) that only take a small percentage of your profits but allow purchasers to choose their payment price. So while you may lose on purchase price, you may earn it back on reduced paid percentages.

Steam, on the other hand, is a massive platform with huge reach but they take 25% (it was 30% for many years until literally the last few months), which is a much larger percentage than Humble's meager 5%.

Other platforms are available as well such as GOG and the newly created Epic system. I'd also be remiss if I didn't mention that you can actually sell finished games on "The GameGuru Store" as well. While that one has a 30% margin for a much smaller reach, it does, however, cater to a specific crowd and has reasonably simple tools to get you started. Each has its own pluses and minuses. These platforms have distinct advantages but you'd be considered a fool not to place your game on every available platform.

As such, you want to plan your launch with great care; have it packaged and ready to go for each platform and get it loaded in as many places as possible. Traditional sales metrics show that you will generally make the most volume in sales in your first few days after launch. However, according to several different industry sources, there are other ways around this as well such as having a special Black Friday sale. Positive press can be timed with a sale to help encourage interested buyers, so keep an eye out on what's going on in the world. A sudden spike in interest can be easily be met with a "special flash sale" to help push more units out the door. Generally, after a year or so, the game's price should be cut significantly to help stimulate long-term buyers; no one wants to spend on "new game prices" for an old title!

Piracy

This is a delicate topic; no one wants to admit their game is going to get stolen, but there it is. It can and will be pirated. You can try to fight it, of course, but there's only so much as an indie gamedev you can do. The trick here is to balance the value of stealing versus the value of paying. According to recent statistics, only 4% of American PC gamers admit to pirating games. This sounds fairly good on paper, but the reality is that lower income nations are almost always massively higher in terms of software theft.

So while GameGuru has certain provisions against piracy, such as encrypted assets to protect your work, it really isn't going to stop anyone who is genuinely determined to steal your game.

The fact is your best mitigation is actually to just price your product well. Think about it—who is going to steal your product? Is it the guy who makes fifty grand a year doing technical support and buys one to three games per month? Not likely. It's likely going to be the guy who makes ten grand a year, is a nearly full-time student, and spends most of his money on beer. You want to price your products around providing a value without providing a reason to steal it. As your price increases, so does the likelihood of having the product stolen.

I generally wouldn't charge more than five dollars for a GameGuru game, honestly speaking. Most of them, even multiyear endeavors, plainly aren't worth that price. Moreover, you're pocketing a good portion of the proceeds that would normally be given to a publisher, so it's really not a bad deal. Plan on pricing between one and three dollars, which puts your game in the realm of "not worth stealing." This is a pretty good place to be. We'll get more into that as we discuss pricing and some of the little tricks you can do to help boost sales.

So as I mentioned, you are definitely going to lose some sales to piracy. This applies even if you are pricing your game well. Pricing is all about mitigation, but the fact is you don't have to take piracy lying down. There are ways to keep on top of it and try to stem the losses. I don't advocate digital rights management (DRM) or obsessively going after every single person who pirated your game. Now, you could, but the reality is that it's really just going to cause you nothing but heartburn and lost sleep.

Other considerations to bear in mind are that if someone is stealing your game, it's also possible they are stealing other elements of your GameGuru game. They could potentially steal your copied Lua files or entities, especially if they break the encryption. Yes, that is a possibility, if someone is truly determined.

Now what are some mitigation strategies you can implement? Luckily for you, I've worked closely with members of several corporate abuse departments and know all of the little secrets you can use to deal with people spreading your game illegally.

So what do you to stop the spread of your game, custom assets, or custom artwork?

Stop it at the source.

Most of the time people distributing games illegally are doing it in such a way that they are trying to obfuscate their identities. It can be maddening to know that someone is using a proxy in the Netherlands to prevent you from taking the fight directly to them. Often it's one or two people doing it, and the real trick is isolating who they are and how they are doing it. So what you want to do is first go after the whois records for the site that is distributing your work. Often, almost every time, they will have an abuse email.

So what is whois? Whois is an old Internet service available for any website. Just search on your favorite search engine for a "whois lookup." Once there, search the site itself for the website of the host and you will be presented with several key bits of information. Often, sites will obscure their name by using protection services, but you can still get other key information here as well. Remember, in almost every circumstance, there's someone who is accountable. The key here is to find out who is accountable and go after them. Let's say you have a site who has protected their whois records and refuses to take down the illegal copy of your game. Well, if you use other Internet tools such as ping, nslookup, or traceroute, you can identify what their IP address is and use something called a … you guessed it an "ip whois" to find out who their Internet provider is. I can tell you from many years in the business that Internet providers are extremely picky about what kind of content is going over their connections. You can almost invariably find their abuse department's information and file a complaint with them. If you do, then often they will notify the siteholder or shut down the entire site altogether. I've seen it firsthand and know for a fact it can be done. If you aren't familiar with the process, don't be afraid to hire a competent Internet geek to do it for you.

You find the person; if you can't find the person, then you go after the site. If you can't go after the site, go after their Internet provider. If you can't get to the Internet provider because they're using a cloud provider, go after the cloud provider. If, after all of that, you still cannot make it work, well… perhaps it wasn't meant to be. Unless you are losing a preponderance of money to that one particular site, then at that point, it's time to cut your losses and move on.

Get notified.

So how do you know when your game is being distributed? The easy answer is to set up an alert that scans the Internet and notifies you every time it meets the proper criteria. I mean that type of service sounds pretty expensive right? I mean scanning the entire Internet must be a really brutal process. If only there was a free answer to such a difficult conundrum?

There is, and it's been around for years. In fact, it's the exact method several Fortune 500 companies use for social media monitoring of certain key terms. It's called Google Alerts. If you go to google.com/alerts and configure a search for a specific term (such as "<your game name> free download"), it will send you daily updates about where those items can be found on the Internet as it does its parses. We call it "scraping" the Internet.

Kind of crazy, right? Incidentally, you can also use this for monitoring about press and news with respect to your games. This way, any time a positive, or negative, review pops up on a gaming magazine site, you'll know.

It's these types of tricks that help keep you "in the game"—no pun intended. You have to think cleverly everywhere, not just when developing your game!

Pricing Your Game

Pricing your game is as much an intuitive exercise as it is a religious experience. You need a good bit of faith to figure out if you're really pricing it right.

The first thing you have to know is a bit of sales figures on what you can likely expect so you can kind of figure out what your time is worth. How much do you estimate you will make on your game? Ten thousand? A hundred thousand? Good; now cut those expectations in half, then half again.

That's how you get a more realistic goal. Estimates, ironically, are about as good as the paper they're printed on. They mean virtually nothing. You never know when you will have a surprise hit or a total flop. So as a result, set a realistic goal for what you want to walk away with. The higher the number, the more you are going to have to work for it.

As you are going to be marketing on multiple platforms, as mentioned earlier, it can be a bear knowing you'll be using steam. You can expect right off the top to lose 25–30% of your proceeds. That's a fact of life in doing business. You are paying them to use their distribution channel and so as a result you pay that flat fee. This means if you intend to walk away with a dollar or two per game, then you need to add a 30% cost on top of that to reach your objective. I learned this the hard way with my wife, who is a professional gallery acrylic painter. Her paintings sell for hundreds to thousands of dollars, and it was a rude awakening for her to go from direct commission to selling in a gallery. Galleries in my area range from a 40 to 60% commission rate just to sell your art through them. This hurts, truly, but it really can't be helped. One must learn to include that as part of your cost, so that the bottom line makes more sense to us as a developer.

That's not even factoring in the losses from materials (in our cases assets, time spent, graphics tools purchased, etc.) or from government income taxes.

At the end of the day, all of this is the cost of doing business (Figure 22.2).

In the end, you are left with a fraction of what you put in and, while that can be disheartening, I promise you it's actually a vastly better deal than what most AAA studios get for their efforts.

So knowing how much we are going to pay out gives us a good sense of how much we need to think about when we are going after our potential sales numbers. I say this because if we can estimate how many sales we are going to get, then we can estimate how much money we want to make. If you recall from

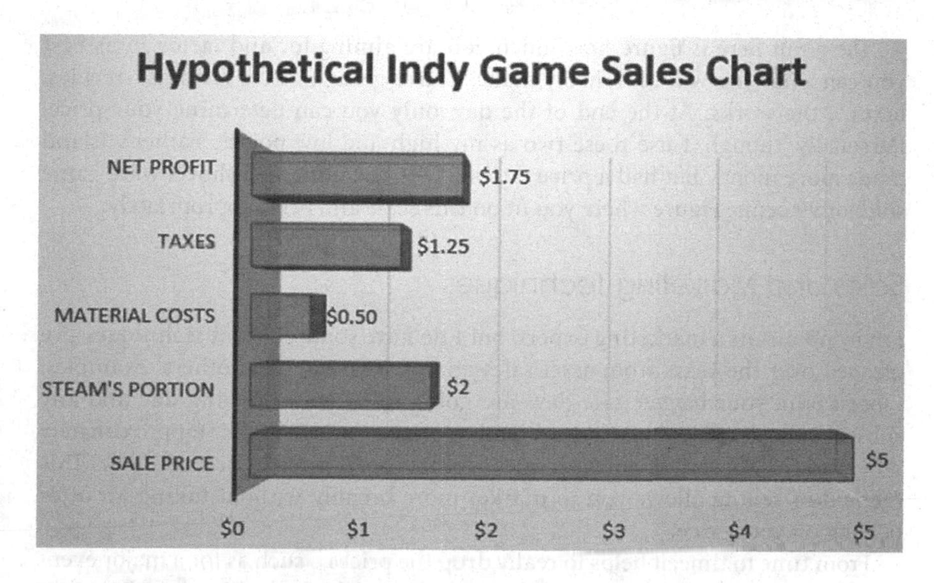

Figure 22.2
Independent publishers can sell less and take home more.

Chapter 22 on piracy that there's a thin line for a game's price point and to when it just becomes more likely an end user will simply pirate it. For instance, would you pay $50 for a new steam game made by a first-time game developer using GameGuru? Not likely. How about $5? Seems much more reasonable, right? Now compare that against other games that cost $5 in the same genre. Do you stack up? Maybe it's more like $3?

Your biggest sale day, in general, will be the launch day, followed by subsequent steam sale days. Eventually, it will then either dry up or settle into a sort of steady residual income stream.

If you look back at the interview with Ivan Ertlov of "Father's Island" fame, you will have your high-water mark. He sold 40,000 copies of his game either direct or in bundles but barely walked away with over a hundred thousand USD after it was all said and done. That means, on average, he was earning approximately $2.50 per copy… for the most successful GameGuru game sold to date.

Now, personally, I don't feel like that's anything to sneeze at. By all accounts, this is a massive accomplishment. More interesting, perhaps, is how a different game, a terrible asset flip, did in GameGuru. This asset flip, which I refuse to name directly, is what many in the GameGuru community would consider a stain on all things holy. Yet even this game sold over a hundred thousand copies. A hundred thousand! The user only charged 99 cents for the game, meaning a maximum of 70,000 was earned. Obviously, this wasn't their takeaway, as most likely there was a huge rash of refunds; but at 99 cents, that's actually in the "why bother" territory of requesting a refund. In my case, I'd just write it off.

The point here is figure how much you are aiming for and factor in as best you can what you will reasonably make. You're going to have refunds, freebies, taxes... the works. At the end of the day, only you can determine your price. Personally, though, I use these two as my high and low points. Father's Island made more money but had a price tag of $4.99; the unnamed shovel ware game sold for 99 cents. Figure where you fit on this scale and price appropriately.

Sales and Marketing Techniques

I'm by no means a marketing expert, but I do have some efficient techniques I've gleaned over the years from asset sales and by learning from others' examples. Once again, your biggest sale days are going to be your opening day and any subsequent sales. For this reason, I tend to price a smidge higher (approximately 20%) and then price it down with sales to what the "normal" price would be. This method of selling allows you to market more broadly without taking an utter beating on your price.

From time to time, it helps to really drop the prices—such as for a major event like Black Friday, Christmas, and the like. This method of selling is risky, obviously, but for those who are unaware of your product, seeing that big fat 50% off sticker is sometimes enough to push them over the edge. In those cases, you are banking on the volume making up for the lower sticker price. I for many years served as a Linux Systems Engineer for the Bon-Ton Corporation in charge of many of their retail website's infrastructure. In working in that role, I learned a lot about how much money was earned on some of those major holidays. Major holidays can be massive from a sales perspective; some businesses rely on them to stay afloat from year to year.

Sales should always be timed in some respect with some meaningful event to help rationalize the sale for the consumer. I've even made one-day sales just for a single customer who asked me about the product to help "facilitate" the sale. That kind of care and attention really gets around, and people enjoy knowing you did something just for them.

Marketing

Marketing is tricky business, with AAA companies investing millions into getting a positive perception for their games and as such to generate sales.

This sometimes has negative repercussions; for instance, if they generate a massive negative perception, then their sales will suffer. Alternately, if you have the aforementioned "swastika" publicity, then negative press can actually INCREASE sales as people buy your game as a cheap curiosity. These are, as always, calculated gambles, but personally, I'd bank on having a quality product with a good reputation versus a poorly made game with a bad reputation.

Your miles will clearly vary.

The big thing with marketing as a small business or indie game developer is to market unapologetically all of the time, any time. You should feel zero shame bringing up your project or product at every opportunity. You need it in people's minds, consciousness, and thoughts at every opportunity. This is how we generate interest in products and keep our work "on boil" in their heads.

Often this means having a social media presence, which can amount to a number of different channels. For some, it's a YouTube channel with a loyal following; for others, it's a blog that covers related topics. The idea here is you want to have fertile ground in which to grow your game's presence. There are numerous web forums on which you can engage with other game developers. While I don't recommend sitting in them all day, I do recommend periodically stopping in and having a dialogue with people who might spread word about a "new, upcoming project." Often other gamedevs might buy your project just to help support you.

It's important to make a grand tour of all the major "indie gaming" sites such as indiedb.com and other associated sites. These sites can help keep potential buyers abreast of your updates and whet the palette, so to speak.

You are going to want a dedicated "studio site" with a site for your game that you can offer press releases at. Alternately, you could make a website for each game; though, realistically, if you're a smaller studio, it will save you some money to have a studio website and make a separate sublocation for the game itself. Even a great many larger studios do this to help save costs. Obviously, if you're not able to put together a decent site yourself, it will probably help to hire someone proficient to do it.

There are, of course, industry experts (Ivan Ertlov is arguably one of them) who can, for a price, actually get your press releases to the proper places and into magazines where you will get even more exposure. This can cost hundreds or thousands of dollars, and so it's important to measure this against what your perceived value of it is. That said, by Ertlov's own admission, there's a huge value in advertising properly.

In speaking with several different game developers, one place of prime import is Facebook advertising. Their system, while somewhat pricey, can really deliver if utilized properly.

Dealing with Customers

Let's fast forward to the future a bit. You've spent months, possibly even years, developing your product. You're proud of it and have released it to at least decent reviews on Steam. Magazines have reviewed it reasonably favorably. Money is starting to come in. You are, for all purposes, a success. Then, the unthinkable happens: Someone writes an absolutely scathing rebuke of your work. Customers begin tearing apart your game on social media, and you are at once downtrodden. Then comes the anger. How dare they destroy your game! How dare they attack your years of hard work!

If you're not familiar with it, I'd highly recommend viewing a documentary called "Indie Game: The Movie." It contains a classic story about a developer who not only didn't reach his own milestones, but he also didn't accurately transmit what he was going to be providing to a very eager audience. The predictably angry fusillades fired back and forth between developer and customers is the stuff of legends at this point.

Experts increasingly agree that online abuse is a problem in the video game development community. It's only natural that you will be a target for it at some point. Luckily, you're not only reading a book from an expert on GameGuru but from someone who also is an expert in dealing with angry customers!

There were two different companies that I helped manage and create their platform for social media presence. One was a $1 billion company and the other was a $10 billion company. At the time, I had been in the right place at the right time with the right information. Regardless, I learned from the $1 billion company the right things to do, so when I got to the $10 billion company, I knew how to best represent them on the Internet. It probably also helped that I did years upon years of Internet technical support as a day job. I've done literally thousands of phone calls, emails, chat sessions, company-sanctioned forum posts, and probably more that I've forgotten. I will do my level best to distill ten years or more of industry experience dealing with angry people in every capacity down to something you can use safely.

The first thing you have to understand is that the less in-person you are, the easier it is for people to be angry with you. Put another way, a former coworker of mine was an explosive ordinance disposal (EOD) military technician in the first Gulf War. So basically, he was the guy who helped disarm bombs and dispose of old explosives. To paraphrase:

> I've never seen people as hysterical as ones who can't get their email. You can tell them, 'this is a bomb' and they might be slightly interested or worried. If they can't get their email, however, the world is ending and you had better watch out.

It's one thing to get an angry phone call, which can be a fairly frequent occurrence in the support industry. It's quite another to deal with the absolutely scathing criticism and curses that you might see launched at you from the deep corners of the Internet.

Internet users are notoriously unhinged and angry. This is because it's a lot easier to vent frustrations virtually than physically. A hyperventilating, red-in-the-face human being at a store counter is a rarer sight than a blaspheming forum user, for instance. This is because we have a sense of public shame; we know what is expected of us in public. This doesn't stop everyone but does act as a filter for our actions.

The Internet is not like that. People will say incredibly coarse things because it's easier to. You don't see your opposition as human beings, rather they are faceless electrons on the Internet with which you are arguing. Throw in the loss of inflection and body language, which accounts for a large portion of what message is actually conveyed, and you have a nasty brew bubbling. Psychologists are not entirely sure what the percentages are with respect to body language. Some say its 60/40 (with 60% being body language and context), others say it's 55/38/7: with 7% being the actual words being spoken. Regardless, you need to keep in mind that an emoticon is not a very good substitute for an actual human expression.

This can cause some severe disagreements over nothing. It can allow arguments to fester where they would normally die. It can cause massive flare-ups and reprisals.

So how, as a social media expert, do you deal with this? I say this because if you are marketing your own game, which you likely are at this point, you will need to be a social media expert. So how do you deal with a negative response on social media? It's easy if you follow these simple rules:

Rule number one: Never be wrong.

You might think this sounds absurd, but it's absolutely critical. Once you open the Pandora's Box of posting on the Internet, you have to realize whatever you put out there is put there in perpetuity. I realize you are not a god and as such you will make mistakes. Your goal is to minimize or eliminate your errors. So if you don't know the answer to something, say so, or say nothing at all. Answer only questions you are 100% certain of the proper answer to.

Do not hypothesize or make guesses. Those will be taken as fact, even if they were simply you making an estimation. The last thing you want to do is provide errors for them to feed off of. This includes your spelling and grammar. It's important to do the best you can with respect to this and not rush your typing. You want to ensure that anything that ends up in a recorded capacity (notably electronic communications) is factual and accurate.

Your goal is to establish a sense of intelligence and authority—to instill a sense of confidence that you are able to resolve this concern for them.

Rule number two: Be apologetic without admitting fault.

This one is tricky. Have you ever called customer support for a problem with your Internet connection? During that call, did the agent (who has the thankless job of dealing with 30–40 disgruntled customers a day) ever say to you: "I'm truly sorry for the inconvenience."

This is a classic way of apologizing to someone without actually apologizing. They're apologizing for the inconvenience caused to you but not necessarily saying "Sorry we broke your Internet connection and caused you to lose thirty thousand dollars in stock trades."

Alternately, if you look at being pulled over by the police for speeding and you apologize to them that is (at least in United States) something that can be construed as an admission of guilt. Your goal here is not to be guilty. The reason for this is because you open a whole can of worms if you admit fault to something, even minor, with respect to your problem. I realize that this goes against what some people feel they need to do, but the reality is you could be opening a much larger door to lawsuits or customers spreading your words around to places you never intended.

So always play your cards close to your vest; keep yourself safe and, at the same time, do your best to satisfy your customers.

Rule number three: Don't argue if you can help it or in other words... don't be a jerk.

This one can be difficult. There are times we feel like picking a fight, as humans. Just because you're right doesn't mean you should act like a rampaging lunatic. Sometimes you need to temper yourself and take a few deep breaths before responding.

Even a valid response, when filled with anger or rage, will seem nuts to people not familiar with the situation. This makes a bad situation worse if it "goes viral" and blows up on social media.

Often times keeping a cool head and not overreacting is really the best plan of action. People will see you being cool as a cucumber while under fire from your opponent (who will often seem more and more unhinged as they ratchet up their anger) and respect you all the more for it.

A prime example of someone failing in this capacity was the "Ocean Marketing vs. Penny Arcade™" row.

In this particularly infamous example, a customer looking for an update on their video game controller becomes increasingly frustrated and the person replying doesn't take it too well. Eventually things reach critical mass, and it ends up becoming a cautionary tale on "what not to do when responding to customers." Regardless of how insane it might seem when reading it, if you take a very open mind to it, you can easily understand why both of them get so upset. Emotions are very powerful things, and you have be mindful of yours when you are replying to paying or potential customers on the Internet.

I highly recommend rereading it here: https://www.penny-arcade.com/news/post/2011/12/26/just-wow1

Just make sure when you do that you try to consider the possibility that both sides are correct. You see it's actually very possible to be in a situation where two opposing parties are both partially correct. This type of situation can be extremely volatile as people's sense of self-righteous pride gets inflamed. Once that occurs, things can get ugly in a hurry.

Rule number four: You are under no obligation to respond.

The last simple rule is just to remember you have the right to remain silent, as it were. As mom always says: "If you've got nothing nice to say, don't say anything at all."

This rule, as simple as it is, can keep you out of more trouble than virtually all of the previous ones. A well-meaning comment getting misconstrued, an angry retort, private information finding its way out of email into the public forum... all of these things can be avoided if you don't respond unless necessary. Obviously, customers need a response for customer-based inquiries. However, sometimes even a bland response is a nonresponse. A simple "We are looking into it and are working on a resolution" is about as benign as you can get. Of course, it's important to maintain the public persona that you are actually looking into it at that point so it helps to update publicly with your findings via patch notes and press releases. Follow-through does matter, and people will be watching to see if you actually did look into it or not.

Abuse, however, has no requirement for being responded to. A customer who is ranting, hollering, and screaming at you is expecting you to stand there and take it. In situations like this, I'd recommend a three-strikes rule. The first strike is a warning along the lines of "Sir, I'm trying to be civil with you, I'd appreciate you being civil with me." The second strike is a "time out." If you're on the phone or a live chat, tell them you are going to give them a few minutes to cool down. Be careful if you are using this that you don't do it in an aggressive fashion as that will only escalate it. Just calmly explain that you are going to put them on hold until they can speak to you in a less abusive fashion. If you're in email, tell them you are going to give them 24–48 hours to cool down before you respond. If you reach three strikes, tell them as impassively as you can that you will not work with someone who is being abusive and to contact you again when they are calmed down. Then hang up or end communication with them.

They will likely come back shortly after, at which point they remain on the third strike. Instantly inform them impassively they are being abusive, that you are not going to communicate with abusive persons until they either relax or stop contacting you. They may well go nuclear at this point, but the reality is you absolutely cannot join them in their hostility. Remain above it and wait for things to relax. In almost every case of having dealt with this, it did relax. In the cases when it does not and they continue to endlessly be hostile, be aware that there are laws for this kind of thing. Use them as a last resort if necessary.

Realize this isn't going to happen a lot of the time. In fact, be happy they are complaining to you. Despite their anger, they are at least willing to communicate with you. Most people will simply ask for a refund and move on.

23

In Closing

Success is a thing difficult to measure. Creating a game is a difficult process with a lot of hours spent getting it just the way you like it. Your success may be as simple as creating a game for a friend or family member that they can enjoy. Perhaps your success will be more tangible, such as making twenty thousand dollars off of it. It's hard to say what parameters you might ascribe to your own personal success.

GameGuru, for all of its simplicity, is a capable tool. When placed in your now-capable hands, you can make miracles and with it find your own success. Above all, the greatest skill you can have as a game developer isn't your proficiency, your budget, your multithousand-dollar toolkits, or even your team. It's your willful stubbornness to complete a project. That is the one single thing that will ensure whether you actually finish the road you start out on. Find that, harness it, and reach your goals!

I wish you great success on your journey!

Appendix and References

Lua Command Reference

The best location to get the most up-to-date information on what's available in Lua is in the globals.lua file in your GameGuru installation\Files\scriptbank folder.

The following is a list that is current as of this writing but is subject to change with additional values and modifications.

Common Functions

GetPlayerDistance (e): Returns the distance from the entity to the player as a real numeric value.

Prompt (string): Prints a simple message at the bottom of the HUD of "string."

PromptDuration (string, time): Prints a simple message at the bottom of the HUD of "string" for a duration specified in milliseconds.

PromptTextSize (size): Sets the prompt text size, values range between 1 and 8, 1 being smallest.

PromptLocalForVR (entity, string): Creates a localized text message near an entity of "string."

GetTimeElapsed (): Returns the float time slice of the current game cycle.

StartTimer (e): Creates relative timer for entity that can be compared against main loop time.

GetTimer (e): Retrieves difference of relative timer vs. "game time."

GetElapsedTime: x=GetElapsedTime (): Returns the elapsed delta time since the last game cycle.

GetTimeElapsed: The same as GetElapsedTime ()!

GetKeyState: x=GetKeyState(y): Returns 1 in x when keycode specified in y is pressed.

Timer (): x=timer (): Returns the global time in milliseconds since the system started.

SwitchScript (e, str): Changes the script used by entity (e) to the one specified in string "str."

Text(x, y, size, txt): Displays text (txt) on the screen in position X/Y of size (size).

TextCenterOnX(x, y, size, txt): The same as text but centered on X position instead of starting at X position.

TextColor(x, y, size, txt, r, g, b): The same as text but this time with an RGB value for color.

TextCenterOnXColor (x, y, size, txt, r, g, b): The same as TextColor but centered on X.

TriggerWaterRipple(x, y, z): A method of triggering a water ripple at a specified coordinate.

GetTerrainHeight: height = GetTerrainHeight(x, z) where X and Z are the coordinates on the terrain you want the height from.

GetGroundHeight: y=GetGroundHeight(x, z): Returns the terrain height of the coordinates specified by x and z.

ResetUnderwaterState (): Resets the underwater subsystem when player emerges from water.

SetUnderwaterOn (): Use this when the player goes underwater for visual changes.

SetUnderwaterOff (): Use this when the player goes above water for visual changes.

SetFont (fontname, fontnum): Example: SetFont ("myFont," 1) to change in game font. Fonts 1–3 are the default ones used.

NOTE: You can place your texture atlas bitmap font file in the Files\fontbank\ folder with the name FPSCR-Font-XX.png where XX is the unique name for your font. When you want to use it, call the command SetFont ("XX," YY) where XX is the unique name above and YY is the index you want to "overwrite." Remember to include the 'FPSCR-Font-XX-Subimages.fnt' file, which describes the coordinates within the texture atlas image for the specific bitmap fonts contained therein.

CurveValue: x=CurveValue (dest, current, smooth): Rreturns the smoothed value based on the smooth factor.

CurveAngle: a=CurveAngle (dest, current, smooth) as CurveValue but handles angles from 0–360 degrees.

WrapValue: x=WrapValue(y): Takes the value y and wraps it to an angle between 0–360 degrees.

NewXValue: x=NewXValue (current, angle, distance): Projects a new x position from the specified angle and distance.

NewZValue: z=NewZValue (current, angle, distance): Projects a new z position from the specified angle and distance.

RayTerrain: r=RayTerrain(x, y, z, x2, y2, z2): Returns 1 if the ray cast hits the terrain geometry.

GetRayCollisionX: x=GetRayCollisionX (): Returns the X position of the terrain hit position.

GetRayCollisionY: y=GetRayCollisionY (): Returns the Y position of the terrain hit position.

GetRayCollisionZ: z=GetRayCollisionZ (): Returns the Z position of the terrain hit position.

IntersectAll: x=IntersectAll(x1, y1, z1, x2, y2, z2, IgnoreObj): Returns 1 if the ray cast hits entity or light mapped geometry.

GetIntersectCollisionX: x=GetIntersectCollisionX (): Returns the X position of the entity hit position.

GetIntersectCollisionY: y=GetIntersectCollisionY (): Returns the Y position of the entity hit position.

GetIntersectCollisionZ: z=GetIntersectCollisionZ (): Returns the Z position of the entity hit position.

SetPreExitValue: SetPreExitValue (e, value): Where e is the entity and a value of 2 will exit preexit function. This is invoked at runtime and allows a function to run code before it runs its final "exit" code.

Input Controls

GetKeyState: x=GetKeyState(y): Returns 1 in x when keycode specified in y is pressed.

MouseMoveX: x=MouseMoveX (): Returns the mouse delta since the last time it was called.

MouseMoveY: y=MouseMoveY (): Returns the mouse delta since the last time it was called.

PositionMouse: PositionMouse(x, y): Repositions the hardware mouse pointer in real time.

GetCharacterControllerDucking: x=GetCharacterControllerDucking (): Returns 1 if the player has been forced to duck.

Graphical Controls

GetDeviceWidth: GetDeviceWidth (): Returns the display width in pixels.

GetDeviceHeight: GetDeviceHeight (): Returns the current display height in pixels.

GetDesktopWidth: GetDesktopWidth (): Returns the current desktop width.

GetDesktopHeight: GetDesktopHeight (): Returns the current desktop height.

SetOcclusion: SetOcclusion (100), control the occluder from script! Sets the occluder from 0 (off) to 100 (max), 10 and under for minimal popping.

GetFogNearest: value = GetFogNearest (): Gets the setting value currently used in the game.

GetFogDistance: value = GetFogDistance (): Gets the setting value currently used in the game.

GetFogRed: value = GetFogRed (): Gets the setting value currently used in the game.

GetFogGreen: value = GetFogGreen (): Gets the setting value currently used in the game.

GetFogBlue: value = GetFogBlue (): Gets the setting value currently used in the game.

GetFogIntensity: value = GetFogIntensity (): Gets the setting value currently used in the game.

GetAmbienceIntensity: value = GetAmbienceIntensity (): Gets the setting value currently used in the game.

GetAmbienceRed: value = GetAmbienceRed (): Gets the setting value currently used in the game.

GetAmbienceGreen: value = GetAmbienceGreen (): Gets the setting value currently used in the game.

GetAmbienceBlue: value = GetAmbienceBlue (): Gets the setting value currently used in the game.

GetSurfaceRed: value = GetSurfaceRed (): Gets the setting value currently used in the game.

GetSurfaceGreen: value = GetSurfaceGreen (): Gets the setting value currently used in the game.

GetSurfaceBlue: value = GetSurfaceBlue (): Gets the setting value currently used in the game.

GetSurfaceIntensity: value = GetSurfaceIntensity (): Gets the setting value currently used in the game.

GetPostVignetteRadius: value = GetPostVignetteRadius (): Gets the setting value currently used in the game.

GetPostVignetteIntensity: value = GetPostVignetteIntensity (): Gets the setting value currently used in the game.

GetPostMotionDistance: value = GetPostMotionDistance (): Gets the setting value currently used in the game.

GetPostMotionIntensity: value = GetPostMotionIntensity (): Gets the setting value currently used in the game.

GetPostDepthOfFieldDistance: value = GetPostDepthOfFieldDistance (): Gets the setting value currently used in the game.

GetPostDepthOfFieldIntensity: value = GetPostDepthOfFieldIntensity (): Gets the setting value currently used in the game.

SetFogNearest (v): Sets the near value for fog (0–255).

SetFogDistance (v): Sets the end value for transitioning fog (0–255).

SetFogRed (v): Sets fog red color (0–255).

SetFogGreen (v): Sets fog green color (0–255).

SetFogBlue (v): Sets fog blue color (0–255).

SetFogIntensity (v): Sets fog intensity (0–255).

SetAmbienceIntensity (v): Sets ambient light intensity (0–100).

SetAmbienceRed (v): Sets ambient light red color (0–255).

SetAmbienceGreen (v): Sets ambient light green color (0–255).

SetAmbienceBlue (v): Sets ambient light blue color (0–255).

SetSurfaceIntensity (v) (v/33): Sets the surface light intensity, ranges from 0–32,767.

SetSurfaceRed (v): Sets surface light level red to value (v) (0–255).

SetSurfaceGreen (v): Sets surface light level green to value (v) (0–255).

SetSurfaceBlue (v): Sets surface light level blue to value (v) (0–255).

SetSurfaceSunFactor (v): Sets "sun surface factor," which affects how bright the sunlight appears on models.

SetGlobalSpecular (v): Sets global specular value. Doesn't affect PBR models as of this writing. Typically 0–100, but it can be set extremely high (up to 10,000).

SetBrightness (v): Sets the brightness, however, it goes in a range of −0.5(0%) to 0.5(100%).

SetContrast (v): Sets the contrast in a range of 0(0%) to 3.33(100%).

SetPostBloom (v): Sets the post-effect bloom shader level.

SetPostVignetteRadius (v): Sets post-effect vignette radius.

SetPostVignetteIntensity (v): Sets post-effect vignette intensity.

SetPostMotionDistance (v): Sets post-effect motion blur distance.

SetPostMotionIntensity (v): Sets post-effect motion blur intensity.

SetPostDepthOfFieldDistance (v): Sets post-effect depth of field starting distance.

SetPostDepthOfFieldIntensity (v): Sets post-effect depth of field intensity.

SetPostLightRayLength (v): Sets post-effect light ray length.

SetPostLightRayQuality (v): Sets post-effect light ray quality.

SetPostLightRayDecay (v): Sets post effect light ray decay.

SetPostSAORadius (v): Sets post effect "screen-space ambient occlusion" radius.

SetPostSAOIntensity (v): Sets post effect "screen-space ambient occlusion" intensity.

SetPostLensFlareIntensity (v): Sets post-effect lens flare intensity.

SetOptionReflection (v): Sets reflection level (correlates with tab settings) slider to v (0–100).

SetOptionShadows (v): Sets shadow level (correlates with tab settings) slider to v (0–100).

SetOptionLightRays (v): Sets light ray level (correlates with tab settings) slider to v (0–100).

SetOptionVegetation (v): Sets vegetation level (correlates with tab settings) slider to v (0–100).

SetOptionOcclusion (v): Sets occlusion level (correlates with tab settings) slider to v (0–100).

SetCameraPanelDistance (v): Sets camera panel distance level (correlates to tab settings) slider to v (0–100).

SetCameraPanelFOV (v): Sets field of view for camera to v (0–359).

SetCameraPanelZoomPercentage (v): Sets camera zoom percentage (0–100).

SetCameraPanelWeaponFOV (v): Sets weapon FOV to v (0–359).

SetTerrainLODNear (v): Sets terrain level of detail slider near to v (0–255). Must be lower than mid and far.

SetTerrainLODMid (v): Sets terrain level of detail slider mid to v (0–255). Must be higher than near and lower than far.

SetTerrainLODFar (v): Sets terrain level of detail slider far to v (0–255). Must be higher than mid and low.

SetTerrainSize (v): Sets terrain maximum displayable size to v.

SetVegetationQuantity (v): Sets vegetation quantity to v (0–100).

SetVegetationWidth (v): Sets vegetation width to v (0–100).

SetVegetationHeight (v): Sets vegetation height to v (0–100).

Level Control Functions

JumpToLevelIfUsed (e): Jump to the level specified in the object's "ifused" field, loading the new level.

JumpToLevel (levelname): Jumps to a level specified in the string "levelname."

FinishLevel (): Finishes the level, ending the game.

Checkpoint (e): Creates a checkpoint for if you return to this level, allowing you to restart at that location.

Disable and Enable Core Functions

HideTerrain (): Hides all terrain.

ShowTerrain (): Shows all terrain.

HideWater (): Hides all water.

ShowWater (): Shows all water.

HideHuds (): Hides all player heads up displays.

ShowHuds (): Shows all player heads up displays.

FreezeAI (): Freezes all AI, even friendly. Is prone to be buggy.

UnFreezeAI (): Unfreezes all frozen AI, even friendly. Is prone to be buggy.

FreezePlayer (): Freezes the player in location. Is prone to be buggy.

UnFreezePlayer (): Allows the player to move again. Is prone to be buggy.

SetFreezePosition(x, y, z): Sets a position for the player to go when frozen. Useful for cutscenes.

SetFreezeAngle (ax, ay, az): Configures the angle they will face when frozen. Useful for cutscenes.

TransportToFreezePosition (): Teleports the player to the position specified by SetFreezePosition. Useful for cutscenes.

TransportToFreezePositionOnly (): Teleports the player to the position specified by SetFreezePosition but only while frozen. Useful for cutscenes in different locations.

ActivateMouse (): Turns on the mouse, if not already active.

DeactivateMouse (): Disables the mouse, if not already disabled.

Player Functions

SetPlayerHealth (v): Sets player's health to direct value (v); 0 is dead.

SetPlayerLives (v): Sets the number of lives a player has to (v).

TransportToIfUsed (e): Transport to the entity specified in this entity's "ifused" field.

AddPlayerWeapon (e): Give the player a weapon specified by the entity #.

ChangePlayerWeapon (str): Change the player's weapon to the one specified in the string "str."

ChangePlayerWeaponID (id): Change the player's weapon based on weapon ID number.

ReplacePlayerWeapon (e): Swap a player's current weapon by entity #.

AddPlayerAmmo (e): Use this entity to give a player ammo.

AddPlayerHealth (e): Use this entity to give a player health.

SetPlayerPower (e, v): Use this entity to set the player's power to v (value).

AddPlayerPower (e, v): Use this entity to add to the player's power by v (value).

RemovePlayerWeapons (e): Use this entity to remove all player weapons.

AddPlayerJetPack (e, fuel): Give the player jetpack fuel specified by variable "fuel."

GetPlayerInZone (e): Use this zone entity to check if player is in the zone and return a 1 if they are.

FireWeapon (e): Fires the player's weapon for them.

HurtPlayer (e, v): Use this entity (e) to hurt the player by value v.

DrownPlayer (e, v): Use this entity (e) to drown the player by value v.

ControlDynamicCharacterController: ControlDynamicCharacterController (iObj, fAngleY, fAngleX, fSpeed, fJump, fDucking, fPushAngle, fPushForce, ThrustUpwards): Controls player physics capsule.

GetCharacterHitFloor: x=GetCharacterHitFloor (): Returns a value if the player hits the floor.

GetCharacterFallDistance: x=GetCharacterFallDistance (): Returns the distance the player fell when it hit the floor.

Player Jetpack

SetGamePlayerControlJetpackMode: SetGamePlayerControlJetpackMode (iValue): Sets the player control data to specified value.

GetGamePlayerControlJetpackMode: iValue=GetGamePlayerControlJetpack Mode (): Gets the specified player control data value.

SetGamePlayerControlJetpackFuel: SetGamePlayerControlJetpackFuel (iValue): Sets the player control data to specified value.

GetGamePlayerControlJetpackFuel: iValue = GetGamePlayerControlJetpackFuel (): Gets the specified player control data value.

SetGamePlayerControlJetpackHidden: SetGamePlayerControlJetpackHidden (iValue): Sets the player control data to specified value.

GetGamePlayerControlJetpackHidden: iValue = GetGamePlayerControlJetpack Hidden (): Gets the specified player control data value.

SetGamePlayerControlJetpackCollected: SetGamePlayerControlJetpackCollected (iValue): Sets the player control data to specified value.

GetGamePlayerControlJetpackCollected: iValue = GetGamePlayerControlJetpack Collected (): Gets the specified player control data value.

SetGamePlayerControlSoundStartIndex: SetGamePlayerControlSoundStartIndex (iValue): Sets the player control data to specified value.

GetGamePlayerControlSoundStartIndex: iValue = GetGamePlayerControlSound StartIndex (): Gets the specified player control data value.

SetGamePlayerControlJetpackParticleEmitterIndex: SetGamePlayerControl JetpackParticleEmitterIndex (iValue): Sets the player control data to specified value.

GetGamePlayerControlJetpackParticleEmitterIndex: iValue = GetGamePlayer ControlJetpackParticleEmitterIndex (): Gets the specified player control data value.

SetGamePlayerControlJetpackThrust: SetGamePlayerControlJetpackThrust (iValue): Sets the player control data to specified value.

GetGamePlayerControlJetpackThrust: iValue = GetGamePlayerControlJetpack Thrust (): Gets the specified player control data value.

Player Weapons

UpdateWeaponStats: UpdateWeaponStats (): Call this to instantly update all g_Weapon* data.

ResetWeaponSystems: ResetWeaponSystems (): Resets any projectiles currently active in game.

SetWeaponSlot: SetWeaponSlot (index, got flag, preference flag): Sets the weapon data directly; index is 1 through 10.

GetWeaponAmmo: quantity = GetWeaponAmmo (index): Sets the weapon data directly; index is 1 through 10.

SetWeaponAmmo: SetWeaponAmmo (index, ammo quantity): Sets the weapon data directly; index is 1 through 10.

GetWeaponClipAmmo: quantity = GetWeaponClipAmmo (index): Sets the weapon data directly; index is 1 through 10.

SetWeaponClipAmmo: SetWeaponClipAmmo (index, clip quantity): Sets the weapon data directly; index is 1 through 10.

GetWeaponPoolAmmo: quantity = GetWeaponPoolAmmo (index): Sets the weapon data directly; index is 1 through 10.

SetWeaponPoolAmmo: SetWeaponPoolAmmo (index, pool ammo quantity): Sets the weapon data directly; index is 1 through 10.

GetWeaponSlot: GetWeaponSlot (index): Gets WeaponID from slot; index is 1 through 10.

GetPlayerWeaponID: WeaponID = GetPlayerWeaponID (): Returns the WeaponID the player is currently carrying.

GetWeaponID: GetWeaponID (GunNameString): Gets WeaponID associated with current GunNameString.

GetEntityWeaponID: GetEntityWeaponID (e): Gets the WeaponID associated with the entity specified.

SetWeaponDamage: SetWeaponDamage (WeaponID, FireModeIndex, Value): Sets damage value of weapon.

SetWeaponAccuracy: SetWeaponAccuracy (WeaponID, FireModeIndex, Value): Sets accuracy value of weapon.

SetWeaponReloadQuantity: SetWeaponReloadQuantity (WeaponID, FireMode Index, Value): Sets reload quantity value of weapon.

SetWeaponFireIterations: SetWeaponFireIterations (WeaponID, FireModeIndex, Value): Sets shot iterations value of weapon.

SetWeaponRange: SetWeaponRange (WeaponID, FireModeIndex, Value): Sets range value of weapon.

SetWeaponDropoff: SetWeaponDropoff (WeaponID, FireModeIndex, Value): Sets drop-off value of weapon.

SetWeaponSpotLighting: SetWeaponSpotLighting (WeaponID, FireModeIndex, Value): Sets whether weapon uses spotlight effect.

GetWeaponDamage: Value = GetWeaponDamage (WeaponID, FireModeIndex): Gets damage value of weapon.

GetWeaponAccuracy: Value = GetWeaponAccuracy (WeaponID, FireModeIndex): Gets accuracy value of weapon.

GetWeaponReloadQuantity: Value = GetWeaponReloadQuantity (WeaponID, FireModeIndex): Gets reload quantity value of weapon.

GetWeaponFireIterations: Value = GetWeaponFireIterations (WeaponID, FireMode Index): Gets shot iterations value of weapon.

GetWeaponRange: Value = GetWeaponRange (WeaponID, FireModeIndex): Gets range value of weapon.

GetWeaponDropoff: Value = GetWeaponDropoff (WeaponID, FireModeIndex): Gets drop-off value of weapon.

GetWeaponSpotLighting: Value = GetWeaponSpotLighting (WeaponID, FireMode Index): Gets whether weapon uses spotlight effect.

SetPlayerWeapons: SetPlayerWeapons (0) disables player weapons. SetPlayerWeapons (1) restores them.

SetAttachmentVisible: SetAttachmentVisible (e, 1): 1 sets the entities attachment to be visible (such as their weapon); 0 switches it off.

SetFlashLight: SetFlashLight (1): 1 switches the flashlight on, 0 off.

SetFlashLightKeyEnabled: SetFlashLightKeyEnabled (1): 1 is for on, 0 for off. Disables the flash light key from being used.

Camera Controls

WrapAngle: V = WrapAngle (Angle, Dest, Smoothing) will smoothly change Angle to Dest, returning in V. Smoothing 0 to 1.

SetCameraOverride: SetCameraOverride (i) where i is 0-off, 1-position only, 2-angle only, 3-position and angle.

SetCameraPosition: SetCameraPosition (c, x, y, z) where c should be zero, and XYZ are 3D coordinates.

SetCameraAngle: SetCameraAngle (c, x, y, z) where c should be zero, and XYZ are Euler angles.

GetCameraPositionX: V = GetCameraPositionX (c) where V is the X coordinate of the specified camera.

GetCameraPositionY: V = GetCameraPositionY (c) where V is the Y coordinate of the specified camera.

GetCameraPositionZ: V = GetCameraPositionZ (c) where V is the Z coordinate of the specified camera.

GetCameraAngleX: V = GetCameraAngleX (c) where V is the X angle of the specified camera.

GetCameraAngleY: V = GetCameraAngleY (c) where V is the Y angle of the specified camera.

GetCameraAngleZ: V = GetCameraAngleZ (c) where V is the Z angle of the specified camera.

PositionCamera: PositionCamera (cam, x, y, z): Positions the specified camera at the xyz position.

PointCamera: PointCamera (cam, x, y, z): Angles the specified camera toward the xyz position.

MoveCamera: MoveCamera (cam, step): Moves the specified camera at its current angle by the step amount.

Physics Commands

ForcePlayer: ForcePlayer (angle, velocity) where angle is the angle and physics velocity to push the player.

PHYSLIB.LUA COMMANDS

getPos3 (): This gets the player's position in x/y/z.

getAng3 (): Returns the angle the player is facing in x/y/z.

ObjectToEntity (obj): Changes object to entity id.

GetObjectDimensions (obj): Returns {w, h, l, m, cx, cy, cz} of an object's dimensions.

AddEntityCollisionCheck (e): Adds a collision check to an entity.

RemoveEntityCollisionCheck (e): Disables the collision check on an entity.

GetEntityTerrainNumCollisions (e): Returns number of terrain collisions stored by collision checking system for a specified entity.

GetTerrainCollisionDetails (obj): Returns nil if no terrain collisions or a table containing the world location of collisions detected in order from oldest to newest.

GetEntityTerrainCollisionDetails (e): Similar to the aforementioned but uses an entity id.

GetEntityObjectNumCollisions (e): Gets the number of object on object collisions for an entity.

GetObjectCollisionDetails (obj): Returns nil if no object on object collisions for the specified entity or a table containing the object id of the colliding object, the world location, and the force of the contact from oldest to newest.

GetEntityObjectCollisionDetails (e): Same thing but with entity to object collisions.

getHingeValues (dims, hingeName, spacing): Gets the value for a specific hinge. Returns w, h, and l.

GetRealWorldYangle (xa, ya, za): A very complex function that returns a real world angle (0–359) based on the Euler angle for the entity.

AddObjectSingleHinge (obj, hingeName, swingAng, offset, spacing): Adds a hinge to "obj" named "hingeName" that has a specific swing angle "swingAng" and is offset from the entity by offset with a spacing of "spacing." Returns a –1 if the joint can't be created.

AddObjectDoubleHinge (objA, objB, hingeNameA, hingeNameB, spacing, noCols): Uses a hinge to connect two objects "objA and objB" and returns a –1 if the joint can't be created.

AddEntityDoubleHinge (e1, e2, hingeName1, hingeName2, spacing, noCols): Uses hinge to connect two entities (e1 and e2), returns a –1 if joint can't be created.

AddObjectSingleJoint (obj, jointName, spacing): Adds a named joint to an object "obj," named joint "JointName," with spacing of "spacing." Returns a –1 if it can't create the hinge.

AddEntitySingleJoint (e, jointName, spacing): Same, only with entities.

AddObjectDoubleJoint (objA, objB, jointNameA, jointNameB, spacing, noCols): Adds a double joint connecting two objects (objA and objB) with two joints named "jointNameA and jointNameB." Returns a –1 if the joint cannot be created.

AddEntityDoubleJoint (e1, e2, jointNameA, jointNameB, spacing, noCols): The same, but with entities.

RemoveEntityConstraints (e): Removes all the hinges, physics constraints, etc. from an entity.

RemoveEntityConstraintsIfDead (e): The same as previous but with a simple health check first.

SetEntityDamping (e, damping, angle): Sets an entity (e)'s damping by "damping" across "angle."

GetViewVector (): Gives the view vector for the player.

ObjectPlayerLookingAt (dist, force): If dist isn't specified, it will default to 2000 units. If force isn't specified, it will default to 0 force. This function is a ray cast for the physics engine from the player. Only returns hits on dynamic entities.

Object Manipulation

ScaleObject: ScaleObject (obj, x, y, z): Scales object in all axis. (Note: Uses object id not entity!)

NOTE: The following four functions return multiple values; if you do not need them all, just replace the ones you don't need with '_'. For example: _, _, _, Ax, Ay, Az = GetEntityPosAng (e) would just give you last three of the six values returned.

GetObjectPosAng: x, y, z, Ax, Ay, Az = GetObjectPosAng (obj): Returns position and Euler angles of object.

GetEntityPosAng: x, y, z, Ax, Ay, Az = GetEntityPosAng (e): Returns position and Euler angles of entity.

GetObjectColBox: xmin, ymin, zmin, xmax, ymax, zmax = GetObjectCollBox (obj): Returns collision cube of object.

GetEntityColBox: xmin, ymin, zmin, xmax, ymax, zmax = GetEntityCollBox (e): Returns collision cube of entity.

GetEntityWeight: weight = GetEntityWeight (e): Returns the physics weight value of the entity.

GetObjectScales: xs, ys, zs = GetObjectScales (obj): Returns scale values of object in all axis. (Note: Uses object id not entity!)

SetRotationYSlowly: SetRotationYSlowly(e, destangle, smoothvalue): Where e is the entity and a smooth value of 100 is immediate, where 50 takes twice as long to rotate to destangle (dest angle).

RotateToPlayerWithOffset (e, angleoffset): Rotates an entity to the player with a Euler angle offset.

SetHoverFactor (e, v): Sets (e) entity's hover factor by (v) value. Used for flying objects.

GetObjectExist: x=GetObjectExist (obj): Returns if the specified object exists.

SetObjectFrame: SetObjectFrame (obj, x): Sets the animation frame of the specified object.

GetObjectFrame: x=GetObjectFrame (obj): Returns the animation frame of the specified object.

SetObjectSpeed: SetObjectSpeed (obj, x): Sets the animation speed of the specified object.

GetObjectSpeed: x=GetObjectSpeed (obj): Returns the animation speed of the specified object.

PositionObject: PositionObject (obj, x, y, z): Sets the position of the specified object.

RotateObject: RotateObject (obj, x, y, z): Sets the angle of the specified object.

GetObjectAngleX: x=GetObjectAngleX (obj): Returns the X position of the specified object.

GetObjectAngleY: y=GetObjectAngleY (obj): Returns the Y position of the specified object.

GetObjectAngleZ: z=GetObjectAngleZ (obj): Returns the Z position of the specified object.

GetFirstEntitySpawn: GetFirstEntitySpawn (): Useful for scripts (such as the radar) that need to deal with entities that can come into existence at any time (returns 0 if no new entity).

GetNextEntitySpawn: GetNextEntitySpawn (): Returns the next new spawn in the list, 0 if the end of the list is reached.

SetEntityHealth (e, v): Sets the health of entity (e) to value (v).

SetEntityHealthSilent (e, v): Sets (e) entity's health to (v) value without applying headshots, physics, or directly damage application. Simply sets the health value. Can cause unpredictable effects.

SetEntityRagdollForce (e, limb, x, y, z, v): Applies ragdoll force to entity (e) on limb (limb) by vector (x/y/y) by value (v).

Destroy (e): Destroys entity (e), removing it from the game until the game is reloaded.

CollisionOn (e): Enables collision detection for entity (e).

CollisionOff (e): Disables collision detection for entity (e).

GetEntityPlayerVisibility (e): Checks if the player is visible to entity (e).

GetEntityInZone (e): Checks if an entity is in the zone (e).

Hide (e): Hides entity (e), temporarily inactivating and hiding it. Does not delete it.

Show (e): Shows a hidden entity (e), activating and showing it.

Spawn (e): Spawns an entity (e) that is not currently spawned.

SetActivated (e, v): Sets entity (e)'s activated flag to value (v).

ResetLimbHit (e): Resets limb hits on entity (e).

ActivateIfUsed (e): Activates the object in entity (e)'s ifused property field.

SpawnIfUsed (e): Spawns the object in entity (e)'s ifused property field.

RefreshEntity (e): Refreshes the entity (e) in case it needs a statistic updated.

Collected (e): Sets the collected flag with the player, indicating entity (e) is collected (for keys and such).

MoveUp (e, v): Physically moves entity (e) by its Y value (v).

MoveForward (e, v): Physically moves entity (e) by its Z value (v).

MoveBackward (e, v): Physically moves entity (e) by its Z value backward (v).

SetPosition (e, x, y, z): Sets an entity (e)'s world position to x/y/z.

ResetPosition (e, x, y, z): Resets entity's position.

SetRotation (e, x, y, z): Sets an entity (e)'s rotation to x/y/z.

ResetRotation (e, x, y, z): Resets entity's rotation.

ModulateSpeed (e, v): Adjusts the entity (e)'s speed to value (v).

RotateX (e, v): Rotates entity (e) by value (v) on the X-axis.

RotateY (e, v): Rotates entity (e) by value (v) on the Y-axis.

RotateZ (e, v): Rotates entity (e) by value (v) on the Z-axis.

SetLimbIndex (e, v): Sets an entity (e)'s limb index to value (v).

RotateLimbX (e, v): Rotates entity limb (e) by on X-axis by value (v).

RotateLimbY (e, v): Rotates entity limb (e) by on Y-axis by value (v).

RotateLimbZ (e, v): Rotates entity limb (e) by on Z-axis by value (v).

Scale (e, v): Scales entity (e) to value (v), which is a percent.

SetAnimation (e): Sets a specific animation.

SetAnimationFrames (e, v): Sets specific animation frames to value for entity E.

PlayAnimation (e): Plays a specific animation once.

LoopAnimation (e): Loops a specific entity animation.

StopAnimation (e): Stops the animation.

MoveWithAnimation (e, v): Allows the entity to move with a specific animation.

SetAnimationSpeed (e, v): Sets the speed of the actual animation.

SetAnimationFrame (e, v): Sets the animation to a specific frame.

GetAnimationFrame (e): Returns the current animation frame of an entity.

GravityOff (e): Disables this entity (e)'s gravity.

GravityOn (e): Enables this entity (e)'s gravity.

LookAtPlayer (e): Faces the entity (e) toward the player.

RotateToPlayer (e): Rotates entity (e) toward the player at moderate speed.

RotateToCamera (e): Rotates entity (e) toward the camera at moderate speed.

RotateToPlayerSlowly (e, v): Rotates the entity (e) to the player by the value (v).

SetEntityActive: SetEntityActive (e, active flag): Sets the entity data directly; e is entity index.

SetEntityActivated: SetEntityActivated (e, activated flag): Sets the entity data directly; e is entity index.

SetEntityCollected: SetEntityCollected (e, collected flag): Sets the entity data directly; e is entity index.

SetEntityHasKey: SetEntityHasKey (e, haskey flag): Sets the entity data directly; e is entity index.

GetEntityVisibility: vis = GetEntityVisibility (e): Where e is the entity number and return vis (0-hidden, 1-shown).

GetEntityActive: flag = GetEntityActive (e): Returns 1 if the entity is active and not in process of dying.

GetEntityPositionX: x = GetEntityPositionX (e): Where e is the entity number and returns the X position.

GetEntityPositionY: y = GetEntityPositionY (e): Where e is the entity number and returns the Y position.

GetEntityPositionZ: z = GetEntityPositionZ (e): Where e is the entity number and returns the Z position.

GetEntityAngleX: x = GetEntityAngleX (e): Where e is the entity number and returns the X angle.

GetEntityAngleY: y = GetEntityAngleY (e): Where e is the entity number and returns the Y angle.

GetEntityAngleZ: z = GetEntityAngleZ (e): Where e is the entity number and returns the Z angle.

GetAnimationSpeed: speed = GetAnimationSpeed (e): Where e is the entity number and speed is the ANIMSPEED of the entity.

SetAnimationSpeedModulation: SetAnimationSpeedModulation (e, speed): Where e is the entity number and speed is animation speed modulator.

GetAnimationSpeedModulation: speed = GetAnimationSpeedModulation (e): Where e is the entity number and speed is the animation speed modulator.

GetMovementDelta: delta = GetMovementDelta (e): Where e is the entity number and delta is the movement distance since the last cycle.

GetEntitySpawnAtStart: state = GetEntitySpawnAtStart (e): Returns the state of the spawn (0-dont spawn at start, 1-spawn at start, 2-spawned during game).

GetEntityFilePath: string = GetEntityFilePath (e): Returns the entity file path to be used for helping inventory image systems.

GetEntityAnimationStart: frame = GetEntityAnimationStart (e, animsetindex): Returns frame (Y) stored in FPE under animX = Y, Z where X is animsetindex.

GetEntityAnimationFinish: frame = GetEntityAnimationFinish (e, animsetindex): Returns frame (Z) stored in FPE under animX = Y, Z where X is animsetindex.

GetAmmoClipMax: ammoclipmax = GetAmmoClipMax (e): Returns the maximum units per ammo clip for the held weapon of the entity.

GetAmmoClip: ammoclip = GetAmmoClip (e): Returns the current ammo in clip for the held weapon of the entity.

SetAmmoClip: SetAmmoClip (e, ammoquantity): Sets the ammo clip quantity for the held weapon of the entity.

FreezeEntity: FreezeEntity (e, mode): Where e is the entity index and mode is reserved. Will freeze entity physics position.

UnFreezeEntity: UnFreezeEntity (e): Where e is the entity index to be unfrozen from a previous call to FreezeEntity.

Particles

ParticlesGetFreeEmitter: iEmitterID = ParticlesGetFreeEmitter (): Returns the index of a free particle emitter object.

StartParticleEmitter (e): Enables the basic particle emitter on the location of entity (e).

StopParticleEmitter (e): Stops the basic particle emitter on the location of entity (e).

ParticlesAddEmitter: ParticlesAddEmitter(particleid,: Creates a particle emitter with the following parameters at the player location: animationSpeed, startsOff RandomAngle, offsetMinX, offsetMinY, offsetMinZ, offsetMaxX, offsetMaxY, offsetMaxZ, scaleStartMin, scaleStartMax, scaleEndMin, scaleEndMax, movementSpeedMinX, movementSpeedMinY, movementSpeedMinZ, movementSpeedMaxX, movementSpeedMaxY, movementSpeedMaxZ, rotateSpeedMinZ, rotateSpeedMaxZ, lifeMin, lifeMax, alphaStartMin, alphaStartMax, alphaEndMin, alphaEndMax, frequency).

ParticlesAddEmitterEX: ParticlesAddEmitterEX(particleid,: Creates a particle emitter with the following parameters at entity location: animationSpeed, starts OffRandomAngle, offsetMinX, offsetMinY, offsetMinZ, offsetMaxX, offsetMaxY, offsetMaxZ, scaleStartMin, scaleStartMax, scaleEndMin, scaleEndMax, movementSpeedMinX, movementSpeedMinY, movementSpeedMinZ, movementSpeedMaxX, movementSpeedMaxY, movementSpeedMaxZ, rotateSpeedMinZ, rotateSpeedMaxZ, lifeMin, lifeMax, alphaStartMin, alphaStartMax, alphaEndMin, alphaEndMax, frequency).

ParticlesDeleteEmitter: ParticlesDeleteEmitter (particleid): Where particleid is the index of the particle emitter.

Sounds, Music, and Video

PlayFootfallSound: snd=PlayFootfallSound (type, x, y, z, lastsnd): Triggers footfall sound and returns raw sound index used.

LoadGlobalSound: LoadGlobalSound (filename, iID): Where iID is an index greater than zero and filename points to a WAV file in your game installation.

DeleteGlobalSound: DeleteGlobalSound (iID): Where iID is the index of the sound loaded in the load command.

PlayGlobalSound: PlayGlobalSound (iID): Where iID is the index of the sound to be played.

LoopGlobalSound: LoopGlobalSound (iID): Where iID is the index of the sound to be looped.

StopGlobalSound: StopGlobalSound (iID): Where iID is the index of the sound to be stopped.

SetGlobalSoundSpeed: SetGlobalSoundSpeed (iID, speed): Where iID is the index of the sound to change the speed of.

SetGlobalSoundVolume: SetGlobalSoundVolume (iID, volume): Where iID is the index of the sound to change the volume of.

GetGlobalSoundExist: GetGlobalSoundExist (iID): Where iID is the index of the sound to check existence of.

GetGlobalSoundPlaying: GetGlobalSoundPlaying (iID): Where iID is the index of the sound to check if playing.

GetGlobalSoundLooping: GetGlobalSoundLooping (iID): Where iID is the index of the sound to check if looping.

PlayRawSound: PlayRawSound (iID): Where iID is the raw engine sound index.

LoopRawSound: LoopRawSound (iID): Where iID is the raw engine sound index.

StopRawSound: StopRawSound (iID): Where iID is the raw engine sound index.

SetRawSoundVolume: SetRawSoundVolume (iID, iVolume): Where iID is the raw engine sound index and iVolume from 0 to 100.

RawSoundExist: iFlag = RawSoundExist (iID): Where iID is the raw engine sound index.

RawSoundPlaying: iFlag = RawSoundPlaying (iID): Where iID is the raw engine sound index.

SetSound (e, v): Sets the sound of entity (e) to value (v), which is in its properties pane.

PlaySound (e, v): Plays the sound of entity (e) at value (v), which is in its properties pane.

PlaySoundIfSilent (e, v): Plays the sound of entity (e) at value (v) in its properties pane if it's silent.

PlayNon3DSound (e, v): Plays the sound of entity (e) at value (v) at maximum volume.

LoopSound (e, v): Loops the sound, endlessly, of entity (e) at value (v), which is in its properties pane.

StopSound (e, v): Stops the sound of entity (e) at value (v) from playing.

SetSoundSpeed (freq): Sets the sound frequency of the sound being played.

SetSoundVolume (vol): Sets the sound volume.

PlayVideo (e, v): Plays video for entity (e) from value (v), which is a string.

PlayVideoNoSkip (e, v): Plays the video for entity (e) from value (v), which is a string; player cannot skip.

StopVideo (e, v): Stops the video played for entity (e) of value (v).

SetCharacterSoundSet(e): Sets a character's sound set (e).

SetCharacterSound (e, str): Changes a character's sound set for entity (e) to string (str), which is a filepath.

PlayCharacterSound (e, str): Plays a different character's sound for entity (e) of string (str), which is a filepath.

PlayCombatMusic (playTime, fadeTime) music_play_timecue (2, playTime, fadeTime): Plays track 2.

PlayFinalAssaultMusic (fadeTime) music_play_cue (3, fadeTime): Plays track 3.

DisableMusicReset (v): Disables music reset.

SetEntityString: SetEntityString (e, slot, string): Where e is the entity number and slot (0–4) to write the string into. This allows you to change sounds or configure them programmatically.

GetEntityString: GetEntityString (e, slot): Where e is the entity number and slot (0–4) is the sound slot index.

LoopNon3DSound (e, v): entity/value: Loops a slotted sound without 3D, so no distance modifiers, just same volume at any distance.

Sprites, Lights, and Images

HideLight (e): Hides a light entity (e).

ShowLight (e): Shows a light entity (e).

LoadImages (str, v): Loads images specified in folder string (str), specifically (v) number of them.

SetImagePosition(x, y): Sets a specific image's position to x/y value.

ShowImage (i): Shows the image (i) on the screen.

HideImage (i): Hides the image (i) on the screen.

SetImageAlignment (i): Sets the image alignment for image (i).

Panel(x, y, x2, y2): Creates a panel starting at x/y and ending at x2/y2.

LoadImage: myImage = LoadImage ("myFolder\\myImage.png"): Anywhere inside GG files folder (however, it is best to put into scriptbank images folder for making standalones).

GetImageWidth: myWidth = GetImageWidth (1): Gets percentage width of image.

GetImageHeight: myHeight = GetImageHeight (1): Gets percentage height of image.

CreateSprite: mySprite = CreateSprite (myImage): Creates a sprite object based off an image definition for later use.

PasteSprite: PasteSprite (mySprite): Pastes the sprite at its current location (good for pasting sprite BEHIND text).

PasteSpritePosition: PasteSpritePosition (mySprite, x, y): Same as previous but pasted at a specified XY coordinate.

DeleteSprite: DeleteSprite (mySprite): Deletes a sprite.

SetSpritePosition: SetSpritePosition (mySprite, x, y): Sets a sprite object to an X/Y position on the screen.

SetSpriteSize: SetSpriteSize (mySprite, sizeX, sizeZ): Passing –1 as one of the params ensures the sprite retains its aspect ratio.

SetSpriteDepth: SetSpriteDepth (mySprite, 10) (0 is front, 100 is back): Sets which layer the sprite operates on with 0 being the closest layer and 100 being the furthest.

SetSpriteColor: SetSpriteColor (mySprite, red, green, blue, alpha): Allows you to change the tint of a sprite along with its alpha value.

SetSpriteAngle: SetSpriteAngle (mySprite, angle): Sets a sprite object to a specific angle.

SetSpriteOffset: SetSpriteOffset (mySprite, 5, -1): Would be the center for a 10% width image assigned to a sprite, passing –1 as one of the params ensures the sprite retains its aspect ratio.

SetSpriteImage: SetSpriteImage (mySprite, myImage): Similar to CreateSprite, allows you to set a sprite object to a new image. Used if you want to adjust the current sprite to a new one.

AI Commands

AIEntityGoToPosition: AIEntityGoToPosition (obj, x, z): Where obj is the object number of the entity. Use this for legacy AI bot movement.

AIEntityGoToPosition: AIEntityGoToPosition (obj, x, z, containerindex): Where obj is the object number of the entity. New decoupled AI bot manual control.

AISetEntityControl: AISetEntityControl (obj, controlmode): Where obj is the object number of the entity. See DarkAI docs for parameter descriptions.

AIEntityStop: AIEntityStop (obj): Where obj is the object number of the entity. See DarkAI docs for parameter descriptions.

AIGetEntityCanSee: AIGetEntityCanSee (obj, x, z, groundflag): Where obj is the object number of the entity. See DarkAI docs for parameter descriptions.

AIGetEntityViewRange: AIGetEntityViewRange (obj): Where obj is the object number of the entity. See DarkAI docs for parameter descriptions.

AIGetEntityHeardSound: AIGetEntityHeardSound (obj): Where obj is the object number of the entity. See DarkAI docs for parameter descriptions.

AICouldSee: AICouldSee (obj, x, y, z): Where obj is the object number of the entity XYZ of the point in space tested line of sight by the AI.

AIGetEntityIsMoving: AIGetEntityIsMoving (obj): Where obj is the object number of the entity. See DarkAI docs for parameter descriptions.

AISetEntityPosition: AISetEntityPosition (obj, x, y, z): Where obj is the object number of the entity and XYZ are the new coordinates.

AISetEntityTurnSpeed: AISetEntityTurnSpeed (obj, speed): Where obj is the object number and speed is the turning speed for navigating entities.

AIGetEntitySpeed: speed = AIGetEntitySpeed (obj): Where obj is the object number of the entity and returns the movement speed of the entity.

AIGetTotalPaths: AIGetTotalPaths (): Returns the number of created paths.

AIGetPathCountPoints: AIGetPathCountPoints (pathnumber): Where pathnumber is the internal number of the path.

AIPathGetPointX: AIPathGetPointX (pathnumber, pointindex): Where obj is the object number of the entity. See DarkAI docs for parameter descriptions.

AIPathGetPointY: AIPathGetPointY (pathnumber, pointindex): Where obj is the object number of the entity. See DarkAI docs for parameter descriptions.

AIPathGetPointZ: AIPathGetPointZ (pathnumber, pointindex): Where obj is the object number of the entity. See DarkAI docs for parameter descriptions.

AIGetTotalCover: AIGetTotalCover (): Returns the number of created cover zones.

AICoverGetPointX: AICoverGetPointX (coverindex): Where coverindex is the index of the cover marker and returns the X position.

AICoverGetPointY: AICoverGetPointY (coverindex): Where coverindex is the index of the cover marker and returns the Y position.

AICoverGetPointZ: AICoverGetPointZ (coverindex): Where coverindex is the index of the cover marker and returns the Z position.

AICoverGetAngle: AICoverGetAngle (coverindex): Where coverindex is the index of the cover marker and returns the Y angle position.

AICoverGetIfUsed: AICoverGetIfUsed (coverindex): Where coverindex is the index of the cover marker and returns string from IFUSED field.

RunCharLoop: RunCharLoop (): Runs the legacy animation system to control character index GetGamePlayerStateCharAnimIndex ().

GetPlrObjectPositionX: x=GetPlrObjectPositionX (): Returns the raw x position of the visible player object.

GetPlrObjectPositionY: x=GetPlrObjectPositionY (): Returns the raw y position of the visible player object.

GetPlrObjectPositionZ: x=GetPlrObjectPositionZ (): Returns the raw z position of the visible player object.

GetPlrObjectAngleX: x=GetPlrObjectAngleX (): Returns the raw x angle of the visible player object.

GetPlrObjectAngleY: x=GetPlrObjectAngleY (): Returns the raw y angle of the visible player object.

GetPlrObjectAngleZ: x=GetPlrObjectAngleZ (): Returns the raw z angle of the visible player object.

Title and Menu System Controls

StartGame (): Starts the game.

LoadGame (): Loads a save state.

SaveGame (): Saves game-related information such as location/ammo/collectibles.

QuitGame (): Closes the game completely.

LeaveGame (): Returns player to main menu.

ResumeGame (): Returns player to their game from the menu.

SwitchPage (strPageName): Changes to a different screen in the menu.

SwitchPageBack (): Switches back to previous, like hitting back on the menu.

LevelFilenameToLoad (strLevelName): Loads a level specified in "strLevelName."

TriggerFadeIn (): Does a fade-in on demand.

SetGameQuality (v): Sets the quality of the game to 1 (lowest), 2 (medium), or 3 (highest); only affects shaders for terrain, entity, and vegetation.

SetPlayerFOV (v): Sets the player's FOV.

SetGameSoundVolume (v): Sets game sound FX volume to value (v), which is a value in decibels 0–100; 60 and lower is silent.

SetGameMusicVolume (v): Sets game music volume to value (v), which is a value in decibels 0–100; 60 and lower is silent.

SetLoadingResource (i, v): Used for setting up the loading bar for the menu system.

Multiplayer Controls

MP_IsServer (): Returns whether you are the multiplayer host or not; 1 = yes, 0 = no.

SetMultiplayerGameMode (mode): Sets a mode flag for the multiplayer game.

GetMultiplayerGameMode (mode): Returns the current game mode flag.

SetServerTimer (t): Sets the timer for the server for synchronization purposes.

GetServerTimer (t): Returns the server's "server time" for synchronization purposes.

GetServerTimerPassed (): Returns the difference between the server time and the current time.

ServerRespawnAll (): Respawns all players.

ServerEndPlay (): Ends the game.

GetShowScores (): Shows the server K/D score.

SetServerKillsToWin (v): Sets a win condition for a map of (v) kills.

GetInKey (): Returns the value of g_InKey, or which key was input.

GetScancode (): Returns the current keyboard scancode.

GetMultiplayerTeamBased (): Returns whether this game is a team game or not.

SetMultiplayerGameFriendlyFireOff (): Turns off friendly fire.

SetNameplatesOff (): Disables nameplates for players.

GetCoOpMode (): Returns whether this is a co-op mode or not.

GetCoOpEnemiesAlive (): Returns how many enemies are left to kill for your team to win the map.

Joystick/Gamepad/VR

JoystickX: JoystickX (): Returns a value between –1000 and +1000 representing X-axis of controller.

JoystickY: JoystickY (): Returns a value between –1000 and +1000 representing Y-axis of controller.

JoystickZ: JoystickZ (): Returns a value between –1000 and +1000 representing trigger of controller.

PromptLocalForVR (e, str, vrmode): Creates localized prompt around entity E for VR systems.

PromptLocal (e, str): Creates a localized prompt around entity E.

JoystickHatAngle: JoystickHatAngle (): Command used by the default player control mechanism.

JoystickFireXL: JoystickFireXL (): Command used by the default player control mechanism.

JoystickTwistX: JoystickTwistX (): Command used by the default player control mechanism.

JoystickTwistY: JoystickTwistY (): Command used by the default player control mechanism.

JoystickTwistZ: JoystickTwistZ (): Command used by the default player control mechanism.

SetGamePlayerStatePlrZoomInChange: SetGamePlayerStatePlrZoomInChange (): Command used by the default player control mechanism.

GetGamePlayerStatePlrZoomInChange: GetGamePlayerStatePlrZoomInChange (): Command used by the default player control mechanism.

GetDynamicCharacterControllerDidJump: x=GetDynamicCharacterControllerDidJump (): Returns 1 if controller jumped.

Water Controls

NOTE: Look into the shader for information about these values (open effectbank/reloaded/water_basic.fx with i.e. notepad).

SetWaterHeight (value): Sets height of water plane.

SetWaterColor (red, green, blue): Sets RGB of water plane.

SetWaterWaveIntensity (value): Sets intensity of waves.

SetWaterTransparancy (value): Sets transparency of waves.

SetWaterReflection (value): Sets reflection value of water surface.

SetWaterReflectionSparkleIntensity (value): Specularity of water surface, I believe.

SetWaterFlowDirection(x, y, speed): Small tip: –1 = east/north; 1= west/south; speed is a multiplier of the flowdirection (higher => fast flow).

SetWaterDistortionWaves (value): Water noise level.

SetRippleWaterSpeed (value): How fast the ripples move.

GetWaterHeight (): Returns height of water.

GetWaterWaveIntensity (): Returns intensity of water.

GetWaterShaderColorRed (): Returns water plane R value.

GetWaterShaderColorGreen (): Returns water plane G value.

GetWaterShaderColorBlue (): Returns water plane B value.

GetWaterTransparancy (): Returns water transparency value.

GetWaterReflection (): Returns water reflection value.

GetWaterReflectionSparkleIntensity (): Returns "water reflection sparkle intensity" value.

GetWaterFlowDirectionX (): Returns water flow direction X.

GetWaterFlowDirectionY (): Returns water flow direction Y.

GetWaterFlowSpeed (): Returns water flow speed.

GetWaterDistortionWaves (): Returns water distortion wave setting.

GetRippleWaterSpeed (): Returns water ripple speed.

Dynamic Light and Sky Controls

SetSkyTo (str): str = folder name of the sky you want to change to; i.e., SetSkyTo ("dark").

GetEntityLightNumber (e): Returns entity light number.

x, y, z = GetLightPosition (lightNum): Presumably returns light XYZ position into three separate variables, needs testing.

r, g, b = GetLightRGB (lightNum): Presumably fills RGB values into three separate variables. Needs testing.

GetLightRange (lightNum): Returns light range.

GetLightAngle: xv, yv, zv = GetLightAngle (LightNum): Returns the angle vector of the dynamic light specified.

SetLightAngle: SetLightAngle (lightNum, xv, yv, zv): Sets the angle vector of the specified light (e.g. 0, 0, 1 would be "North" or +Z-axis).

SetLightPosition (lightNum, x, y, z): LightNum=entity light number. Sets physical position.

SetLightRGB (lightNum, r, g, b): LightNum=entity light number. Sets RBG value of light.

SetLightRange (lightNum, range): Range is 1… 10000; values outside range are capped; configures output range of light.

Error Codes

The following is a full list of error codes with some basic ideas as to what is causing them. "Code issues" are generally problems with the actual GameGuru code itself and are typically only seen in Beta releases or public preview releases. Report them online if you encounter them. Many of these are completely undocumented and as such I cannot advise on a proper course of action for them. They are listed as "unknown," so you'd want to take those to the forums as well get assistance from the developers.

//General Codes

#define RUNTIMEERROR_GENERICERROR 0: A default error caused when it fits no other criteria.

#define RUNTIMEERROR_TRIEDTORUNFUNCTIONHEADER 21: Improperly formatted code for function.

#define RUNTIMEERROR_ARRAYACCESSEDOUTOFBOUNDS 51: Accessed an array out of bounds, code issue.

#define RUNTIMEERROR_ARRAYINDEXINVALID 52: Array's index invalid, code issue.

#define RUNTIMEERROR_ARRAYEMPTY 53: Array was improperly empty, code issue.

#define RUNTIMEERROR_ARRAYTYPEINVALID 54: Array's "type" was invalid, code issue.

#define RUNTIMEERROR_ARRAYMUSTBESINGLEDIM 55: Array has to be a single dimension, code issue.

#define RUNTIMEERROR_NOTENOUGHMEMORY 101: You ran out of memory (see Chapter 21 on optimization).

#define RUNTIMEERROR_INVALIDARRAYUSE 102: An array was improperly used, code issue.

#define RUNTIMEERROR_FILETOOLARGE 103: You used a file that exceeded memory limits. Try a smaller texture size, smaller sound sample, model with less polys, etc.

#define RUNTIMEERROR_INVALIDFILE 104: You pointed to a file that wasn't openable (i.e., said open this JPG file and it was a .WAV).

#define RUNTIMEERROR_FILENOTEXIST 105: File couldn't be found where you told it to look.

#define RUNTIMEERROR_FILEEXISTS 106: File ALREADY exists and you're reloading it again!

#define RUNTIMEERROR_STRINGLENGTHOVERFLOW 107: Your string is too long for memory.

#define RUNTIMEERROR_STACKOVERFLOW 108: The stack was overwritten, code issue likely.

#define RUNTIMEERROR_INVALIDARRAY 109: The array was invalid, code issue.

#define RUNTIMEERROR_MUSTBEPOSITIVEVALUE 110: You gave an incorrect value to something that only takes positive numeric values.

#define RUNTIMEERROR_DIVIDEBYZERO 111: You divided by zero.

#define RUNTIMEERROR_SYNCRATEINVALID 112: Unknown.

#define RUNTIMEERROR_RANDOMVALUEPOSITIVE 113: Unknown.

#define RUNTIMEERROR_CANONLYINCREMENTVARIABLE 114: Code issue.

#define RUNTIMEERROR_CANONLYDECREMENTVARIABLE 115: Code issue.

#define RUNTIMEERROR_COMMANDNOWOBSOLETE 116: A command was called that is no longer used, code issue.

#define RUNTIMEERROR_FILEISLOCKED 117: The file was already in use by another application in the operating system.

#define RUNTIMEERROR_SPRITEERROR 300: A generic sprite error, check your sprites and Lua.

#define RUNTIMEERROR_SPRITEILLEGALNUMBER 301: You didn't use a valid number for your sprite.

#define RUNTIMEERROR_SPRITENOTEXIST 302: Sprite graphic couldn't be found.

#define RUNTIMEERROR_SPRITEBACKSAVEILLEGAL 303: Unknown.

#define RUNTIMEERROR_SPRITETRANSPARENCYILLEGAL 304: Sprite transparency is improper format.

#define RUNTIMEERROR_SPRITEROTATIONILLEGAL 310: Your math is probably bad on your sprite rotation.

#define RUNTIMEERROR_SPRITESCALEILLEGAL 311: You are using invalid values for your sprite scaling.

#define RUNTIMEERROR_SPRITESIZEILLEGAL 312: Your sprite is too big or too small.

#define RUNTIMEERROR_SPRITEANGLEILLEGAL 313: Your sprite is using invalid values for the angle.

#define RUNTIMEERROR_SPRITEALPHAVALUEILLEGAL 314: Your sprite has an invalid alpha value. Probably a file corruption or bad save.

#define RUNTIMEERROR_SPRITERGBCOMPONENTILLEGAL 315: Your sprite's RGB data are incorrect, probably a file corruption or bad save.

#define RUNTIMEERROR_SPRITEANIMDELAYILLEGAL 316: Your sprite's animation delay is incorrectly set.

#define RUNTIMEERROR_SPRITEVERTEXILLEGAL 317: The sprite's vertex amount is illegal.

#define RUNTIMEERROR_SPRITEWIDTHILLEGAL 318: The sprite's width is too big or small.

#define RUNTIMEERROR_SPRITEHEIGHTILLEGAL 319: The sprite's height is too big or too small.

#define RUNTIMEERROR_SPRITEHANIMCOUNTILLEGAL 320: The sprite's animation count is invalid; check your Lua code.

#define RUNTIMEERROR_SPRITEALREADYTEXISTS 321: The sprite already is loaded in memory or is being used.

#define RUNTIMEERROR_IMAGEERROR 500: A generic image error for when no others apply.

#define RUNTIMEERROR_IMAGEILLEGALNUMBER 501: You assigned an invalid image handle number to the image in your Lua code.

#define RUNTIMEERROR_IMAGENOTEXIST 502: The image doesn't exist where you said it would be in your Lua code.

#define RUNTIMEERROR_IMAGEGRABTOOLARGE 503: Unknown.

#define RUNTIMEERROR_IMAGEAREAILLEGAL 504: The image is using too big of an area for the resolution of the screen.

#define RUNTIMEERROR_IMAGETOOBIGASTEXTURE 505: The image texture size is way too large to fit into memory. Try changing it to a smaller resolution (say 1024 × 1024 pixels) and use a better compression system such as JPG or DDS.

#define RUNTIMEERROR_IMAGELOADFAILED 506: The file wasn't able to be loaded but was able to be found. It's probably a graphic format issue or you pointed it to the wrong file.

#define RUNTIMEERROR_IMAGELOCKED 507: The file is in use and locked by another program on your system.

#define RUNTIMEERROR_BITMAPERROR 1000: Bitmap generic error for when no others apply.

#define RUNTIMEERROR_BITMAPILLEGALNUMBER 1001: You assigned a bitmap to an invalid image handle in your Lua code.

#define RUNTIMEERROR_BITMAPNOTEXIST 1002: The bitmap wasn't where you said it would be in your Lua code.

#define RUNTIMEERROR_BITMAPLOADFAILED 1003: The bitmap was found but unable to be loaded. You probably are trying to load a format that isn't actually a bitmap (BMP).

#define RUNTIMEERROR_BITMAPSAVEFAILED 1004: Couldn't save the bitmap file.

#define RUNTIMEERROR_BITMAPCREATEFAILED 1005: Couldn't create a new bitmap file.

#define RUNTIMEERROR_BITMAPZERONODELETE 1006: Unknown.

#define RUNTIMEERROR_BITMAPBOTHSAME 1007: Unknown.

#define RUNTIMEERROR_BITMAPSOURCETOOLARGE 1008: The bitmap's source file is too large. Bitmaps are uncompressed so if you are using a large JPG, this will generate this error. Resize the JPG to a smaller resolution.

#define RUNTIMEERROR_BITMAPZERORESERVED 1009: A property in your bitmap file is incorrect.

#define RUNTIMEERROR_BITMAPREGIONEXCEEDED 1010: A property in your bitmap file is incorrect.

#define RUNTIMEERROR_BITMAPAREASINVALID 1011: A property in your bitmap file is incorrect.

#define RUNTIMEERROR_BITMAPBLURVALUEILLEGAL 1012: A property in your bitmap file is incorrect.

#define RUNTIMEERROR_BITMAPFADEVALUEILLEGAL 1013: A property in your bitmap file is incorrect.

#define RUNTIMEERROR_BITMAPGAMMAILLEGAL 1014: A property in your bitmap file is incorrect.

#define RUNTIMEERROR_SCREEN 1500: A generic screen resolution error.

#define RUNTIMEERROR_SCREENSIZEILLEGAL 1501: You chose an invalid screen resolution in your Lua code.

#define RUNTIMEERROR_SCREENDEPTHILLEGAL 1502: You chose an invalid bit depth in your Lua code.

#define RUNTIMEERROR_SCREENMODEINVALID 1503: You chose an invalid screen mode in your Lua code.

#define RUNTIMEERROR_NOTSUPPORTDISPLAY 1504: Your display is unsupported (generic error).

#define RUNTIMEERROR_NOTSUPPORTDISPLAY16B 1505: Your display doesn't support 16-bit output.

#define RUNTIMEERROR_NOTSUPPORTDISPLAY24B 1506: Your display doesn't support 24-bit output.

#define RUNTIMEERROR_NOTSUPPORTDISPLAY32B 1507: Your display doesn't support 32-bit output.

#define RUNTIMEERROR_NOTSUPPORTDISPLAYVB 1508: Unknown.

#define RUNTIMEERROR_NOTSUPPORTDISPLAYLOCK 1509: Your display cannot be locked for use; there is likely a driver or operating system (OS) level issue with your video card.

#define RUNTIMEERROR_NOTSUPPORTDISPLAYNODX 1510: You don't have DirectX installed.

#define RUNTIMEERROR_NOTSUPPORTDISPLAYINVALID 1511: Unknown.

#define RUNTIMEERROR_NOTSUPPORTDISPLAYNOTAVAIL 1512: Your video card is unavailable for use.

#define RUNTIMEERROR_NOTSUPPORTDISPLAYNOVID 1513: Your video card is unavailable for use.

#define RUNTIMEERROR_24BITNOTSUPPORTED 1514: Your video card is probably in need of a driver update or a replacement.

#define RUNTIMEERROR_ANIMERROR 2000: A generic video animation error where no others applied.

#define RUNTIMEERROR_ANIMNUMBERILLEGAL 2001: Your video handle number is not valid in your Lua code.

#define RUNTIMEERROR_ANIMLOADFAILED 2002: The animation couldn't be loaded despite being found, not already loaded, and everything else working. This is probably a format issue. Make sure you aren't trying to load a video using something such as Digital Video Express or DIVX, which is unsupported.

#define RUNTIMEERROR_ANIMALREADYEXISTS 2003: The video file is already loaded.

#define RUNTIMEERROR_ANIMNOTEXIST 2004: The video file doesn't exist where the Lua code said it would be.

#define RUNTIMEERROR_ANIMVOLUMEILLEGAL 2005: The video file's volume data are corrupt.

#define RUNTIMEERROR_ANIMFREQILLEGAL 2006: The video file's frequency rate is corrupt.

#define RUNTIMEERROR_ANIMALREADYPLAYING 2007: The video is already playing.

#define RUNTIMEERROR_ANIMNOTPLAYING 2008: Unknown.

#define RUNTIMEERROR_ANIMALREADYPAUSED 2009: The video is already paused.

#define RUNTIMEERROR_ANIMNOTPAUSED 2010: Unknown.

#define RUNTIMEERROR_SOUNDERROR 3000: A generic error from the sound system where no other errors applied.

#define RUNTIMEERROR_SOUNDNUMBERILLEGAL 3001: Your handle number for the sound file in Lua was invalid.

#define RUNTIMEERROR_SOUNDLOADFAILED 3002: The sound file could not be loaded despite existing and not failing any other checks. Probably a format issue. Make sure it is a valid wav or ogg file.

#define RUNTIMEERROR_SOUNDALREADYEXISTS 3003: The sound file already exists in memory; you are attempting to load it again in your Lua code.

#define RUNTIMEERROR_SOUNDNOTEXIST 3004: The sound file does not exist where you said it would be in your Lua code.

#define RUNTIMEERROR_SOUNDVOLUMEILLEGAL 3005: The sound file's volume data are corrupt.

#define RUNTIMEERROR_SOUNDFREQILLEGAL 3006: The sound file's frequency rate is corrupt.

#define RUNTIMEERROR_SOUNDPANVALUEILLEGAL 3007: The sound file's pan value is corrupt.

#define RUNTIMEERROR_SOUNDSAVEFAILED 3008: The sound file cannot be saved by the OS. Probably a read/write issue on the folder involved in Windows itself.

#define RUNTIMEERROR_SOUNDCANNOTBECLONED 3021: Unknown.

#define RUNTIMEERROR_SOUNDMUSTSPECIFYSOUND 3022: Unknown.

#define RUNTIMEERROR_SOUNDMUSTSPECIFYCLONE 3023: Unknown.

#define RUNTIMEERROR_NOSPEECHENGINE 3201: Unknown.

#define RUNTIMEERROR_MUSICERROR 3500: Generic music system error where no other errors applied.

#define RUNTIMEERROR_MUSICNUMBERILLEGAL 3501: Your music handle number in Lua was incorrect.

#define RUNTIMEERROR_MUSICLOADFAILED 3502: Your music could not be loaded despite existing and passing other checks. Make sure your music is saved in a compatible format.

#define RUNTIMEERROR_MUSICALREADYEXISTS 3503: Your music is already loaded in memory.

#define RUNTIMEERROR_MUSICNOTEXIST 3504: The music file was not where you said it would be in your Lua code.

#define RUNTIMEERROR_MUSICVOLUMEILLEGAL 3505: The music file's volume data are corrupt.

#define RUNTIMEERROR_MUSICSPEEDILLEGAL 3506: The music file's speed data are corrupt.

#define RUNTIMEERROR_MUSICNOTPLAYING 3507: The music is not playing, despite being loaded. This is another generic error.

#define RUNTIMEERROR_MUSICTRACKILLEGAL 3508: The music track you are attempting to call in your Lua code does not exist or is out of bounds.

#define RUNTIMEERROR_INPUTCONTROLLERNOTAVAIL 4001: The input controller specified is not available at a system level. Verify you are pointing to a valid device.

#define RUNTIMEERROR_INPUTNOCONTROLLERSELECTED 4002: No controller was selected for input at all. Check your Lua code.

#define RUNTIMEERROR_INPUTFORCEFEEDBACKNOTAVAIL 4101: You are attempting to use the force feedback system on a device that doesn't support it. Check your Lua code.

#define RUNTIMEERROR_INPUTFFMAGNITUDEERROR 4102: The magnitude given to force feedback was out of bounds; check your Lua code.

#define RUNTIMEERROR_INPUTFFDURATIONERROR 4103: The duration given to force feedback was out of bounds; check your Lua code.

#define RUNTIMEERROR_INPUTFFANGLEERROR 4104: The angle given to force feedback was out of bounds; check your Lua code.

#define RUNTIMEERROR_MEMBLOCKRANGEILLEGAL 5101: Code issue.

#define RUNTIMEERROR_MEMBLOCKALREADYEXISTS 5102: Code issue.

#define RUNTIMEERROR_MEMBLOCKNOTEXIST 5103: Code issue.

#define RUNTIMEERROR_MEMBLOCKCREATIONFAILED 5104: Code issue.

#define RUNTIMEERROR_MEMBLOCKOUTSIDERANGE 5105: Code issue.

#define RUNTIMEERROR_MEMBLOCKSIZEINVALID 5106: Code issue.

#define RUNTIMEERROR_MEMBLOCKNOTABYTE 5107: Code issue.

#define RUNTIMEERROR_MEMBLOCKNOTAWORD 5108: Code issue.

#define RUNTIMEERROR_MEMBLOCKNOTADWORD 5109: Code issue.

#define RUNTIMEERROR_B3DERROR 7000: All of these Blitz3D (B3D) errors are depreciated and should never be seen.

#define RUNTIMEERROR_B3DMESHNUMBERILLEGAL 7001: All of these B3D errors are depreciated and should never be seen.

#define RUNTIMEERROR_B3DMESHLOADFAILED 7002: All of these B3D errors are depreciated and should never be seen.

#define RUNTIMEERROR_B3DMESHNOTEXIST 7003: All of these B3D errors are depreciated and should never be seen.

#define RUNTIMEERROR_B3DMESHDARKENILLEGAL 7004: All of these B3D errors are depreciated and should never be seen.

#define RUNTIMEERROR_B3DMESHLIGHTENILLEGAL 7005: All of these B3D errors are depreciated and should never be seen.

#define RUNTIMEERROR_B3DMODELNUMBERILLEGAL 7006: All of these B3D errors are depreciated and should never be seen.

#define RUNTIMEERROR_B3DMODELALREADYEXISTS 7007: All of these B3D errors are depreciated and should never be seen.

#define RUNTIMEERROR_B3DMODELNOTEXISTS 7008: All of these B3D errors are depreciated and should never be seen.

#define RUNTIMEERROR_B3DMATRIXALREADYEXISTS 7009: All of these B3D errors are depreciated and should never be seen.

#define RUNTIMEERROR_B3DMATRIXNUMBERILLEGAL 7010: All of these B3D errors are depreciated and should never be seen.

#define RUNTIMEERROR_B3DMATRIXDIMENSIONWRONG 7011: All of these B3D errors are depreciated and should never be seen.

#define RUNTIMEERROR_B3DMATRIXSEGMENTWRONG 7012: All of these B3D errors are depreciated and should never be seen.

#define RUNTIMEERROR_B3DMATRIXNOTEXISTS 7013: All of these B3D errors are depreciated and should never be seen.

#define RUNTIMEERROR_B3DMATRIXNOHEIGHTMAX 7014: All of these B3D errors are depreciated and should never be seen.

#define RUNTIMEERROR_B3DMATRIXTOOLARGE 7015: All of these B3D errors are depreciated and should never be seen.

#define RUNTIMEERROR_B3DMATRIXTILEILLEGAL 7016: All of these B3D errors are depreciated and should never be seen.

#define RUNTIMEERROR_B3DMATRIXTILECOORDSWRONG 7017: All of these B3D errors are depreciated and should never be seen.

#define RUNTIMEERROR_B3DOBJECTLOADFAILED 7018: All of these B3D errors are depreciated and should never be seen.

#define RUNTIMEERROR_B3DANGLERANGEERROR 7019: All of these B3D errors are depreciated and should never be seen.

#define RUNTIMEERROR_B3DOBJECTTOOMANYLIMBS 7020: All of these B3D errors are depreciated and should never be seen.

#define RUNTIMEERROR_B3DMEMORYERROR 7029: All of these B3D errors are depreciated and should never be seen.

#define RUNTIMEERROR_B3DMUSTUSEDBOEXTENSION 7030: All of these B3D errors are depreciated and should never be seen.

#define RUNTIMEERROR_CAMERANUMBERILLEGAL 7201: The camera handle number you specified in Lua was invalid.

#define RUNTIMEERROR_CAMERAALREADYEXISTS 7202: The camera you are attempting to create already exists; check your Lua code.

#define RUNTIMEERROR_CAMERANOTEXIST 7203: The camera you are attempting to use does not exist; check your Lua code.

#define RUNTIMEERROR_CAMERACANNOTCREATE 7204: A generic error caused when no other applies (only when attempting to make a new camera).

#define RUNTIMEERROR_CAMERANOZERO 7205: The camera number cannot be a zero.

#define RUNTIMEERROR_B3DLIGHTNUMBERILLEGAL 7301: All of these B3D errors are depreciated and should never be seen.

#define RUNTIMEERROR_B3DLIGHTALREADYEXISTS 7302: All of these B3D errors are depreciated and should never be seen.

#define RUNTIMEERROR_B3DLIGHTNOTEXIST 7303: All of these B3D errors are depreciated and should never be seen.

#define RUNTIMEERROR_B3DLIGHTCANNOTCREATE 7304: All of these B3D errors are depreciated and should never be seen.

#define RUNTIMEERROR_B3DLIGHTNOZERO 7305: All of these B3D errors are depreciated and should never be seen.

#define RUNTIMEERROR_LIMBNUMBERILLEGAL 7021: The limb number specified was invalid. Check your code, FPE file, and model.

#define RUNTIMEERROR_LIMBADDNUMBERILLEGAL 7022: The limb you are attempting to add is using an invalid number. Check your Lua code.

#define RUNTIMEERROR_LIMBNOTEXIST 7023: The limb you are referencing doesn't exist.

#define RUNTIMEERROR_LIMBALREADYEXISTS 7024: You are attempting to create a limb that already exists.

#define RUNTIMEERROR_LINKNOTPOSSIBLE 7025: You are attempting to link two limbs that aren't connected to each other.

#define RUNTIMEERROR_LIMBMUSTCHAININSEQUENCE 7026: You are attempting to link two limbs that aren't chained together.

#define RUNTIMEERROR_LINKSHOULDBENEW 7027: The limb's link should be one that doesn't already exist.

#define RUNTIMEERROR_B3DMESHTOOLARGE 7028: All of these B3D errors are depreciated and should never be seen.

#define RUNTIMEERROR_B3DMEMORYERROR 7029: All of these B3D errors are depreciated and should never be seen.

#define RUNTIMEERROR_B3DMUSTUSEDBOEXTENSION 7030: All of these B3D errors are depreciated and should never be seen.#define RUNTIMEERROR_B3DMODELFADEINVALID 7031: All of these B3D errors are depreciated and should never be seen.

#define RUNTIMEERROR_B3DLIMBBUTNOMESH 7032: All of these B3D errors are depreciated and should never be seen.

#define RUNTIMEERROR_PARTICLESALREADYEXISTS 7101: The particle emitter you are attempting to use already exists. Check your Lua code.

#define RUNTIMEERROR_PARTICLESNOTEXIST 7102: The particle emitter you are referencing doesn't exist. Check your Lua code.

#define RUNTIMEERROR_PARTICLESERROR 7103: A generic particle engine error. Check your Lua code.

#define RUNTIMEERROR_PARTICLESNUMBERILLEGAL 7104: Your particle emitter handle number is invalid. Check your Lua code.

#define RUNTIMEERROR_PARTICLESCOULDNOTBECREATED 7105: A generic particle engine error. Check your Lua code.

#define RUNTIMEERROR_TERRAINFAILEDCREATE 7126: The terrain engine failed to create terrain. Try validating your Steam installation again and replacing corrupt files.

#define RUNTIMEERROR_TERRAINALREADYEXIST 7127: The terrain engine failed to create terrain. Try validating your Steam installation again and replacing corrupt files.

#define RUNTIMEERROR_TERRAINNOTEXIST 7128: The terrain engine failed to create terrain. Try validating your Steam installation again and replacing corrupt files.

#define RUNTIMEERROR_TERRAINFILEMUSTBESQUARE 7129: The terrain engine failed to create terrain. Try validating your Steam installation again and replacing corrupt files.

#define RUNTIMEERROR_TERRAINNUMBERILLEGAL 7130: The terrain engine failed to create terrain. Try validating your Steam installation again and replacing corrupt files.

#define RUNTIMEERROR_BSPLOADFAILED 7151: An engine error, contact support.

#define RUNTIMEERROR_BSPNOTEXIST 7152: An engine error, contact support.

#define RUNTIMEERROR_BSPALREADYEXIST 7153: An engine error, contact support.

#define RUNTIMEERROR_BSPCOLLISIONNUMBERILLEGAL 7154: An engine error, contact support.

#define RUNTIMEERROR_B3DMODELDOESNOTANIMATE 7601: All of these B3D errors are depreciated and should never be seen.

#define RUNTIMEERROR_B3DKEYFRAMENOTEXIST 7602: All of these B3D errors are depreciated and should never be seen.

#define RUNTIMEERROR_B3DANIMSPEEDERROR 7603: All of these B3D errors are depreciated and should never be seen.

#define RUNTIMEERROR_B3DANIMINTERPERROR 7604: All of these B3D errors are depreciated and should never be seen.

#define RUNTIMEERROR_B3DOBJECTAPPENDFAILED 7605: All of these B3D errors are depreciated and should never be seen.

#define RUNTIMEERROR_B3DOBJECTAPPENDTOOLOW 7606: All of these B3D errors are depreciated and should never be seen.

#define RUNTIMEERROR_FAILEDTOCOMPILECSG 7607: Unknown.

#define RUNTIMEERROR_B3DVSHADERNUMBERILLEGAL 7701: All of these B3D errors are depreciated and should never be seen.

#define RUNTIMEERROR_B3DVSHADERCOUNTILLEGAL 7702: All of these B3D errors are depreciated and should never be seen.

#define RUNTIMEERROR_B3DVSHADERCANNOTCREATE 7703: All of these B3D errors are depreciated and should never be seen.

#define RUNTIMEERROR_B3DVSHADERSTREAMPOSINVALID 7704: All of these B3D errors are depreciated and should never be seen.

#define RUNTIMEERROR_B3DVSHADERDATAINVALID 7705: All of these B3D errors are depreciated and should never be seen.

#define RUNTIMEERROR_B3DVSHADERINVALIDSTREAM 7706: All of these B3D errors are depreciated and should never be seen.

#define RUNTIMEERROR_B3DVSHADERCANNOTASSEMBLE 7707: All of these B3D errors are depreciated and should never be seen.

#define RUNTIMEERROR_B3DVSHADERINVALID 7708: All of these B3D errors are depreciated and should never be seen.

#define RUNTIMEERROR_B3DEFFECTNUMBERILLEGAL 7721: All of these B3D errors are depreciated and should never be seen.

#define RUNTIMEERROR_B3DEFFECTNOTEXISTS 7722: All of these B3D errors are depreciated and should never be seen.

#define RUNTIMEERROR_B3DEFFECTALREADYEXISTS 7723: All of these B3D errors are depreciated and should never be seen.

#define RUNTIMEERROR_VECTORNOTEXIST 7801: Your vector specified doesn't exist. Check your Lua code.

#define RUNTIMEERROR_MATRIX4NOTEXIST 7802: Your matrix4 doesn't exist. Check your Lua code.

#define RUNTIMEERROR_VECTORNUMBERILLEGAL 7803: Your vector number specified doesn't exist. Check your Lua code.

#define RUNTIMEERROR_MATRIX4NUMBERILLEGAL 7804: Your matrix4 number does not exist. Check your Lua code.

#define RUNTIMEERROR_B3DFOGNOTABLE 7901: All of these B3D errors are depreciated and should never be seen.

#define RUNTIMEERROR_B3DAMBIENTPERCENTAGEERROR 7911: All of these B3D errors are depreciated and should never be seen.

#define RUNTIMEERROR_B3DCAMERARANGEERROR 7912: All of these B3D errors are depreciated and should never be seen.

#define RUNTIMEERROR_B3DSOURCEMUSTBE3DS 7931: All of these B3D errors are depreciated and should never be seen.

#define RUNTIMEERROR_B3DDESTMUSTBEX 7932: All of these B3D errors are depreciated and should never be seen.

#define RUNTIMEERROR_CANNOTSCANCURRENTDIR 8001: Unknown.

#define RUNTIMEERROR_NOMOREFILESINDIR 8002: Unknown.

#define RUNTIMEERROR_PATHCANNOTBEFOUND 8003: A very common error caused by your Lua or FPE file pointing to something that isn't there.

#define RUNTIMEERROR_CANNOTMAKEFILE 8021: Cannot write to destination folder; make sure the folder isn't set to read only in Windows.

#define RUNTIMEERROR_CANNOTDELETEFILE 8022: Cannot delete file from destination folder; make sure the folder isn't set to read only in Windows.

#define RUNTIMEERROR_CANNOTCOPYFILE 8023: Cannot copy file to destination folder; make sure the folder isn't set to ready only in Windows.

#define RUNTIMEERROR_CANNOTRENAMEFILE 8024: Cannot rename file from destination folder; make sure the folder isn't set to read only in Windows.

#define RUNTIMEERROR_CANNOTMOVEFILE 8025: Cannot move the file into destination folder; make sure that folder isn't set to ready only in Windows.

#define RUNTIMEERROR_CANNOTMAKEDIR 8101: A generic error when a directory couldn't be created; often caused by read-only errors or because you specified an invalid path.

#define RUNTIMEERROR_CANNOTDELETEDIR 8102: Cannot delete the destination directory; make sure the folder isn't set to read only in Windows.

#define RUNTIMEERROR_CANNOTEXECUTEFILE 8103: Cannot execute specified destination file; verify it's a valid path to the file and a valid format for execution (exe, com, and bat).

#define RUNTIMEERROR_CANNOTOPENFILEFORREADING 8201: File system error—couldn't find the file to open or couldn't open it for a generic reason.

#define RUNTIMEERROR_CANNOTOPENFILEFORWRITING 8202: File system error—couldn't find the file to write to or couldn't write to it for a generic reason. Also, verify that it's not set to read only.

#define RUNTIMEERROR_FILEALREADYOPEN 8203: This file is already open for being written to by GameGuru. Check your Lua code.

#define RUNTIMEERROR_FILENOTOPEN 8204: A generic file opening error. Check your Lua code.

#define RUNTIMEERROR_CANNOTREADFROMFILE 8211: Cannot read from the file specified, possibly due to data corruption or bad Lua code.

#define RUNTIMEERROR_CANNOTWRITETOFILE 8212: Cannot write to the file specified, possibly due to read-only permissions or bad Lua code.

#define RUNTIMEERROR_FILENUMBERINVALID 8213: The file number handle specified was invalid. Check your Lua code.

#define RUNTIMEERROR_FTPCONNECTIONFAILED 8301: Issue connecting to the store.

#define RUNTIMEERROR_FTPPATHCANNOTBEFOUND 8302: Issue connecting to the store caused by your machine. Validate steam installation.

#define RUNTIMEERROR_FTPCANNOTPUTFILE 8303: Issue connecting to the store.

#define RUNTIMEERROR_FTPCANNOTDELETEFILE 8304: Issue connecting to the store.

#define RUNTIMEERROR_FTPCANNOTGETFILE 8305: Issue connecting to the store.

#define RUNTIMEERROR_MPFAILEDTOCONNECT 8501: Failed to connect to multiplayer game. Check IP address, firewall configurations, and port accessibility.

#define RUNTIMEERROR_MPFAILEDTOFINDSESSION 8502: Failed to find the session, usually caused by firewalls and a partially blocked connection.

#define RUNTIMEERROR_MPFAILEDTOSETSESSION 8503: Failed to set session data, usually caused by firewalls and a partially blocked connection.

#define RUNTIMEERROR_MPFAILEDTOCREATEGAME 8504: Failed to create multiplayer game server, generic error.

#define RUNTIMEERROR_MPFAILEDTOJOINGAME 8505: Failed to join multiplayer game server, generic error.

#define RUNTIMEERROR_MPFAILEDTOSENDMESSAGE 8506: Failed to send data packet to server, usually caused by bad connectivity or firewalls.

#define RUNTIMEERROR_MPCREATEBETWEEN2AND255 8507: Unknown.

#define RUNTIMEERROR_MPMUSTGIVEPLAYERNAME 8508: Multiplayer error where player didn't specify their name properly.

#define RUNTIMEERROR_MPMUSTGIVEGAMENAME 8509: Server didn't properly specify game server name.

#define RUNTIMEERROR_MPCONNECTIONNUMINVALID 8510: Unknown.

#define RUNTIMEERROR_MPSESSIONNUMINVALID 8511: Unknown.

#define RUNTIMEERROR_MPPLAYERNUMINVALID 8512: Unknown.

#define RUNTIMEERROR_MPNOTINSESSION 8513: Unknown.

#define RUNTIMEERROR_MPPLAYERNOTEXIST 8514: Unknown.

#define RUNTIMEERROR_MPSESSIONEXISTS 8515: The server is still holding onto your previous connection; try again in a few minutes or reboot the server.

#define RUNTIMEERROR_MPNOTCREATEDPLAYER 8516: Unknown.

#define RUNTIMEERROR_MPCANNOTDELETEPLAYER 8517: Server had an error where it couldn't delete a player.

#define RUNTIMEERROR_MPTOOMANYPLAYERS 8518: Server exceeded number of supported players.

#define RUNTIMEERROR_CHECKLISTILLEGALNUMBER 9001: Code issue.

#define RUNTIMEERROR_CHECKLISTNUMBERWRONG 9002: Code issue.

#define RUNTIMEERROR_CHECKLISTONLYVALUES 9003: Code issue.

#define RUNTIMEERROR_CHECKLISTONLYSTRINGS 9004: Code issue.

#define RUNTIMEERROR_CHECKLISTNOTEXIST 9005: Code issue.

#define RUNTIMEERROR_SYSCARDNOTFOUND 9011: Hardware error, video card couldn't be found.

#define RUNTIMEERROR_SYSCOULDNOTGETTEXMEM 9012: Hardware or driver error. GameGuru couldn't access your texture memory. Update drivers and try again.

#define RUNTIMEERROR_SYSCOULDNOTGETVIDMEM 9013: Hardware or driver error. GameGuru couldn't access your video memory. Update drivers and try again.

#define RUNTIMEERROR_SYSCOULDNOTGETSYSMEM 9014: Hardware or driver error. GameGuru couldn't access your system memory. Update Windows and try again.

#define RUNTIMEERROR_SYSCOULDNOTLOADDLL 9701: Often means your Windows is out of date (typically Windows 7) and needs a specific update to fix it.

#define RUNTIMEERROR_SYSDLLNOTEXIST 9702: The specified dynamic link library (DLL)file (usually listed with the error) is not being found. This is often a computer issue or OS issue.

#define RUNTIMEERROR_SYSDLLALREADYEXISTS 9703: The specified DLL file is duplicated for some reason. This is often a computer issue or OS issue.

#define RUNTIMEERROR_SYSDLLCALLFAILED 9704: This is often a computer issue or OS issue.

#define RUNTIMEERROR_SYSDLLINDEXINVALID 9705: This is often a computer issue or OS issue.

#define RUNTIMEERROR_OBJECTMANAGERFAILED 9706: This is often a computer issue or OS issue.

FPI/FPE File Definitions

FPE files are an important part of GameGuru but as they are often in flux with subtle changes under the hood, it is virtually impossible to keep a proper up-to-date list of them. As a result, I've got the most stable and consistent ones here for your perusal with a brief description of each. That said, you may need to dig a bit to find more specific or niche ones that are not listed here.

Commenting is done with a ";" so, for example, a line with a ";" preceding it is automatically ignored by the engine. Thus we can say:

; I like to eat chicken

Yet nothing will happen in the engine. It is, however, useful to provide headers or tags for people reading your file.

Actual commands are done in the format similar to Lua with a variable assigned a value. So this list will have a format of "type=value" as that is how it will be within the actual FPE file.

Variable list

description = "A description of the entity: ex: A large green box."

texture = The filename of your primary _d or _color texture file. For multitexture objects, separate textures get their own line with a corresponding number like texture38=zxy_d.dds.

reducetexture = A divisor that reduces the quality of the texture by dividing it by a number. Lowest acceptable value is 1. See Chapter 21 on optimization.

effect = Configures which shader you use for your entity. Must specify in this format: (effect=entitybank\reloaded\shadername_type.fx).

model = This tells what file to load for the model. Supports several formats (see section on model importer in Chapter 4).

aimain = This lists which Lua file is used by the entity. It automatically assumes it's in files\scriptbank as its default location.

defaultstatic = 0 is for dynamic entities, 1 is for static entities.

immobile = 0 allows the object freedom of movement, 1 locks it in position.

alwaysactive = 0 sets the object as not always active (default) and requires a player be within 3000 units before activating. 1 makes the object always active. See Chapter 21 on optimization.

strength = This is a numeric value signifying a raw HP value. Can range from 1 to 10000 or higher.

explodable = 0 if you want the object to die normally and leave a body, 1 if you want it to blow up and remove a body when it's dead.

castshadow = Configures if the object will show a basic circular shadow. Useful if you have shadows disabled but want them for dynamic entities: –1 ignores all lightmapping, 0 is disabled (default), and 1 enables this shadow.

cullmode = Default 0: 0 does back face culling, 1 does not.

scale = Default 100. This is a raw scale value in percentage. This can go up to at least 5000 percent. Do not use a percent symbol, just a raw numeric value.

forwardfacing = This is mostly for posters and wall coverings; 0 is default and doesn't snap to anything; 1 will snap it to a wall and face it outward.

offx = A numeric value corresponding to a position offset on the x-axis.

offy = A numeric value corresponding to a position offset on the y-axis.

offz = A numeric value corresponding to a position offset on the z-axis.

rotx = A numeric value corresponding to a rotation on the x-axis.

roty = A numeric value corresponding to a rotation on the y-axis.

rotz = A numeric value corresponding to a rotation on the z-axis.

defaultheight = This is a numeric value for an object's initial starting position above the ground it's placed on. This can be used as a positive or negative value, with 0 being the default and original height.

fixnewy = This is a rotation value used to fix the y angle orientation; if your model is facing the wrong way put a 180 in this. Otherwise, leave it blank.

ischaracter = Default 0. This specifies if this is a valid character for the game with a 0 for no and 1 for yes.

collisionmode = 0 is a default box for collision and physics; 1 is a polygon map of the object for collision but uses a box for physics; 2 is a sphere for collision and physics; 3 is a cylinder for collision and physics; 11 disables collision and physics; 12 disables collision and physics but can still be checked with "intersectall," and 21 is a "repel player feature." Special options are for 1000–1999 with 1000 being limb zero and using collision boxes for all limbs. Each one must have its own number; 2000–2999 are the same but with polygon collision boxes but box-type physics. When "ischaracter=1," physics are overridden by a character capsule (like a cylinder).

Forcesimpleobstacle = Default 0. –1 for no obstacle, 0 is default and uses collisionmode (see earlier), 1 is a box, 2 is contour, and 3 is a full poly scan.

ismarker = Specifies if this is a "marker entity." 0 = not a marker, 1 = player start, 2 = light, 3 = zone, 4 = decal or particle emitter, 5 = entitylight, 6 = checkpoint, 7 = multiplayer start marker.

materialindex = Primarily uses 0 for generic "soft" noises, 1 for stone, 2 for metal, 3 for wood, 4 for glass, 5 for wet splash, 6 is flesh, 7 is hollow drum, 8 is high pitch tinny, 9 low pitch tinny, 10 is silly material, 11 is marble, 12 is cobble, 13 is gravel, 14 is soft metal, 15 is old stone, 16 is old wood, 17 is shallow water, 18 is underwater. Most of these were working but recently ceased as of this writing; for now, stick to 0–3 to be safe.

transparency = Default 0. Configures if transparencies are in this texture. 0 is no transparency. 1 is first phase with alpha masking; 2 and 3 are second phase, which overlaps solid geometry; 4 is a test value; 5 is a water line alpha depth sorted automatically; 6 is a combination of 3 and 4 for falling LOD leaves; 7 is early draw phase, no alpha.

isoccluder = Default 1. Configures whether this entity can "occlude entities" behind it (1) or not (0). See Chapter 21 on optimization.

isoccludee = Default 1. Configures whether this entity may BE occluded by entities in front of it (1) or not (0). See Chapter 21 on optimization.

invertnormal = Default 0. Allows artists to toggle green channel of normal without changing texture (1) or not (0).

preservetangents = Default 0. Tells the shader not to generate new tangents/binomials (1) or not (0).

endcollision = Default 1. Defines whether ragdoll collisions are allowed (1) or not (0) on death.

soundset = This corresponds to a file path (ex: soundset=mysounds\soldier), which is a folder containing sounds for a character.

soundset1, 2, 3, 4, 5, 6 = This also corresponds to a file path (ex: soundset3=mysounds\soldier_rpg), which is a folder containing a second bank of sounds for the character.

uvscroll = Default 0,0. Used for UV scrolling on U-axis. Per Lee Bamber: The usage is UVSCROLL = u,v. When used, it will pass this value into any shader that uses the constant "ScrollScaleUV." It's up to the shader to use this value.

uvscale = Default 1,0. Floating point numeric value for amount to scale UV. Works like uvscroll and is reliant on a shader reading the appropriate value to operate.

ragdoll = Default 0. Use 0 if you want ragdoll physics, 1 if it is not compatible with ragdoll.

physics = Use 0 for no physics, 1 for physics.

phyweight = A percentage value based on the volume of the model's collision box. Default is 100.

phyfriction = A percentage value that determines how much the object will be affected by friction on the terrain system.

phyalways = Always on yes/no. Default 0, is no. 1 is yes.

speed = A raw speed value for the entity when moving.

hurtfall = A raw numeric value that gives a damage value for how much it will do when it falls.

usekey = Allows you to specify whether it uses a key or not.

ifused = Allows you to specify a default value for the ifused field.

ifusednear = No longer used in GameGuru.

spawnmax = Sets a maximum spawn limit. Unknown if this still works.

spawndelay = Sets a default spawn delay. Unknown if this still works.

spawnqty = Sets a default spawn quantity. Unknown if this still works.

autoflatten = Default 0. 0 means this object will interface normally with the terrain. 1 will cause it to auto-flatten the terrain around the object.

resetlimbmatrix = Default 0. 0 for no, 1 to reset the limb matrix.

reverseframes = Default 0. 0 for no, 1 to reverse animation frames.

zdepth = Default 1. Determines zdepth render order. You can display the object like a HUD object if desired.

isebe = Default 0. Used by the EBE when saving as an entity.

noxzrotation = Default 0. Enables XZ rotation (0) or disables it (1) when spraying the entity using the spray tool.

offyoverride = Default 0. Allows an override that can change Y offset to correct models.

fullbounds = Default 0. Detect limbs that move out of range of the original frame zero bound box.

hasweapon = Points to a specific gun in the gamecore folder that is used by the entity (ex: modern\colt1911).

cantakeweapon = 0 means it doesn't drop a weapon, 1 means it does.

isobjective = 0 specifies this is not a necessary objective toward completion, 1 means it is.

headlimbs = Only used on characters with limbs, this specifies which limb allows critical hits.

cpuanims = Default 0. 0 configures GPU animation, 1 configures CPU animation for accurate ray detection, and 2 configures 1 but hides meshes without animations.

ignoredefanim = Default 0. Toggles whether to ignore default animations (1) or not (0).

debrisshape = 0 specifies a standard debris type. Other debris types exist but don't actually change anything.

disablebatch = Default 0. Either enables LOD system (1) or disables it (0).

uselodmodifier = Default 0. Numeric value that determines whether to use an LOD modifier (1) or not (0).

lod1distance = Default 0. Configures level of detail distance transition. Numeric value for how far away in units. Requires disablebatch=1.

lod2distance = Default 0. Configures level of detail distance second transition (further). Numeric value for how far away in units. Requires disablebatch=1.

nothrowscript = Default 0. Prevented ragdoll effects. A depreciated command from FPSC.

coneheight = Numeric value related to cone-shaped visibility for AI.

coneangle = Numeric value related to cone-shaped visibility for AI.

conerange = Numeric value related to cone-shaped visibility for AI.

canseethrough = Default 0 (no). Configures whether an entity can see through it or not.

specular = Default setting is 0. 0—uses _S texture based off diffuse filename, 1—uses effectbank\reloaded\media\blank_none_S.dds, 2—uses effectbank\reloaded\media\blank_low_S.dds, — uses effectbank\reloaded\media\blank_medium_S.dds, 4—uses effectbank\reloaded\media\blank_high_S.dds.

specularperc = Specular percent. Configures the default specular value. This is defaulted at 100, for 100%. It can be tuned up much higher, though, to make DNIS entities much shinier.

smoothangle = Default 0. Configures whether you want to use "smooth normal" (1) or not (0).

lives = A numeric value that shows upon collection whether it will give extra lives to the player.

animspeed = Default 100. This is a numeric percentage value that configures how fast the animation processes.

isviolent = Default 1. Enables blood effects on model for 1, 0 disables.

isthirdperson = Configures if you can use this as a third-person control. No longer used.

jumpmodifier = Default 1.0. Floating point numeric value, used for third person as the time to stay in the air. Required for 3 pv.

jumphold = Default 0. Numeric value, used for third person as the frame to hold while "hanging." Required for 3 pv.

jumpresume = Default 0. Numeric value, used for third person perspective (3PV) games and denotes which keyframe is used for when the feet of the character touch the ground after the jump. Required for 3PV.

jumpvaulttrim = Default 1. Numeric value, used for third person. Required for 3PV.

meleerange = Default 80. Numeric value, used for third-person attacks.

meleehitangle = Default 30. Numeric value, used for third-person attacks.

meleestrikest = Default 0. Numeric value, defines "deadly" melee anim frame start.

meleestrikefn = Default 30. Numeric value, defines "deadly" melee anim frame finish.

meleedamagest = Sets a starting value for third-person melee damage per strike (range).

meleedamagefn = Sets an ending value for third-person melee damage per strike.

forceobstaclepolysize = Default 30.0. Floating point value. Controls "obstacle slice resolution." Used to keep small poly objects from affecting AI.

forceobstaclesliceheight = Default 14.0. Floating point value. Allows AI obstacle plane height to be set.

forceobstaclesliceminsize = Default 5.0. Floating point value. Allows AI obstacle plane height to be set with minimum threshold.

effectprofile = Default 0. Zero is the default non-PBR effect profile, 1 is new PBR texture arrangement.

explodedamage = Default 100. Allows you to configure a set HP damage for explosions as a raw numeric damage value.

hoverfactor = Default 0. A numeric value controlling a hover value for entities, measured in units.

dontfindfloor = A toggle (0 off, 1 on) that allows you to disable the floor finder for roof entities.

collisionscaling = Default 100. Configures physics box collision scaling on percentage basis.

canfight = Default 1. Depreciated command.

custombiped = Unknown.

isweapon = 0 means it's not a weapon; 1 means it is a collectible weapon for the player.

rateoffire = Default 85. Sets a rate of fire for the object. Higher is slower, lower is faster.

ishudlayer = Configures whether this object when collected has a custom HUD layer. For an example, see "jet pack" under collectibles in your entity bank.

isequipment = Similar to adding a weapon, but adds equipment such as a jetpack. This makes the item always active so it's droppable.

isammo = 0 means this isn't a valid form of ammo. 1 makes it a valid form of ammo.

ishealth = 0 means this isn't a healthkit; 1 means it is and is collectable.

isflak = This is no longer used in GameGuru.

quantity = Default −1. This relies on isammo, ishealth, and others to be available. Sets a specific quantity of ammo, health, etc. you will receive or not (−1).

hasequipment = This specifies with a 0 or 1 if it has a jetpack it can drop.

fatness = Default 50. A numeric value that configures the "capsule size" for a character, if capsules are being used.

markerindex = A marker-related numeric index. Unknown use.

skipfvfconvert = Default 0. 0 is off, 1 is on. Can fix character import issues by skipping flexible vertex format (FVF) conversion for the DBO file generated by GameGuru.

matrixmode = Default 0. Adds a transform with the original model matrix per limb.

addhandle = Points to a specific file that acts as a decal handle, *example*: *addhandle = decalhandle.dds.*

addhandlelimb = Default 0. Specifies which limb should act as a handle.

usespotlighting = Default 0. Defines whether a light is a spot light (1) or not (0).

muzzlecolorR = X – Muzzle flash RED light value (0–255).

muzzlecolorG = X – Muzzle flash GREEN light value (0–255).

muzzlecolorB = X – Muzzle flash BLUE light value (0–255).

lightcolor = Allows you to configure an RGB value for a light entity.

lightrange = Allows you to configure a default light range.

lightoffsetup = Allows you to configure an offset for the light.

lightoffsetz = Allows you to set the value of the offset on the Z-axis.

stylecolor = A trigger-related color. Internal game engine function.

decalangle = Default 0. An extra decal offset, configures angle.

decaldist= Default 0. An extra decal offset, configures distance.

decaly= Default 0. An extra decal offset, configures how far away on Y-axis it is.

decal# = Allows you to specify the specific decal to apply. Can use multiple decals based on # being individual decal number. *Example: decal8=mydecal.dds.*

decalmax = Default 0. Numeric value for maximum number of decals.

limb# = Limb specific information, with # being the individual limb number. *Example: limb32=<your info here>.*

limbmax = Default 0. Configure maximum limb.

spine = Default –1. Defines a spine for modern animation.

spine2 = Default –1. Defines a second spine for modern animation.

isspinetracker = Default 0. Allows you to control new spine tracker for modern character animations.

firespotlimb = Default –1, configures which limb holds a gun.

headlimb = Default –1. Configure if limb is a head.

hairlimbs = Configure if limb is a hair component.

The following commands also work but have no documentation available:

appendanimfinal = Specifies which appended animation is the final frame.

appendanimmax = Default 0. Specifies which appended animation is the maximum.

appendanim# = Allows you to append the animation, with # being an individual animation number. *Example: appendanim24=<your animation info here>.*

appendanimframe# = Allows you to append the animation frame, with # being an individual animation frame number. *Example: appendanim24=<your animation frame info here>.*

ignorecsirefs = Default 0. A flag that allows you to skip old computer generated imagery (CGI) animation references in favor of original animation fields.

ischaractercreator = Default 0. Created by the character creator, sets 1 if it's a character creator entity, 0 if it isn't.

physicscount = Created by the file importer, defines quantity of custom physics entities.

physics# = Defines the bounding box of the individual physics entities when generated by the importer for bulletphysics.

playaniminededitor = Unknown use.

animstyle = Default 0. Unknown use.

animmax = Default 0. Specifies which animation is the maximum.

anim# = Specify a specific animation, with # being the individual animation number. *Example: anim11=<your animation info here>.*

footfallmax = Default 0. Specifies which footfall is the maximum. Previous command allows entities to specify keyframes that would trigger a footfall sound effect (maximum value).

footfall# = Allows you to specify a footfall, with # being the individual footfall number. Earmarked for future implementation. Previous command allows entities to specify keyframes that would trigger a footfall sound effect, specified on an individual #. *Example: footfall21=<Your animation frame info here>.*

Light Value Charts

These light values are derived from other sources, such as pixel emporium's great guide online, and are modified to be more accurate for GameGuru light sources. There are three major sections: human-made lights, ambient/surface light values for sun, and atmospheric fog values. The first is for static and dynamic lights, the other two are for either the ambient and surface values or fog, respectively.

Human Made Lights

Type of Light & RGB Color Code for GG

Candle: 0079f2

40W standard tungsten bulb: 8fc5dc

100W standard tungsten bulb: aad6fff

Halogen: e0f1ff

LED: fff1e0

Carbon Arc: e6f4ff

Standard Fluorescent: fafff4

Cool Fluorescent: ffecd7

Full Spectrum Fluorescent: f2f4ff

Black Light: ff009b

Mercury Vapor: fff7d8

Metal Halide: f9fadc

Sodium Vapor: 0ed1ff

High-Pressure Sodium: 4cb7ff

Ambient/Surface Light Values from Sun

(Ambient Red%, Green%, Blue%, Fog Red%, Green, Blue%, Intensity%, Near, Distant)

Nighttime 0%, 0%, 0%, 0%, 0%, 0%, 100%, 0, 1

Astronomical twilight 2%, 4%, 5%, 1%, 4%, 5%, 94%, 0, 2

Nautical twilight 2%, 9%, 11%, 2%, 9%, 11%, 86%, 0, 7

Civil twilight 20%, 16%, 12%, 89%, 68%, 65%, 70%, 1, 10

Sunup 97%, 94%, 87%, 94%, 86%, 62%, 79%, 1, 10

Early sun 68%, 72%, 79%, 88%, 88%, 93%, 50%, 1, 7

Midday sun 78%, 78%, 82%, 78%, 78%, 82%, 40%, 1, 15

Late-day sun 64%, 58%, 58%, 78%, 74%, 70%, 62%, 0, and 10

Golden hour 68%, 58%, 58%, 78%, 70%, 58%, 70%, 0, 7

Rose hour 78%, 51%, 42%, 48%, 41%, 37%, 80%, 0, 7

Blue hour 22,19,56,15,9,30, 240, 0, 6

Atmospheric Values for Fog

(Near, Distance, R%, G%, B%, Intensity %)

Daytime city haze 5, 20, 54%, 60%, 65%, 75%

Heat haze in desert 0, 4, 68%, 62%, 45%, 80%

Winter snowstorm 0, 10, 71%, 79%, 89%, 100%

Rainy day 0, 15, 71%, 79%, 89, 85%

Nighttime haze 0, 2, 0%, 0%, 0%, 95%

Pitch black 0, 1, 0%, 0%, 0%, 100%

Standard atmospheric haze 5, 25, 54%, 61%, 67%, 70%

Moderate fog 0, 7, 71%, 74%, 80%, 85%

Heavy fog 0, 4, 71%, 74%, 80%, 90%

Spooky fog 0, 3, 100%, 100%, 100%, 94%

Gunspec.txt File

This follows a similar format as with the FPE files since the actual file itself uses a "type=value" arrangement. Please note that, for accuracy settings, lower values are better.

textured = <name>: File name of the diffuse texture (e.g., gun_D.dds).

effect = effectbank\reloaded\weapon_bone.fx.

weapontype = X – 1: Pistol, 2: RPG, 3: Shotgun, 4: Submachine gun, 5: Rifle, 51: Melee.

statuspanelcode = X – Sets the code used by the status panel.

vweaptex = <name>: The name of a texture for a held weapon.

decal = <name>: The name of the decal folder.

decalforward = X – How far forward from the player is the decal?

invertnormal = X – Sets to 1 to flag for Y-axis normal maps.

preservetangents = X – Sets to 1 to disable normal tangent shifting.

boostintensity = X – Boost illumination effect by setting to 1.

poolammo = foldername\ammotype.

damage = Raw damage done for each successful hitscan test done. With shotguns, this is per pellet.

range = The range of the weapon in # of GameGuru units.

force = The physics value for a successful hit.

iterate = The number of projectiles firing each time the gun is fired. Normally, this is one unless it's a shotgun.

scorchtype = X – A currently disabled setting that configures bullet damage decals on hits.

altscorchtype = X – A currently disabled setting that configures bullet damage decals on hits for alt fire.

noscorch = X – Setting 1 disables decal (for when they are added later).

meleedamage = X – Raw damage for successful melee hits.

meleerange = X – A range in GameGuru units of the melee attack.

meleeforce = X – The physics value of a successful melee hit.

meleescorch = X – Enable or disable wall hit decals (not functional at the moment).

rotx = Change gun rotation angle on X-axis. Accepts positive, negative, and decimal values.

roty = Change gun rotation angle on Y-axis. Accepts positive, negative, and decimal values.

rotz = Change gun rotation angle on Z-axis. Accepts positive, negative, and decimal values.

NOTE: Vertical horizontal and forward commands will change gun position also.

shotgun = X – If X = 1, then performs shotgun-style reloading. Uses reload start, reload loop, and reload end animations.

empty shotgun = X – If X = 1, then performs shotgun-style reloading on an empty weapon. Uses reload start, reload loop, and reload end animations.

burst = X – Only works on automatic weapons. If X is larger than 0, then the weapon will burst fire X number of shots.

firerate = X – Sets the number of loops between shots on automatic weapons to X divided by 2. Default is 12. Four is approximately 600 RPM for a rate of fire. Lower is faster, higher is slower. For semiauto fire, rate is defined by animation length.

disablemovespeedmod = X – If set to 1, will disable the animation speed change applied to the move animation while walking/running/crouching.

altflak = X – Name of flak to use for alternate fire. Note: This currently is the same as "flak = X" and is only provided for compatibility with stock FPSC at this time.

chamberedround = X – If set to 1, the player will be able to reload the weapon if it is full in order to receive one extra round.

noautoreload = X – If set to 1, will not automatically reload the weapon when the clip runs dry.

nofullreload = X – If set to 1, the player will not be able to reload when the weapon is full. NOTE: If chambered round = 1, they will still be able to reload with full ammo to obtain 1 extra round. They will not be able to reload if they already have the additional round.

overheatafter = X – A numeric value that says how many shots you can take before the weapon can potentially jam. The higher the number, the better a chance before jamming.

cooldown = X – A time in milliseconds the player must wait before it resets the overheatafter chance.

jamchance = X – A percentage chance on each shot taken after the overheatafter threshold is reached.

runx = X – An X offset to use while running (holding shift and moving). NOTE: The weapon is smoothly transitioned to this position using SIMPLEZOOMSPEED.

runy = X – A Y offset to use while running (holding shift and moving). NOTE: The weapon is smoothly transitioned to this position using SIMPLEZOOMSPEED.

runacc = X – Accuracy of the weapon while running.

horiz = X – A simple horizontal positional offset.

vert = X – A simple vertical positional offset.

forward = A simple Z-axis positional offset for depth.

simplezoom = X – Used for iron sights. X is the amount that the player should zoom in when pressing right click.

simplezoommode = X – Used for iron sights. High values for X mean the weapon does not move backward as much when the player zooms in. Negative values mean it moves forward. A value of zero means it does not move.

simplezoomacc = X – Used for iron sights. Accuracy when in simple zoom.

simplezoomx = X – An X offset to use when in simple zoom. NOTE: The weapon is smoothly transitioned to this position using SIMPLEZOOMSPEED.

simplezoomy = X – A Y offset to use when in simple zoom. NOTE: The weapon is smoothly transitioned to this position using SIMPLEZOOMSPEED.

simplezoomspeed = X – The speed at which the weapon is smoothed to the X/Y values. Higher values mean it goes slower.

simplezoomanim = X – If set to 1, the weapon will use the zoom animation set when in simple zoom.

simplezoomflash = X – If set to 1, the muzzle flash will use the zoom alignment coordinates.

gunlagspeed = X – The speed at which the gun should lag behind the camera movement. Higher values mean it moves slower and further.

gunlagxmax = X – The maximum amount the gun can lag behind on the X-axis.

gunlagymax = X – The maximum amount the gun can lag behind on the Y-axis.

zoomgunlagspeed = X – Same as gunlagspeed but used while in simple zoom.

zoomgunlagxmax = X – Same as gunlagxmax but used while in simple zoom.

zoomgunlagymax = X – Same as gunlagymax but used while in simple zoom.

zoomwalkspeed = X – The modifier for the player's walk speed while zoomed. Higher values mean the player will move slower.

zoomturnspeed = X – The modifier for the player's looking speed while zoomed. Higher values mean the player will look around slower.

plrmovespeedmod = X – Base move speed multiplier for the player.

plremptyspeedmod = X – Move speed modifier with an empty gun.

plrturnspeedmod = X – Player turn speed modifier.

plrjumpspeedmod = X – Player jump speed modifier.

plrreloadspeedmod = X – Player speed modifier when reloading.

reloadspeed = X – Animation speed of the weapon's reload.

soundstrength = X – The percentage of sound the player's weapon will make in the AI system. A value of 0 means it will make no sound, while 100 would be normal.

alternateisflak = X – If X is 1, the weapon's alternate fire is the defined flak.

alternateisray = X – If X is 1, the weapon's alternate fire uses ray casting (bullets).

reloadqty = X – The number of cartridges in the magazine for primary fire.

altreloadqty = X – The number of rounds per magazine for alternate fire.

addtospare = X – If ammo is collected, it goes to the pool of ammo not the gun itself.

npcignorereload = X – Determines whether an NPC using this gun spawns with an empty weapon.

altiterate = X – The number of bullets that should be shot if alternateisray = 1.

altrange = X – The range of the bullets if alternateisray = 1.

accuracy = The base accuracy of your primary weapons fire.

altaccuracy = X – The accuracy of the bullets if alternateisray = 1.

altdamage = X – The damage of the bullets if alternateisray = 1.

muzzleflash = X – The muzzle flash id for primary fire.

altmuzzleflash = X – The muzzle flash id for alternate fire (like muzzleflash = X).

muzzlesize = X – Size of the muzzle flash.

smokedecal = <name>: Filename of the bullet puff effect.

recoily = X – The amount of recoil on the Y-axis.

recoilx = X – The amount of recoil on the X-axis (randomly selects left or right).

recoilyreturn = X – The percentage of the recoil that should be compensated for on the y-axis (0: 100).

recoilxreturn = X – The percentage of the recoil that should be compensated for on the x-axis (0: 100).

zoomaccuracy = X – Your accuracy with primary fire while zoomed.

zoomaccuracybreathhold = X – Enables or disables steadier aim when holding the key configured in setup.ini as [zoomholdbreath].

zoomaccuracybreath = X – A time in milliseconds of how long the key will function for holding breath before it ceases function.

zoomaccuracyheld = X – Accuracy of fire while holding in breath.

zoomrecoily = X – Same as recoily but while zoomed in (works with simplezoom).

zoomrecoilx = X – Same as recoilx but while zoomed in (works with simplezoom).

zoomrecoilyreturn – X – Same as recoilyreturn but while zoomed in (works with simplezoom).

zoomrecoilxreturn = X – Same as recoilxreturn but while zoomed in (works with simplezoom).

disablerunandshoot = X – Setting this to 1 means a player cannot fire the gun while running.

altrecoily = X – Same as recoily but while in alternate fire.

altrecoilx = X – Same as recoilx but while in alternate fire.

altrecoilyreturn = X – Same as recoilyreturn but while in alternate fire.

altrecoilxreturn = X – Same as recoilxreturn but while in alternate fire.

forcezoomout = X – If X is 1, then forces zoom out on reload for scoped weapons. Automatic on simplezoom.

Gunspec Muzzle Flash Alignments

zoomalignx = X – Alignment of muzzle flash while in simplezoom.

zoomaligny = X – Alignment of muzzle flash while in simplezoom.

zoomalignz = X – Alignment of muzzle flash while in simplezoom.

alignx = X – Alignment of muzzle flash while in primary fire.

aligny = X – Alignment of muzzle flash while in primary fire.

alignz = X – Alignment of muzzle flash while in primary fire.

altalignx = X – Alignment of muzzle flash while in alternatefire.

altaligny = X – Alignment of muzzle flash while in alternatefire.

altalignz = X – Alignment of muzzle flash while in alternatefire.

brass = X – The ID of the brass model used for case ejections.

brasslife = X – Time in MS for the brass to live before being despawned.

brassangle = X – Angle of the brass casing's ejection.

brassanglerand = X – A random value to modify the ejection by.

brassspeed = X – How fast the brass ejections occur in MS.

brassspeedrand = X – A random modification to brass speed ejection.

brassupward = X – How fast the brass moves vertically.

brassupwardrand = X – A random modification to brass vertical speed.

brassrotx = X – The spin rate of brass on the X-axis.

brassrotxrand = X – A random modifier for brass X-axis rotation.

brassroty = X – The spin rate of brass on the Y-axis.

brassrotyrand = X – A random modifier for brass Y-axis rotation.

brassrotz = X – The spin rate of brass on the Z-axis.

brassrotzrand = X – A random modifier for brass Z-axis rotation.

brassdelay = X – The spawn delay of brass in milliseconds.

zoombrassdelay = The spawn delay of brass while zoomed in milliseconds.

sound1 = <name>: Gunfire sound effect.

sound2 = <name>: Reload sound effect.

sound3 = <name>: Dry firing sound effect.

sound4 = <name>: Sound effect of weapon being put away.

sound5 = <name>: Melee sound effect.

sound6 = <name>: Pump shotgun full sound effect.

sound7 = <name>: Pump shotgun starting reload sound effect.

sound8 = <name>: Pump shotgun end of animation sound effect.

fireloop = X – Time in MS before sound effect plays again for firing.

soundstrength = X – Volume in decibels of sound effects (60–100).

soundframes = X – Number of frames for sounds to match animation.

sframe<num> = X – A range of animations to match a specific sound. Example: sframe1=22,3.

Gunspec Animation Ranges

block = X,X – Sets right click to block and plays animation. Affects plrblocking state.

start fire 2 = X,X || end fire 2 = X,X – Randomly selected alternate fire animation.

start fire 3 = X,X || end fire 3 = X,X – Randomly selected alternate fire animation.

zoomto = X,X – Animation played when entering simplezoom.

zoomfrom = X,X – Animation played when leaving simplezoom.

zoom start fire = X,X – Animation played when starting to shoot in simple zoom.

zoom automatic fire = X,X – Animation looped in auto fire in simple zoom.

zoom end fire = X,X – Animation played when stopping shooting in simple zoom.

zoom idle = X,X – Idle animation for simple zoom.

zoom move = X,X – Move animation for simple zoom.

altto = X,X – Animation played when entering alternate fire.

altfrom = X,X – Animation played when leaving alternate fire.

alt start fire = X,X – Beginning of shooting in alternate fire.

alt end fire = X,X – End of shooting in alternate fire.

alt idle = X,X – Alternate fire idle animation.

alt move = X,X – Alternate fire move animation.

alt reload = X,X – Alternate fire reload animation.

Hyperlink Reference Guide

http://gamegurureport.blogspot.com: The author's weekly report on all things GameGuru.

On lighting

https://www.youtube.com/watch?v=IyUgHPs86XM: John Carmack, "The principles of lighting and rendering"

https://www.youtube.com/watch?v=B0sM7ZU0Nwo: "Lighting Mirror's Edge"

Tools

https://forum.game-guru.com/thread/215728?page=5: FBX2GG

https://forum.game-guru.com/thread/218348: Make FPE from X files

https://forum.game-guru.com/thread/218876: Heightmap 2 GameGuru

https://forum.game-guru.com/thread/214389

https://www.amigapd.com/interview-lee-bamber.html: Lee Bamber's Amiga interview.

On games improving cognition

http://www.medicaldaily.com/video-games-improve-memory-and-problem-solving-try-cut-rope-yourself-290382: Samantha Olsen, "Video Games Improve Memory And Problem Solving; Try 'Cut the Rope' For Yourself," 2014.

http://www.rochester.edu/news/show.php?id=3679: Rochester.Edu, "Video Games Lead to Faster Decisions that are No Less Accurate," 2010.

https://medium.com/peak-play/5-games-with-surprising-benefits-for-your-brain-fea1501e0fee: Peak in Peak Play, "5 Games With Surprising Benefits for Your Brain," 2016.

https://www.psychologytoday.com/us/blog/freedom-learn/201502/cognitive-benefits-playing-video-games: Peter Gray, "Cognitive Benefits of Playing Video Games," 2015.

Customer service

https://www.forbes.com/sites/forbesagencycouncil/2017/06/20/13-golden-rules-of-pr-crisis-management/: Forbes Agency Council, "13 Golden Rules of PR Crisis Management," 2017.

Optimization

https://forum.game-guru.com/thread/218003 – Optimization for end users

https://forum.game-guru.com/thread/220336 – Memory management with audio

Particles

https://forum.game-guru.com/thread/220349

https://forum.game-guru.com/thread/220140#msg2606716

AI (cover zones)

https://forum.game-guru.com/thread/209401

AI (waypoint circuits)

https://forum.game-guru.com/thread/218257#msg2581688

Sales

http://www.ign.com/articles/2006/05/06/the-economics-of-game-publishing: Ralph Edwards, The Economics of Game Publishing, 2006.

https://splinternews.com/man-addicted-to-fallout-4-is-suing-game-developer-after-1793853675: Charles Pulliam-Moore, "Man addicted to 'Fallout 4' is suing game developer after losing his job and wife," 2015.

http://www.gamesbrief.com/2013/03/why-do-game-devs-need-professional-indemnity-insurance/

http://www.dailymail.co.uk/news/article-4571492/Cash-outside-teen-sues-game-developers-1million.html

https://kotaku.com/how-a-successful-kickstarter-lost-half-a-million-dollar-1608877998

https://www.gamasutra.com/blogs/JakeBirkett/20180206/314393/Blog_Can_weekone_Steam_sales_predict_firstyear_sales.php

https://en.wikipedia.org/wiki/Video_game_controversies

Piracy

https://kotaku.com/5533615/another-view-of-video-game-piracy

https://www.dvsgaming.org/a-look-into-video-game-piracy/ (deleted since accessed July 15, 2018).

FPE files

http://freetoronto.org/gameguru/tutorial_fpe.html

https://github.com/TheGameCreators/GameGuruRepo/wiki/FPE-Entity-Properties-Reference-Guide

https://forum.thegamecreators.com/thread/192239

Level design

https://forum.game-guru.com/thread/214049

https://www.mcvuk.com/development/getting-started-with-gameguru

https://3dexport.com/blog/making-of-final-stand/

Math

https://www.gamedev.net/articles/programming/math-and-physics/practical-use-of-vector-math-in-games-r2968/

http://nic-gamedev.blogspot.com/2011/11/using-vector-mathematics-cross-products.html

Sounds

https://forum.game-guru.com/thread/220002

Glossary

3D: Three-dimensional space consisting of X, Y, and Z coordinates.

Anti-aliasing: A graphic effect that smooths edges and can improve graphic quality. Various types of anti-aliasing exist such as fast approximate anti-aliasing (FXAA), enhanced subpixel morphological anti-aliasing (SMAA), and morphological anti-aliasing (MLAA), which are post-effects. There are also other methods that increase sample rates such as multisample anti-aliasing (MSAA) and super sampling anti-aliasing (SSAA). GameGuru uses FXAA by default.

Biome: A natural environment that encompasses a specific location and has a community of plants and animals common to it.

BSP: Binary space partitioning. Dividing areas in a binary fashion that allows rapid data traversal.

CC3: Creative Commons 3 license, requires attribution of the original author by the user.

CPU: Central processing unit, your computer's primary math and information processor.

DNSI or DNIS: Diffuse, normal, specular, and illumination. A method of texture mapping that includes a diffuse texture for colors, normal mapping, specularity mapping for shininess, and illumination for self-illuminated textures.

DX9: Direct X 9, a graphics coding library provided by Microsoft that allows for less-complicated graphic functions done through Windows via a common method. Was used in earlier versions of GameGuru.

DX11: Direct X 11, a graphics coding library provided by Microsoft that allows for complicated graphics functions done through Windows via a common method. It is used in later and current versions of GameGuru.

Entity: An interactive object that can be placed and used in GameGuru.

Euler: Euler is the name of a man (Leonhard Euler, 18th century) who wrote a significant amount of mathematical theorems specifically regarding physics, geometry, calculus, and number theory. Often used descriptively with respect to his ideas such as Euler angles, Euler's formula, etc.

FPS (first person shooter): A gaming type where the player assumes the first-person view of a player and often uses weapons as a puzzle and problem-solving implement. Use of FPS for first person shooter as acronym depends on context.

FPS (frames per second): A measure of how fast the rendering system can display a "frame," or full screen, of data per second. The human eye sees at anywhere from 25–60 frames per second, with the vast majority falling into the range of 45 frames per second.

Fractal: A mathematical equation that produces geometric shapes and patterns that are highly irregular. These shapes and patterns are similar to the larger object and are often used to model natural characteristics.

GPL: GNU public license, a common licensing platform that allows free software licensing.

GPU: Graphics processing unit, a type of specialized graphics processor that helps take the load off the CPU by handling more graphics intensive tasks.

HD: Hard disk, a type of long-term storage for a computer.

Heightmap: A raster that is transformed into a 3D surface by rendering the high and low points based off the color values using a terrain system.

Hit-scan: A method of hit detection that uses a ray cast out from one location to another while performing a scan to see if it actually hit the object in question. Typically used for weapons fire or line of sight. There is no discernable delay or travel time.

IP: Intellectual property. This represents the ownership of an idea or concept by a particular person or party and forms the foundation of most copyright law.

PBR: Physically based rendering. This method of rendering a model relies on a large number of secondary texture maps to provide significant detail to a model, thus allowing greater graphical fidelity.

PD: Public domain. This type of licensing or ownership implies that it is available freely for anyone without a license.

Plane: A flat two-dimensional geometric surface.

Quaternion: Quaternions are a method of math that is used to represent rotations in 3D math.

RAM: Random access memory, a type of short-term computer memory.

Raster: A raster is a geometric plane of data that contains graphical information to be rendered.

Ray-tracing: A method where an invisible ray is drawn out from an origination point (typically, the player) and then it detects whether it is intersecting a wall, object, etc. This is useful for hit detection, lighting, and wall detection. Also called ray casting.

Render: Rendering is the process of displaying an image or graphic element.

Shader: A programming system that allows a specialized function relating to computer special effects.

SSAO: Screen space ambient occlusion. This is a graphic effect that creates small micro shadows on a surface.

Terrain: The rendering system that configures the land surface in GameGuru.

Texture map: The process of taking a raster and applying it over a series of polygons on a model via something called a UV wrap.

UV wrap: UV coordinates correlate to XY coordinates except they are for textures.

Vector: Also known as a Euclidean vector. Defines a magnitude and direction in 3D space.

Vegetation: The vegetation system that allows you to spray plants in GameGuru.

Index

Note: Page numbers in *italics* indicate figures.

F

M

N

Q

R

U

V

W

X

Y

Z

Printed in the United States
by Baker & Taylor Publisher Services

Printed in the United States
by Baker & Taylor Publisher Services